The Good Life

The Good Life

Edited, with Introductions, by
Charles Guignon

Hackett Publishing Company, Inc.
Indianapolis/Cambridge

Copyright © 1999 by Hackett Publishing Company, Inc.

22 21 20 19   6 7 8 9

For further information, please address
  Hackett Publishing Company, Inc.
  P.O. Box 44937
  Indianapolis, IN 46244–0937

  www.hackettpublishing.com

Cover design by John Pershing

Library of Congress Cataloging-in-Publication Data

The good life / edited with introduction by Charles Guignon.
      p.   cm. —(Hackett readings in philosophy)
  Includes bibliographical references.
  ISBN 0-87220-439-1 (cloth.)—ISBN 0-87220-438-3 (pbk.)
  1. Happiness.   2. Conduct of life.   I. Guignon, Charles B., 1944–
II. Series.
BJ1481.G626   1999
170—dc21   98-50831
                                                        CIP

ISBN-13: 978-0-87220-439-3 (cloth)
ISBN-13: 978-0-87220-438-6 (pbk.)

Contents

Introduction

What is the good life? This is one of the oldest questions asked by philosophers, and it is a question that has received renewed interest in recent years.[1] Asking about the good life for humans is not the same—or is not obviously the same—as asking what it is to be a good human, where good is understood in the ethical sense of acting decently to others, doing the right thing, and having the right motives. In a vocabulary that might seem a bit dated, we could say that the question of the good life is concerned with prudential rather than ethical issues—in other words, it is "self-directed," addressing questions about what is good for one's self, in contrast to the typically "other-directed" matters of modern ethics. The question of the good life aims at identifying the most fulfilling, meaningful, and satisfying life possible for humans, a life which may be described as thriving, flourishing, and (to use a still older vocabulary) "blessed." It focuses on the personal question of how I might best achieve happiness or fulfill my potential, how I might do something important with my life.

1. One main impetus to the renewed interest in this question is the line of inquiry opened toward the end of his life by Michel Foucault in his *The Use of Pleasure* and *The Care of the Self*, Vols. 2 and 3 of *The History of Sexuality*, trans. R. Hurley (New York: Random House, 1985 and 1986). The influence of Foucault's creative readings of ancient Greek and Roman philosophers is evident in Pierre Hadot's *Philosophy as a Way of Life: Spiritual Exercises from Socrates to Foucault*, trans. M. Chase, with an excellent Introduction by A. I. Davidson (Oxford: Blackwell, 1995); Alexander Nehamas' *The Art of Living: Socratic Reflections from Plato to Foucault* (Berkeley: University of California Press, 1998); and Richard Shusterman's *Practicing Philosophy: Pragmatism and the Philosophical Life* (New York: Routledge, 1997). But this traditional question had always been central to the thought of philosophers working in the field of ancient philosophy: one need only think of Julia Annas' *The Morality of Happiness* (Oxford: Oxford University Press, 1993) and such works by Martha C. Nussbaum as *The Fragility of Goodness: Luck and Ethics in Greek Tragedy and Philosophy* (Cambridge: Cambridge University Press, 1986) and *The Therapy of Desire: Theory and Practice in Hellenistic Ethics* (Princeton: Princeton University Press, 1994). It also appears in the work of a philosopher specializing in seventeenth-century rationalist thought, John Cottingham, who examines different views of the good life from the ancient Greeks to the twentieth century in *Philosophy and the Good Life: Reason and the Passions in Greek, Cartesian and Psychoanalytic Ethics* (Cambridge: Cambridge University Press, 1998). And the question is central to such contemporary North American writers as Charles Taylor, *Sources of the Self: The Making of the Modern Identity* (Cambridge, MA: Harvard University Press, 1989), John Kekes, *Moral Wisdom and Good Lives* (Ithaca: Cornell University Press, 1995), and Harry G. Frankfurt, *The Importance of What We Care About: Philosophical Essays* (Cambridge: Cambridge University Press, 1988).

And there is no reason to presume at the outset that finding the answers to such personal questions will show us anything about the need to be a good person as this is understood today by the field called "ethics." Indeed, there is one old strand of thought, referred to by Plato in the second selection in this book, which holds that the good life is a matter of looking out for number one, doing whatever you can get away with, and not caring about what anyone else thinks. If one sees the good life this way, then concerns about what is good *for me* will always be at odds with concerns about what I ought to do in my relations with others.

But it is not at all easy to maintain these distinctions. From the earliest times, philosophers have held that living a rich and fruitful life is inseparable from being a decent, just, and caring person. And there is a broad conception of ethics that embraces both self-directed and other-directed value judgments. If the fundamental question asked by ethics is "How should one live?" then there is no way to draw a sharp line between prudential and ethical questions. Construed in this broad way, ethics deals not just with our obligations to others, but with "questions about how I am going to live my life which touch on the issue of what kind of life is worth living, or what kind of life would fulfill the promise implicit in my particular talents, . . . or of what constitutes a rich, meaningful life—as against one concerned with secondary matters or trivia."[2] For most ancient philosophers, and for many contemporary philosophers, our ability to answer questions of this sort has a direct bearing on our ability to understand our obligations as participants in a shared world.

Throughout the course of history, thoughtful people have tried to characterize the good life by presenting lists of features that such a life should have. One of the oldest and most profound is that described by the prophet Micah (6:8) in the Old Testament: "He has showed you, O man, what is good; and what does the Lord require of you but to do justice, and to love kindness, and to walk humbly with your God?" Socrates held that the good life, which he saw as the same as a life lived honorably or rightly, includes five virtues: temperance, courage, piety, justice, and wisdom.[3] A contemporary ethicist, George Sher, lists six features of a good life: knowledge, rational activity, close personal relations, an appreciation of true beauty, the development of one's capabilities, and moral goodness.[4] But

---

2. Charles Taylor, *Sources of the Self,* p. 14.

3. See John Kekes, *Moral Wisdom and Good Lives,* p. 32.

4. George Sher, *Beyond Neutrality: Perfectionism and Politics* (Cambridge: Cambridge University Press, 1997), chapter 9. Sher points out that his list is based on a list of values drawn up by Derek Parfit.

even though most of us would agree with the ideals found on such lists, the question of the good life does not seem to be clarified by lists alone. What we need to get clear about is what asking about the good life involves and what sorts of reasons can be given in favor of particular visions of the good life.

A good way to get clear about the assumptions underlying this question is to think about a well-known passage from Plato's *Crito* (48b) where Socrates remarks that what is most important is not just to live, but to live well. Here Socrates is drawing a distinction between simply living— getting by from day to day, satisfying one's basic needs—and living a higher, more meaningful, more worthy life—one characterizable as noble or fulfilling or flourishing. This distinction assumes that we can rise above brute "existing"—a level at which we are not much different from the animals—in order to reach a form of life in which we maximize our potential as humans and achieve a higher quality of life. According to this picture, we can rise above our basic desires and needs—for example, our innate drives to survive and reproduce our species and our basic desires for pleasure and comfort—and direct ourselves toward realizing higher goals and ideals—possibilities defined by our most distinctive potential as humans. Reaching this superior level of existence is the most important thing for us, Socrates suggests, because it is only by attaining these greater goals that we achieve a form of life that is genuinely worthwhile and fulfilling. Only by being all you can be (in the now hackneyed phrase) can you have a warranted self-esteem and so feel genuine satisfaction with your life. The effort to arrive at the best possible life for oneself calls for self-discipline (*askesis*) and a willingness to do the work involved in "caring for the self."

To such an austere and demanding conception of life we might imagine a natural objection. Why, one might ask, should we make such a big deal out of the issue of the good life? For one thing, Socrates' whole notion of "higher" goals beyond those of ordinary life seems suspect. Perhaps in earlier times people believed there were commandments and ideals determined by the gods or by nature that everyone had to follow. But if we agree with Nietzsche's claim that modern science makes such belief impossible, then there no longer seems to be any reason to believe in a transcendent source of commandments or values whose ideals are binding on us. Given our contemporary view of the world, it seems that it is up to each of us to pick and choose the values we will embrace. And that means we can simply refuse to buy into any heavy-duty value judgments. For objective, rigorous-minded people today, talk about "the meaning of life" and "higher values" begins to look like a fraud: as Sigmund Freud said, "The moment one inquires about the meaning or value of life one is sick, since objectively neither of them has any existence."[5] Moreover, all dwelling on life seems like a waste of time. Why not just follow the adage *Carpe diem!* (Seize the day!) and live fully in the present, without worrying about bigger things? Isn't the important thing to enjoy yourself, finding whatever pleasures you can get along the way and avoiding hassles? If there are no big meanings and values that hold for everyone, if the only values are the personal ones you decide to adopt from day to day, then you might as well be a free spirit and go with whatever floats your boat.

This is a serious objection, one that manifests a pervasive outlook in contemporary life, and there are no easy answers. One possible line of reply has been put forward by Charles Taylor, who tries to show that the position of the objector is not clearly tenable.[6] In his view, the person who advocates such a subjectivist and hedonistic way of life needs to carefully think through what motivates and underlies a position of this sort. On close inspection, it seems that the ideal of throwing off all constraints in order to become a free spirit rests on a fairly elaborate conception of the good life. The free spirit has set a very high value on living a life that is freed from all comforting illusions and externally imposed ideals. He or she takes personal freedom as the highest value, and that means resisting the temptation to slide into the uncritical attitudes and ways of living circulating in the social world. There is an ideal of personal integrity here, a notion of authentic existence, which calls for steadiness and self-control if it is to be sustained. Moreover, the hedonistic goal of maintaining a durable sense of well-being requires a considerable amount of effort to achieve. If you are going to maintain a steady, good feeling throughout your life, it is probably necessary to avoid getting too attached to things, for people and things can disappoint you and disturb your equilibrium. But avoiding attachments itself requires effort and discipline: the Stoic philosopher Epictetus describes the rigorous exercises one must employ to avoid getting hung up on anything.

What these observations suggest is that the project of being a free spirit, of living in the present, having fun, and not worrying about anything, is not so much a way to escape from all concerns about the good life as it is one more vision of the good life, one that is as loaded down with assumptions and as demanding of *askesis* as any other. In Taylor's language, living a human life always involves operating with some framework of values and meanings that provide orientation and guidelines for one's life, and these

5. Cited in Philip Rieff, *Freud: The Mind of the Moralist*, 3rd ed. (Chicago: The University of Chicago Press, 1979), p. 390; translation slightly modified.

6. *Sources of the Self*, Part I; see also *The Ethics of Authenticity* (Cambridge, MA: Harvard University Press, 1991), chapter IV.

frameworks are inescapable. And if this is the case, then the question concerning the good life remains pressing even for today's free spirits.

Of course, philosophers like Charles Taylor are fully aware that many people do not consciously reflect on their lives in the way intellectually inclined people do. Many people probably just drift into publicly accepted ways of thinking and responding and never step back and ask whether this way of living is really the best. But it is also the case that many people do, at least once in their lives, stop and ask themselves what their lives are all about and whether they are living well. There is a "point of reflection," according to Julia Annas, when people ask: "Am I satisfied with my life as a whole, with the way it has developed and promises to continue?"[7] And she adds, "For most of us are dissatisfied with both our achievement and our promise, and it is only the dissatisfied who have the urge to live differently, and hence the need to find out what ways of living differently would be improvements."[8] We might agree with Annas that dissatisfaction with one's life can be a powerful incentive to reflect on the question of the good life, but still feel it is not a necessary prerequisite. It is possible, even in the course of a contented and successful existence, to step back and ask whether one is living the best possible life, and at that point the age-old question of the good life comes into play. The fact that this question does arise is sufficient reason to look at what some of the greatest thinkers of all time have said about the subject.

One more observation might be made to show why this question is of pressing importance in the modern world. Counseling psychologists have often observed that people seeking professional help today seem to suffer from problems that are quite different from those treated by earlier therapists. E. H. Erikson noted this trend a half a century ago when he pointed out that, whereas "the patient of early psychoanalysis suffered most under inhibitions which prevented him from being what and who he thought he knew he was," the contemporary patient "suffers most under the problem of what he should believe in and who he should—or, indeed, might—be or become."[9] Those seeking help today suffer not so much from classical neuroses as from "feelings of meaninglessness, feelings of emptiness, pervasive depression, lack of sustaining interests, goals, ideals, and values, and feelings of unrelatedness," problems which seem to be rooted in "the lack of stable ideologies and values" and the "atmosphere of

---

7. *The Morality of Happiness*, pp. 28–29.

8. Ibid., p. 29.

9. E. H. Erikson, *Childhood and Society*, 2nd ed. (New York: W. W. Norton, 1963), p. 279, cited in Morris Eagle, *Recent Developments in Psychoanalysis: A Critical Evaluation* (New York: McGraw-Hill, 1984), p. 73.

disillusionment and cynicism in the surrounding society."[10] The result is that, in today's society, people are prone to "self disorders" in which, even though one might be successful in one's career and personal life, one swings between moods of grandiosity and depression, or feels a deep-seated sense of purposelessness and hopelessness. In this atmosphere, psychologists have expressed the need for reflection on basic life values and ideals. As this situation shows, the question of the good life is more than just an optional entertainment for the leisured elite; it is a dire necessity for those trying to go on living in a harsh and often baffling world.

My aim in putting together this collection of readings is to offer a representative sampling of ways of understanding the good life which have been proposed by great thinkers from various times and places. The term "sampling" seems quite apt here, for the final product is more like a chocolate sampler, containing bits and pieces of what is available, than it is an exhaustive compendium of writings on this topic. In an area where so many valuable texts exist, selection is a painful process, and a great deal has to be left out. In particular, I have omitted the works of thinkers—for example, David Hume, Arthur Schopenhauer, Ludwig Wittgenstein— whose thoughts on the good life are so rich and dispersed throughout their writings that no passages can be isolated and treated as representative. In the case of other texts I hoped to include—for example, Søren Kierke- gaard, Malcolm X—permissions to quote were prohibitively expensive. I also decided to leave out the texts of authors who have written very extensively on the good life—for example, Confucius, Plotinus, Cicero, Boethius, Martin Heidegger—on the assumption that their works should be made separate objects of study. Further, no effort has been made to include every cultural and religious perspective: such a collection either would be mammoth and unwieldy or would turn into a collection of snippets that ill serves both readers and authors. Finally, I have left out the works of psychologists and psychotherapy theorists who are perhaps our modern world's most insightful and profound interpreters of the good life—figures like Sigmund Freud, Carl Jung, Alfred Adler, Karen Horney, and Alice Miller—as these seem to deserve a study of their own.[11]

Even when the readings had been cut back to the small sampling that makes up this volume, the collection seemed in need of some division into basic categories. My principle for organizing the readings was basically

10. Eagle, *Recent Developments in Psychoanalysis*, p. 73.

11. See Frank C. Richardson, Blaine Fowers, and Charles Guignon, *Re-envisioning Psychology* (San Francisco: Jossey-Bass, 1999).

historical, but as I tried to group essays according to themes and orientations, I found it necessary to mix more recent works in with older writings. The categories are therefore supposed to identify basic themes running through the readings in the section. But it should be said in advance that these categories are extremely artificial, and they tend to disguise both similarities among readings across categories and deep differences within categories. What is most striking in looking at the great wealth of writings on the topic of the good life is how different generations of writers are concerned to place their views in relation to those of earlier writers, with the result that they embrace some ideas from predecessors while ignoring or rejecting others. Because of this complex story of influence, the history of reflections on the good life is more like a tapestry of overlapping and interweaving strands than it is like a set of boxes, each containing a distinctive point of view.

Granting that the section divisions are suspect, something should be said about the assumptions underlying the divisions. The first set of readings, which I have described as examples of "the classical model," have in common the assumption that philosophy (or, in general, reflective thought) has important consequences for the practice of one's life, and that understanding the way things are (in the broadest sense of that term) can help us see how we ought to live our lives. These writings also seem to share a particular vision of what the good life involves, namely, the idea that nature or the cosmos has certain inbuilt characteristics, and that achieving the best possible life (a life of happiness or inner peace) is a matter of living in harmony with the cosmic order, which means at the same time achieving harmony within oneself. Representatives of the classical model tend to see the happiest, most flourishing and fulfilled life as one that is "healthy" because it is in tune with nature and at peace within itself.

The religious ways of life presented in the second section often take over many of the themes central to the classical model, but they are distinct in their concern with the possibility of achieving what Louis Dumont has called an "outworldly" orientation toward life,[12] that is, a way of life that looks beyond the everyday world to a standpoint outside or beyond the familiar world. However, not all the writings in this section are "outworldly" in this sense. Dostoyevsky presents a view of Christianity that is quite consciously "this-worldly," and the religious attitudes dis-

---

12. Louis Dumont, "A Modified View of Our Origins: The Christian Beginnings of Modern Individualism," in M. Carrithers, S. Collins, and S. Lukes, eds., *Anthropology, Philosophy, History* (Cambridge: Cambridge University Press, 1985).

cussed by William James seem to be solely concerned with the benefits they will reap for the here and now. What binds these selections together, then, is their place in a tradition that made the "outworldly" a central question.

A commitment to using reason in living the best possible life was central to many thinkers of the classical model, but reason comes to have a very special significance beginning with the rise of the scientific worldview in the sixteenth and seventeenth centuries. For the mechanistic and materialistic conception of the universe in modern science works to undermine the belief, shared by most classical models, that there is an order in nature that gives us guidance on how we ought to determine the course of our lives. As a result, reason in the modern period is thought of not as a faculty that gives us a vision of the Good, but as a tool that can be used to regulate factors that might cut us off from living a comfortable and relatively painless life. What the readings on the use of reason have in common is the idea that a cool, dispassionate, rational approach to life will enable us to achieve self-mastery and live intelligently.

The section called "Self-Exploration" brings together a group of authors from the modern period who were concerned not so much with rational self-mastery as with an open-ended exploration of one's self and a willingness to follow the quest wherever it might lead. What unites these authors, as I see it, is a refusal to assume anything in advance about what this quest will produce and a recognition that there might be some surprises along the way.

It should be obvious that the section called "Self-Realization" cannot be sharply contrasted with the self-exploratory approach. What I had in mind by the concept of self-realization is a relatively new idea in our civilization, the ideal of "authenticity," where this is understood as a matter of (1) identifying what is most truly oneself and (2) courageously making a commitment to be true to that self. But the specific form this ideal takes in existentialist authors (whose texts make up the section called "Self-Realization") is the idea that what defines us as humans is nothing other than our complete and unlimited freedom—our lack of being predefined in any. For these writers, then, the demand that we be true to ourselves is the demand that we be true to (and realize) freedom itself. As Sartre says, we are "condemned to be free"—the only thing with respect to which we are not free is our own total freedom. Thus, while all the authors in this volume are concerned with self-realization in some sense, existentialism has defined a very specific, and very compelling, idea of what that involves.

The central concern with self-realization and authentic existence provides a contrast to the readings that make up the final section, called

"Social Involvement." These writings, while developing themes found in the other sections, place a special emphasis on our being with others as agents in a shared, social world, and therefore bring to light the resources and hardships that are found in the actual, concrete world in which we live.

Special thanks are owed to a number of people who devoted their time and ideas to the preparation of this volume. I would like to thank Ray Boisvert, Julie Gifford, David Hiley, Don Loeb, Bill Mann, Alexander Nehamas, Derk Pereboom, Richard Polt, Frank Richardson, and Bob Taylor for their excellent suggestions and thoughtful advice in various stages of the composition of *The Good Life*.

CLASSICAL SOURCES:
THE IDEAL OF HARMONY

1

Lao Tzu,
Tao Te Ching

The author of the Chinese masterpiece Tao Te Ching *is lost in the gray mists of antiquity. The name Lao Tzu means "Old Master," and it is not clear whether the* Tao Te Ching *(pronounced roughly "dow deh jing"), which stems from the fourth or third century* B.C.E., *was composed by one old master or is a composite of the teachings of several masters. The book itself is one of the core works of Taoism, an ancient school of thought that rejected the moral rigor and concern with action of Confucianism and Mohism and, instead, advocated a "let-it-be" approach to worldy affairs, a way of life characterized by attunement to nature and the cultivation of quietude and inner peace. The classic or book* (Ching) *deals with the two concepts,* Tao *and* Te. Tao *means "way" or "path" and refers to the principle underlying all things, the primordial One that is the source and sustainer of all that exists. Because only things can be named, that which is the source of all things is itself unnameable, but it can be grasped through images and intuitive reflection on the whole of what is.* Te *refers to the personal characteristics of a person who acts in the right way, and it points to the mode of existence of one whose life is in tune with the* Tao *rather than at odds with it. The* Tao Te Ching *presents an image of a life lived in accord with the Way of nature, a life in which one abjures show and ceremony and instead is in touch with who one truly is.*

8.

Highest good is like water. Because water excels in benefiting the myriad creatures without contending with them and settles where none would like to be, it comes close to the way.

In a home it is the site that matters;
In quality of mind it is depth that matters;
In an ally it is benevolence that matters;
In speech it is good faith that matters;
In government it is order that matters;
In affairs it is ability that matters;
In action it is timeliness that matters.

It is because it does not contend that it is never at fault.

16.

I do my utmost to attain emptiness;
I hold firmly to stillness.
The myriad creatures all rise together
And I watch their return.
The teeming creatures
All return to their separate roots.
Returning to one's roots is known as stillness.
This is what is meant by returning to one's destiny.
Returning to one's destiny is known as the constant.
Knowledge of the constant is known as discernment.
Woe to him who wilfully innovates
While ignorant of the constant,
But should one act from knowledge of the constant
One's action will lead to impartiality,
Impartiality to kingliness,
Kingliness to heaven,
Heaven to the way,
The way to perpetuity,
And to the end of one's days one will meet with no danger.

Lao Tzu, *Tao Te Ching*, trans. by D. C. Lau (London: Penguin, 1963). Reprinted by permission.

19.

Exterminate the sage, discard the wise,
And the people will benefit a hundredfold;
Exterminate benevolence, discard rectitude,
And the people will again be filial;
Exterminate ingenuity, discard profit,
And there will be no more thieves and bandits.
These three, being false adornments, are not enough
And the people must have something to which they can attach themselves:
Exhibit the unadorned and embrace the uncarved block,
Have little thought of self and as few desires as possible.

21.

In his every movement a man of great virtue
Follows the way and the way only.
As a thing the way is
Shadowy, indistinct.
Indistinct and shadowy,
Yet within it is an image;
Shadowy and indistinct,
Yet within it is a substance.
Dim and dark,
Yet within it is an essence.
This essence is quite genuine
And within it is something that can be tested.
From the present back to antiquity
Its name never deserted it.
It serves as a means for inspecting the fathers of the multitude.

How do I know that the fathers of the multitude are like that? By means of this.

22.

Bowed down then preserved;
Bent then straight;
Hollow then full;
Worn then new;
A little then benefited;
A lot then perplexed.
Therefore the sage embraces the One and is a model for the empire.
He does not show himself, and so is conspicuous;
He does not consider himself right, and so is illustrious;
He does not brag, and so has merit;
He does not boast, and so endures.

It is because he does not contend that no one in the empire is in a position
to contend with him.
The way the ancients had it, "Bowed down then preserved," is no empty
saying. Truly it enables one to be preserved to the end.

37.

The way never acts yet nothing is left undone.
Should lords and princes be able to hold fast to it,
The myriad creatures will be transformed of their own accord.
After they are transformed, should desire raise its head,
I shall press it down with the weight of the nameless uncarved block.
The nameless uncarved block
Is but freedom from desire,
And if I cease to desire and remain still,
The empire will be at peace of its own accord.

38.

A man of the highest virtue does not keep to virtue and that is why he has virtue. A man of the lowest virtue never strays from virtue and that is why he is without virtue. The former never acts yet leaves nothing undone. The latter acts but there are things left undone. A man of the highest benevolence acts, but from no ulterior motive. A man of the highest rectitude acts, but from ulterior motive. A man most conversant in the rites acts, but when no one responds rolls up his sleeves and resorts to persuasion by force.

Hence when the way was lost there was virtue; when virtue was lost there was benevolence; when benevolence was lost there was rectitude; when rectitude was lost there were the rites.

The rites are the wearing thin of loyalty and good faith
And the beginning of disorder;
Foreknowledge is the flowery embellishment of the way
And the beginning of folly.

Hence the man of large mind abides in the thick not in the thin, in the fruit not in the flower.
Therefore he discards the one and takes the other.

41.

When the best student hears about the way
He practises it assiduously;
When the average student hears about the way
It seems to him one moment there and gone the next;
When the worst student hears about the way
He laughs out loud.
If he did not laugh
It would be unworthy of being the way.

Hence the *Chien yen* has it:

The way that is bright seems dull;
The way that leads forward seems to lead backward;
The way that is even seems rough.
The highest virtue is like the valley;
The sheerest whiteness seems sullied;
Ample virtue seems defective;
Vigorous virtue seems indolent;
Plain virtue seems soiled;
The great square has no corners.
The great vessel takes long to complete;
The great note is rarefied in sound;
The great image has no shape.
The way conceals itself in being nameless.
It is the way alone that excels in bestowing and in accomplishing.

44.

Your name or your person,
Which is dearer?
Your person or your goods,
Which is worth more?
Gain or loss,
Which is a greater bane?
That is why excessive meanness
Is sure to lead to great expense;
Too much store
Is sure to end in immense loss.
Know contentment
And you will suffer no disgrace;
Know when to stop
And you will meet with no danger.
You can then endure.

49.

The sage has no mind of his own. He takes as his own the mind of the people.

Those who are good I treat as good. Those who are not good I also treat as good. In so doing I gain in goodness. Those who are of good faith I have faith in. Those who are lacking in good faith I also have faith in. In so doing I gain in good faith.

The sage in his attempt to distract the mind of the empire seeks urgently to muddle it. The people all have something to occupy their eyes and ears, and the sage treats them all like children.

56.

One who knows does not speak; one who speaks does not know.

Block the openings;
Shut the doors.
Blunt the sharpness;
Untangle the knots;
Soften the glare;
Let your wheels move only along old ruts.

This is known as mysterious sameness.
Hence you cannot get close to it, nor can you keep it at arm's length; you cannot bestow benefit on it, nor can you do it harm; you cannot ennoble it, nor can you debase it.
Therefore it is valued by the empire.

71.

To know yet to think that one does not know is best;
Not to know yet to think that one knows will lead to difficulty.

It is by being alive to difficulty that one can avoid it. The sage meets with no difficulty. It is because he is alive to it that he meets with no difficulty.

74.

When the people are not afraid of death, wherefore frighten them with death? Were the people always afraid of death, and were I able to arrest and put to death those who innovate, then who would dare? There is a regular executioner whose charge it is to kill. To kill on behalf of the executioner is what is described as chopping wood on behalf of the master carpenter. In chopping wood on behalf of the master carpenter, there are few who escape hurting their own hands instead.

81.

Truthful words are not beautiful; beautiful words are not truthful. Good words are not persuasive; persuasive words are not good. He who knows has no wide learning; he who has wide learning does not know. The sage does not hoard.

Having bestowed all he has on others, he has yet more;
Having given all he has to others, he is richer still.

The way of heaven benefits and does not harm; the way of the sage is bountiful and does not contend.

Plato,
Republic

Born into an aristocratic Athenian family, Plato (427–347 B.C.E.) was groomed to play a central role in politics. As a young man, however, he came under the influence of Socrates and, as result, spent the rest of his life carrying forward the kinds of philosophical questioning Socrates had begun. After an unsuccessful attempt to advise the tyrant of Syracuse on governing, Plato returned to Athens and founded the Academy, one of the greatest centers of learning of the ancient world. Many of Plato's writings take the form of dialogues between a central figure (whom, in honor of his teacher, he calls Socrates) and others about topics such as the nature of piety, beauty, or knowledge. In these dialogues, Socrates presses his interlocutors to define the terms they use, and in the course of the discussion he leads them to see that their initial understanding was inadequate, with the result that they move toward a better understanding by the end of the dialogue.

The Republic, *one of Plato's greatest and longest works, is written as a report by Socrates about conversations he had concerning the nature of justice. The* Republic *focuses on the question "What is justice?" where the just person is one we would think of as morally upstanding: a person who acts decently to others, does the right thing, tells the truth, keeps promises, and so forth. At the outset of the dialogue, Socrates' opponents argue that justice in this sense is not usually good for a person, where what is good is understood as what makes you happy or what is to your advantage. In the following passage, the character Glaucon defends the commonly accepted view that people are never just because they want to be, and that being just is something we do in order to reap rewards (e.g., praise, respect, recognition) and not for its own sake. To prove his point, Glaucon presents the famous story of a ring that makes its wearer invisible. What this story suggests is that morality is a sucker's game: in other words, so long as you know you cannot be caught, the smart money is on doing whatever is to your own advantage—looking out for number one, getting yours while the getting's good—and this usually means acting in self-centered ways that are regarded as immoral or unjust.*

They say that to do injustice is naturally good and to suffer injustice   *358e*
bad, but that the badness of suffering it so far exceeds the goodness of
doing it that those who have done and suffered injustice and tasted both,
but who lack the power to do it and avoid suffering it, decide that it is
profitable to come to an agreement with each other neither to do injustice   *359*
nor to suffer it. As a result, they begin to make laws and covenants, and
what the law commands they call lawful and just. This, they say, is the
origin and essence of justice. It is intermediate between the best and the
worst. The best is to do injustice without paying the penalty; the worst is
to suffer it without being able to take revenge. Justice is a mean between
these two extremes. People value it not as a good but because they are too
weak to do injustice with impunity. Someone who has the power to do this,
however, and is a true man wouldn't make an agreement with anyone not   *b*
to do injustice in order not to suffer it. For him that would be madness.
This is the nature of justice, according to the argument, Socrates, and
these are its natural origins.

We can see most clearly that those who practice justice do it unwillingly
and because they lack the power to do injustice, if in our thoughts we grant   *c*
to a just and an unjust person the freedom to do whatever they like. We can
then follow both of them and see where their desires would lead. And we'll
catch the just person red-handed travelling the same road as the unjust.
The reason for this is the desire to outdo others and get more and more.
This is what anyone's nature naturally pursues as good, but nature is
forced by law into the perversion of treating fairness with respect.

The freedom I mentioned would be most easily realized if both people
had the power they say the ancestor of Gyges of Lydia possessed. The
story goes that he was a shepherd in the service of the ruler of Lydia.   *d*
There was a violent thunderstorm, and an earthquake broke open the
ground and created a chasm at the place where he was tending his sheep.
Seeing this, he was filled with amazement and went down into it. And
there, in addition to many other wonders of which we're told, he saw a
hollow bronze horse. There were windowlike openings in it, and, peeping
in, he saw a corpse, which seemed to be of more than human size, wearing
nothing but a gold ring on its finger. He took the ring and came out of the   *e*
chasm. He wore the ring at the usual monthly meeting that reported to the
king on the state of the flocks. And as he was sitting among the others, he
happened to turn the setting of the ring towards himself to the inside of his
hand. When he did this, he became invisible to those sitting near him, and
they went on talking as if he had gone. He wondered at this, and, fingering   *360*

From Plato, *Republic*, trans. by G. M. A. Grube, rev. by C. D. C. Reeve (Indianapolis: Hackett Publishing Co., 1992). Reprinted by permission of the publisher.

the ring, he turned the setting outwards again and became visible. So he
experimented with the ring to test whether it indeed had this power—and
it did. If he turned the setting inward, he became invisible; if he turned it
outward, he became visible again. When he realized this, he at once
arranged to become one of the messengers sent to report to the king. And
b   when he arrived there, he seduced the king's wife, attacked the king with
her help, killed him, and took over the kingdom.

  Let's suppose, then, that there were two such rings, one worn by a just
and the other by an unjust person. Now, no one, it seems, would be so
incorruptible that he would stay on the path of justice or stay away from
other people's property, when he could take whatever he wanted from the
marketplace with impunity, go into people's houses and have sex with
c   anyone he wished, kill or release from prison anyone he wished, and do all
the other things that would make him like a god among humans. Rather
his actions would be in no way different from those of an unjust person,
and both would follow the same path. This, some would say, is a great
proof that one is never just willingly but only when compelled to be. No
one believes justice to be a good when it is kept private, since, wherever
either person thinks he can do injustice with impunity, he does it. Indeed,
every man believes that injustice is far more profitable to himself than
d   justice. And any exponent of this argument will say he's right, for someone
who didn't want to do injustice, given this sort of opportunity, and who
didn't touch other people's property would be thought wretched and
stupid by everyone aware of the situation, though, of course, they'd praise
him in public, deceiving each other for fear of suffering injustice.

Plato's project in the Republic *is to reply to ordinary views about justice
like the one presented by Glaucon. To do this, he must show that being
moral and just is in a person's best interests, and that an individual is altogether happier and leads a better life if he or she is a just person. This
means that Socrates must formulate a vision of the good life in which it is
evident that justice is indeed a necessary component of a maximally good
life. But to show this he must refute the ordinary view that a happy or good
life consists in getting what one wants when one wants it. In other words,
Socrates must show that a life devoted to pleasure and the satisfaction of
appetites is not really a happy and fulfilling life.*

  *Socrates undertakes this project by developing an extended analogy be-
tween a person and an ideal political community, on the assumption that in
the city-state one can see justice written large. A state, he suggests, is made
up of three distinct types of people. The first group, consisting of the
farmers, merchants, craftsmen, builders, and so on, will be involved in producing and selling goods, and they will be motivated by the love of wealth*

and success. The second group consists of the guardians, soldier-police who enforce the laws, defend the state, and are motivated by a desire for honor. The third group, the smallest, consists of the rulers of the state, people who are motivated by the desire for order and the well-being of all. The ideal or virtuous state, according to this account, is one in which each group does its proper job: the rulers rule wisely and fairly, the guardians courageously uphold the rulers' commands, and the producers are orderly and law-abiding. Such a state will have the virtues of wisdom, courage, moderation, and justice.

Extending the analogy to the individual, Socrates argues that a person's soul contains three components—the appetitive, the spirited (the part of us that manifests competitiveness, anger, and pride), and the rational— corresponding to the major groups in the city—producers, guardians, and rulers. In the person who lives well, each part functions in the way it should: reason rules, the assertive part provides the force needed to act, and the appetites desire only what reason dictates. The following passage tries to show (1) that the virtuous or good life is one in which the elements of the soul are coordinated in the proper way, (2) that a virtuous life is a "healthy" life characterized by wisdom, courage, moderation, and justice, and (3) that a good life of this sort is one which is truly happy or blessed. Thus, the argument moves a long way toward answering the crucial question of the Re-public: Is it more profitable to be just or unjust? Socrates is speaking.

Well, then, we've now made our difficult way through a sea of argu-   *441c*
ment. We are pretty much agreed that the same number and the same
kinds of classes as are in the city are also in the soul of each individual.

That's true.

Therefore, it necessarily follows that the individual is wise in the same
way and in the same part of himself as the city.

That's right.

And isn't the individual courageous in the same way and in the same
part of himself as the city? And isn't everything else that has to do with   *d*
virtue the same in both?

Necessarily.

Moreover, Glaucon, I suppose we'll say that a man is just in the same
way as a city.

That too is entirely necessary.

And we surely haven't forgotten that the city was just because each of
the three classes in it was doing its own work.

I don't think we could forget that.

Then we must also remember that each one of us in whom each part is
doing its own work will himself be just and do his own.   *e*

Of course, we must.

Therefore, isn't it appropriate for the rational part to rule, since it is really wise and exercises foresight on behalf of the whole soul, and for the spirited part to obey it and be its ally?

It certainly is.

And isn't it, as we were saying, a mixture of music and poetry, on the one hand, and physical training, on the other, that makes the two parts harmonious, stretching and nurturing the rational part with fine words and learning, relaxing the other part through soothing stories, and making
442   it gentle by means of harmony and rhythm?

That's precisely it.

And these two, having been nurtured in this way, and having truly learned their own roles and been educated in them, will govern the appetitive part, which is the largest part in each person's soul and is by nature most insatiable for money. They'll watch over it to see that it isn't filled with the so-called pleasures of the body and that it doesn't become so big and strong that it no longer does its own work but attempts to enslave and
b   rule over the classes it isn't fitted to rule, thereby overturning everyone's whole life.

That's right.

Then, wouldn't these two parts also do the finest job of guarding the whole soul and body against external enemies—reason by planning, spirit by fighting, following its leader, and carrying out the leader's decisions through its courage?

Yes, that's true.

And it is because of the spirited part, I suppose, that we call a single
c   individual courageous, namely, when it preserves through pains and pleasures the declarations of reason about what is to be feared and what isn't.

That's right.

And we'll call him wise because of that small part of himself that rules in him and makes those declarations and has within it the knowledge of what is advantageous for each part and for the whole soul, which is the community of all three parts.

Absolutely.

And isn't he moderate because of the friendly and harmonious relations between these same parts, namely, when the ruler and the ruled believe in common that the rational part should rule and don't engage in civil war
d   against it?

Moderation is surely nothing other than that, both in the city and in the individual.

And, of course, a person will be just because of what we've so often mentioned, and in that way.

Necessarily.

Well, then, is the justice in us at all indistinct? Does it seem to be something different from what we found in the city?

It doesn't seem so to me.

If there are still any doubts in our soul about this, we could dispel them altogether by appealing to ordinary cases.   *e*

Which ones?

For example, if we had to come to an agreement about whether someone similar in nature and training to our city had embezzled a deposit of gold or silver that he had accepted, who do you think would consider him to have done it rather than someone who isn't like him?   *443*

No one.

And would he have anything to do with temple robberies, thefts, betrayals of friends in private life or of cities in public life?

No, nothing.

And he'd be in no way untrustworthy in keeping an oath or other agreement.

How could he be?

And adultery, disrespect for parents, and neglect of the gods would be more in keeping with every other kind of character than his.

With every one.

And isn't the cause of all this that every part within him does its own work, whether it's ruling or being ruled?   *b*

Yes, that and nothing else.

Then, are you still looking for justice to be something other than this power, the one that produces men and cities of the sort we've described?

No, I certainly am not.

Then the dream we had has been completely fulfilled—our suspicion that, with the help of some god, we had hit upon the origin and pattern of justice right at the beginning in founding our city.   *c*

Absolutely.

Indeed, Glaucon, the principle that it is right for someone who is by nature a cobbler to practice cobblery and nothing else, for the carpenter to practice carpentry, and the same for the others is a sort of image of justice—that's why it's beneficial.

Apparently.

And in truth justice is, it seems, something of this sort. However, it isn't concerned with someone's doing his own externally, but with what is inside him, with what is truly himself and his own. One who is just does   *d* not allow any part of himself to do the work of another part or allow the various classes within him to meddle with each other. He regulates well what is really his own and rules himself. He puts himself in order, is his

own friend, and harmonizes the three parts of himself like three limiting notes in a musical scale—high, low, and middle. He binds together those parts and any others there may be in between, and from having been many
e   things he becomes entirely one, moderate and harmonious. Only then does he act. And when he does anything, whether acquiring wealth, taking care of his body, engaging in politics, or in private contracts—in all of these, he believes that the action is just and fine that preserves this inner harmony and helps achieve it, and calls it so, and regards as wisdom the knowledge that oversees such actions. And he believes that the action that
444   destroys this harmony is unjust, and calls it so, and regards the belief that oversees it as ignorance.

That's absolutely true, Socrates.

Well, then, if we claim to have found the just man, the just city, and what the justice is that is in them, I don't suppose that we'll seem to be telling a complete falsehood.

No, we certainly won't.

Shall we claim it, then?

We shall.

So be it. Now, I suppose we must look for injustice.

Clearly.

b   Surely, it must be a kind of civil war between the three parts, a meddling and doing of another's work, a rebellion by some part against the whole soul in order to rule it inappropriately. The rebellious part is by nature suited to be a slave, while the other part is not a slave but belongs to the ruling class. We'll say something like that, I suppose, and that the turmoil and straying of these parts are injustice, licentiousness, cowardice, ignorance, and, in a word, the whole of vice.

That's what they are.

So, if justice and injustice are really clear enough to us, then acting
c   justly, acting unjustly, and doing injustice are also clear.

How so?

Because just and unjust actions are no different for the soul than healthy and unhealthy things are for the body.

In what way?

Healthy things produce health, unhealthy ones disease.

Yes.

And don't just actions produce justice in the soul and unjust ones
d   injustice?

Necessarily.

To produce health is to establish the components of the body in a natural relation of control and being controlled, one by another, while to produce disease is to establish a relation of ruling and being ruled contrary to nature.

That's right.

Then, isn't to produce justice to establish the parts of the soul in a natural relation of control, one by another, while to produce injustice is to establish a relation of ruling and being ruled contrary to nature?

Precisely.

Virtue seems, then, to be a kind of health, fine condition, and well-being of the soul, while vice is disease, shameful condition, and weakness.   *e*

That's true.

And don't fine ways of living lead one to the possession of virtue, shameful ones to vice?

Necessarily.

So it now remains, it seems, to enquire whether it is more profitable to act justly, live in a fine way, and be just, whether one is known to be so or   *445* not, or to act unjustly and be unjust, provided that one doesn't pay the penalty and become better as a result of punishment.

But, Socrates, this inquiry looks ridiculous to me now that justice and injustice have been shown to be as we have described. Even if one has every kind of food and drink, lots of money, and every sort of power to rule, life is thought to be not worth living when the body's nature is ruined. So even if someone can do whatever he wishes, except what will   *b* free him from vice and injustice and make him acquire justice and virtue, how can it be worth living when his soul—the very thing by which he lives—is ruined and in turmoil?

The final passage appears near the end of the Republic *where Socrates argues that the best or happiest life possible for humans is one in which reason rules the passions and the individual lives in harmony with the natural order of the cosmos. Plato's conception of the good life served as the model for many different ideals in the ancient world, and it strongly influenced early visions of the good life in Christianity. It gives us a picture of a life characterized by order, harmony, balance, and focus—a life that is self-possessed and grounded—in contrast to a life that is torn apart, agitated, dissociated, conflicted, and pushed in all directions by relentless cravings and passions.*

Since we've reached this point in the argument, let's return to the first   *588b* things we said, since they are what led us here. I think someone said at some point that injustice profits a completely unjust person who is believed to be just. Isn't that so?

It certainly is.

Now, let's discuss this with him, since we've agreed on the respective powers that injustice and justice have.

How?

By fashioning an image of the soul in words, so that the person who says this sort of thing will know what he is saying.

c   What sort of image?

One like those creatures that legends tell us used to come into being in ancient times, such as the Chimera, Scylla, Cerberus,[1] or any of the multitude of others in which many different kinds of things are said to have grown together naturally into one.

Yes, the legends do tell us of such things.

Well, then, fashion a single kind of multicolored beast with a ring of many heads that it can grow and change at will—some from gentle, some from savage animals.

d   That's work for a clever artist. However, since words are more malleable than wax and the like, consider it done.

Then fashion one other kind, that of a lion, and another of a human being. But make the first much the largest and the other second to it in size.

That's easier—the sculpting is done.

Now join the three of them into one, so that they somehow grow together naturally.

They're joined.

Then, fashion around them the image of one of them, that of a human being so that anyone who sees only the outer covering and not what's

e   inside will think it is a single creature, a human being.

It's done.

Then, if someone maintains that injustice profits this human being and that doing just things brings no advantage, let's tell him that he is simply saying that it is beneficial for him, first, to feed the multiform beast well and make it strong, and also the lion and all that pertains to him; second,

589 to starve and weaken the human being within, so that he is dragged along wherever either of the other two leads; and, third, to leave the parts to bite and kill one another rather than accustoming them to each other and making them friendly.

Yes, that's absolutely what someone who praises injustice is saying.

---

1. The Chimera was "lion in the front, serpent in the back, and she-goat in the middle" (*Iliad* 6.181). Scylla had six heads, each with three rows of teeth, and twelve feet (see *Odyssey* 12.85 ff., 245 ff.). Cerberus was a huge dog guarding the entrance to Hades; he had three heads and a serpent's tail.

But, on the other hand, wouldn't someone who maintains that just things are profitable be saying, first, that all our words and deeds should insure that the human being within this human being has the most control; second, that he should take care of the many-headed beast as a farmer *b* does his animals, feeding and domesticating the gentle heads and preventing the savage ones from growing; and, third, that he should make the lion's nature his ally, care for the community of all his parts, and bring them up in such a way that they will be friends with each other and with himself?

Yes, that's exactly what someone who praises justice is saying.

From every point of view, then, anyone who praises justice speaks truly, and anyone who praises injustice speaks falsely. Whether we look at the matter from the point of view of pleasure, good reputation, or advantage, a praiser of justice tells the truth, while one who condemns it has nothing *c* sound to say and condemns without knowing what he is condemning.

In my opinion, at least, he knows nothing about it.

Then let's persuade him gently—for he isn't wrong of his own will— by asking him these questions. Should we say that this is the original basis for the conventions about what is fine and what is shameful? Fine things are those that subordinate the beastlike parts of our nature to the human— or better, perhaps, to the divine; shameful ones are those that enslave the *d* gentle to the savage? Will he agree or what?

He will, if he takes my advice.

In light of this argument, can it profit anyone to acquire gold unjustly if, by doing so, he enslaves the best part of himself to the most vicious? If he got the gold by enslaving his son or daughter to savage and evil men, it wouldn't profit him, no matter how much gold he got. How, then, could he *e* fail to be wretched if he pitilessly enslaves the most divine part of himself to the most godless and polluted one and accepts golden gifts in return for a more terrible destruction than Eriphyle's when she took the necklace in *590* return for her husband's soul?[2]

A much more terrible one, Glaucon said. I'll answer for him.

And don't you think that licentiousness has long been condemned for just these reasons, namely, that because of it, that terrible, large, and multiform beast is let loose more than it should be?

Clearly.

---

2. Eriphyle was bribed by Polynices to persuade her husband, Amphiaraus, to take part in an attack on Thebes. He was killed, and she was murdered by her son in revenge. See *Odyssey* 11.326–27; Pindar, *Nemean* 9.37 ff.

And aren't stubbornness and irritability condemned because they in-
b harmoniously increase and stretch the lionlike and snakelike[3] part?
Certainly.
And aren't luxury and softness condemned because the slackening and
loosening of this same part produce cowardice in it?
Of course.
And aren't flattery and slavishness condemned because they subject the
spirited part to the moblike beast, accustoming it from youth on to being
insulted for the sake of the money needed to satisfy the beast's insatiable
appetites, so that it becomes an ape instead of a lion?
c   They certainly are.
Why do you think that the condition of a manual worker is despised? Or
is it for any other reason than that, when the best part is naturally weak in
someone, it can't rule the beasts within him but can only serve them and
learn to flatter them?
Probably so.
Therefore, to insure that someone like that is ruled by something similar to what rules the best person, we say that he ought to be the slave of
that best person who has a divine ruler within himself. It isn't to harm the
d slave that we say he must be ruled, which is what Thrasymachus thought
to be true of all subjects, but because it is better for everyone to be ruled by
divine reason, preferably within himself and his own, otherwise imposed
from without, so that as far as possible all will be alike and friends,
governed by the same thing.
Yes, that's right.
This is clearly the aim of the law, which is the ally of everyone. But it's
also our aim in ruling our children, we don't allow them to be free until we
establish a constitution in them, just as in a city, and—by fostering their
best part with our own—equip them with a guardian and ruler similar to
591 our own to take our place. Then, and only then, we set them free.
Clearly so.
Then how can we maintain or argue, Glaucon, that injustice, licentiousness, and doing shameful things are profitable to anyone, since, even
though he may acquire more money or other sort of power from them,
they make him more vicious?
There's no way we can.

---

3. The snakelike part hasn't been previously mentioned, although it may be
included in "all that pertains to" the lion (588e). It symbolizes some of the meaner
components of the spirited part, such as irritability, which it would be unnatural to
attribute to the noble lion.

Or that to do injustice without being discovered and having to pay the penalty is profitable? Doesn't the one who remains undiscovered become even more vicious, while the bestial part of the one who is discovered is *b* calmed and tamed and his gentle part freed, so that his entire soul settles into its best nature, acquires moderation, justice, and reason, and attains a more valuable state than that of having a fine, strong, healthy body, since the soul itself is more valuable than the body?

That's absolutely certain.

Then won't a person of understanding direct all his efforts to attaining that state of his soul? First, he'll value the studies that produce it and *c* despise the others.

Clearly so.

Second, he won't entrust the condition and nurture of his body to the irrational pleasure of the beast within or turn his life in that direction, but neither will he make health his aim or assign first place to being strong, healthy, and beautiful, unless he happens to acquire moderation as a result. Rather, it's clear that he will always cultivate the harmony of his body for the sake of the consonance in his soul. *d*

He certainly will, if indeed he's to be truly trained in music and poetry.

Will he also keep order and consonance in his acquisition of money, with that same end in view? Or, even though he isn't dazzled by the size of the majority into accepting their idea of blessed happiness, will he increase his wealth without limit and so have unlimited evils?

Not in my view.

Rather, he'll look to the constitution within him and guard against *e* disturbing anything in it, either by too much money or too little. And, in this way, he'll direct both the increase and expenditure of his wealth, as far as he can.

That's exactly what he'll do.

And he'll look to the same thing where honors are concerned. He'll willingly share in and taste those that he believes will make him better, but *592* he'll avoid any public or private honor that might overthrow the established condition of his soul.

Aristotle,
Nicomachean Ethics

Son of the court physician to the King of Macedonia, Aristotle (384–322 B.C.E.) was a member of Plato's Academy in Athens for twenty years. After Plato's death, he traveled, engaged in extensive investigations into nature, and occasionally taught, his most famous student being the thirteen-year-old who became Alexander the Great. Returning to Athens in 335, he founded his school, the Lyceum, and wrote extensively on a wide variety of topics. Many of his most polished writings have been lost, and the extant texts are mostly drafts or lecture notes edited with the aid of students—the Nicomachean Ethics *presumably with the aid of Aristotle's son, Nicomachus.*

Aristotle begins the Nicomachean Ethics *with a series of reflections that lead from the plausible idea that human life is directed to achieving certain aims to the astounding claim that the highest and best possible life is one characterized by excellence of character or ethical virtue. One central move in this reasoning is the claim that our highest goal in life (what we all regard as good) is* happiness. *It is important to see that the Greek word translated as "happiness,"* eudaimonia, *does not quite coincide in meaning with our idea of happiness. Where we usually think of happiness as a good feeling accompanying some activity or state, similar to pleasure, the Greeks regarded the feeling as only part of what constitutes happiness. For them,* eudaimonia *refers primarily to what Aristotle calls "living well and doing well," that is, living a life that is satisfying and worthwhile because it is full, abundant, and deserving of praise. This is why* eudaimonia *is often translated as "flourishing" or "thriving." What is at issue in this conception of happiness is not how one happens to feel at any moment, but the quality of one's life as a whole, with all its ties to the social world in which it unfolds.*

Another key move in Aristotle's reasoning is the claim that everything in the universe has a proper function, and that the proper function of humans is to act and deliberate in a way that is guided by reason. Humans are creatures who can take charge of their animal instincts and shape them in ways prescribed by reason. For Aristotle, this means forming good habits or character traits, the "virtues," where these are defined in terms of a "golden mean" between extremes. Thus, the mean between the vices of being a doormat and being a pompous fool is the virtue of having a good, healthy pride in oneself. The mean between being a cold fish and being a pig is enjoying a

*hearty sensuality. In this way, Aristotle is able to generate a list of virtues
that should regulate our active lives.*

*Aristotle's conception of the good life as a matter of character-building
and acting in accordance with virtue has had a profound and lasting impact
on Western thought. It not only gives us a powerful image of a self-
controlled, dignified, and upbeat person, it suggests that the best possible life
is one that is lived according to the highest rational ideals.*

1. The Highest Good: Happiness

1.1 The Highest Good Is Supreme in the Hierarchy of Goods

Every craft and every investigation, and likewise every action and decision, seems to aim at some good; hence the good has been well described as
that at which everything aims.

However, there is an apparent difference among the ends aimed at. For
the end is sometimes an activity, sometimes a product beyond the activity;
and when there is an end beyond the action, the product is by nature
better than the activity.

Since there are many actions, crafts and sciences, the ends turn out to be
many as well; for health is the end of medicine, a boat of boatbuilding,
victory of generalship, and wealth of household management.

But whenever any of these sciences are subordinate to some one
capacity—as e.g., bridlemaking and every other science producing equipment for horses are subordinate to horsemanship, while this and every
action in warfare are in turn subordinate to generalship, and in the same
way other sciences are subordinate to further ones—in each of these the
end of the ruling science is more choiceworthy than all the ends subordinate to it, since it is the end for which those ends are also pursued. And
here it does not matter whether the ends of the actions are the activities
themselves, or some product beyond them, as in the sciences we have
mentioned.

Suppose, then, that (a) there is some end of the things we pursue in our
actions which we wish for because of itself, and because of which we wish
for the other things; and (b) we do not choose everything because of
something else, since (c) if we do, it will go on without limit, making desire
empty and futile; then clearly (d) this end will be the good, i.e. the best
good.

From Aristotle, *Nicomachean Ethics*, trans. by T. H. Irwin (Indianapolis: Hackett
Publishing Co., 1985). Reprinted by permission of the publisher.

1.2 The Ruling Science Studying the Highest Good Is Political Science

Then surely knowledge of this good is also of great importance for the conduct of our lives, and if, like archers, we have a target to aim at, we are more likely to hit the right mark. If so, we should try to grasp, in outline at any rate, what the good is, and which science or capacity is concerned with it.

It seems to concern the most controlling science, the one that, more than any other, is the ruling science. And political science apparently has this character.

(1) For it is the one that prescribes which of the sciences ought to be studied in cities, and which ones each class in the city should learn, and how far.

(2) Again, we see that even the most honoured capacities, e.g., generalship, household management and rhetoric, are subordinate to it.

(3) Further, it uses the other sciences concerned with action, and moreover legislates what must be done and what avoided.

Hence its end will include the ends of the other sciences, and so will be the human good.

[This is properly called political science;] for though admittedly the good is the same for a city as for an individual, still the good of the city is apparently a greater and more complete good to acquire and preserve. For while it is satisfactory to acquire and preserve the good even for an individual, it is finer and more divine to acquire and preserve it for a people and for cities. And so, since our investigation aims at these [goods, for an individual and for a city], it is a sort of political science.

1.3 The Method of Political Inquiry

Our discussion will be adequate if its degree of clarity fits the subject-matter; for we should not seek the same degree of exactness in all sorts of arguments alike, any more than in the products of different crafts.

Moreover, what is fine and what is just, the topics of inquiry in political science, differ and vary so much that they seem to rest on convention only, not on nature. Goods, however, also vary in the same sort of way, since they cause harm to many people; for it has happened that some people have been destroyed because of their wealth, others because of their bravery.

Since these, then, are the sorts of things we argue from and about, it will be satisfactory if we can indicate the truth roughly and in outline; since [that is to say] we argue from and about what holds good usually [but not universally], it will be satisfactory if we can draw conclusions of the same sort.

Each of our claims, then, ought to be accepted in the same way [as claiming to hold good usually], since the educated person seeks exactness in each area to the extent that the nature of the subject allows; for apparently it is just as mistaken to demand demonstrations from a rhetorician as to accept [merely] persuasive arguments from a mathematician.

Further, each person judges well what he knows, and is a good judge about that; hence the good judge in a particular area is the person educated in that area, and the unconditionally good judge is the person educated in every area.

This is why a youth is not a suitable student of political science; for he lacks experience of the actions in life which political science argues from and about.

Moreover, since he tends to be guided by his feelings, his study will be futile and useless; for its end is action, not knowledge. And here it does not matter whether he is young in years or immature in character, since the deficiency does not depend on age, but results from being guided in his life and in each of his pursuits by his feelings; for an immature person, like an incontinent person, gets no benefit from his knowledge.

If, however, we are guided by reason in forming our desires and in acting, then this knowledge will be of great benefit.

These are the preliminary points about the student, about the way our claims are to be accepted, and about what we intend to do.

1.4 Common Beliefs about the Highest Good Are Inadequate

Let us, then, begin again. Since every sort of knowledge and decision pursues some good, what is that good which we say is the aim of political science? What [in other words] is the highest of all the goods pursued in action?

As far as its name goes, most people virtually agree [about what the good is], since both the many and the cultivated call it happiness, and suppose that living well and doing well are the same as being happy. But they disagree about what happiness is, and the many do not give the same answer as the wise.

For the many think it is something obvious and evident, e.g., pleasure, wealth or honour, some thinking one thing, others another; and indeed the same person keeps changing his mind, since in sickness he thinks it is health, in poverty wealth. And when they are conscious of their own

ignorance, they admire anyone who speaks of something grand and beyond them.

[Among the wise,] however, some used to think that besides these many
goods there is some other good that is something in itself, and also causes
all these goods to be goods.

Presumably, then, it is rather futile to examine all these beliefs, and it is
enough to examine those that are most current or seem to have some
argument for them.

We must notice, however, the difference between arguments from origins and arguments towards origins. For indeed Plato was right to be
puzzled about this, when he used to ask if [the argument] set out from the
origins or led towards them—just as on a race course the path may go
from the starting-line to the far end, or back again.

For while we should certainly begin from origins that are known, things
are known in two ways; for some are known to us, some known unconditionally [but not necessarily known to us]. Presumably, then, the origin *we*
should begin from is what is known to *us*.

This is why we need to have been brought up in fine habits if we are to
be adequate students of what is fine and just, and of political questions
generally. For the origin we begin from is the belief that something is true,
and if this is apparent enough to us, we will not, at this stage, need the
reason why it is true in addition; and if we have this good upbringing, we
have the origins to begin from, or can easily acquire them. Someone who
neither has them nor can acquire them should listen to Hesiod: "He who
understands everything himself is best of all; he is noble also who listens to
one who has spoken well; but he who neither understands it himself nor
takes to heart what he hears from another is a useless man."

But let us begin again from [the common beliefs] from which we
digressed. For, it would seem, people quite reasonably reach their conception of the good, i.e., of happiness, from the lives [they lead]; for there are
roughly three most favoured lives—the lives of gratification, of political
activity, and, third, of study.

The many, the most vulgar, seemingly conceive the good and happiness
as pleasure, and hence they also like the life of gratification. Here they
appear completely slavish, since the life they decide on is a life for grazing
animals; and yet they have some argument in their defence, since many in
positions of power feel the same way as Sardanapallus [and also choose this
life].

The cultivated people, those active [in politics], conceive the good as
honour, since this is more or less the end [normally pursued] in the
political life. This, however, appears to be too superficial to be what we are
seeking, since it seems to depend more on those who honour than on the

one honoured, whereas we intuitively believe that the good is something of our own and hard to take from us.

Further, their aim in pursuing honour is seemingly to convince themselves that they are good; at any rate, they seek to be honoured by intelligent people, among people who know them, and for virtue. It is clear, then, that in the view of active people at least, virtue is superior [to honour].

Perhaps, indeed, one might conceive virtue more than honour to be the end of the political life. However, this also is apparently too incomplete [to be the good]. For, it seems, someone might possess virtue but be asleep or inactive throughout his life; or, further, he might suffer the worst evils and misfortunes; and if this is the sort of life he leads, no one would count him happy, except to defend a philosopher's paradox. Enough about this, since it has been adequately discussed in the popular works also.

The third life is the life of study, which we will examine in what follows.

The money-maker's life is in a way forced on him [not chosen for itself]; and clearly wealth is not the good we are seeking, since it is [merely] useful, [choiceworthy only] for some other end. Hence one would be more inclined to suppose that [any of] the goods mentioned earlier is the end, since they are liked for themselves. But apparently they are not [the end] either; and many arguments have been presented against them. Let us, then, dismiss them.

. . .

1.5 Characteristics of the Good

But let us return once again to the good we are looking for, and consider just what it could be, since it is apparently one thing in one action or craft, and another thing in another; for it is one thing in medicine, another in generalship, and so on for the rest.

What, then, is the good in each of these cases? Surely it is that for the sake of which the other things are done; and in medicine this is health, in generalship victory, in house-building a house, in another case something else, but in every action and decision it is the end, since it is for the sake of the end that everyone does the other things.

And so, if there is some end of everything that is pursued in action, this will be the good pursued in action; and if there are more ends than one, these will be the goods pursued in action.

Our argument has progressed, then, to the same conclusion [as before, that the highest end is the good]; but we must try to clarify this still more.

Though apparently there are many ends, we choose some of them, e.g., wealth, flutes and, in general, instruments, because of something else; hence it is clear that not all ends are complete. But the best good is apparently something complete. Hence, if only one end is complete, this will be what we are looking for; and if more than one are complete, the most complete of these will be what we are looking for.

An end pursued in itself, we say, is more complete than an end pursued because of something else; and an end that is never choiceworthy because of something else is more complete than ends that are choiceworthy both in themselves and because of this end; and hence an end that is always [choiceworthy, and also] choiceworthy in itself, never because of something else, is unconditionally complete.

Now happiness more than anything else seems unconditionally complete, since we always [choose it, and also] choose it because of itself, never because of something else.

Honour, pleasure, understanding and every virtue we certainly choose because of themselves, since we would choose each of them even if it had no further result, but we also choose them for the sake of happiness, supposing that through them we shall be happy. Happiness, by contrast, no one ever chooses for their sake, or for the sake of anything else at all.

The same conclusion [that happiness is complete] also appears to follow from self-sufficiency, since the complete good seems to be self-sufficient.

Now what we count as self-sufficient is not what suffices for a solitary person by himself, living an isolated life, but what suffices also for parents, children, wife and in general for friends and fellow-citizens, since a human being is a naturally political [animal]. Here, however, we must impose some limit; for if we extend the good to parents' parents and children's children and to friends of friends, we shall go on without limit; but we must examine this another time.

Anyhow, we regard something as self-sufficient when all by itself it makes a life choiceworthy and lacking nothing; and that is what we think happiness does.

Moreover, [the complete good is most choiceworthy, and] we think happiness is most choiceworthy of all goods, since it is not counted as one good among many. If it were counted as one among many, then, clearly, we think that the addition of the smallest of goods would make it more choiceworthy; for [the smallest good] that is added becomes an extra quantity of goods [so creating a good larger than the original good], and the larger of two goods is always more choiceworthy. [But we do not think any addition can make happiness more choiceworthy; hence it is most choiceworthy.]

Happiness, then, is apparently something complete and self-sufficient, since it is the end of the things pursued in action.

But presumably the remark that the best good is happiness is apparently something [generally] agreed, and what we miss is a clearer statement of what the best good is.

Well, perhaps we shall find the best good if we first find the function of a human being. For just as the good, i.e., [doing] well, for a flautist, a sculptor, and every craftsman, and, in general, for whatever has a function and [characteristic] action, seems to depend on its function, the same seems to be true for a human being, if a human being has some function.

Then do the carpenter and the leatherworker have their functions and actions, while a human being has none, and is by nature idle, without any function? Or, just as eye, hand, foot and, in general, every [bodily] part apparently has its functions, may we likewise ascribe to a human being some function besides all of theirs?

What, then, could this be? For living is apparently shared with plants, but what we are looking for is the special function of a human being; hence we should set aside the life of nutrition and growth. The life next in order is some sort of life of sense-perception; but this too is apparently shared, with horse, ox and every animal. The remaining possibility, then, is some sort of life of action of the [part of the soul] that has reason.

Now this [part has two parts, which have reason in different ways], one as obeying the reason [in the other part], the other as itself having reason and thinking. [We intend both.] Moreover, life is also spoken of in two ways [as capacity and as activity], and we must take [a human being's special function to be] life as activity, since this seems to be called life to a fuller extent.

(a) We have found, then, that the human function is the soul's activity that expresses reason [as itself having reason] or requires reason [as obeying reason]. (b) Now the function of F, e.g., of a harpist, is the same in kind, so we say, as the function of an excellent F, e.g., an excellent harpist. (c) The same is true unconditionally in every case, when we add to the function the superior achievement that expresses the virtue; for a harpist's function, e.g., is to play the harp, and a good harpist's is to do it well. (d) Now we take the human function to be a certain kind of life, and take this life to be the soul's activity and actions that express reason. (e) [Hence by (c) and (d)] the excellent man's function is to do this finely and well. (f) Each function is completed well when its completion expresses the proper virtue. (g) Therefore [by (d), (e) and (f)] the human good turns out to be the soul's activity that expresses virtue.

And if there are more virtues than one, the good will express the best and most complete virtue. Moreover, it will be in a complete life. For one swallow does not make a spring, nor does one day; nor, similarly, does one day or a short time make us blessed and happy.

. . .

1.7 Defence of Our Account of the Good, from Common Beliefs

However, we should examine the origin not only from the conclusion and premises [of a deductive argument], but also from what is said about it; for all the facts harmonize with a true account, whereas the truth soon clashes with a false one.

Goods are divided, then, into three types, some called external, some goods of the soul, others goods of the body; and the goods of the soul are said to be goods to the fullest extent and most of all, and the soul's actions and activities are ascribed to the soul. Hence the account [of the good] is sound, to judge by this belief anyhow—and it is an ancient belief agreed on by philosophers.

Our account is also correct in saying that some sort of actions and activities are the end; for then the end turns out to be a good of the soul, not an external good.

The belief that the happy person lives well and does well in action also agrees with our account, since we have virtually said that the end is a sort of living well and doing well in action.

Further, all the features that people look for in happiness appear to be true of the end described in our account. For to some people it seems to be virtue; to others intelligence; to others some sort of wisdom; to others again it seems to be these, or one of these, involving pleasure or requiring its addition; and others add in external prosperity as well.

Some of these views are traditional, held by many, while others are held by a few reputable men; and it is reasonable for each group to be not entirely in error, but correct on one point at least, or even on most points.

First, our account agrees with those who say happiness is virtue [in general] or some [particular] virtue; for activity expressing virtue is proper to virtue. Presumably, though, it matters quite a bit whether we suppose that the best good consists in possessing or in using, i.e., in a state or in an activity [that actualizes the state]. For while someone may be in a state that achieves no good, if, e.g., he is asleep or inactive in some other way, this cannot be true of the activity; for it will necessarily do actions and do well in them. And just as Olympic prizes are not for the finest and strongest, but for contestants, since it is only these who win; so also in life [only] the fine and good people who act correctly win the prize.

Moreover, the life of these [active] people is also pleasant in itself. For being pleased is a condition of the soul, [hence included in the activity of the soul]. Further, each type of person finds pleasure in whatever he is called a lover of, so that a horse, e.g., pleases the horse-lover, a spectacle the lover of spectacles, and similarly what is just pleases the lover of justice, and in general what expresses virtue pleases the lover of virtue. Hence the things that please most people conflict, because they are not pleasant by nature, whereas the things that please lovers of what is fine are things pleasant by nature; and actions expressing virtue are pleasant in this way; and so they both please lovers of what is fine and are pleasant in themselves.

Hence their life does not need pleasure to be added [to virtuous activity] as some sort of ornament; rather, it has its pleasure within itself. For besides the reasons already given, no one is good if he does not enjoy fine actions; for no one would call him just, e.g., if he did not enjoy doing just actions, or generous if he did not enjoy generous actions, and similarly for the other virtues. If this is so, then actions expressing the virtues are pleasant in themselves.

Moreover, these actions are good and fine as well as pleasant; indeed, they are good, fine and pleasant more than anything else, since on this question the excellent person has good judgement, and his judgement agrees with our conclusions.

Happiness, then, is best, finest and most pleasant, and these three features are not distinguished in the way suggested by the Delian inscription: "What is most just is finest; being healthy is most beneficial; but it is most pleasant to win our heart's desire." For all three features are found in the best activities, and happiness we say is these activities, or [rather] one of them, the best one.

Nonetheless, happiness evidently also needs external goods to be added [to the activity], as we said, since we cannot, or cannot easily, do fine actions if we lack the resources.

For, first of all, in many actions we use friends, wealth and political power just as we use instruments. Further, deprivation of certain [externals]—e.g., good birth, good children, beauty—mars our blessedness; for we do not altogether have the character of happiness if we look utterly repulsive or are ill-born, solitary or childless, and have it even less, presumably, if our children or friends are totally bad, or were good but have died.

And so, as we have said, happiness would seem to need this sort of prosperity added also; that is why some people identify happiness with good fortune, while others [reacting from one extreme to the other] identify it with virtue.

. . .

[Happiness needs a complete life.] For life includes many reversals of fortune, good and bad, and the most prosperous person may fall into a terrible disaster in old age, as the Trojan stories tell us about Priam; but if someone has suffered these sorts of misfortunes and comes to a miserable end, no one counts him happy.

Then should we count no human being happy during his lifetime, but follow Solon's advice to wait to see the end? And if we should hold that, can he really be happy during the time after he has died? Surely that is completely absurd, especially when we say happiness is an activity.

· · ·

If, then, we must wait to see the end, and must then count someone blessed, not as being blessed [during the time he is dead] but because he previously was blessed, surely it is absurd if at the time when he is happy we will not truly ascribe to him the happiness he has.

[We hesitate] out of reluctance to call him happy during his lifetime, because of the variations, and because we suppose happiness is enduring and definitely not prone to fluctuate, whereas the same person's fortunes often turn to and fro. For clearly, if we are guided by his fortunes, so that we often call him happy and then miserable again, we will be representing the happy person as a kind of chameleon, insecurely based.

But surely it is quite wrong to be guided by someone's fortunes. For his doing well or badly does not rest on them; though a human life, as we said, needs these added, it is the activities expressing virtue that control happiness, and the contrary activities that control its contrary.

Still, it is apparently rather unfriendly and contrary to the [common] beliefs to claim that the fortunes of our descendants and all our friends contribute nothing. But since they can find themselves in many and various circumstances, some of which affect us more, some less, it is apparently a long, indeed endless, task to differentiate all the particular cases, and perhaps a general outline will be enough of an answer.

Misfortunes, then, even to the person himself, differ, and some have a certain weight and influence on his life, while others would seem to be lighter. The same is true for the misfortunes of his friends; and it matters whether they happen to living or to dead people—much more than it matters whether lawless and terrible crimes are committed before a tragic drama begins or in the course of it. In our reasoning, then, we should also take account of this difference, and even more, presumably, of the puzzle about whether the dead share in any good or evil.

For if we consider this, anything good or evil penetrating to the dead would seem to be weak and unimportant, either unconditionally or for them; and even if it is not, still its size and character are not enough to make people happy who are not happy, or to take away the blessedness of those who are happy. And so, when friends do well, and likewise when they

do badly, it appears to contribute something to the dead, but of a character
and size that neither makes happy people not happy nor anything else of
this sort.

. . .

1.9 Introduction to the Account of Virtue

Since happiness is an activity of the soul expressing complete virtue, we
must examine virtue; for that will perhaps also be a way to study happiness
better.

. . .

It is clear that the virtue we must examine is human virtue, since we are
also seeking the human good and human happiness. And by human virtue
we mean virtue of the soul, not of the body, since we also say that happiness is an activity of the soul. If this is so, then it is clear that the politician
must acquire some knowledge about the soul, just as someone setting out
to heal the eyes must acquire knowledge about the whole body as well.
This is all the more true to the extent that political science is better and
more honourable than medicine—and even among doctors the cultivated
ones devote a lot of effort to acquiring knowledge about the body. Hence
the politician as well [as the student of nature] must study the soul.

But he must study it for the purpose [of inquiring into virtue], as far as
suffices for what he seeks; for a more exact treatment would presumably
take more effort than his purpose requires. [We] have discussed the soul
sufficiently [for our purposes] in [our] popular works as well [as our less
popular], and we should use this discussion.

We have said, e.g., that one [part] of the soul is nonrational, while one
has reason. Are these distinguished as parts of a body and everything
divisible into parts are? Or are they two only in account, and inseparable
by nature, as the convex and the concave are in a surface? It does not
matter for present purposes.

Consider the nonrational [part]. One [part] of it, i.e., the cause of
nutrition and growth, is seemingly plant-like and shared [with other living
things]: for we can ascribe this capacity of the soul to everything that is
nourished, including embryos, and the same one to complete living things,
since this is more reasonable than to ascribe another capacity to them.

. . .

Another nature in the soul would also seem to be nonrational, though in
a way it shares in reason.

[Clearly it is nonrational.] For in the continent and the incontinent person we praise their reason, i.e., the [part] of the soul that has reason, because it exhorts them correctly and towards what is best; but they evidently also have in them some other [part] that is by nature something besides reason, conflicting and struggling with reason.

For just as paralysed parts of a body, when we decide to move them to the right, do the contrary and move off to the left, the same is true of the soul; for incontinent people have impulses in contrary directions. In bodies, admittedly, we see the part go astray, whereas we do not see it in the soul; nonetheless, presumably, we should suppose that the soul also has a [part] besides reason, contrary to and countering reason. The [precise] way it is different does not matter.

However, this [part] as well [as the rational part] appears, as we said, to share in reason. At any rate, in the continent person it obeys reason; and in the temperate and the brave person it presumably listens still better to reason, since there it agrees with reason in everything.

The nonrational [part], then, as well [as the whole soul] apparently has two parts. For while the plant-like [part] shares in reason not at all, the [part] with appetites and in general desires shares in reason in a way, in so far as it both listens to reason and obeys it.

It listens in the way in which we are said to "listen to reason" from father or friends, not in the way in which we ["give the reason"] in mathematics.

The nonrational part also [obeys and] is persuaded in some way by reason, as is shown by chastening, and by every sort of reproof and exhortation.

If we ought to say, then, that this [part] also has reason, then the [part] that has reason, as well [as the nonrational part] will have two parts, one that has reason to the full extent by having it within itself, and another [that has it] by listening to reason as to a father.

The distinction between virtues also reflects this difference. For some virtues are called virtues of thought, other virtues of character; wisdom, comprehension and intelligence are called virtues of thought, generosity and temperance virtues of character.

For when we speak of someone's character we do not say that he is wise or has good comprehension, but that he is gentle or temperate. [Hence these are the virtues of character.] And yet, we also praise the wise person for his state, and the states that are praiseworthy are the ones we call virtues. [Hence wisdom is also a virtue.]

2. Virtues of Character in General

2.1 How a Virtue of Character Is Acquired

Virtue, then, is of two sorts, virtue of thought and virtue of character. Virtue of thought arises and grows mostly from teaching, and hence needs experience and time. Virtue of character [i.e. of *ēthos*] results from habit [*ethos*]; hence its name "ethical," slightly varied from "*ethos*."

Hence it is also clear that none of the virtues of character arises in us naturally.

For if something is by nature [in one condition], habituation cannot bring it into another condition. A stone, e.g., by nature moves downwards, and habituation could not make it move upwards, not even if you threw it up ten thousand times to habituate it; nor could habituation make fire move downwards, or bring anything that is by nature in one condition into another condition.

Thus the virtues arise in us neither by nature nor against nature, but we are by nature able to acquire them, and reach our complete perfection through habit.

Further, if something arises in us by nature, we first have the capacity for it, and later display the activity. This is clear in the case of the senses; for we did not acquire them by frequent seeing or hearing, but already had them when we exercised them, and did not get them by exercising them.

Virtues, by contrast, we acquire, just as we acquire crafts, by having previously activated them. For we learn a craft by producing the same product that we must produce when we have learned it, becoming builders, e.g., by building and harpists by playing the harp; so also, then, we become just by doing just actions, temperate by doing temperate actions, brave by doing brave actions.

What goes on in cities is evidence for this also. For the legislator makes the citizens good by habituating them, and this is the wish of every legislator; if he fails to do it well he misses his goal. [The right] habituation is what makes the difference between a good political system and a bad one.

Further, just as in the case of a craft, the sources and means that develop each virtue also ruin it. For playing the harp makes both good and bad harpists, and it is analogous in the case of builders and all the rest; for building well makes good builders, building badly, bad ones. If it were not so, no teacher would be needed, but everyone would be born a good or a bad craftsman.

It is the same, then, with the virtues. For actions in dealings with [other] human beings make some people just, some unjust; actions in terrifying situations and the acquired habit of fear or confidence make some brave and others cowardly. The same is true of situations involving appetites and anger; for one or another sort of conduct in these situations makes some people temperate and gentle, others intemperate and irascible.

To sum up, then, in a single account: A state [of character] arises from [the repetition of] similar activities. Hence we must display the right activities, since differences in these imply corresponding differences in the states. It is not unimportant, then, to acquire one sort of habit or another, right from our youth; rather, it is very important, indeed all-important.

Our present inquiry does not aim, as our others do, at study; for the purpose of our examination is not to know what virtue is, but to become good, since otherwise the inquiry would be of no benefit to us. Hence we must examine the right way to act, since, as we have said, the actions also control the character of the states we acquire.

First, then, actions should express correct reason. That is a common [belief], and let us assume it; later we will say what correct reason is and how it is related to the other virtues.

But let us take it as agreed in advance that every account of the actions we must do has to be stated in outline, not exactly. As we also said at the start, the type of accounts we demand should reflect the subject-matter; and questions about actions and expediency, like questions about health, have no fixed [and invariable answers].

And when our general account is so inexact, the account of particular cases is all the more inexact. For these fall under no craft or profession, and the agents themselves must consider in each case what the opportune action is, as doctors and navigators do.

The account we offer, then, in our present inquiry is of this inexact sort; still, we must try to offer help.

First, then, we should observe that these sorts of states naturally tend to be ruined by excess and deficiency. We see this happen with strength and health, which we mention because we must use what is evident as a witness to what is not. For both excessive and deficient exercises ruin strength; and likewise, too much or too little eating or drinking ruins health, while the proportionate amount produces, increases and preserves it.

The same is true, then, of temperance, bravery and the other virtues. For if, e.g., someone avoids and is afraid of everything, standing firm against nothing, he becomes cowardly, but if he is afraid of nothing at all and goes to face everything, he becomes rash. Similarly, if he gratifies himself with every pleasure and refrains from none, he becomes intemperate, but if he avoids them all, as boors do, he becomes some sort of insensible person. Temperance and bravery, then, are ruined by excess and deficiency but preserved by the mean.

The same actions, then, are the sources and causes both of the emergence and growth of virtues and of their ruin; but further, the activities of the virtues will be found in these same actions. For this is also true of more evident cases, e.g., strength, which arises from eating a lot and from withstanding much hard labour, and it is the strong person who is most able to do these very things. It is the same with the virtues. Refraining from pleasures make us become temperate, and when we have become temperate we are most able to refrain from pleasures. And it is similar with bravery; habituation in disdaining what is fearful and in standing firm against it makes us become brave, and when we have become brave we shall be most able to stand firm.

But [actions are not enough]; we must take as a sign of someone's state his pleasure or pain in consequence of his action. For if someone who abstains from bodily pleasures enjoys the abstinence itself, then he is temperate, but if he is grieved by it, he is intemperate. Again, if he stands firm against terrifying situations and enjoys it, or at least does not find it painful, then he is brave, and if he finds it painful, he is cowardly.

[Pleasures and pains are appropriately taken as signs] because virtue of character is concerned with pleasures and pains.

. . .

However, someone might raise this puzzle: "What do you mean by saying that to become just we must first do just actions and to become temperate we must first do temperate actions? For if we do what is grammatical or musical, we must already be grammarians or musicians. In the same way, then, if we do what is just or temperate, we must already be just or temperate."

But surely this is not so even with the crafts, for it is possible to produce something grammatical by chance or by following someone else's instructions. To be a grammarian, then, we must both produce something grammatical and produce it in the way in which the grammarian produces it, i.e., expressing grammatical knowledge that is in us.

Moreover, in any case what is true of crafts is not true of virtues. For the products of a craft determine by their own character whether they have been produced well; and so it suffices that they are in the right state when they have been produced. But for actions expressing virtue to be done temperately or justly [and hence well] it does not suffice that they are themselves in the right state. Rather, the agent must also be in the right state when he does them. First, he must know [that he is doing virtuous actions]; second, he must decide on them, and decide on them for themselves; and, third, he must also do them from a firm and unchanging state.

As conditions for having a craft these three do not count, except for the knowing itself. As a condition for having a virtue, however, the knowing counts for nothing, or [rather] for only a little, whereas the other two conditions are very important, indeed all-important. And these other two conditions are achieved by the frequent doing of just and temperate actions.

Hence actions are called just or temperate when they are the sort that a just or temperate person would do. But the just and temperate person is not the one who [merely] does these actions, but the one who also does them in the way in which just or temperate people do them.

It is right, then, to say that a person comes to be just from doing just actions and temperate from doing temperate actions; for no one has even a prospect of becoming good from failing to do them.

The many, however, do not do these actions but take refuge in arguments, thinking that they are doing philosophy, and that this is the way to become excellent people. In this they are like a sick person who listens attentively to the doctor, but acts on none of his instructions. Such a course of treatment will not improve the state of his body; any more than will the many's way of doing philosophy improve the state of their souls.

2.2 A Virtue of Character Is a State Intermediate between Two Extremes, and Involving Decision

Next we must examine what virtue is. Since there are three conditions arising in the soul—feelings, capacities and states—virtue must be one of these.

By feelings I mean appetite, anger, fear, confidence, envy, joy, love, hate, longing, jealousy, pity, in general whatever implies pleasure or pain.

By capacities I mean what we have when we are said to be capable of these feelings—capable of, e.g., being angry or afraid or feeling pity.

By states I mean what we have when we are well or badly off in relation to feelings. If, e.g., our feeling is too intense or slack, we are badly off in relation to anger, but if it is intermediate, we are well off; and the same is true in the other cases.

First, then, neither virtues nor vices are feelings. (a) For we are called excellent or base in so far as we have virtues or vices, not in so far as we have feelings. (b) We are neither praised nor blamed in so far as we have feelings; for we do not praise the angry or the frightened person, and do not blame the person who is simply angry, but only the person who is angry in a particular way. But we are praised or blamed in so far as we have virtues or vices. (c) We are angry and afraid without decision; but the virtues are decisions of some kind, or [rather] require decision. (d) Besides, in so far as we have feelings, we are said to be moved; but in so far as we have virtues or vices, we are said to be in some condition rather than moved.

For these reasons the virtues are not capacities either; for we are neither called good nor called bad in so far as we are simply capable of feelings. Further, while we have capacities by nature, we do not become good or bad by nature; we have discussed this before.

If, then, the virtues are neither feelings nor capacities, the remaining possibility is that they are states. And so we have said what the genus of virtue is.

But we must say not only, as we already have, that it is a state, but also what sort of state it is.

It should be said, then, that every virtue causes its possessors to be in a good state and to perform their functions well; the virtue of eyes, e.g., makes the eyes and their functioning excellent, because it makes us see well; and similarly, the virtue of a horse makes the horse excellent, and thereby good at galloping, at carrying its rider and at standing steady in the face of the enemy. If this is true in every case, then the virtue of a human being will likewise be the state that makes a human being good and makes him perform his function well.

We have already said how this will be true, and it will also be evident from our next remarks, if we consider the sort of nature that virtue has.

In everything continuous and divisible we can take more, less and equal, and each of them either in the object itself or relative to us; and the equal is some intermediate between excess and deficiency.

By the intermediate in the object I mean what is equidistant from each extremity; this is one and the same for everyone. But relative to us the intermediate is what is neither superfluous nor deficient; this is not one, and is not the same for everyone.

If, e.g., ten are many and two are few, we take six as intermediate in the object, since it exceeds [two] and is exceeded [by ten] by an equal amount, [four]; this is what is intermediate by numerical proportion. But that is not how we must take the intermediate that is relative to us. For if, e.g., ten pounds [of food] are a lot for someone to eat, and two pounds a little, it does not follow that the trainer will prescribe six, since this might also be either a little or a lot for the person who is to take it—for Milo [the athlete] a little, but for the beginner in gymnastics a lot; and the same is true for running and wrestling. In this way every scientific expert avoids excess and deficiency and seeks and chooses what is intermediate—but intermediate relative to us, not in the object.

This, then, is how each science produces its product well, by focusing on what is intermediate and making the product conform to that. This, indeed, is why people regularly comment on well-made products that nothing could be added or subtracted, since they assume that excess or deficiency ruins a good [result] while the mean preserves it. Good craftsmen also, we say, focus on what is intermediate when they produce their product. And since virtue, like nature, is better and more exact than any craft, it will also aim at what is intermediate.

By virtue I mean virtue of character; for this [pursues the mean because] it is concerned with feelings and actions, and these admit of excess, deficiency and an intermediate condition. We can be afraid, e.g., or be confident, or have appetites, or get angry, or feel pity, in general have pleasure or pain, both too much and too little, and in both ways not well; but [having these feelings] at the right times, about the right things, towards the right people, for the right end, and in the right way, is the intermediate and best condition, and this is proper to virtue. Similarly, actions also admit of excess, deficiency and the intermediate condition.

Now virtue is concerned with feelings and actions, in which excess and deficiency are in error and incur blame, while the intermediate condition is correct and wins praise, which are both proper features of virtue. Virtue, then, is a mean, in so far as it aims at what is intermediate.

Moreover, there are many ways to be in error, since badness is proper to what is unlimited, as the Pythagoreans pictured it, and good to what is limited; but there is only one way to be correct. That is why error is easy and correctness hard, since it is easy to miss the target and hard to hit it. And so for this reason also excess and deficiency are proper to vice, the mean to virtue; "for we are noble in only one way, but bad in all sorts of ways."

Virtue, then, is (a) a state that decides, (b) [consisting] in a mean, (c) the mean relative to us, (d) which is defined by reference to reason, (e) i.e., to the reason by reference to which the intelligent person would define it. It is a mean between two vices, one of excess and one of deficiency.

It is a mean for this reason also: Some vices miss what is right because they are deficient, others because they are excessive, in feelings or in actions, while virtue finds and chooses what is intermediate.

Hence, as far as its substance and the account stating its essence are concerned, virtue is a mean; but as far as the best [condition] and the good [result] are concerned, it is an extremity.

But not every action or feeling admits of the mean. For the names of some automatically include baseness, e.g., spite, shamelessness, envy [among feelings], and adultery, theft, murder, among actions. All of these and similar things are called by these names because they themselves, not their excesses or deficiencies, are base.

Hence in doing these things we can never be correct, but must invariably be in error. We cannot do them well or not well—e.g., by committing adultery with the right woman at the right time in the right way; on the contrary, it is true unconditionally that to do any of them is to be in error.

[To think these admit of a mean], therefore, is like thinking that unjust or cowardly or intemperate action also admits of a mean, an excess and a deficiency. For then there would be a mean of excess, a mean of deficiency, an excess of excess and a deficiency of deficiency.

Rather, just as there is no excess or deficiency of temperance or of bravery, since the intermediate is a sort of extreme [in achieving the good], so also there is no mean of these [vicious actions] either, but whatever way anyone does them, he is in error. For in general there is no mean of excess or of deficiency, and no excess or deficiency of a mean.

Lucretius,
On the Order of Things

The epic poem On the Order of Things (De Rerum Natura), *by the Roman poet and philosopher Lucretius (c. 99–c. 55* B.C.E.*), lays out the core ideas of Epicureanism, the doctrine originated by the Greek philosopher Epicurus (341–271* B.C.E.*). Almost nothing is known about Lucretius himself—there is no corroboration for St. Jerome's report that Lucretius, driven mad by a love potion, wrote his epic poem while insane and committed suicide at the age of forty-three. Like Epicurus before him, Lucretius begins with the physical theory of Atomism: the view that the universe is made up of physical atoms in a void, and that everything that exists, including humans and whatever gods there might be, are compounds of these atoms. Since everything that happens is the result of the collisions of atoms and the laws of nature, there is no divine guidance, purpose, or providence in the universe. According to this view, humans are entirely composed of physical stuff, and so there is no part of us that can survive the death of the body. This means that there is no consciousness after death and, hence, no reason to fear death. Moreover, since the gods are as much a part of the physical universe as anything else, they are not to be feared. Understanding these things can liberate us from fear and bring us acceptance of the way things are.*

Epicureans hold that the desire for pleasure and the avoidance of pain are the ultimate motivating factors behind all human action. The best way to attain a durable sense of well-being and prevent pain, according to this doctrine, is to achieve a clear view of the way things are and, using that knowledge, train ourselves so that we desire nothing beyond what is natural and necessary for humans. To live in tune with nature, we should adopt a simple way of life in which our chief aim is to release ourselves from pointless needs and desires so as to achieve "serenity" or "freedom from disturbance" (ataraxia). This ideal accounts for Lucretius' criticism of sexual pursuits as producing only transient pleasures and as ultimately insatiable. The wise person is one who can transcend the preoccupation with satisfying basic needs, achieve detachment from worldly involvements, and, in the company of like-minded friends, live a life of equilibrium, tranquillity, and contentment.

Book Two

What joy it is, when out at sea the stormwinds are lashing the waters, to gaze from the shore at the heavy stress some other man is enduring! Not that anyone's afflictions are in themselves a source of delight; but to realize from what troubles you yourself are free is joy indeed. What joy, again, to watch opposing hosts marshalled on the field of battle when you have yourself no part in their peril! But this is the greatest joy of all: to possess a quiet sanctuary, stoutly fortified by the teaching of the wise, and to gaze down from that elevation on others wandering aimlessly in search of a way of life, pitting their wits one against another, disputing for precedence, struggling night and day with unstinted effort to scale the pinnacles of wealth and power. O joyless hearts of men! O minds without vision! How dark and dangerous the life in which this tiny span is lived away! Do you not see that nature is barking for two things only, a body free from pain, a mind released from worry and fear for the enjoyment of pleasurable sensations?

So we find that the requirements of our bodily nature are few indeed, no more than is necessary to banish pain, and also to spread out many pleasures for ourselves. Nature does not periodically seek anything more gratifying than this, not complaining if there are no golden images of youths about the house, holding flaming torches in their right hands to illumine banquets prolonged into the night. What matter if the hall does not sparkle with silver and gleam with gold, and no carved and gilded rafters ring to the music of the lute? Nature does not miss these luxuries when men recline in company on the soft grass by a running stream under the branches of a tall tree and refresh their bodies pleasurably at small expense. Better still if the weather smiles upon them, and the season of the year stipples the green herbage with flowers. Burning fevers flee no swifter from your body if you toss under figured counterpanes and coverlets of crimson than if you must lie in rude homespun.

If our bodies are not profited by treasures or titles or the majesty of kingship, we must go on to admit that neither are our minds. Or tell me, Memmius, when you see your legions thronging the Campus Martius in the ardour of mimic warfare, supported by ample auxiliaries and a force of cavalry, magnificently armed and fired by a common purpose, does that sight scare the terrors of superstition from your mind? Does the fear of death retire from your breast and leave it carefree? Or do we not find such resources absurdly ineffective? The fears and anxieties that dog the human breast do not shrink from the clash of arms or the fierce rain of missiles.

From Lucretius, *On the Nature of the Universe,* trans. by R. E. Latham (London: Penguin Books, 1994). Reprinted by permission of the publisher.

They stalk unabashed among princes and potentates. They are not awe-
struck by the gleam of gold or the bright sheen of purple robes.

Can you doubt then that this power rests with reason alone? All life is a
struggle in the dark. As children in blank darkness tremble and start at
everything, so we in broad daylight are oppressed at times by fears as
baseless as those horrors which children imagine coming upon them in the
dark. This dread and darkness of the mind cannot be dispelled by the
sunbeams, the shining shafts of day, but only by an understanding of the
outward form and inner workings of nature.

Book Three

. . . I have already shown what the component bodies of everything are
like: how they vary in shape: how they fly spontaneously through space,
impelled by a perpetual motion: and how from these all objects can be
created. The next step now is evidently to elucidate in my verses the
nature of mind and of spirit. In so doing I must throw out the fear of
Acheron head over heels—that fear which blasts the life of man from its
very foundations, sullying everything with the blackness of death and
leaving no pleasure pure and unalloyed. I know that men often speak of
sickness or of shameful life as more to be dreaded than the lowest pit of
death; they claim to know that the mind consists of blood, or maybe wind,
if that is how the whim takes them, and to stand in no need whatever of our
reasoning. But all this talk is based more on a desire to show off than on
actual proof, as you may infer from their conduct. These same men,
though they may be exiled from home, banished far from the sight of their
fellows, soiled with the accusation of some filthy crime, a prey to every
torment, still cling to life. Wherever they come in their tribulation, they
make propitiatory sacrifices, slaughter black cattle and despatch offerings
to the Departed Spirits. The heavier their afflictions, the more devoutly
they turn their minds to superstition. Look at a man in the midst of
trouble and danger, and you will learn in his hour of adversity what he
really is. It is then that true utterances are wrung from the depths of his
heart. The mask is torn off; the reality remains.

Consider too the greed and blind lust of status that drive pathetic men
to overstep the bounds of right and may even turn them into accomplices
or instruments of crime, struggling night and day with unstinted effort to
scale the pinnacles of wealth. These running sores of life are fed in no
small measure by the fear of death. For abject ignominy and irksome
poverty seem far indeed from the joy and assurance of life, loitering
already in effect at the gateway of death. From such a fate men revolt in
groundless terror and long to escape far, far away. So in their greed of gain

they amass a fortune out of civil bloodshed; piling wealth on wealth, they heap carnage on carnage. With heartless glee they welcome a brother's tragic death. They hate and fear the hospitable board of their own kin. Often, in the same spirit and influenced by the same fear, they are consumed with envy at the sight of another's success: he walks in a blaze of glory, looked up to by all, while they curse the dingy squalor in which their own lives are bogged. Some sacrifice life itself for the sake of statues and a title. Often from fear of death mortals are gripped by such a hate of living and looking on the light that with anguished hearts they do themselves to death. They forget that this fear is the very fountainhead of their troubles: this it is that harasses conscience, snaps the bonds of friendship and in a word utterly destroys all moral responsibility. For many a time before now men have betrayed their country and their beloved parents in an effort to escape the halls of Acheron.

As children in blank darkness tremble and start at everything, so we in broad daylight are oppressed at times by fears as baseless as those horrors which children imagine coming upon them in the dark. This dread and darkness of the mind cannot be dispelled by the sunbeams, the shining shafts of day, but only by an understanding of the outward form and inner workings of nature.

. . .

From all this it follows that *death is nothing to us* and no concern of ours, since the nature of the mind is now held to be mortal. In days of old, we felt no disquiet when the hosts of Carthage poured in to battle on every side—when the whole earth, dizzied by the convulsive shock of war, reeled sickeningly under the high ethereal vault, and between realm and realm the empire of mankind by land and sea trembled in the balance. So, when we shall be no more—when the union of body and spirit that engenders us has been disrupted—to us, who shall then be nothing, nothing by any hazard will happen any more at all. Nothing will have power to stir our senses, not though earth be fused with sea and sea with sky.

If any feeling remains in mind or spirit after it has been torn from our body, that is nothing to us, who are brought into being by the wedlock of body and spirit, conjoined and coalesced. Or even if the matter that composes us should be reassembled by time after our death and brought back into its present state—if the light of life were given to us anew—even that contingency would still be no concern of ours once the chain of our identity had been snapped. We who are now are not concerned with ourselves in any previous existence: the sufferings of those selves do not touch us. When you look at the immeasurable extent of time gone by and the multiform movements of matter, you will readily credit that these same atoms that compose us now must many a time before have entered into the selfsame combinations as now. But our mind cannot recall this to remembrance. For between then and now is interposed a break in life, and all the atomic motions have been wandering far astray from sentience.

If the future holds misery and anguish in store, the self must be in existence, when that time comes, in order to be miserable. But from this fate we are redeemed by death, which denies existence to the self that might have suffered these tribulations. Rest assured, therefore, that we have nothing to fear in death. One who no longer is cannot suffer, or differ in any way from one who has never been born, when once this mortal life has been usurped by death the immortal.

When you find a man treating it as a grievance that after death he will either moulder in the grave or fall a prey to flames or to the jaws of predatory beasts, be sure that his utterance does not ring true. Subconsciously his heart is stabbed by a secret dread, however loudly the man himself may disavow the belief that after death he will still experience sensation. I am convinced that he does not grant the admission he professes, nor the grounds of it; he does not oust and pluck himself root and branch out of life, but all unwittingly makes something of himself linger on. When a living man confronts the thought that after death his body will be mauled by birds and beasts prey, he is filled with self-pity. He does not banish himself from the scene nor distinguish sharply enough between himself and that abandoned carcass. He visualizes that object as himself and infects it with his own feelings as an onlooker. That is why he is aggrieved at having been created mortal. He does not see that in real death there will be no other self alive to mourn his own decease—no other self standing by to flinch at the agony he suffers lying there being mangled, or indeed being cremated. For if it is really a bad thing after death to be mauled and crunched by ravening jaws, I cannot see why it should not be disagreeable to roast in the scorching flames of a funeral pyre, or to lie embalmed in honey, stifled and stiff with cold, on the surface of a chilly slab, or to be squashed under a crushing weight of earth.

. . .

Suppose that Nature herself were suddenly to find a voice and round upon one of us in these terms: "What is your grievance, mortal, that you give yourself up to this whining and repining? Why do you weep and wail over death? If the life you have lived till now has been a pleasant thing—if all its blessings have not leaked away like water poured into a cracked pot and run to waste unrelished—why then, you stupid man, do you not retire like a dinner guest who has eaten his fill of life, and take your carefree rest with a quiet mind? Or, if all your gains have been poured profitless away and life has grown distasteful, why do you seek to swell the total? The new can but turn out as badly as the old and perish as unprofitably. Why not rather make an end of life and trouble? Do you expect me to invent some new contrivance for your pleasure? I tell you, there is none. All things are always the same. If your body is not yet withered with age, nor your limbs decrepit and flagging, even so there is nothing new to look forward to—not though you should outlive all living creatures, or even though you should never die at all." What are we to answer, except that Nature's rebuttal is justified and the plea she puts forward is a true one?

But suppose it is some man of riper years who complains—some dismal greybeard who laments over his approaching end far more than he ought. Would she not have every right to protest more vehemently and repulse him in stern tones: "Away with your tears, old reprobate! Have done with your grumbling! You are withering now after tasting all the joys of life. But because you are always pining for what is not and unappreciative of the things at hand, your life has slipped away unfulfilled and unprized. Death has stolen upon you unawares, before you are ready to retire from life's banquet filled and satisfied. Come now, put away all that is unbecoming to your years and compose your mind to make way for others. You have no choice." I cannot question but that she would have right on her side; her censure and rebuke would be well merited. The old is always thrust aside to make way for the new, and one thing must be built out of the wreck of others. There is no murky pit of Tartarus awaiting anyone. There is need of matter, so that later generations may arise; when they have lived out their span, they will all follow you. Bygone generations have taken your road, and those to come will take it no less. So one thing will never cease to spring from another. To none is life given in freehold; to all on lease. Look back at the eternity that passed before we were born, and mark how utterly it counts to us as nothing. This is a mirror that Nature holds up to us, in which we may see the time that shall be after we are dead. Is there anything terrifying in the sight—anything depressing—anything that is not more restful than the soundest sleep?

．　．　．

And the master himself, when his daylit race was run, Epicurus himself died, whose genius outshone the race of men and dimmed them all, as the stars are dimmed by the rising of the fiery sun. And will *you* kick and protest against your sentence? You, whose life is next-door to death although you still live and look on the light. You, who waste the major part of your time in sleep and, when you are awake, are snoring still and dreaming. You, who bear a mind hag-ridden by baseless fear and cannot find the commonest cause of your distress, hounded as you are, pathetic creature, by a pack of troubles and drifting in a drunken stupor upon a wavering tide of fantasy.

Men feel plainly enough within their minds a heavy burden, whose weight depresses them. If only they perceived with equal clearness the causes of this depression, the origin of this lump of evil within their breasts, they would not lead such a life as we now see all too commonly— no one knowing what he really wants and everyone for ever trying to get away from where he is, as though travel alone could throw off the load. Often the owner of some stately mansion, bored stiff by staying at home, takes his departure, only to return as speedily when he feels himself no better off out of doors. Off he goes to his country seat, driving his Gaulish ponies hotfoot, as though rushing to save a house on fire. No sooner has he crossed its doorstep than he starts yawning or retires moodily to sleep and courts oblivion, or else rushes back to revisit the city. In so doing the individual is really running away from himself. Since he remains reluctantly wedded to the self whom he cannot of course escape, he grows to hate him, because he is a sick man ignorant of the cause of his malady. If he did but see this, he would cast other thoughts aside and devote himself first to studying the nature of the universe. It is not the fortune of an hour that is in question, but of all time—the lot in store for mortals throughout the eternity that awaits them after death.

What is this deplorable lust for life that holds us trembling in bondage to such uncertainties and dangers? A fixed term is set to the life of mortals, and there is no way of dodging death. In any case the setting of our lives remains the same throughout, and by going on living we do not mint any new coin of pleasure. So long as the object of our craving is unattained, it seems more precious than anything besides. Once it is ours, we crave for something else. So an unquenchable thirst for life keeps us always on the gasp. There is no telling what fortune the future may bring—what chance may throw in our way, or what upshot lies in waiting. By prolonging life, we cannot subtract or whittle away one jot from the duration of our death. The time after our taking off remains constant. However many generations you may add to your store by living, there waits for you none the less the same eternal death. The period of not-being will be no less for him who made an end of life with today's daylight than for him who perished many a moon and many a year before.

Book Four

. . . Little boys often fancy when fast asleep that they are standing at a lavatory or a chamber pot and lifting up their clothes. Then they discharge all the filtered fluid of their body, and even the costly splendour of oriental coverlets does not escape a soaking. Those boys in whom the seed is for the first time working its way into the choppy waters of their youth are invaded from without by images emanating from some body or other with tidings of an alluring face and a delightful complexion. This stimulates the organs swollen with an accumulation of seed. Often, as though their function were actually fulfilled, they discharge a flood of fluid and stain their clothes.

In this last case, as I have explained, the thing in us that responds to the stimulus is the seed that comes with ripening years and stiffening limbs. For different things respond to different stimuli or provocations. *The one stimulus that evokes human seed from the human body is a human form.* As soon as this seed is evicted from its abodes, it travels through every member of the body, concentrating at certain reservoirs in the loins, and promptly awakens the generative organs. These organs are stimulated and swollen by the seed. Hence follows the will to eject it in the direction in which tyrannical lust is tugging. The body makes for the source from which the mind is pierced by love. For the wounded normally fall in the direction of their wound: the blood spurts out towards the source of the blow; and the enemy who delivered it, if he is fighting at close quarters, is bespattered by the crimson stream. So, when a man is pierced by the shafts of Venus, whether they are launched by a lad with womanish limbs or a woman radiating love from her whole body, he strives towards the source of the wound and craves to be united with it and to ejaculate the fluid drawn from out of his body into that body. His speechless yearning foretells his pleasure.

This, then, is what we term Venus. This is the origin of the thing called love—that drop of Venus' honey that first drips into our heart, to be followed by icy heartache. Though the object of your love may be absent, images of it still haunt you and the beloved name rings sweetly in your ears. If you find yourself thus passionately enamoured of an individual, you should keep well away from such images. Thrust from you anything that might feed your passion, and turn your mind elsewhere. Ejaculate the build-up of seed promiscuously and do not hold on to it—by clinging to it you assure yourself the certainty of heartsickness and pain. With nourishment the festering sore quickens and strengthens. Day by day the madness heightens and the grief deepens. Your only remedy is to lance the first wound with new incisions; to salve it, while it is still fresh, with promiscuous attachments or to guide the motions of your mind into a different direction.

Do not think that by avoiding romantic love you are missing the delights of sex. Rather, you are reaping the sort of profits that carry with them no penalty. Rest assured that this pleasure is enjoyed in a purer form by the sane than by the lovesick. Lovers' passion is storm-tossed, even in the moment of possession, by waves of delusion and incertitude. They cannot make up their mind what to enjoy first with eye or hand. They clasp the object of their longing so tightly that the embrace is painful. They kiss so fiercely that teeth are driven into lips. All this because their pleasure is not pure, but they are goaded by an underlying impulse to hurt the thing, whatever it may be, that gives rise to these budding shoots of madness.

In the actual presence of love Venus gives a slight break in the penalties she imposes, and her sting is assuaged by an admixture of alluring pleasure. For in love there is the hope that the flame of passion may be quenched by the same body that kindled it. But this runs clean counter to the course of nature. This is the one thing of which the more we have, the more our breast burns with the evil lust of having. Food and fluid are taken into our body; since they can fill their allotted places, the desire for meat and drink is thus easily appeased. But a pretty face or a pleasing complexion gives the body nothing to enjoy but insubstantial images, which all too often pathetic hope scatters to the winds.

When a thirsty man tries to drink in his dreams but is given no drop to quench the fire in his limbs, he clutches at images of water with fruitless effort and in the middle of a rushing stream he remains thirsty as he drinks. Just so in the midst of love Venus teases lovers with images. They cannot glut their eyes by gazing on the beloved form, however closely. Their hands can rub nothing from off those dainty limbs in their aimless roving over all the body. Then comes the moment when with limbs entwined they pluck the flower of youth. Their bodies thrill with the joy to come, and Venus is just about to sow the seed in the female fields. Body clings greedily to body; they mingle the saliva of their mouths and breathe hard down each other's mouths pressing them with their teeth. But all to no purpose. One can remove nothing from the other by rubbing, nor enter right in and be wholly absorbed, body in body; for sometimes it seems that that is what they are craving and striving to do, so hungrily do they cling together in Venus' fetters, while their limbs are unnerved and liquefied by the intensity of pleasure. At length, when the build-up of lust has burst out of their groin, there comes a slight intermission in the raging fever. But not for long. Soon the same frenzy returns. The madness is upon them once more. They ask themselves what it is they are craving for, but find no device that will master their malady. In aimless bewilderment they rot away, stricken by a secret sore.

Add to this that they waste their strength and work themselves to death.

Their days are passed at the mercy of another's whim. Their wealth slips from them, transmuted to Babylonian brocades. Their duties are neglected. Their reputation totters and goes into a decline. Perfumes and lovely slippers from Sicyon laugh on her dainty feet; settings of gold enclasp huge emeralds aglow with green fire, and sea-tinted garments are worn thin with constant use and drink the sweat of Venus in their exertions. A hard-won patrimony is metamorphosed into coronets and tiaras or, it may be, into robes from the looms of Malta or Cos. No matter how lavish the décor and the cuisine—drinking parties (with no lack of drinks), entertainments, perfumes, garlands, festoons and all—they are still a waste of time. From the very heart of the fountain of delight there rises a jet of bitterness that poisons the fragrance of the flowers. Perhaps the guilty conscience frets itself remorsefully with the thought of life's best years squandered slothfully in brothels. Perhaps the beloved has let fly some two-edged word, which lodges in the impassioned heart and glows there like a living flame. Perhaps he thinks she is rolling her eyes too freely and turning them upon another, or he catches in her face a hint of mockery.

And these are the evils inherent in love that prospers and fulfils its hopes. In starved and unrequited love the evils you can see plainly without even opening your eyes are past all counting. How much better to be on your guard beforehand, as I have advised, and take care that you are not enmeshed!

To avoid enticement into the snares of love is not so difficult as, once entrapped, to escape out of the toils and snap the tenacious knots of Venus. And yet, be you never so tightly entangled and embrangled, you can still free yourself from the danger unless you stand in the way of your own freedom. First, you should concentrate on all the faults of mind or body of her whom you pursue and lust after. For men often behave as though blinded by love and credit the beloved with charms to which she has no valid title. This is why we see foul and disgusting women basking in a lover's adoration! One man scoffs at another and urges him to propitiate Venus because he is the victim of such a degrading infatuation; yet as like as not the poor devil is in the same pathetic plight himself, but does not realize it. A filthy stinking slut is admired for her "beauty unadorned." Her eyes are never green, but grey as Athene's. If she is stringy and woody, she is lithe as a gazelle. A stunted runt is "one of the Graces," a "sheer delight from top to toe." A massive dragon is "a knockout—a fine figure of a woman." She cannot speak for stammering—a charming lisp, of course. She's as mute as a stockfish—what modesty! A hateful blazing gossip is a "livewire"; she's "slender," "a little love" when she is almost too skinny to live; she is "delicate" when she is half-dead with coughing. The fat girl with enormous breasts is "Ceres suckling Bacchus." The girl with the stumpy little nose is "a Faun," then or "a lady Satyr." The one with balloon lips is "all one big kiss." It would be a wearisome task to run through the whole catalogue of euphemisms. But suppose her face in fact is all that could be desired and the charm of Venus radiates from her whole body. Even so, there are still others. Even so, we lived without her before. Even so, in her physical nature she is no different, as we well know, from the ugly slut. She too has to fumigate her pathetic body with its disgusting smells. Her maids keep well away from her and snigger behind her back. The tearful lover, locked out from her presence, heaps the threshold with flowers and garlands, anoints the disdainful doorposts with marjoram, and plants rueful kisses on the door. Often enough, were he admitted, one whiff would promptly make him cast round for some decent pretext to clear off. His fond elegy, long-pondered and drawn from the bottom of his heart, would fall dismally flat. He would curse himself for a fool to have endowed her with qualities above human imperfection.

To the daughters of Venus themselves all this is no secret. Hence they are at pains to hide all the backstage activities of life from those whom they wish to keep fast bound in the bonds of love. But their pains are wasted, since your mind has power to drag all these mysteries into the daylight and get at the truth behind all the giggling. Then, if the woman is good-hearted and void of malice, it is up to you in your turn to accept unpleasant facts and make allowance for human imperfection.

Do not imagine that a woman is always sighing with feigned love when she clings to a man in a close embrace, body to body, and prolongs his kisses by the tension of moist lips. Often she is acting from the heart and is longing for a shared delight when she stimulates him to run love's race to the end. So, too, with birds and beasts, both tame and wild. Cows and mares would never submit to the males, were it not that their female nature in its superabundance is all aglow thrusting in delight against the penis of the leaping male. Have you never noticed, again, how couples linked by mutual rapture are often tormented in their common bondage? How often dogs at a street corner, wishing to separate, tug lustily with all their might in opposite directions and yet remain united by the constraining fetters of Venus? This they would never do unless they knew the mutual joys which could entice them into the trap and hold them enchained. Here then is proof upon proof for my contention that the pleasure of sex is shared.

Epictetus,
Encheiridion, or *The Handbook*

*Epictetus (*A.D. *c. 55–c. 135) is a representative of Stoicism, a philosophical movement that flourished in the ancient world from the time it was founded in Greece by Zeno of Citium (334–262* B.C.E.*) until the demise of the Roman emperor and philosopher Marcus Aurelius (*A.D. *121–180). Not too much is known about the life of Epictetus: he was a slave who was freed by his master, he studied Stoic philosophy and then taught it in Rome and later in Greece, and he dictated the* Encheiridion, or The Handbook, *to a disciple. This short work embodies many of the core ideas of Stoicism about the place of humans in the universe and the proper conduct of life. The Stoics believed that the world is a physical totality which is like an organism whose parts all work for the good of the whole. Everything that happens in the world is governed by divine reason (logos) and therefore is good, though humans, restricted as they are to a limited point of view, may not be able to see the purpose and providence in the world. The only thing that has ultimate worth in life is virtue, that is, action in accordance with reason; all other things valued by people (health, money, wealth, pleasure, fame) are either instruments to attaining the supreme good or are worthless things we would do well not to desire. Emotions are generally regarded as harmful because they keep us from living according to the dictates of reason. As Epictetus points out, we should try to get a dispassionate understanding of what is truly within our power (e.g., our beliefs, attitudes, and inclinations) and what is not (e.g., worldly success, health), and calmly accept the things we cannot control while changing what we can. Once we are freed from counterproductive desires and emotions, Stoics believe, we can live in accord with the underlying order and reason of nature. Such a life is characterized by equanimity and inner peace.*

1

Some things are up to us and some are not up to us. Our opinions are up to us, and our impulses, desires, aversions—in short, whatever is our own doing. Our bodies are not up to us, nor are our possessions, our reputations, or our public offices, or, that is, whatever is not our own doing. The

From Epictetus, *The Handbook of Epictetus,* trans. by Nicholas White (Indianapolis: Hackett Publishing Co., 1983). Reprinted by permission of the publisher.

things that are up to us are by nature free, unhindered, and unimpeded; the things that are not up to us are weak, enslaved, hindered, not our own. So remember, if you think that things naturally enslaved are free or that things not your own are your own, you will be thwarted, miserable, and upset, and will blame both gods and men. But if you think that only what is yours is yours, and that what is not your own is, just as it is, not your own, then no one will ever coerce you, no one will hinder you, you will blame no one, you will not accuse anyone, you will not do a single thing unwillingly, you will have no enemies, and no one will harm you, because you will not be harmed at all.

As you aim for such great goals, remember that you must not undertake them by acting moderately,[1] but must let some things go completely and postpone others for the time being. But if you want both those great goals and also to hold public office and to be rich then you may perhaps not get even the latter just because you aim at the former too; and you certainly will fail to get the former, which are the only things that yield freedom and happiness.[2]

From the start, then, work on saying to each harsh appearance,[3] "You are an appearance, and not at all the thing that has the appearance." Then examine it and assess it by these yardsticks that you have, and first and foremost by whether it concerns the things that are up to us or the things that are not up to us. And if it is about one of the things that is not up to us, be ready to say, "You are nothing in relation to me."

2

Remember, what a desire proposes is that you gain what you desire, and what an aversion proposes is that you not fall into what you are averse to. Someone who fails to get what he desires is *un*fortunate, while someone

---

1. This may mean simply that the proposed undertaking is difficult. (Oldfather's translation suggests this), or it may mean (as I believe) that the aim cannot be achieved by the Aristotelian policy of pursuing a mean or middle course between extremes.—N.W.

2. Epictetus recommends aiming to have one's state of mind in accord with nature, in the sense explained in the previous paragraph and in c. 8. His point here is that if you aim for that and also simultaneously for certain "externals" like wealth, you will probably have neither and clearly will not have the former.

3. The word "appearance" translates *phantasia*, which some translators render by "impression" or "presentation." An appearance is roughly the immediate experience of sense or feeling, which may or may not represent an external state of affairs. (The Stoics held, against the Sceptics, that some appearances self-evidently do represent external states of affairs correctly.)

who falls into what he is averse to has met *mis*fortune. So if you are averse only to what is against nature among the things that are up to you, then you will never fall into anything that you are averse to; but if you are averse to illness or death or poverty, you will meet misfortune. So detach your aversion from everything not up to us, and transfer it to what is against nature among the things that are up to us. And for the time being eliminate desire completely, since if you desire something that is not up to us, you are bound to be unfortunate, and at the same time none of the things that are up to us, which it would be good to desire, will be available to you. Make use only of impulse and its contrary, rejection,[4] though with reservation, lightly, and without straining.

3

In the case of everything attractive or useful or that you are fond of, remember to say just what sort of thing it is, beginning with the least little things. If you are fond of a jug, say "I am fond of a jug!" For then when it is broken you will not be upset. If you kiss your child or your wife, say that you are kissing a human being; for when it dies you will not be upset.

4

When you are about to undertake some action, remind yourself what sort of action it is. If you are going out for a bath, put before your mind what happens at baths—there are people who splash, people who jostle, people who are insulting, people who steal. And you will undertake the action more securely if from the start you say of it, "I want to take a bath and to keep my choices in accord with nature;" and likewise for each action. For that way if something happens to interfere with your bathing you will be ready to say, "Oh, well, I wanted not only this but also to keep my choices in accord with nature, and I cannot do that if I am annoyed with things that happen."

5

What upsets people is not things themselves but their judgments about the things. For example, death is nothing dreadful (or else it would have appeared dreadful to Socrates), but instead the judgment about death that it is dreadful—*that* is what is dreadful. So when we are thwarted or upset

---

4. Impulse and rejection (*hormē* and *aphormē*) are, in Stoic terms, natural and non-rational psychological movements, so to speak, that are respectively toward or away from external objects.

or distressed, let us never blame someone else but rather ourselves, that is, our own judgments. An uneducated person accuses others when he is doing badly; a partly educated person accuses himself, an educated person accuses neither someone else nor himself.

6

Do not be joyful about any superiority that is not your own. If the horse were to say joyfully, "I am beautiful," one could put up with it. But certainly you, when you say joyfully, "I have a beautiful horse," are joyful about the good of the horse. What, then, is your own? Your way of dealing with appearances. So whenever you are in accord with nature in your way of dealing with appearances, then be joyful, since then you are joyful about a good of your own.

7

On a voyage when your boat has anchored, if you want to get fresh water you may pick up a small shellfish and a vegetable by the way, but you must keep your mind fixed on the boat and look around frequently in case the captain calls. If he calls you must let all those other things go so that you will not be tied up and thrown on the ship like livestock. That is how it is in life too: if you are given a wife and a child instead of a vegetable and a small shellfish, that will not hinder you; but if the captain calls, let all those things go and run to the boat without turning back; and if you are old, do not even go very far from the boat, so that when the call comes you are not left behind.

8

Do not seek to have events happen as you want them to, but instead want them to happen as they do happen, and your life will go well.

9

Illness interferes with the body, not with one's faculty of choice,[5] unless that faculty of choice wishes it to. Lameness interferes with the limb, not with one's faculty of choice. Say this at each thing that happens to you, since you will find that it interferes with something else, not with you.

5. "Faculty of choice" translates "*proairesis,*" which designates a rational faculty of the soul (cf. n. 4).

10

At each thing that happens to you, remember to turn to yourself and ask what capacity you have for dealing with it. If you see a beautiful boy or woman, you will find the capacity of self-control for that. If hardship comes to you, you will find endurance. If it is abuse, you will find patience. And if you become used to this, you will not be carried away by appearances.

11

Never say about anything, "I have lost it," but instead, "I have given it back." Did your child die? It was given back. Did your wife die? She was given back. "My land was taken." So this too was given back. "But the person who took it was bad!" How does the way the giver[6] asked for it back concern you? As long as he gives it, take care of it as something that is not your own, just as travelers treat an inn.

12

If you want to make progress,[7] give up all considerations like these: "If I neglect my property I will have nothing to live on," "If I do not punish my slave boy he will be bad." It is better to die of hunger with distress and fear gone than to live upset in the midst of plenty. It is better for the slave boy to be bad than for you to be in a bad state. Begin therefore with little things. A little oil is spilled, a little wine is stolen: say, "This is the price of tranquillity; this is the price of not being upset." Nothing comes for free. When you call the slave boy, keep in mind that he is capable of not paying attention, and even if he does pay attention he is capable of not doing any of the things that you want him to. But he is not in such a good position that your being upset or not depends on him.

13

If you want to make progress, let people think you are a mindless fool about externals, and do not desire a reputation for knowing about them. If people think you amount to something, distrust yourself. Certainly it is

---

6. The "giver" can be taken to be nature, or the natural order of the cosmos, or god, which the Stoics identified with each other.

7. "Making progress" (*prokoptein*) is the Stoic expression for movement in the direction of the ideal condition for a human being, embodied by the Stoic "sage" (cf. c. 15, n. 8).

not easy to be on guard both for one's choices to be in accord with nature
and also for externals, and a person who concerns himself with the one will
be bound to neglect the other.

14

You are foolish if you want your children and your wife and your friends
to live forever, since you are wanting things to be up to you that are not up
to you, and things to be yours that are not yours. You are stupid in the
same way if you want your slave boy to be faultless, since you are wanting
badness not to be badness but something else. But wanting not to fail to
get what you desire—*this* you are capable of. A person's master is someone
who has power over what he wants or does not want, either to obtain it or
take it away. Whoever wants to be free, therefore, let him not want or avoid
anything that is up to others. Otherwise he will necessarily be a slave.

15

Remember, you must behave as you do at a banquet. Something is
passed around and comes to you: reach out your hand politely and take
some. It goes by: do not hold it back. It has not arrived yet: do not stretch
your desire out toward it, but wait until it comes to you. In the same way
toward your children, in the same way toward your wife, in the same way
toward public office, in the same way toward wealth, and you will be fit to
share a banquet with the gods. But if when things are set in front of you,
you do not take them but despise them, then you will not only share a
banquet with the gods but also be a ruler along with them. For by acting in
this way Diogenes and Heraclitus[8] and people like them were deservedly
gods and were deservedly called gods.

16

When you see someone weeping in grief at the departure of his child or
the loss of his property, take care not to be carried away by the appearance
that the externals he is involved in are bad, and be ready to say immediately, "What weighs down on this man is not what has happened (since it
does not weigh down on someone else), but his judgment about it." Do

8. Diogenes the Cynic (the one who with his lantern looked for an honest man)
and Heraclitus of Ephesus, the presocratic philosopher, were along with Socrates
and Zeno people whom the Stoics said might possibly have reached the perfect
condition of being sages, which the Stoics took to be conceptually no different
from the perfect condition of a god.

not hesitate, however, to sympathise with him verbally, and even to moan with him if the occasion arises; but be careful not to moan inwardly.

17

Remember that you are an actor in a play, which is as the playwright wants it to be: short if he wants it short, long if he wants it long. If he wants you to play a beggar, play even this part skillfully, or a cripple, or a public official, or a private citizen. What is yours is to play the assigned part well. But to choose it belongs to someone else.

18

When a raven gives an unfavorable sign by croaking,[9] do not be carried away by the appearance, but immediately draw a distinction to yourself and say, "None of these signs is for me, but only for my petty body or my petty property or my petty judgments or children or wife. For all signs are favorable if I wish, since it is up to me to be benefited by whichever of them turns out correct."

19

You can be invincible if you do not enter any contest in which victory is not up to you. See that you are not carried away by the appearance, in thinking that someone is happy when you see him honored ahead of you or very powerful or otherwise having a good reputation. For if the really good things are up to us, neither envy nor jealousy has a place, and you yourself will want neither to be a general or a magistrate or a consul, but to be free. And there is one road to this: despising what is not up to us.

20

Remember that what is insulting is not the person who abuses you or hits you, but the judgment about them that they *are* insulting. So when someone irritates you be aware that what irritates you is your own belief. Most importantly, therefore, try not to be carried away by appearance, since if you once gain time and delay you will control yourself more easily.

9. Most people in antiquity believed in fortune-telling of various kinds, involving bird-calls, the flight of birds, inspection of entrails, stars, and whatnot. Many Stoics, notably Chrysippus, believed in such things, not least because they saw in them manifestations of the order of the cosmos and the tight and intricate interconnections within it, and thus saw them as scientific rather than superstitious.

21

Let death and exile and everything that is terrible appear before your eyes every day, especially death; and you will never have anything contemptible in your thoughts or crave anything excessively.

22

If you crave philosophy prepare yourself on the spot to be ridiculed, to be jeered at by many people who will say, "Here he is again, all of a sudden turned philosopher on us!" and "Where did he get that high brow?" But don't *you* put on a high brow, but hold fast to the things that appear best to you, as someone assigned by god to this place. And remember that if you hold to these views, those who previously ridiculed you will later be impressed with you, but if you are defeated by them you will be doubly ridiculed.

23

If it ever happens that you turn outward to want to please another person, certainly you have lost your plan of life. Be content therefore in everything to be a philosopher, and if you want to seem to be one, make yourself appear so to yourself, and you will be capable of it.

24

Do not be weighed down by the consideration, "I shall live without any honor, everywhere a nobody!" For if lack of honors is something bad, I cannot be in a bad state because of another person any more than I can be in a shameful one. It is not your task[10] to gain political office, or be invited to a banquet, is it? Not at all. How then is that a lack of honor? And how will you be a nobody everywhere, if you need to be a somebody only in things that are up to you—in which it is open to you to be of the greatest worth? "But your friends will be without help!" What do you mean, "without help?" Well, they will be without a little cash from you, and you will not make them Roman citizens. Who told you, then, that these things are up to you and not the business of someone else? Who can give to someone else what he does not have himself? "Get money," someone says, "so that we may have some." If I can get it while keeping self-respect and trustworthiness and high-mindedness, show me the way and I will get it.

10. The word translated "task" here and below is *ergon*, which might also be translated by "function."

But if you demand that I lose the good things that are mine so that you may acquire things that are not good, see for yourselves how unfair and inconsiderate you are. Which do you want more, money or a self-respecting and trustworthy friend? Then help me more toward this, and do not expect me to do things that will make me lose these qualities. "But my country," he says, "will be without help, in so far as it depends on me!" Again, what sort of "help" is this? So it will not have porticos and baths by your efforts. What does that amount to? For it does not have shoes because of the blacksmith or weapons because of the cobbler, but it is enough if each person fulfills his own task. And if you furnished for it another citizen who was trustworthy and self-respecting, would you in no way be helpful to it? "Yes, I would be." Then neither would you yourself be unhelpful to it. "Then what place," he says "will I have in the city?" The one you can have by preserving your trustworthiness and self-respect. And if while wanting to help it you throw away these things, what use will you be to it if you turn out shameless and untrustworthy?

26

It is possible to learn the will of nature from the things in which we do not differ from each other. For example, when someone else's little slave boy breaks his cup we are ready to say, "It's one of those things that just happen." Certainly, then, when your own cup is broken you should be just the way you were when the other person's was broken. Transfer the same idea to larger matters. Someone else's child is dead, or his wife. There is no one would not say, "It's the lot of a human being." But when one's own dies, immediately it is, "Alas! Poor me!" But we should have remembered how we feel when we hear of the same thing about others.

27

Just as a target is not set up to be missed, in the same way nothing bad by nature happens in the world.[11]

28

If someone turned your body over to just any person who happened to meet you, you would be angry. But are you not ashamed that you turn over

11. According to the Stoic view, the universe as a whole is perfect and everything in it has a place in its overall design, so that nothing can exist or occur that is bad in its relation to that overall design.

your own faculty of judgment to whoever happens along, so that if he abuses you it is upset and confused?

29

For each action, consider what leads up to it and what follows it, and approach it in the light of that. Otherwise you will come to it enthusiastically at first, since you have not borne in mind any of what will happen next, but later when difficulties turn up you will give up disgracefully. You want to win an Olympic victory? I do too, by the gods, since that is a fine thing. But consider what leads up to it and what follows it, and undertake the action in the light of that. You must be disciplined, keep a strict diet, stay away from cakes, train according to strict routine at a fixed time in heat and in cold, not drink cold water, not drink wine when you feel like it, and in general you must have turned yourself over to your trainer as to a doctor, and then in the contest "dig in,"[12] sometimes dislocate your hand, twist your ankle, swallow a lot of sand, sometimes be whipped, and, after all that, lose. Think about that and then undertake training, if you want to. Otherwise you will be behaving the way children do, who play wrestlers one time, gladiators another time, blow trumpets another time, then act a play. In this way you too are now an athlete, now a gladiator, then an orator, then a philosopher, yet you are nothing wholeheartedly, but like a monkey you mimic each sight that you see, and one thing after another is to your taste, since you do not undertake a thing after considering it from every side, but only randomly and half-heartedly.

In the same way when some people watch a philosopher and hear one speaking like Euphrates[13] (though after all who can speak like him?), they want to be philosophers themselves. Just you consider, as a human being, what sort of thing it is; then inspect your own nature and whether you can bear it. You want to do the pentathlon, or to wrestle? Look at your arms, your thighs, inspect your loins. Different people are naturally suited for different things. Do you think that if you do those things you can eat as you now do, drink as you now do, have the same likes and dislikes? You must go without sleep, put up with hardship, be away from your own people, be looked down on by a little slave boy, be laughed at by people who meet you, get the worse of it in everything, honor, public office, law course, every little thing. Think about whether you want to exchange these things for tranquillity, freedom, calm. If not, do not embrace philosophy, and do not like children be a philosopher at one time, later a tax-collector,

---

12. Nobody knows just what this expression means in this context.

13. Euphrates was a Stoic lecturer noted for his eloquence.

then an orator, then a procurator of the emperor. These things do not go together. You must be one person, either good or bad. You must either work on your ruling principle,[14] or work on externals, practise the art either of what is inside or of what is outside, that is, play the role either of a philosopher or of a non-philosopher.

30

Appropriate actions[15] are in general measured by relationships. He is a father: that entails taking care of him, yielding to him in everything, putting up with him when he abuses you or strikes you. "But he is a bad father." Does nature then determine that you have a good father? No, only that you have a father.[16] "My brother has done me wrong." Then keep your place in relation to him; do not consider his action, but instead consider what you can do to bring your own faculty of choice[17] into accord with nature. Another person will not do you harm unless you wish it; you will be harmed at just that time at which you take yourself to be harmed. In this way, then, you will discover the appropriate actions to expect from a neighbor, from a citizen, from a general, if you are in the habit of looking at relationships.

31

The most important aspect of piety toward the gods is certainly both to have correct beliefs about them, as beings that arrange the universe well and justly, and to set yourself to obey them and acquiesce in everything that happens and to follow it willingly, as something brought to completion by the best judgment. For in this way you will never blame the gods or accuse them of neglecting you. And this piety is impossible unless you detach the good and the bad from what is not up to us and attach it

14. The "ruling principle" (or "governing principle"), the *hēgemonikon*, in the rather complicated psychological theory adopted by the Stoics, is that central part of the soul that can understand what is good and decide to act on that understanding.

15. "Appropriate actions" are *kathēkonta*, which Cicero called *officia*, and are in English translations often called "duties," though the notion is actually somewhat different from that of duty. They are the actions that are of a type generally in accord with nature, or with a particular sort of person's place in it.

16. The idea here is, roughly, that there are certain relationships of affinity established by the natural order, and that having a father represents one of them, but that having a good father is not entailed by it.

17. Cf. c. 9, n. 5, and c. 29, n. 14.

exclusively to what is up to us, because if you think that any of what is not up to us is good or bad, then when you fail to get what you want and fall into what you do not want, you will be bound to blame and hate those who cause this. For every animal by nature flees and turns away from things that are harmful and from what causes them, and pursues and admires things that are beneficial and what causes them. There is therefore no way for a person who thinks he is being harmed to enjoy what he thinks is harming him, just as it is impossible to enjoy the harm itself. Hence a son even abuses his father when the father does not give him a share of things that he thinks are good; and thinking that being a tyrant was a good thing is what made enemies of Polyneices and Eteocles.[18] This is why the farmer too abuses the gods, and the sailor, and the merchant, and those who have lost their wives and children. For wherever someone's advantage lies, there he also shows piety. So whoever takes care to have desires and aversions as one should also in the same instance takes care about being pious. And it is always appropriate to make libations and sacrifices and give firstfruits according to the custom of one's forefathers, in a manner that is pure and neither slovenly nor careless, nor indeed cheaply nor beyond one's means.

33

Set up right now a certain character and pattern for yourself which you will preserve when you are by yourself and when you are with people. Be silent for the most part, or say what you have to in a few words. Speak rarely, when the occasion requires speaking, but not about just any topic that comes up, not about gladiators, horse-races, athletes, eating or drinking—the things that always come up; and especially if it is about people, talk without blaming or praising or comparing. Divert by your own talk, if you can, the talk of those with you to something appropriate. If you happen to be stranded among strangers, do not talk. Do not laugh a great deal or at a great many things or unrestrainedly. Refuse to swear oaths, altogether if possible, or otherwise as circumstances allow. Avoid banquets given by those outside philosophy. But if the appropriate occasion arises, take great care not to slide into their ways, since certainly if a person's companion is dirty the person who spends time with him, even if he happens to be clean, is bound to become dirty too. Take what has to do with the body to the point of bare need, such as food, drink, clothing, house, household slaves, and cut out everything that is for reputation or luxury. As for sex stay pure as far as possible before marriage, and if you

18. The story of the conflict between the brothers Polyneices and Eteocles is best known to modern readers from Sophocles' tragedy, *Antigone*.

have it do only what is allowable. But do not be angry or censorious toward those who do engage in it, and do not always be making an exhibition of the fact that you do not.

If someone reports back to you that so-and-so is saying bad things about you, do not reply to them but answer, "Obviously he didn't know my other bad characteristics, since otherwise he wouldn't just have mentioned these."

34

Whenever you encounter some kind of apparent pleasure, be on guard, as in the case of other appearances, not to be carried away by it, but let the thing wait for you and allow yourself to delay. Then bring before your mind two times, both the time when you enjoy the pleasure and the time when after enjoying it you later regret it and berate yourself; and set against these the way you will be pleased and will praise yourself if you refrain from it. But if the right occasion appears for you to undertake the action, pay attention so that you will not be overcome by its attractiveness and pleasantness and seductiveness, and set against it how much better it is to be conscious of having won this victory against it.

35

When you do something that you determine is to be done, never try not to be seen doing it, even if most people are likely to think something bad about it. If you are not doing it rightly, avoid the act itself; if you are doing it rightly, why do you fear those who will criticize you wrongly?

36

Just as the propositions "It is day" and "It is night" have their full value when disjoined [*sc.*, in "It is day *or* it is night"] but have negative value when conjoined [*sc.*, in "It is day *and* it is night"], in the same way, granted that taking the larger portion has value for one's body, it has negative value for preserving the fellowship of a banquet in the way one should.[19] So when you eat with another, remember not merely to see the value for your body of what lies in front of you, but also to preserve your respect for your host.

19. Very roughly, the idea is that the value of an action has to be judged from all features of the context. The parallel is that allegedly the meaningfulness of a sentence depends in a way on its context.

37

If you undertake some role beyond your capacity, you both disgrace yourself by taking it and also thereby neglect the role that you were unable to take.

38

Just as in walking about you pay attention so as not to step on a nail or twist your foot, pay attention in the same way so as not to harm your ruling principle.[20] And if we are on guard about this in every action, we shall set about it more securely.

39

The measure of possessions for each person is the body, as the foot is of the shoe. So if you hold to this principle you will preserve the measure; but if you step beyond it, you will in the end be carried as if over a cliff; just as in the case of the shoe, if you go beyond the foot, you get a gilded shoe, and then a purple embroidered one. For there is no limit to a thing once it is beyond its measure.

41

It shows lack of natural talent to spend time on what concerns the body, as in exercising a great deal, eating a great deal, drinking a great deal, moving one's bowels or copulating a great deal. Instead you must do these things in passing, but turn your whole attention toward your faculty of judgment.[21]

42

When someone acts badly toward you or speaks badly of you, remember that he does or says it in the belief that it is appropriate for him to do so. Accordingly he cannot follow what appears to you but only what appears

20. Cf. c. 29, n. 14.
21. Cf. c. 29, n. 14. The claim is in effect that one should be concerned wholly with the state of the ruling part of one's soul, and not with external states of affairs or with those aspects of the soul, such as one's affective feelings or desires, that are directly dependent on external states of affairs. One can see here the Stoic view, which seems paradoxical to many, that one's feelings and non-rational desires are in a crucial sense external to one's true self (cf. c. 6 and Introd.).

to him, so that if things appear badly to him, he is harmed in as much as he has been deceived. For if someone thinks that a true conjunctive proposition[22] is false, the conjunction is not harmed but rather the one who is deceived. Starting from these considerations you will be gentle with the person who abuses you. For you must say on each occasion, "That's how it seemed to him."

43

Everything has two handles, one by which it may be carried and the other not. If your brother acts unjustly toward you, do not take hold of it by this side, that he has acted unjustly (since this is the handle by which it may not be carried), but instead by this side, that he is your brother and was brought up with you, and you will be taking hold of it in the way that it can be carried.

44

These statements are not valid inferences: "I am richer than you; therefore I am superior to you," or "I am more eloquent than you; therefore I am superior to you." But rather these are valid: "I am richer than you; therefore my property is superior to yours," or "I am more eloquent than you; therefore my speaking is superior to yours." But you are identical neither with your property nor with your speaking.

45

Someone takes a bath quickly; do not say that he does it badly but that he does it quickly. Someone drinks a great deal of wine; do not say that he does it badly but that he does a great deal of it. For until you have discerned what his judgment was, how do you know whether he did it badly? In this way it will not turn out that you receive convincing appearances of some things but give assent to quite different ones.[23]

22. Cf. c. 36. A proposition of this sort consists of two component propositions conjoined by "and."

23. A "convincing appearance" is a *kataléptiké phantasia*, the sort of appearance that according to the Stoics is a self-evidently correct representation of the way things actually are (cf. n. 3). "Assent" is *synkatathesis*. Correct assent would of course be assent to self-evidently correct appearances. The line of thought here is, however, quite compressed, and the student will find it a difficult exercise to explain it.

46

Never call yourself a philosopher and do not talk a great deal among non-philosophers about philosophical propositions, but do what follows from them. For example, at a banquet do not say how a person ought to eat, but eat as a person ought to. Remember that Socrates had so completely put aside ostentation that people actually went to him when they wanted to be introduced to philosophers, and he took them.[24] He was that tolerant of being overlooked. And if talk about philosophical propositions arises among non-philosophers, for the most part be silent, since there is a great danger of your spewing out what you have not digested. And when someone says to you that you know nothing and you are not hurt by it, then you know that you are making a start at your task. Sheep do not show how much they have eaten by bringing the feed to the shepherds, but they digest the food inside themselves, and outside themselves they bear wool and milk. So in your case likewise do not display propositions to non-philosophers but instead the actions that come from the propositions when they are digested.

47

When you have become adapted to living cheaply as far as your body is concerned, do not make a show of it, and if you drink water do not say at every opening that you drink water. If you wish to train yourself to hardship, do it for yourself and not for those outside. Do not throw your arms around statues.[25] Instead, when you are terribly thirsty, take cold water into your mouth, and spit it out, and do not tell anyone about it.

48

The position and character of a non-philosopher: he never looks for benefit or harm to come from himself but from things outside. The position and character of a philosopher: he looks for all benefit and harm to come from himself.

Signs of someone's making progress: he censures no one; he praises no one; he blames no one; he never talks about himself as a person who amounts to something or knows something. When he is thwarted or prevented in something, he accuses himself. And if someone praises him

24. The allusion is perhaps to the events in the early part of Plato's *Protagoras*.
25. According to a story in Diogenes Laertius 6.23, Diogenes, the Cynic did this nude in cold weather, to toughen himself. But the statues were outdoors, and Diogenes was a bit of a show-off (but cf. n. 8!).

he laughs to himself at the person who has praised him; and if someone censures him he does not respond. He goes around like an invalid, careful not to move any of his parts that are healing before they have become firm. He has kept off all desire from himself, and he has transferred all aversion onto what is against nature among the things that are up to us. His impulses toward everything are diminished. If he seems foolish or ignorant, he does not care. In a single phrase, he is on guard against himself as an enemy lying in wait.

49

When someone acts grand because he understands and can expound the works of Chrysippus,[26] say to yourself, "If Chrysippus had not written unclearly, this man would have nothing to be proud of."

But what do *I* want? To learn to understand nature and follow it. So I try to find out who explains it. And I hear that Chrysippus does, and I go to him. But I do not understand the things that he has written, so I try to find the person who explains them. Up to this point there is nothing grand. But when I do find someone who explains them, what remains is to carry out what has been conveyed to me. This alone is grand. But if I am impressed by the explaining itself, what have I done but ended up a grammarian instead of a philosopher—except that I am explaining Chrysippus instead of Homer. Instead, when someone says to me, "Read me some Chrysippus," I turn red when I cannot exhibit actions that are similar to his words and in harmony with them.

50

Abide by whatever task is set before you as if it were a law, and as if you would be committing sacrilege if you went against it. But pay no attention to whatever anyone says about you, since that falls outside what is yours.

51

How long do you put off thinking yourself worthy of the best things, and never going against the definitive capacity of reason?[27] You have received the philosophical propositions that you ought to agree to and you have agreed to them. Then what sort of teacher are you still waiting for, that you put off improving yourself until he comes? You are not a boy any

26. Chrysippus was the third head of the Stoic school at Athens.

27. In brief, the capacity of reason here is that of distinguishing different things from each other and defining them.

more, but already a full-grown man. If you now neglect things and are lazy
and are always making delay after delay and set one day after another as the
day for paying attention to yourself, then without realizing it you will
make no progress but will end up a non-philosopher all through life and
death. So decide now that you are worthy of living as a full-grown man
who is making progress, and make everything that seems best be a law that
you cannot go against. And if you meet with any hardship or anything
pleasant or reputable or disreputable, then remember that the contest is
now and the Olympic games are *now* and you cannot put things off any
more and that your progress is made or destroyed by a single day and a
single action. Socrates became fully perfect in this way, by not paying
attention to anything but his reason in everything that he met with. You,
even if you are not yet Socrates, ought to live as someone wanting to be
Socrates.

52

The first and most necessary aspect of philosophy is that of dealing with
philosophical propositions, such as "not to hold to falsehood." The second is that of demonstrations, for example, "How come one must not hold
to falsehood?" The third is that of the confirmation and articulation of
these, for example. "How come this is a demonstration? What is
demonstration? What is entailment? What is conflict? What is truth?
What is falsity?" Therefore the third is necessary because of the second,
and the second because of the first; but the most necessary, and the one
where one must rest, is the first. We, however, do it backwards, since we
spend time in the third and all of our effort goes into it, and we neglect the
first completely. Therefore we hold to falsehood, but we are ready to
explain how it is demonstrated that one must not hold to falsehood.

53

On every occasion you must have these thoughts ready:

Lead me, Zeus, and you too, Destiny,
Wherever I am assigned by you;
I'll follow and not hesitate,
But even if I do not wish to,
Because I'm bad, I'll follow anyway.

Whoever has complied well with necessity
Is counted wise by us, and understands divine affairs.

Well, Crito, if it is pleasing to the gods this way, then let it happen this way. Anytus and Meletus can kill me, but they can't harm me.[28]

---

28. These four bits of poetry have the following origins. The first is by Cleanthes, who was head of the Stoic school at Athens between Zeno and Chrysippus. The second is a fragment of Euripides (fr. 965 Nauck). The third is Plato, *Crito* 43d, and the fourth is Plato, *Apology* 30c–d (slightly modified as compared with our manuscript texts), both purporting to be quotations from Socrates (cf. n. 8).

6

Siddhattha Gotama Buddha, "The Foundation of the Kingdom of Righteousness"

The founder of Buddhism, Siddhattha Gotama (c. fifth century B.C.E.; in Sanskrit, Siddhārtha Gautama), bears the title "Buddha," meaning "the enlightened one." Born into a noble family, most likely in what is now Nepal, Siddhattha left home at the age of twenty-nine to seek enlightenment. Having found enlightenment at the age of thirty-five, he spent the remaining forty-five years of his life as a wandering teacher. From traditional Indian belief he took the ideas of samsara *(wheel of rebirth) and* karma *(consequences of actions), and the concern with finding a way to escape from the cycle of rebirth. The source of the problem, he taught, is desire or craving: for riches, health, influence, pleasure, and so forth. To eliminate these cravings, we must follow the "eightfold path" and accept that existence is unsatisfying and impermanent, that the enduring self is an illusion, that all is transient, and that everything is dependent upon everything else in the universe. The following passage contains some core Buddhist teachings: the eightfold path and the noble truths about suffering. Since no enduring things exist, according to Buddhism, there can be no "God" as it is conceived in Western religions, though there are gods who live a long time and have various powers. Buddhism's sensitivity to suffering calls for a strong sense of compassion for all things as well as a willingness to alleviate suffering wherever possible.*

Dhamma-cakka-ppavattana-sutta

Reverence to the Blessed One, the Holy One, the Fully-Enlightened One.

1. Thus have I heard. The Blessed One was once staying at Benares, at

From *The Sacred Books of the East*, trans. by T. W. Rhys Davids, vol. XI (Oxford: Clarendon Press, 1881).

the hermitage called Migadāya. And there the Blessed One addressed the company of the five Bhikkhus,[1] and said:

2. "There are two extremes, O Bhikkhus, which the man who has given up the world[2] ought not to follow—the habitual practice, on the one hand, of those things whose attraction depends upon the passions, and especially of sensuality—a low and pagan[3] way (of seeking satisfaction) unworthy, unprofitable, and fit only for the worldly-minded—and the habitual practice, on the other hand, of asceticism (or self-mortification), which is painful, unworthy, and unprofitable.

3. "There is a middle path, O Bhikkhus, avoiding these two extremes, discovered by the Tathāgata[4]—a path which opens the eyes, and bestows understanding, which leads to peace of mind, to the higher wisdom, to full enlightenment, to Nirvāna!

4. "What is that middle path, O Bhikkhus, avoiding these two extremes, discovered by the Tathāgata—that path which opens the eyes, and bestows understanding, which leads to peace of mind, to the higher wisdom, to full enlightenment, to Nirvāna? Verily! it is this noble eightfold path; that is to say:

"Right views;
Right aspirations;
Right speech;
Right conduct;
Right livelihood;
Right effort;
Right mindfulness; and
Right contemplation.

1. These are the five mendicants who had waited on the Bodisat during his austerities, as described in "Buddhist Birth Stories."

2. Pabbajito, one who has gone forth, who has renounced worldly things, a "religious."

3. Gamma, a word of the same derivation as, and corresponding meaning to, our word "pagan."

4. The Tathāgata is an epithet of a Buddha. It is interpreted by Buddhaghosa, in the Samangala Vilāsinī, to mean that he came to earth for the same purposes, after having passed through the same training in former births, as all the supposed former Buddhas; and that, when he had so come, all his actions corresponded with theirs.

"Avoiding these two extremes" should perhaps be referred to the Tathāgata, but I prefer the above rendering.

"This, O Bhikkhus, is that middle path, avoiding these two extremes, discovered by the Tathāgata—that path which opens the eyes, and bestows understanding, which leads to peace of mind, to the higher wisdom, to full enlightenment, to Nirvāna!

. . .

5. "Now[5] this, O Bhikkhus, is the noble truth concerning suffering.

"Birth is attended with pain,[6] decay is painful, disease is painful, death is painful. Union with the unpleasant is painful, painful is separation from the pleasant; and any craving that is unsatisfied, that too is painful. In brief, the five aggregates which spring from attachment (the conditions of individuality and their cause)[7] are painful.

"This then, O Bhikkhus, is the noble truth concerning suffering.

6. "Now this, O Bhikkhus, is the noble truth concerning the origin of suffering.

"Verily, it is that thirst (or craving), causing the renewal of existence, accompanied by sensual delight, seeking satisfaction now here, now there—that is to say, the craving for the gratification of the passions, or the craving for (a future) life, or the craving for success (in this present life).[8]

5. On the following "four truths" compare Dhammapada, verse 191, and Mahā-parinibbāna Sutta II, 2, 3, and IV, 7, 8.

6. Or "is painful."

7. One might express the central thought of this First Noble Truth in the language of [today] by saying that pain results from existence as an individual. It is the struggle to maintain one's individuality which produces pain—a most pregnant and far-reaching suggestion.

8. "The lust of the flesh, the lust of the eye, and the pride of life" correspond very exactly to the first and third of these three tanhās. "The lust of the flesh, the lust of life, and the pride of life," or "the lust of the flesh, the lust of life, and the love of this present world," would be not inadequate renderings of all three.

The last two are in Pāli bhava-tanhā and vibhava-tanhā, on which Childers, on the authority of Vijesinha, says: "The former applies to the sassata-ditthi, and means a desire for an eternity of existence; the latter applies to the uccheda-ditthi, and means a desire for annihilation in the very first (the present) form of existence." Sassata-ditthi may be called the "everlasting life heresy," and uccheda-ditthi the "let-us-eat-and-drink-for-to-morrow-we-die heresy." These two heresies thus implicitly condemned, have very close analogies to theism and materialism.

Spence Hardy says (*"Manual of Buddhism"*): "Bhawatanhā signifies the pertinacious love of existence induced by the supposition that transmigratory existence is not only eternal, but felicitous and desirable. Wibhawa-tanhā is the love of

"This then, O Bhikkhus, is the noble truth concerning the origin of suffering.

7. "Now this, O Bhikkhus, is the noble truth concerning the destruction of suffering.

"Verily, it is the destruction, in which no passion remains, of this very thirst; the laying aside of, the getting rid of, the being free from, the harbouring no longer of this thirst.

"This then, O Bhikkhus, is the noble truth concerning the destruction of suffering.

8. "Now this, O Bhikkhus, is the noble truth concerning the way[9] which leads to the destruction of sorrow. Verily! it is this noble eightfold path;[10] that is to say:

"Right views;
Right aspirations;
Right speech;
Right conduct;
Right livelihood;
Right effort;
Right mindfulness; and
Right contemplation.

"This then, O Bhikkhus, is the noble truth concerning the destruction of sorrow.

                              . . .

21. "So long, O Bhikkhus, as my knowledge and insight were not quite clear, regarding each of these four noble truths in this triple order, in this twelve-fold manner—so long was I uncertain whether I had attained to the full insight of that wisdom which is unsurpassed in the heavens or on earth, among the whole race of Samanas and Brāhmans, or of gods or men.

22. "But as soon, O Bhikkhus, as my knowledge and insight were quite clear regarding each of these four noble truths, in this triple order, in this twelvefold manner—then did I become certain that I had attained to the

---

the present life, under the notion that existence will cease therewith, and that there is to be no future state."

Vibhava in Sanskrit means, 1. development; 2. might, majesty, prosperity; and 3. property: but the technical Buddhist sense, as will be seen from the above, is something more than this.

9. Patipadā.

10. Ariyo atangiko Maggo.

full insight of that wisdom which is unsurpassed in the heavens or on earth, among the whole race of Samanas and Brāhmans, or of gods or men.

23. "And now this knowledge and this insight has arisen within me. Immovable is the emancipation of my heart. This is my last existence. There will now be no rebirth for me!"

. . .

24. Thus spake the Blessed One. The company of the five Bhikkhus, glad at heart, exalted the words of the Blessed One. And when the discourse had been uttered, there arose within the venerable Kondañña the eye of truth, spotless, and without a stain, (and he saw that) whatsoever has an origin, in that is also inherent the necessity of coming to an end.[11]

. . .

25. And when the royal chariot wheel of the truth had thus been set rolling onwards by the Blessed One, the gods of the earth gave forth a shout, saying:

"In Benāres, at the hermitage of the Migadāya, the supreme wheel of the empire of Truth has been set rolling by the Blessed One—that wheel which not by any Samana or Brāhman, not by any god, not by any Brahma or Māra, not by any one in the universe, can ever be turned back!"

. . .

28. And thus, in an instant, a second, a moment, the sound went up even to the world of Brahmā: and this great ten-thousand-world-system quaked and trembled and was shaken violently, and an immeasurable bright light appeared in the universe, beyond even the power of the gods!

. . .

29. Then did the Blessed One give utterance to this exclamation of joy: "Kondañña hath realised it. Kondañña hath realised it!" And so the venerable Kondañña acquired the name of Aññāta-Kondañña ("the Kondañña who realised").[12]

11. It is the perception of this fact which is the Dhammacakkhu, the Eye of Truth, or the Eye of Qualities as it might be rendered with reference to the meaning of Dhamma in the words that follow.

They are in Pāli, yam kiñci samudaya-dhammam, sabbam tam nirodha-dhammam, literally, "whatever has the quality of beginning, that has the quality of ceasing."

12. The Mahā Vagga completes the narrative as follows: "And then the venerable Aññāta-Kondañña having seen the truth, having arrived at the truth, having

. . .

End of the Dhamma-cakka-ppavattana-sutta.

---

known the truth, having penetrated the truth, having past beyond doubt, having laid aside uncertainty, having attained to confidence, and being dependent on no one beside himself for knowledge of the religion of the teacher, spake thus to the Blessed One:

"'May I become, O my Lord, a novice under the Blessed One, may I receive full ordination!'

"'Welcome, O brother!' said the Blessed One, 'the truth has been well laid down. Practice holiness to the complete suppression of sorrow!'

"And that was the ordination of the Venerable One."

The other four, Vappa, Bhaddiya, Mahānāma, and Assaji, were converted on the following days, according to the "Buddhist Birth Stories."

It is there also said that "myriads of the angels (devas) had been converted simultaneously with Kondanya."

Augustine,
Confessions

St. Augustine (354–430), bishop and Church father, was born to a Christian family in what today is Algeria but was known to the Roman empire as part of "the province of Africa." In Carthage, where he studied rhetoric, he converted to Manicheanism, a religion that pictured God as present in the material world and portrayed the universe as an ongoing battle between good and evil forces. While teaching rhetoric in Milan, Augustine came under the influence of St. Ambrose and "certain Platonic texts," and as a result embraced Christianity in 387. Returning to his homeland, he was ordained Bishop of Hippo and spent the rest of his life there writing and serving the Church.

Confessions (397) was written at a time when poor health led the forty-three-year-old Augustine to feel the need to sum up his life. The book is first and foremost a "confession of faith," a testimony of devotion to God. But it is also a confession in the more familiar sense of examining one's conscience and admitting one's sins. As we read this remarkable book, we experience a sense of intense self-reflection that seems truly modern. In the opening words of the book Augustine says to God: You have made us toward Yourself, and our hearts are restless until they rest in you. The implication here is that humans have been created in such a way that their proper orientation is to be turned toward God, worshipping Him and glorifying His name. Thus, we are only fully human when we stand in the right relation to God. But even though our natural state is orientation toward God, we are normally inclined to turn away from God toward the sensual world, where we throw ourselves into a life of carnal pleasures and are tempted to sin. This life of worldly attachments, twisted away from its proper orientation, is experienced as dispersed, torn apart, and ultimately wretched. What is necessary, then, is to accept God's grace and, using our free will, to turn away from worldly things and surrender ourselves to God. This is the path to bliss and salvation.

One of Augustine's greatest contributions to the Judeo-Christian strand of Western thought is his emphasis on the need for inward-turning. His view, influenced by Platonic thought, holds that God is found within each of us. We must turn away from the material world and its temptations in order to get in touch with the divine spiritual realm deep inside us. There is, thus, a sharp distinction in Augustine's thought between "this world" and the "other

world," the physical and the spiritual, body and soul, carnal desire and the
love of God. Confessions *gives us a picture of the need to grasp the divine
Truth through inward-turning in order to know what we are and to thereby
realize our humanity.*

Book I

Chapter I

Great art Thou, *O Lord, and greatly to be praised; great Thy power, and of
Thy wisdom there is no number.* And man desires to praise Thee. He is but a
tiny part of all that Thou hast created. He bears about him his mortality,
the evidence of his sinfulness, and the evidence that *Thou dost resist the
proud:* yet this tiny part of all that Thou hast created desires to praise
Thee.

Thou dost so excite him that to praise Thee is his joy. For Thou hast
made us for Thyself and our hearts are restless till they rest in Thee.

Book II

Chapter IV

Your law, O Lord, punishes theft; and this law is so written in the hearts
of men that not even the breaking of it blots it out: for no thief bears
calmly being stolen from—not even if he is rich and the other steals
through want. Yet I chose to steal, and not because want drove me to it—
unless a want of justice and contempt for it and an excess of iniquity. For I
stole things which I already had in plenty and of better quality. Nor had I
any desire to enjoy the things I stole, but only the stealing of them and the
sin. There was a pear tree near our vineyard, heavy with fruit, but fruit
that was not particularly tempting either to look at or to taste. A group of
young blackguards, and I among them, went out to knock down the pears
and carry them off late one night, for it was our bad habit to carry on our
games in the streets till very late. We carried off an immense load of pears,
not to eat—for we barely tasted them before throwing them to the hogs.
Our only pleasure in doing it was that it was forbidden. Such was my
heart, O God, such was my heart: yet in the depth of the abyss You had
pity on it. Let that heart now tell You what it sought when I was thus evil
for no object, having no cause for wrongdoing save my wrongness. The
malice of the act was base and I loved it—that is to say I loved my own

From Augustine, *Confessions,* trans. by F. J. Sheed (Indianapolis: Hackett Publishing Co., 1992). Reprinted by permission of the publisher.

undoing, I loved the evil in me—not the thing for which I did the evil, simply the evil: my soul was depraved and hurled itself down from security in You into utter destruction, seeking no profit from wickedness but only to be wicked.

Chapter V

There is an appeal to the eye in beautiful things, in gold and silver and all such; the sense of touch has its own powerful pleasures; and the other senses find qualities in things suited to them. Worldly success has its glory, and the power to command and to overcome: and from this springs the thirst for revenge. But in our quest of all these things, we must not depart from You, Lord, or deviate from Your Law. This life we live here below has its own attractiveness, grounded in the measure of beauty it has and its harmony with the beauty of all lesser things. The bond of human friendship is admirable, holding many souls as one. Yet in the enjoyment of all such things we commit sin if through immoderate inclination to them— for though they are good, they are of the lowest order of good—things higher and better are forgotten, even You, O Lord our God, and Your Truth and Your Law. These lower things have their delights but not such as my God has, for He made them all: *and in Him doth the righteous delight, and He is the joy of the upright of heart.*

Chapter VI

What was it then that in my wretched folly I loved in You, O theft of mine, deed wrought in that dark night when I was sixteen? For you were not lovely: you were a theft. Or are you anything at all, that I should talk with you? The pears that we stole were beautiful for they were created by Thee, Thou most Beautiful of all, Creator of all, Thou good God, my Sovereign and true Good. The pears were beautiful but it was not pears that my empty soul desired. For I had any number of better pears of my own, and plucked those only that I might steal. For once I had gathered them I threw them away, tasting only my own sin and savouring that with delight; for if I took so much as a bite of any one of those pears, it was the sin that sweetened it. And now, Lord my God, I ask what was it that attracted me in that theft, for there was no beauty in it to attract. I do not mean merely that it lacked the beauty that there is in justice and prudence, or in the mind of man or his senses and vegetative life: or even so much as the beauty and glory of the stars in the heavens, or of earth and sea with their oncoming of new life to replace the generations that pass. It had not even that false show or shadow of beauty by which sin tempts us.

[For there *is* a certain show of beauty in sin.] Thus pride wears the mask of loftiness of spirit, although You alone, O God, are high over all. Ambition seeks honor and glory, although You alone are to be honored before all and glorious forever. By cruelty the great seek to be feared, yet who is to be feared but God alone: from His power what can be wrested away, or when or where or how or by whom? The caresses by which the lustful seduce are a seeking for love: but nothing is more caressing than Your charity, nor is anything more healthfully loved than Your supremely lovely, supremely luminous Truth. Curiosity may be regarded as a desire for knowledge, whereas You supremely know all things. Ignorance and sheer stupidity hide under the names of simplicity and innocence: yet no being has simplicity like to Yours: and none is more innocent than You, for it is their own deeds that harm the wicked. Sloth pretends that it wants quietude: but what sure rest is there save the Lord? Luxuriousness would be called abundance and completeness; but You are the fullness and inexhaustible abundance of incorruptible delight. Wastefulness is a parody of generosity: but You are the infinitely generous giver of all good. Avarice wants to possess overmuch: but You possess all. Enviousness claims that it strives to excel: but what can excel before You? Anger clamors for just vengeance: but whose vengeance is so just as Yours? Fear is the recoil from a new and sudden threat to something one holds dear, and a cautious regard for one's own safety: but nothing new or sudden can happen to You, nothing can threaten Your hold upon things loved, and where is safety secure save in You? Grief pines at the loss of things in which desire delighted: for it wills to be like to You from whom nothing can be taken away.

Thus the soul is guilty of fornication when she turns from You and seeks from any other source what she will nowhere find pure and without taint unless she returns to You. Thus even those who go from You and stand up against You are still perversely imitating You. But by the mere fact of their imitation, they declare that You are the creator of all that is, and that there is nowhere for them to go where You are not.

So once again what did I enjoy in that theft of mine? Of what excellence of my Lord was I making perverse and vicious imitation? Perhaps it was the thrill of acting against Your law—at least in appearance, since I had no power to do so in fact, the delight a prisoner might have in making some small gesture of liberty—getting a deceptive sense of omnipotence from doing something forbidden without immediate punishment. I was that slave, who fled from his Lord and pursued his Lord's shadow. O rottenness, O monstrousness of life and abyss of death! Could you find pleasure only in what was forbidden, and only because it was forbidden?

Chapter X

Who can unravel that complex twisted knottedness? It is unclean, I hate to think of it or look at it. I long for Thee, O Justice and Innocence; Joy and Beauty of the clear of sight, I long for Thee with unquenchable longing. There is sure repose in Thee and life untroubled. He that enters into Thee, enters into the joy of his Lord and shall not fear and shall be well in Him who is the Best. I went away from Thee, my God, in my youth I strayed too far from Thy sustaining power, and I became to myself a barren land.

Book III

Chapter I

I came to Carthage, where a cauldron of illicit loves leapt and boiled about me. I was not yet in love, but I was in love with love, and from the very depth of my need hated myself for not more keenly feeling the need. I sought some object to love, since I was thus in love with loving; and I hated security and a life with no snares for my feet. For within I was hungry, all for the want of that spiritual food which is Thyself, my God; yet [though I was hungry for want of it] I did not hunger for it: I had no desire whatever for incorruptible food, not because I had it in abundance but the emptier I was, the more I hated the thought of it. Because of all this my soul was sick, and broke out in sores, whose itch I agonized to scratch with the rub of carnal things—carnal, yet if there were no soul in them, they would not be objects of love. My longing then was to love and to be loved, but most when I obtained the enjoyment of the body of the person who loved me.

Thus I polluted the stream of friendship with the filth of unclean desire and sullied its limpidity with the hell of lust. And vile and unclean as I was, so great was my vanity that I was bent upon passing for clean and courtly. And I did fall in love, simply from wanting to. O my God, my Mercy, with how much bitterness didst Thou in Thy goodness sprinkle the delights of that time! I was loved, and our love came to the bond of consummation: I wore my chains with bliss but with torment too, for I was scourged with the red hot rods of jealousy, with suspicions and fears and tempers and quarrels.

Chapter VI

I fell in with a sect of men [the Manicheans] talking high-sounding nonsense, carnal and wordy men. The snares of the devil were in their mouths, to trap souls with an arrangement of the syllables of the names of

God the Father and of the Lord Jesus Christ and of the Paraclete, the Holy
Ghost, our Comforter. These names were always on their lips, but only as
sounds and tongue noises; for their heart was empty of the true meaning.
They cried out "Truth, truth;" they were forever uttering the word to me,
but the thing was nowhere in them; indeed they spoke falsehood not only
of You, who are truly Truth, but also of the elements of this world, Your
creatures. Concerning these I ought to have passed beyond even the
philosophers who spoke truly, for love of You, O my supreme and good
Father, Beauty of all things beautiful. O Truth, Truth, how inwardly did
the very marrow of my soul pant for You when time and again I heard
them sound Your name. But it was all words—words spoken, words
written in many huge tomes. In these dishes—while I hungered for You—
they served me up the sun and the moon, beautiful works of Yours, but
works of Yours all the same and not Yourself: not even Your mightiest
works. For Your spiritual creation is greater than these material things,
brilliantly as they shine in the sky. . . .

Where then were You and how far from me? I had indeed straggled far
from You, not even being allowed to eat the husks of the swine whom I was
feeding with husks. How much better were the sheer fables of the poets
and literary men than all the traps [that Manes set for souls]. Verses, and
poems, and Medea flying, were less harmful than the Five Elements,
variously transformed in strife with the five Dens of Darkness, which have
no being whatsoever and are death to the soul that believes them. It is
possible to get real food for the mind out of verses and poems; and though
I sang of Medea flying, I did not think it was true; and when I heard it
sung I did not believe it. But these fantasies of the Manichees I did believe.
Alas, by what stages was I brought down to the deepest depths of the pit,
giving myself needless labour and turmoil of spirit for want of the truth: in
that I sought You my God—to You I confess it, for You had pity on me
even when I had not yet confessed—in that I sought You not according to
the understanding of the mind by which You have set us above the beasts,
but according to the sense of the flesh. Yet all the time You were more
inward than the most inward place of my heart and loftier than the
highest.

Book VII

Chapter IX

And first you willed to show me how You resist the proud and give grace
to the humble, and with how great mercy You have shown men the way of
humility in that the Word was made flesh and dwelt among men. There-

fore You brought in my way by means of a certain man—an incredibly conceited man—some books of the Platonists translated from Greek into Latin. In them I found, though not in the very words, yet the thing itself and proved by all sorts of reasons: that *in the beginning was the Word and the Word was with God and the Word was God: the same was in the beginning with God; all things were made by Him and without him was made nothing that was made; in Him was life and the life was the light of men, and the light shines in darkness and the darkness did not comprehend it.* . . .

Chapter X

Being admonished by all this to return to myself, I entered into my own depths, with You as guide; and I was able to do it because You were my helper. I entered, and with the eye of my soul, such as it was, I saw Your unchangeable Light shining over that same eye of my soul, over my mind. It was not the light of everyday that the eye of flesh can see, nor some greater light of the same order, such as might be if the brightness of our daily light should be seen shining with a more intense brightness and filling all things with its greatness. Your Light was not that, but other, altogether other, than all such lights. Nor was it above my mind as oil above the water it floats on, nor as the sky is above the earth; it was above because it made me, and I was below because made by it. He who knows the truth knows that Light, and he that knows the Light knows eternity. Charity knows it. O eternal truth and true love and beloved eternity! Thou art my God, I sigh to Thee by day and by night. When first I knew Thee, Thou didst lift me up so that I might see that there was something to see, but that I was not yet the man to see it. And Thou didst beat back the weakness of my gaze, blazing upon me too strongly, and I was shaken with love and with dread. And I knew that I was far from Thee in the region of unlikeness. . . .

Book VIII

Chapter III

. . . What is it in the soul, I ask again, that makes it delight more to have found or regained the things it loves than if it had always had them? Creatures other than man bear the same witness, and all things are filled with testimonies acclaiming that it is so. The victorious general has his triumph; but he would not have been victorious if he had not fought; and the greater danger there was in the battle, the greater rejoicing in the triumph. The storm tosses the sailors and threatens to wreck the ship; all are pale with the threat of death. But the sky grows clear, the sea calm, and now they are as wild with exultation as before with fear. A friend is sick and his pulse threatens danger; all who want him well feel as if they shared his sickness. He begins to recover, though he cannot yet walk as strongly as of old: and there is more joy than there was before, when he was still well and could walk properly. Note too that men procure the actual pleasures of human life by way of pain—I mean not only the pain that comes upon us unlooked for and beyond our will, but unpleasantness planned and willingly accepted. There is no pleasure in eating or drinking, unless the discomfort of hunger and thirst come before. Drunkards eat salty things to develop a thirst so great as to be painful, and pleasure arises when the liquor quenches the pain of the thirst. And it is the custom that promised brides do not give themselves at once lest the husband should hold the gift cheap unless delay had set him craving.

We see this in base and dishonourable pleasure, but also in the pleasure that is licit and permitted, and again in the purest and most honourable friendship. We have seen it in the case of him who had been dead and was brought back to life, who had been lost and was found. Universally the greater joy is heralded by greater pain. What does this mean, O Lord my God, when Thou art an eternal joy to Thyself, Thou Thyself art joy itself, and things about Thee ever rejoice in Thee? What does it mean that this part of creation thus alternates between need felt and need met, between discord and harmony? Is this their mode of being, this what Thou didst give them, when from the heights of heaven to the lowest earth, from the beginning of time to the end, from the angel to the worm, from the first movement to the last, Thou didst set all kinds of good things and all Thy just works each in its place, each in its season? Alas for me, how high art Thou in the highest, how deep in the deepest! And Thou dost never depart from us, yet with difficulty do we return to Thee.

Chapter V

Now when this man of Yours, Simplicianus, had told me the story of Victorinus, I was on fire to imitate him: which indeed was why he had told me. He added that in the time of the emperor Julian, when a law was made prohibiting Christians from teaching Literature and Rhetoric, Victorinus had obeyed the law, preferring to give up his own school of words rather than Your word, by which You make eloquent the tongues of babes. In this he seemed to me not only courageous but actually fortunate, because it gave him the chance to devote himself wholly to You. I longed for the same chance, but I was bound not with the iron of another's chains, but by my own iron will. The enemy held my will; and of it he made a chain and bound me. Because my will was perverse it changed to lust, and lust yielded to become habit, and habit not resisted became necessity. These were like links hanging one on another—which is why I have called it a chain—and their hard bondage held me bound hand and foot. The new will which I now began to have, by which I willed to worship You freely and to enjoy You, O God, the only certain Joy, was not yet strong enough to overcome that earlier will rooted deep through the years. My two wills, one old, one new, one carnal, one spiritual, were in conflict and in their conflict wasted my soul.

Thus, with myself as object of the experiment, I came to understand what I had read, how the *flesh lusts against the spirit and the spirit against the flesh.* I indeed was in both camps, but more in that which I approved in myself than in that which I disapproved. For in a sense it was now no longer I that was in this second camp, because in large part I rather suffered it unwillingly than did it with my will. Yet habit had grown stronger against me by my own act, since I had come willingly where I did not now will to be. Who can justly complain when just punishment overtakes the sinner? I no longer had the excuse which I used to think I had for not yet forsaking the world and serving You, the excuse namely that I had no certain knowledge of the truth. By now I was quite certain; but I was still bound to earth and refused to take service in Your army; I feared to be freed of all the things that impeded me, as strongly as I ought to have feared the being impeded by them. I was held down as agreeably by this world's baggage as one often is by sleep; and indeed the thoughts with which I meditated upon You were like the efforts of a man who wants to get up but is so heavy with sleep that he simply sinks back into it again. There is no one who wants to be asleep always—for every sound judgment holds that it is best to be awake—yet a man often postpones the effort of shaking himself awake when he feels a sluggish heaviness in the limbs, and settles pleasurably into another doze though he knows he should not, because it is time to get up. Similarly I regarded it as settled that it would be better to give myself to Your love rather than go on yielding to my own lust; but the first course delighted and convinced my mind, the second delighted my body and held it in bondage. For there was nothing I could reply when You called me: *Rise, thou that sleepest and arise from the dead: and Christ shall enlighten thee;* and whereas You showed me by every evidence that Your words were true, there was simply nothing I could answer save only laggard lazy words: "Soon," "Quite soon," "Give me just a little while." But "soon" and "quite soon" did not mean any particular time; and "just a little while" went on for a long while. It was in vain that *I delighted in Thy law according to the inner man, when that other law in my members rebelled against the law of my mind and led me captive in the law of sin that was in my members.* For the law of sin is the fierce force of habit, by which the mind is drawn and held even against its will, and yet deservedly because it had fallen wilfully into the habit. *Who then should deliver me from the body of this death, but Thy grace only, through Jesus Christ Our Lord?*

Book IX

Chapter IV

. . . I read, *Be angry and sin not.* And by this I was much moved, O my God, for I had by then learned to be angry with myself for the past, that I might not sin in what remained of life: and to be angry with good reason, because it was not some other nature of the race of darkness that had sinned in me, as the Manichees say: and they are not angry at themselves, but treasure up to themselves wrath against the day of wrath and of the revelation of the just judgement of God.

The good I now sought was not in things outside me, to be seen by the eye of flesh under the sun. For those that find their joy outside them easily fall into emptiness and are spilled out upon the things that are seen and the things of time, and in their starved minds lick shadows. If only they could grow weary of their own hunger and say: *Who shall show us good things?* And we should say and they should hear: *The light of Thy countenance is sealed upon us,* O Lord. For we are not *the Light that enlightens every man* but we are enlightened by *Thee that as we were heretofore darkness we are now light in Thee.* If they could but see the Light interior and eternal: for now that I had known it, I was frantic that I could not make them see it even were they to ask: *Who shall show us good things?* For the heart they would bring me would be in their eyes, eyes that looked everywhere but at You. But there, where I had been angry with myself, in my own room where I had been pierced, where I had offered my sacrifice, slaying the self that I had been, and, in the newly-taken purpose of newness of life, hoping in You—there You began to make me feel Your love and to give *gladness in my heart.* I cried out as I read this aloud and realized it within: and I no longer wished any increase of earthly goods, in which a man wastes time and is wasted by time, since in the simplicity of the Eternal I had other corn and wine and oil.

Book X

Chapter VI

It is with no doubtful knowledge, Lord, but with utter certainty that I love You. You have stricken my heart with Your word and I have loved You. And indeed heaven and earth and all that is in them tell me wherever I look that I should love You, and they cease not to tell it to all men, so that there is no excuse for them. For *You will have mercy on whom You will have mercy, and You will show mercy to whom You will show mercy:* otherwise heaven and earth cry their praise of You to deaf ears.

But what is it that I love when I love You? Not the beauty of any bodily thing, nor the order of seasons, not the brightness of light that rejoices the eye, nor the sweet melodies of all songs, nor the sweet fragrance of flowers and ointments and spices: not manna nor honey, not the limbs that carnal love embraces. None of these things do I love in loving my God. Yet in a sense I do love light and melody and fragrance and food and embrace when I love my God—the light and the voice and the fragrance and the food and embrace in the soul, when that light shines upon my soul which no place can contain, that voice sounds which no time can take from me, I breathe that fragrance which no wind scatters, I eat the food which is not lessened by eating, and I lie in the embrace which satiety never comes to sunder. This it is that I love, when I love my God.

Chapter XX

How then do I seek You, O Lord? For in seeking You, my God, it is happiness that I am seeking. I shall seek You, that my soul may live. For my body lives by my soul and my soul lives by You. What *is* the way to seek for happiness, then? Because I have no happiness till I can say, and say rightly: "Enough, it is there." . . .

Chapter XXII

Far be it, O Lord, far be it from the heart of Thy servant who makes this confession to Thee, far be it from me to think that I am happy for any or every joy that I may have. For there is a joy which is not given to the ungodly but only to those who love Thee for Thy own sake, whose joy is Thyself. And this is happiness, to be joyful in Thee and for Thee and because of Thee, this and no other. Those who think happiness is any other, pursue a joy that is apart from Thee and is no true joy. Yet their will is not wholly without some image of joy.

Chapter XXVIII

When once I shall be united to Thee with all my being, there shall be no more grief and toil, and my life will be alive, filled wholly with Thee. Thou dost raise up him whom Thou dost fill; whereas being not yet filled with Thee I am a burden to myself. The pleasures of this life for which I should weep are in conflict with the sorrows of this life in which I should rejoice, and I know not on which side stands the victory. Woe is me, Lord, have pity on me! For I have likewise sorrows which are evil and these are in conflict with joys that are good, and I know not on which side stands the victory. Woe is me, Lord have mercy upon me! Woe is me! See, I do not hide my wounds: Thou art the physician, I the sick man; Thou art merciful, I need mercy. Is not the life of man on earth a trial? Who would choose trouble and difficulty? Thou dost command us to endure them, not to love them. No one loves what he endures, though he may love to endure. For though he rejoices at his endurance, yet he would rather that there were nothing to endure. In adversity I desire prosperity, in prosperity I fear adversity. Yet what middle place is there between the two, where man's life may be other than trial? There is woe and woe again in the prosperity of this world, woe from the fear of adversity, woe from the corruption of joy! There is woe in the adversity of this world, and a second woe and a third, from the longing for prosperity, and because adversity itself is hard, and for fear that endurance may break! Is not man's life upon earth trial without intermission?

Chapter XXIX

All my hope is naught save in Thy great mercy. Grant what Thou dost command, and command what Thou wilt. Thou dost command continence. And *when I knew*, as it is said, *that no one could be continent unless God gave it, even this was a point of wisdom, to know whose gift it was.* For by continence we are collected and bound up into unity within ourself, whereas we had been scattered abroad in multiplicity. Too little does any man love Thee, who loves some other thing together with Thee, loving it not on account of Thee, O Thou Love, who art ever burning and never extinguished! O Charity, my God, enkindle me! Thou dost command continence: grant what Thou dost command and command what Thou wilt.

Chapter XXXVIII

I am poor and needy: yet I am better when with anguish of soul I see myself as hateful and seek your mercy, till what is damaged in me is repaired and made perfect, to the attaining of that peace which the eye of the proud knows not. The report of men's mouths, and deeds known to men, bring with them a most perilous temptation from the love of praise, which goes round almost begging for compliments and piles them up for our own personal glory. Love of praise tempts me even when I reprove it in myself, indeed in the very fact that I do reprove it: a man often glories the more vainly for his very contempt of vainglory: for which reason he does not really glory in his contempt of glory; in that he glories in it, he does not contemn it.

8

Martin Luther,
"The Freedom of a Christian"

Martin Luther (1483–1546), the German religious reformer whose protests led to Protestantism, was one of the most influential figures in Western history. A priest assigned to the University of Wittenberg, he became disillusioned with the corruption in the Church during a visit to Rome in 1510, and in 1517, protesting the sale of indulgences, Luther posted his ninety-five Theses on the door of the castle church in Wittenberg, thereby creating the division between Roman Catholics and Protestants that characterizes Western Christianity to this day. When the Roman Curia issued a bull of condemnation in 1520 threatening to excommunicate Luther in sixty days if he did not recant, Luther wrote "The Freedom of a Christian" in a conciliatory effort to explain his views. At the end of the sixty days, Luther burned the bull, canon law, and books supporting the pope, and was excommunicated.

"The Freedom of a Christian" spells out a key point in Luther's opposition to Catholic doctrine. Drawing on Scriptures, and especially St. Paul, Luther argues that it is not through works that one is saved—not through doing good deeds or performing rituals—but rather through the inner condition of faith alone. The true Christian is free from sin through faith in God, but is nevertheless bound through love to serve his or her neighbor. This image of human salvation as depending on the inner condition of the individual is one of the main sources of the avid emphasis on inwardness and the individualism that is definitive of the modern understanding of the self.

Many people have considered Christian faith an easy thing, and not a few have given it a place among the virtues. They do this because they have not experienced it and have never tasted the great strength there is in faith. It is impossible to write well about it or to understand what has been written about it unless one has at one time or another experienced the courage which faith gives a man when trials oppress him. But he who has had even a faint taste of it can never write, speak, meditate, or hear enough concerning it. It is a living "spring of water welling up to eternal life," as Christ calls it in John 4 [:14].

As for me, although I have no wealth of faith to boast of and know how scant my supply is, I nevertheless hope that I have attained to a little faith, even though I have been assailed by great and various temptations; and I hope that I can discuss it, if not more elegantly, certainly more to the point, than those literalists and subtile disputants have previously done, who have not even understood what they have written.

To make the way smoother for the unlearned—for only them do I serve—I shall set down the following two propositions concerning the freedom and the bondage of the spirit:

A Christian is a perfectly free lord of all, subject to none.

A Christian is a perfectly dutiful servant of all, subject to all.

These two theses seem to contradict each other. If, however, they should be found to fit together they would serve our purpose beautifully. Both are Paul's own statements, who says in I Cor. 9 [:19], "For though I am free from all men, I have made myself a slave to all," and in Rom. 13 [:8], "Owe no one anything, except to love one another." Love by its very nature is ready to serve and be subject to him who is loved. So Christ, although he was Lord of all, was "born of woman, born under the law" [Gal. 4:4], and therefore was at the same time a free man and a servant, "in the form of God" and "of a servant" [Phil. 2:6–7].

Let us start, however, with something more remote from our subject, but more obvious. Man has a twofold nature, a spiritual and a bodily one. According to the spiritual nature, which men refer to as the soul, he is called a spiritual, inner, or new man. According to the bodily nature, which men refer to as flesh, he is called a carnal, outward, or old man, of whom the Apostle writes in II Cor. 4 [:16], "Though our outer nature is wasting away, our inner nature is being renewed every day." Because of this diversity of nature the Scriptures assert contradictory things concerning the same man, since these two men in the same man contradict each other, "for the desires of the flesh are against the Spirit, and the desires of the Spirit are against the flesh," according to Gal. 5 [:17].

First, let us consider the inner man to see how a righteous, free, and pious Christian, that is, a spiritual, new, and inner man, becomes what he is. It is evident that no external thing has any influence in producing Christian righteousness or freedom, or in producing unrighteousness or servitude. A simple argument will furnish the proof of this statement. What can it profit the soul if the body is well, free, and active, and eats, drinks, and does as it pleases? For in these respects even the most godless slaves of vice may prosper. On the other hand, how will poor health or imprisonment or hunger or thirst or any other external misfortune harm the soul? Even the most godly men, and those who are free because of clear consciences, are afflicted with these things. None of these things touch either the freedom or the servitude of the soul. It does not help the soul if the body is adorned with the sacred robes of priests or dwells in sacred places or is occupied with sacred duties or prays, fasts, abstains from certain kinds of food, or does any work that can be done by the body and in the body. The righteousness and the freedom of the soul require something far different, since the things which have been mentioned could be done by any wicked person. Such works produce nothing but hypocrites. On the other hand, it will not harm the soul if the body is clothed in secular dress, dwells in unconsecrated places, eats and drinks as others do, does not pray aloud, and neglects to do all the above-mentioned things which hypocrites can do.

Furthermore, to put aside all kinds of works, even contemplation, meditation, and all that the soul can do, does not help. One thing, and only one thing, is necessary for Christian life, righteousness, and freedom. That one thing is the most holy Word of God, the gospel of Christ, as Christ says, John 11 [:25], "I am the resurrection and the life; he who believes in me, though he die, yet shall he live"; and John 8 [:36], "So if the Son makes you free, you will be free indeed"; and Matt. 4 [:4], "Man shall not live by bread alone, but by every word that proceeds from the mouth of God." Let us then consider it certain and firmly established that the soul can do without anything except the Word of God and that where the Word of God is missing there is no help at all for the soul. If it has the Word of God it is rich and lacks nothing, since it is the Word of life, truth, light, peace, righteousness, salvation, joy, liberty, wisdom, power, grace, glory, and of every incalculable blessing. This is why the prophet in the entire Psalm [119] and in many other places yearns and sighs for the Word of God and uses so many names to describe it.

On the other hand, there is no more terrible disaster with which the wrath of God can afflict men than a famine of the hearing of his Word, as he says in Amos [8:11]. Likewise there is no greater mercy than when he sends forth his Word, as we read in Psalm 107 [:20]: "He sent forth his word, and healed them, and delivered them from destruction." Nor was Christ sent into the world for any other ministry except that of the Word. Moreover, the entire spiritual estate—all the apostles, bishops, and priests—has been called and instituted only for the ministry of the Word.

You may ask, "What then is the Word of God, and how shall it be used, since there are so many words of God?" I answer: The Apostle explains this in Romans 1. The Word is the gospel of God concerning his Son, who was made flesh, suffered, rose from the dead, and was glorified through the Spirit who sanctifies. To preach Christ means to feed the soul, make it righteous, set it free, and save it, provided it believes the preaching. Faith alone is the saving and efficacious use of the Word of God, according to

Rom. 10 [:9]: "If you confess with your lips that Jesus is Lord and believe in your heart that God raised him from the dead, you will be saved." Furthermore, "Christ is the end of the law, that every one who has faith may be justified" [Rom. 10:4]. Again, in Rom. 1 [:17], "He who through faith is righteous shall live." The Word of God cannot be received and cherished by any works whatever but only by faith. Therefore it is clear that, as the soul needs only the Word of God for its life and righteousness, so it is justified by faith alone and not any works; for if it could be justified by anything else, it would not need the Word, and consequently it would not need faith.

This faith cannot exist in connection with works—that is to say, if you at the same time claim to be justified by works, whatever this character— for that would be the same as "limping with two different opinions" [I Kings 18:21], as worshiping Baal and kissing one's own hand [Job 31:27– 28], which, as Job says, is a very great iniquity. Therefore the moment you begin to have faith you learn that all things in you are altogether blame- worthy, sinful, and damnable, as the Apostle says in Rom. 3 [:23], "Since all have sinned and fall short of the glory of God," and, "None is righ- teous, no, not one; . . . all have turned aside, together they have gone wrong" (Rom. 3:10–12). When you have learned this you will know that you need Christ, who suffered and rose again for you so that, if you believe in him, you may through this faith become a new man in so far as your sins are forgiven and you are justified by the merits of another, namely, of Christ alone.

Since, therefore, this faith can rule only in the inner man, as Rom. 10 [:10] says, "For man believes with his heart and so is justified," and since faith alone justifies, it is clear that the inner man cannot be justified, freed, or saved by any outer work or action at all, and that these works, whatever their character, have nothing to do with this inner man. On the other hand, only ungodliness and unbelief of heart, and no outer work, make him guilty and a damnable servant of sin. Wherefore it ought to be the first concern of every Christian to lay aside all confidence in works and increas- ingly to strengthen faith alone and through faith to grow in the knowledge, not of works, but of Christ Jesus, who suffered and rose for him, as Peter teaches in the last chapter of his first Epistle (I Pet. 5:10). No other work makes a Christian. Thus when the Jews asked Christ, as related in John 6 [:28], what they must do "to be doing the work of God," he brushed aside the multitude of works which he saw they did in great profusion and suggested one work, saying, "This is the work of God, that you believe in him whom he has sent" [John 6:29]; "for on him has God the Father set his seal" [John 6:27].

Therefore true faith in Christ is a treasure beyond comparison which brings with it complete salvation and saves man from every evil, as Christ says in the last chapter of Mark [16:16]: "He who believes and is baptized will be saved; but he who does not believe will be condemned." Isaiah contemplated this treasure and foretold it in chapter 10: "The Lord will make a small and consuming word upon the land, and it will overflow with righteousness" [Cf. Isa. 10:22]. This is as though he said, "Faith, which is a small and perfect fulfillment of the law, will fill believers with so great a righteousness that they will need nothing more to become righteous." So Paul says, Rom. 10 [:10], "For man believes with his heart and so is justified."

Should you ask how it happens that faith alone justifies and offers us such a treasure of great benefits without works in view of the fact that so many works, ceremonies, and laws are prescribed in the Scriptures, I answer: First of all, remember what has been said, namely, that faith alone, without works, justifies, frees, and saves; we shall make this clearer later on. Here we must point out that the entire Scripture of God is divided into two parts: commandments and promises. Although the commandments teach things that are good, the things taught are not done as soon as they are taught, for the commandments show us what we ought to do but do not give us the power to do it. They are intended to teach man to know himself, that through them he may recognize his inability to do good and may despair of his own ability. That is why they are called the Old Testament and constitute the Old Testament. For example, the commandment, "You shall not covet" [Exod. 20:17], is a command which proves us all to be sinners, for no one can avoid coveting no matter how much he may struggle against it. Therefore, in order not to covet and to fulfill the commandment, a man is compelled to despair of himself, to seek the help which he does not find in himself elsewhere and from someone else, as stated in Hosea [13:9]: "Destruction is your own, O Israel: your help is only in me." As we fare with respect to one commandment, so we fare with all, for it is equally impossible for us to keep any one of them.

Now when a man has learned through the commandments to recognize his helplessness and is distressed about how he might satisfy the law— since the law must be fulfilled so that not a jot or tittle shall be lost, otherwise man will be condemned without hope—then, being truly humbled and reduced to nothing in his own eyes, he finds in himself nothing whereby he may be justified and saved. Here the second part of Scripture comes to our aid, namely, the promises of God which declare the glory of God, saying, "If you wish to fulfill the law and not covet, as the law demands, come, believe in Christ in whom grace, righteousness, peace, liberty, and all things are promised you. If you believe, you shall have all things; if you do not believe, you shall lack all things." That which is impossible for you to accomplish by trying to fulfill all the works of the law—many and useless as they all are—you will accomplish quickly and easily through faith. God our Father has made all things depend on faith so that whoever has faith will have everything, and whoever does not have faith will have nothing. "For God has consigned all men to disobedience, that he may have mercy upon all," as it is stated in Rom. 11 [:32]. Thus the promises of God give what the commandments of God demand and fulfill what the law prescribes so that all things may be God's alone, both the commandments and the fulfilling of the commandments. He alone commands, he alone fulfills. Therefore the promises of God belong to the New Testament. Indeed, they are the New Testament.

Since these promises of God are holy, true, righteous, free, and peaceful words, full of goodness, the soul which clings to them with a firm faith will be so closely united with them and altogether absorbed by them that it not only will share in all their power but will be saturated and intoxicated by them. If a touch of Christ healed, how much more will this most tender spiritual touch, this absorbing of the Word, communicate to the soul all things that belong to the Word. This, then, is how through faith alone without works the soul is justified by the Word of God, sanctified, made true, peaceful, and free, filled with every blessing and truly made a child of God, as John 1 [:12] says: "But to all who . . . believed in his name, he gave power to become children of God."

From what has been said it is easy to see from what source faith derives such great power and why a good work or all good works together cannot equal it. No good work can rely upon the Word of God or live in the soul, for faith alone and the Word of God rule in the soul. Just as the heated iron glows like fire because of the union of fire with it, so the Word imparts its qualities to the soul. It is clear, then, that a Christian has all that he needs in faith and needs no work to justify him; and if he has no need of works, he has no need of the law; and if he has no need of the law, surely he is free from the law. It is true that "the law is not laid down for the just" [I Tim. 1:9]. This is that Christian liberty, our faith, which does not induce us to live in idleness or wickedness but makes the law and works unnecessary for any man's righteousness and salvation.

This is the first power of faith. Let us now examine also the second. It is a further function of faith that it honors him whom it trusts with the most reverent and highest regard since it considers him truthful and trustworthy. There is no other honor equal to the estimate of truthfulness with which we honor him whom we trust. Could we ascribe to a man anything greater than truthfulness and righteousness and perfect goodness? On the other hand, there is no way in which we can show greater contempt for a man than to regard him as false and wicked and to be suspicious of him, as we do when we do not trust him. So when the soul firmly trusts God's promises, it regards him as truthful and righteous. Nothing more excellent than this can be ascribed to God. The very highest worship of God is this that we ascribe to him truthfulness, righteousness, and whatever else should be ascribed to one who is trusted. When this is done, the soul consents to his will. Then it hallows his name and allows itself to be treated according to God's good pleasure for, clinging to God's promises, it does not doubt that he who is true, just, and wise will do, dispose, and provide all things well.

Is not such a soul most obedient to God in all things by this faith? What commandment is there that such obedience has not completely fulfilled? What more complete fulfillment is there than obedience in all things? This obedience, however, is not rendered by works, but by faith alone. On the other hand, what greater rebellion against God, what greater wickedness, what greater contempt of God is there than not believing his promise? For what is this but to make God a liar or to doubt that he is truthful?—that is, to ascribe truthfulness to one's self but lying and vanity to God? Does not a man who does this deny God and set himself up as an idol in his heart? Then of what good are works done in such wickedness, even if they were the works of angels and apostles? Therefore God has rightly included all things, not under anger or lust, but under unbelief, so that they who imagine that they are fulfilling the law by doing the works of chastity and mercy required by the law (the civil and human virtues) might not be saved. They are included under the sin of unbelief and must either seek mercy or be justly condemned.

When, however, God sees that we consider him truthful and by the faith of our heart pay him the great honor which is due him, he does us that great honor of considering us truthful and righteous for the sake of our faith. Faith works truth and righteousness by giving God what belongs to him. Therefore God in turn glorifies our righteousness. It is true and just that God is truthful and just, and to consider and confess him to be so is the same as being truthful and just. Accordingly he says in I Sam. 2 [:30], "Those who honor me I will honor, and those who despise me shall be lightly esteemed." So Paul says in Rom. 4 [:3] that Abraham's faith "was reckoned to him as righteousness" because by it he gave glory most perfectly to God, and that for the same reason our faith shall be reckoned to us as righteousness if we believe.

The third incomparable benefit of faith is that it unites the soul with Christ as a bride is united with her bridegroom. By this mystery, as the Apostle teaches, Christ and the soul become one flesh [Eph. 5:31–32]. And if they are one flesh and there is between them a true marriage— indeed the most perfect of all marriages, since human marriages are but poor examples of this one true marriage—it follows that everything they have they hold in common, the good as well as the evil. Accordingly the believing soul can boast of and glory in whatever Christ has as though it were its own, and whatever the soul has Christ claims as his own. Let us compare these and we shall see inestimable benefits. Christ is full of grace, life, and salvation. The soul is full of sins, death, and damnation. Now let faith come between them and sins, death, and damnation will be Christ's, while grace, life, and salvation will be the soul's; for if Christ is a bride-groom, he must take upon himself the things which are his bride's and bestow upon her the things that are his. If he gives her his body and very self, how shall he not give her all that is his? And if he takes the body of the bride, how shall he not take all that is hers?

. . .

That we may examine more profoundly that grace which our inner man has in Christ, we must realize that in the Old Testament God consecrated to himself all the first-born males. The birthright was highly prized for it involved a twofold honor, that of priesthood and that of kingship. The first-born brother was priest and lord over all the others and a type of Christ, the true and only first-born of God the Father and the Virgin Mary and true king and priest, but not after the fashion of the flesh and the world, for his kingdom is not of this world [John 18:36]. He reigns in heavenly and spiritual things and consecrates them—things such as righteousness, truth, wisdom, peace, salvation, etc. This does not mean that all things on earth and in hell are not also subject to him—otherwise how could he protect and save us from them?—but that his kingdom consists neither in them nor of them. Nor does his priesthood consist in the outer splendor of robes and postures like those of the human priesthood of Aaron and our present-day church; but it consists of spiritual things through which he by an invisible service intercedes for us in heaven before God, there offers himself as a sacrifice, and does all things a priest should do, as Paul describes him under the type of Melchizedek in the Epistle to the Hebrews [Heb. 6–7]. Nor does he only pray and intercede for us but he teaches us inwardly through the living instruction of his Spirit, thus performing the two real functions of a priest, of which the prayers and the preaching of human priests are visible types.

Now just as Christ by his birthright obtained these two prerogatives, so he imparts them to and shares them with everyone who believes in him according to the law of the above-mentioned marriage, according to which the wife owns whatever belongs to the husband. Hence all of us who believe in Christ are priests and kings in Christ, as I Pet. 2 [:9] says: "You

are a chosen race, God's own people, a royal priesthood, a priestly kingdom, that you may declare the wonderful deeds of him who called you out
of darkness into his marvelous light."

The nature of this priesthood and kingship is something like this: First,
with respect to the kingship, every Christian is by faith so exalted above all
things that, by virtue of a spiritual power, he is lord of all things without
exception, so that nothing can do him any harm. As a matter of fact, all
things are made subject to him and are compelled to serve him in obtain-
ing salvation. Accordingly Paul says in Rom. 8 [:28], "All things work
together for good for the elect," and in I Cor. 3 [:21–23], "All things are
yours whether . . . life or death or the present or the future, all are yours;
and you are Christ's. . . ." This is not to say that every Christian is placed
over all things to have and control them by physical power—a madness
with which some churchmen are afflicted—for such power belongs to
kings, princes, and other men on earth. Our ordinary experience in life
shows us that we are subjected to all, suffer many things, and even die. As a
matter of fact, the more Christian a man is, the more evils, sufferings, and
deaths he must endure, as we see in Christ the first-born prince himself,
and in all his brethren, the saints. The power of which we speak is spiritual. It rules in the midst of enemies and is powerful in the midst of
oppression. This means nothing else than that "power is made perfect in
weakness" [II Cor. 12:9] and that in all things I can find profit toward
salvation [Rom. 8:28], so that the cross and death itself are compelled to
serve me and to work together with me for my salvation. This is a splendid
privilege and hard to attain, a truly omnipotent power, a spiritual dominion in which there is nothing so good and nothing so evil but that it shall
work together for good to me, if only I believe. Yes, since faith alone
suffices for salvation, I need nothing except faith exercising the power and
dominion of its own liberty. Lo, this is the inestimable power and liberty of
Christians.

Not only are we the freest of kings, we are also priests forever, which is
far more excellent than being kings, for as priests we are worthy to appear
before God to pray for others and to teach one another divine things.
These are the functions of priests, and they cannot be granted to any
unbeliever. Thus Christ has made it possible for us, provided we believe in
him, to be not only his brethren, coheirs, and fellow-kings, but also his
fellow-priests. Therefore we may boldly come into the presence of God in
the spirit of faith [Heb. 10:19, 22] and cry "Abba, Father!" pray for one
another, and do all things which we see done and foreshadowed in the
outer and visible works of priests.

He, however, who does not believe is not served by anything. On the
contrary, nothing works for his good, but he himself is a servant of all, and

all things turn out badly for him because he wickedly uses them to his own advantage and not to the glory of God. So he is no priest but a wicked man whose prayer becomes sin and who never comes into the presence of God because God does not hear sinners [John 9:31]. Who then can comprehend the lofty dignity of the Christian? By virtue of his royal power he rules over all things, death, life, and sin, and through his priestly glory is omnipotent with God because he does the things which God asks and desires, as it is written, "He will fulfill the desire of those who fear him; he also will hear their cry and save them" [Cf. Phil. 4:13]. To this glory a man attains, certainly not by any works of his, but by faith alone.

From this anyone can clearly see how a Christian is free from all things and over all things so that he needs no works to make him righteous and save him, since faith alone abundantly confers all these things. Should he grow so foolish, however, as to presume to become righteous, free, saved, and a Christian by means of some good work, he would instantly lose faith and all its benefits, a foolishness aptly illustrated in the fable of the dog who runs along a stream with a piece of meat in his mouth and, deceived by the reflection of the meat in the water, opens his mouth to snap at it and so loses both the meat and the reflection.[1]

. . .

Repentance proceeds from the law of God, but faith or grace from the promise of God, as Rom. 10 [:17] says: "So faith comes from what is heard, and what is heard comes by the preaching of Christ." Accordingly man is consoled and exalted by faith in the divine promise after he has been humbled and led to a knowledge of himself by the threats and the fear of the divine law. So we read in Psalm 30 [:5]: "Weeping may tarry for the night, but joy comes with the morning."

Let this suffice concerning works in general and at the same time concerning the works which a Christian does for himself. Lastly, we shall also speak of the things which he does toward his neighbor. A man does not live for himself alone in this mortal body to work for it alone, but he lives also for all men on earth; rather, he lives only for others and not for himself. To this end he brings his body into subjection that he may the more sincerely and freely serve others, as Paul says in Rom. 14 [:7–8], "None of us lives to himself, and none of us dies to himself. If we live, we live to the Lord, and if we die, we die to the Lord." He cannot ever in this life be idle and without works toward his neighbors, for he will necessarily speak, deal with, and exchange views with men, as Christ also, being made

1. Luther was fond of Aesop's Fables, of which this is one.

in the likeness of men [Phil. 2:7], was found in form as a man and conversed with men, as Baruch 3 [:37] says.

Man, however, needs none of these things for his righteousness and salvation. Therefore he should be guided in all his works by this thought and contemplate this one thing alone, that he may serve and benefit others in all that he does, considering nothing except the need and the advantage of his neighbor. Accordingly the Apostle commands us to work with our hands so that we may give to the needy, although he might have said that we should work to support ourselves. He says, however, "that he may be able to give to those in need" [Eph. 4:28]. This is what makes caring for the body a Christian work, that through its health and comfort we may be able to work, to acquire, and lay by funds with which to aid those who are in need, that in this way the strong member may serve the weaker, and we may be sons of God, each caring for and working for the other, bearing one another's burdens and so fulfilling the law of Christ [Gal. 6:2]. This is a truly Christian life. Here faith is truly active through love [Gal. 5:6], that is, it finds expression in works of the freest service, cheerfully and lovingly done, with which a man willingly serves another without hope of reward; and for himself he is satisfied with the fullness and wealth of his faith.

Accordingly Paul, after teaching the Philippians how rich they were made through faith in Christ, in which they obtained all things, thereafter teaches them, saying, "So if there is any encouragement in Christ, any incentive of love, any participation in the Spirit, any affection and sympathy, complete my joy by being of the same mind, having the same love, being in full accord and of one mind. Do nothing from selfishness or conceit, but in humility count others better than yourselves. Let each of you look not only to his own interests, but also to the interests of others" [Phil. 2:1–4]. Here we see clearly that the Apostle has prescribed this rule for the life of Christians, namely, that we should devote all our works to the welfare of others, since each has such abundant riches in his faith that all his other works and his whole life are a surplus with which he can by voluntary benevolence serve and do good to his neighbor.

Fyodor Dostoyevsky, "The Russian Monk," from *The Brothers Karamazov*

In 1849, the Russian novelist Fyodor Dostoyevsky (1821–1881) was arrested for his involvement in a secret political group and was exiled to Siberia, where he spent four years at hard labor and five as a soldier. His harsh experiences there led him to abandon his youthful liberal outlook, with its emphasis on individual rights and untrammeled freedom, in favor of a more communitarian conception of shared responsibilities in God's world. This religious vision is developed in his last and greatest novel, The Brothers Karamazov (1880), on the surface a story about three brothers and the murder of their father. With extraordinary psychological insight, Dostoyevsky shows how political radicalism and Western liberal thought tend to undermine the fundamental Russian commitment to cooperation and brotherly love, leading to selfishness and ultimately nihilism (the complete disbelief in all values). In a key passage near the middle of the book, Dostoyevsky provides an account of the last words of the monk and spiritual guide, Father Zossima, who formulates Dostoyevsky's own view of the meaning of the Russian essence and the teachings of the Eastern Church. What is crucial here is not so much the issue of individual salvation as the ideal of contributing to the realization of God's plan for earth—the goal, expressed in the Lord's Prayer, that it shall be "on earth as it is in heaven"—through selfless, active love for others.

Notes of the Life in God of the Deceased Priest and Monk, the Elder Zossima, Taken from His Own Words

Father Zossima's Brother

Beloved fathers and teachers, I was born in a distant province in the north, in the town of V. My father was a gentleman by birth, but of no great consequence or position. He died when I was only two years old, and I don't remember him at all. He left my mother a small house built of wood, and an income, not large, but sufficient to keep her and her children

From Fyodor Dostoyevsky, *The Brothers Karamazov*, trans. by Constance Garnett. (London: Heinemann, 1912).

in comfort. There were two of us, my elder brother Markel and I. He was eight years older than I was, of hasty, irritable temperament, but kind-hearted and never ironical. He was remarkably silent, especially at home with me, his mother, and the servants. He did well at school, but did not get on with his schoolfellows, though he never quarrelled, at least so my mother has told me. Six months before his death, when he was seventeen, he made friends with a political exile who had been banished from Moscow to our town for freethinking, and led a solitary existance there. He was a good scholar who had gained distinction in philosophy in the university. Something made him take a fancy to Markel, and he used to ask him to see him. The young man would spend whole evenings with him during that winter, until the exile was summoned to Petersburg to take up his post again at his own request, as he had powerful friends.

It was the beginning of Lent, and Markel would not fast; he was rude and laughed at it. "That's all silly twaddle and there is no God," he said, horrifying my mother, the servants, and me too. For though I was only nine, I too was aghast at hearing such words. We had four servants, all serfs. I remember my mother selling one of the four, the cook Afimya, who was lame and elderly, for sixty paper roubles, and hiring a free servant to take her place.

In the sixth week in Lent, my brother, who was never strong and had a tendency to consumption, was taken ill. He was tall but thin and delicate-looking, and of very pleasing countenance. I suppose he caught cold; anyway, the doctor who came soon whispered to my mother that it was galloping consumption, that he would not live through the spring. My mother began weeping, and careful not to alarm my brother she entreated him to go to church, to confess, and to take the sacrament, as he was still able to move about. This made him angry, and he said something profane about the church. He grew thoughtful, however; he guessed at once that he was seriously ill, and that that was why his mother was begging him to confess and take the sacrament. He had been aware, indeed, for a long time past that he was far from well, and had a year before coolly observed at dinner to our mother and me, "My life won't be long among you; I may not live another year," which seemed now like a prophecy.

Three days passed and Holy Week had come. And on Tuesday morning my brother began going to church. "I am doing this simply for your sake, mother, to please and comfort you," he said. My mother wept with joy and grief; "his end must be near," she thought, "if there's such a change in him." But he was not able to go to church long; he took to his bed, so he had to confess and take the sacrament at home.

It was a late Easter, and the days were bright, fine, and full of fragrance. I remember he used to cough all night and sleep badly, but in the morning he dressed and tried to sit up in an armchair. That's how I remember him sitting, sweet and gentle, smiling, his face bright and joyous, in spite of his illness. A marvellous change passed over him; his spirit seemed transformed. The old nurse would come in and say, "Let me light the lamp before the holy image, my dear." And once he would not have allowed it and would have blown it out.

"Light it, light it, dear, I was a wretch to have prevented you doing it. You are praying when you light the lamp, and I am praying when I rejoice seeing you. So we are praying to the same God."

Those words seemed strange to us, and mother would go to her room and weep, but when she went in to him she wiped her eyes and looked cheerful. "Mother, don't weep, darling," he would say, "I've long to live yet, long to rejoice with you, and life is glad and joyful."

"Ah, dear boy, how can you talk of joy when you lie feverish at night, coughing as though you would tear yourself to pieces."

"Don't cry, mother," he would answer, "life is paradise, and we are all in paradise, but we don't see it; if we did we should have heaven on earth the next day."

Every one wondered at his words; he spoke so strangely and positively, we were all touched and wept. Friends came to see us. "Dear ones," he would say to them, "what have I done that you should love me so; how can you love any one like me, and how was it I did not know, I did not appreciate it before?"

When the servants came in to him, he would say continually, "Dear, kind people, why are you doing so much for me; do I deserve to be waited on? If it were God's will for me to live, I would wait on you, for all men should wait on one another."

Mother shook her head as she listened. "My darling, it's your illness makes you talk like that."

"Mother darling," he would say, "there must be servants and masters, but if so I will be the servant of my servants, the same as they are to me. And another thing, mother, every one of us has sinned against all men, and I more than any."

Mother positively smiled at that and smiled through her tears. "Why, how could you have sinned against all men, more than all? Robbers and murderers have done that, but what sin have you committed yet that you hold yourself more guilty than all?"

"Mother, little heart of mine," he said (he had begun using such strange caressing words at that time), "little heart of mine, my joy, believe me, every one is really responsible to all men for all men and for everything. I don't know how to explain it to you, but I feel it is so, painfully even. And how is it we went on then living, getting angry and not knowing?"

So he would get up every day, more and more sweet and joyous and full of love. When the doctor, an old German called Eisenschmidt, came: "Well, doctor, have I another day in this world?" he would ask, joking.

"You'll live many days yet," the doctor would answer, "and months and years too."

"Months and years!" he would exclaim. "Why reckon the days? One day is enough for a man to know all happiness. My dear ones, why do we quarrel, try to outshine each other, and keep grudges against each other? Let's go straight into the garden, walk and play there, love, appreciate, and kiss each other, and glorify life."

"Your son cannot last long," the doctor told my mother, as she accompanied him to the door. "The disease is affecting his brain."

The windows of his room looked out into the garden, and our garden was a shady one, with old trees in it which were coming into bud. The first birds of spring were flitting in the branches, chirruping and singing at the windows. And looking at them and admiring them, he began suddenly begging their forgiveness too, "Birds of heaven, happy birds, forgive me, for I have sinned against you too." None of us could understand that at the time, but he shed tears of joy. "Yes," he said, "there was such a glory of God all about me; birds, trees, meadows, sky, only I lived in shame and dishonored it all and did not notice the beauty and glory."

"You take too many sins on yourself," mother used to say, weeping.

"Mother, darling, it's for joy, not for grief I am crying. Though I can't explain it to you, I like to humble myself before them, for I don't know how to love them enough. If I have sinned against everyone, yet all forgive me, too, and that's heaven. Am I not in heaven now?"

And there was a great deal more I don't remember. I remember I went once into his room when there was no one else there. It was a bright evening; the sun was setting, and the whole room was lighted up. He beckoned me, and I went up to him. He put his hands on my shoulders and looked into my face tenderly, lovingly; he said nothing for a minute, only looked at me like that.

"Well," he said, "run and play now, enjoy life for me too."

I went out then and ran to play. And many times in my life afterwards I remembered even with tears how he told me to enjoy life for him too. There were many other marvellous and beautiful sayings of his, though we did not understand them at the time. He died the third week after Easter. He was fully conscious, though he could not talk; up to his last hour he did not change. He looked happy; his eyes beamed and sought us; he smiled at us, beckoned us. There was a great deal of talk even in the town about his death. I was impressed by all this at the time, but not too much so, though I cried a great deal at his funeral. I was young then, a child; but a lasting impression, a hidden feeling of it all, remained in my heart, ready to rise up and respond when the time came. So indeed it happened.

Of the Holy Scriptures in the life of Father Zossima

I was left alone with my mother. Her friends began advising her to send me to Petersburg as other parents did. "You have only one son now," they said, "and have a fair income, and you will be depriving him perhaps of a brilliant career if you keep him here." They suggested I should be sent to Petersburg to the Cadet Corps, that I might afterwards enter the Imperial Guard. My mother hesitated for a long time; it was awful to part with her only child, but she made up her mind to it at last, though not without many tears, believing she was acting for my happiness. She brought me to Petersburg and put me into the Cadet Corps, and I never saw her again. For she too died three years afterwards. She spent those three years mourning and grieving for both of us.

From the house of my childhood I have brought nothing but precious memories, for there are no memories more precious than those of early childhood in one's first home. And that is almost always so if there is any love and harmony in the family at all. Indeed, precious memories may remain even of a bad home, if only the heart knows how to find what is precious. With my memories of home I count, too, my memories of the Bible, which, child as I was, I was very eager to read at home. I had a book of Scripture history then with excellent pictures, called *A Hundred and Four Stories from the Old and New Testament,* and I learned to read from it. I have it lying on my shelf now; I keep it as a precious relic of the past. But even before I learned to read, I remember first being moved to devotional feeling at eight years old. My mother took me alone to mass (I don't remember where my brother was at the time) on the Monday before Easter. It was a fine day, and I remember today, as though I saw it now, how the incense rose from the censer and softly floated upwards and, overhead in the cupola, mingled in rising waves with the sunlight that streamed in at the little window. I was stirred by the sight, and for the first time in my life I consciously received the seed of God's word in my heart. A youth came out into the middle of the church carrying a big book, so large that at the time I fancied he could scarcely carry it. He laid it on the reading desk, opened it, and began reading, and suddenly for the first time I understood something read in the church of God. In the land of Uz, there lived a man, righteous and God-fearing, and he had great wealth, so many camels, so many sheep and asses, and his children feasted, and he loved them very much and prayed for them. "It may be that my sons have sinned in their feasting." Now the devil came before the Lord, together with the sons of

God, and said to the Lord that he had gone up and down the earth and under the earth. "And hast thou considered my servant Job?" God asked of him. And God boasted to the devil, pointing to his great and holy servant. And the devil laughed at God's words. "Give him over to me and Thou wilt see that Thy servant will murmur against Thee and curse Thy name." And God gave up the just man He loved so, to the devil. And the devil smote his children and his cattle and scattered his wealth, all of a sudden like a thunderbolt from heaven. And Job rent his mantle and fell down upon the ground and cried aloud, "Naked came I out of my mother's womb, and naked shall I return into the earth; the Lord gave and the Lord has taken away. Blessed be the name of the Lord forever and ever."

Fathers and teachers, forgive my tears now, for all my childhood rises up again before me, and I breathe now as I breathed then, with the breast of a little child of eight, and I feel as I did then, awe and wonder and gladness. The camels at that time caught my imagination, and Satan, who talked like that with God, and God who gave His servant up to destruction, and His servant crying out, "Blessed be Thy name although Thou dost punish me," and then the soft and sweet singing in the Church, "Let my prayer rise up before Thee," and again incense from the priest's censer and the kneeling and the prayer. Ever since then—only yesterday I took it up— I've never been able to read that sacred tale without tears. And how much that is great, mysterious, and unfathomable there is in it! Afterwards I heard the words of mockery and blame, proud words: "How could God give up the most loved of His saints for the diversion of the devil, take from him his children, smite him with sore boils so that he cleansed the corruption from his sores with a potsherd—and for no object except to boast to the devil! 'See what My saint can suffer for My sake.'" But the greatness of it lies just in the fact that it is a mystery—that the passing earthly show and the eternal verity are brought together in it. In the face of the earthly truth, the eternal truth is accomplished. The Creator, just as on the first days of creation He ended each day with praise, "that is good that I have created," looks upon Job and again praises His creation. And Job, praising the Lord, serves not only Him but all His creation for generations and generations, and forever and ever, since for that he was ordained. Good heavens, what a book it is, and what lessons there are in it! What a book the Bible is; what a miracle; what strength is given with it to man. It is like a mould cast of the world and man and human nature; everything is there, and a law for everything for all the ages. And what mysteries are solved and revealed; God raises Job again, gives him wealth again. Many years pass by, and he has other children and loves them. But how could he love those new ones when those first children are no more, when he has lost them? Remembering them, how could he be fully happy with those new ones, however dear the new ones might be? But he could, he could. It's the great mystery of human life that old grief passes gradually into quiet tender joy. The mild serenity of age takes the place of the riotous blood of youth. I bless the rising sun each day and, as before, my heart sings to meet it, but now I love even more its setting, its long slanting rays and the soft tender gentle memories that come with them, the dear images from the whole of my long happy life—and over all the Divine Truth, softening, reconciling, forgiving! My life is ending, I know that well, but every day that is left me I feel how my earthly life is in touch with a new infinite, unknown, but approaching life, the nearness of which sets my soul quivering with rapture, my mind glowing and my heart weeping with joy.

· · ·

Recollections of Father Zossima's youth before he became a monk. The duel

I spent a long time, almost eight years, in the military cadet school at Petersburg, and in the novelty of my surroundings there, many of my childish impressions grew dimmer, though I forgot nothing. I picked up so many new habits and opinions that I was transformed into a cruel, absurd, almost savage creature. A surface polish of courtesy and society manners I did acquire together with the French language.

But we all, myself included, looked upon the soldiers in our service as cattle. I was perhaps worse than the rest in that respect, for I was so much more impressionable than my companions. By the time we left the school as officers, we were ready to lay down our lives for the honor of the regiment, but no one of us had any knowledge of the real meaning of honor, and if any one had known it, he would have been the first to ridicule it. Drunkenness, debauchery, and devilry were what we prided ourselves on. I don't say that we were bad by nature; all these young men were good fellows, but they behaved badly, and I worst of all. What made it worse for me was that I had come into my own money, and so I flung myself into a life of pleasure, and plunged headlong into all the recklessness of youth.

I was fond of reading, yet strange to say the Bible was the one book I never opened at that time, though I always carried it about with me, and I was never separated from it; in very truth I was keeping that book "for the day and the hour, for the month and the year," though I did not know it.

After four years of this life, I chanced to be in the town of K. where our regiment was stationed at the time. We found the people of the town hospitable, rich, and fond of entertainments. I met with a cordial reception everywhere, as I was of a lively temperament and was known to be well off, which always goes a long way in the world. And then a circumstance happened which was the beginning of it all.

I formed an attachment to a beautiful and intelligent young girl of noble and lofty character, the daughter of people much respected. They were well-to-do people of influence and position. They always gave me a cordial and friendly reception. I fancied that the young lady looked on me with favor and my heart was aflame at such an idea. Later on I saw and fully realized that I perhaps was not so passionately in love with her at all, but only recognized the elevation of her mind and character, which I could not indeed have helped doing. I was prevented, however, from making her an offer at the time by my selfishness; I was loath to part with the allurements of my free and licentious bachelor life in the heyday of my youth, and with my pockets full of money. I did drop some hint as to my feelings, however, though I put off taking any decisive step for a time. Then, all of a sudden, we were ordered off for two months to another district.

On my return two months later, I found the young lady already married to a rich neighboring landowner, a very amiable man, still young, though older than I was, connected with the best Petersburg society, which I was not, and of excellent education, which I also was not. I was so overwhelmed at this unexpected circumstance that my mind was positively clouded. The worst of it all was that, as I learned then, the young landowner had been a long while betrothed to her, and I had met him indeed many times in her house, but blinded by my conceit I had noticed nothing. And this particularly mortified me; almost everybody had known all about it, while I knew nothing. I was filled with sudden, irrepressible fury. With flushed face, I began recalling how often I had been on the point of declaring my love to her, and as she had not attempted to stop me or to warn me, she must, I concluded, have been laughing at me all the time. Later on, of course, I reflected and remembered that she had been very far from laughing at me; on the contrary, she used to turn off any courting on my part with a joke and begin talking of other subjects; but at that moment I was incapable of reflecting and was all eagerness for revenge. I am surprised to remember that my wrath and revengeful feelings were extremely repugnant to my own nature, for being of an easy temper, I found it difficult to be angry with anyone for long, and so I had to work myself up artificially and became at last revolting and absurd.

I waited for an opportunity and succeeded in insulting my "rival" in the presence of a large company. I insulted him on a perfectly extraneous pretext, jeering at his opinion upon an important public event—it was in the year 1826[1]—and my jeer was, so people said, clever and effective. Then I forced him to ask for an explanation, and behaved so rudely that he accepted my challenge in spite of the vast inequality between us, as I was younger, a person of no consequence, and of inferior rank. I learned afterwards for a fact that it was from a jealous feeling on his side also that my challenge was accepted; he had been rather jealous of me on his wife's account before their marriage; he fancied now that if he submitted to being insulted by me and refused to accept any challenge, and if she heard of it, she might begin to despise him and waver in her love for him. I soon found a second in a comrade, an ensign of our regiment. In those days, though duels were severely punished, yet duelling was a kind of fashion among the officers—so strong and deeply rooted will a brutal prejudice sometimes be.

It was the end of June, and our meeting was to take place at seven o'clock the next day on the outskirts of the town—and then something happened that in very truth was the turning-point of my life. In the evening, returning home in a savage and brutal humor, I flew into a rage with my orderly, Afanasy, and gave him two blows in the face with all my might, so that it was covered with blood. He had not long been in my service and I had struck him before, but never with such ferocious cruelty. And, believe me, though it's forty years ago, I recall it now with shame and pain. I went to bed and slept for about three hours; when I woke up, the day was breaking. I got up—I did not want to sleep any more—I went to the window—opened it; it looked out upon the garden; I saw the sun rising; it was warm and beautiful; the birds were singing.

What's the meaning of it, I thought? I feel in my heart something vile and shameful. Is it because I am going to shed blood? No, I thought, I feel it's not that. Can it be that I am afraid of death, afraid of being killed? No, that's not it, that's not it at all . . . And all at once I knew what it was: it was because I had beaten Afanasy the evening before! It all rose before my mind; it all was, as it were, repeated over again; he stood before me and I was beating him straight on the face and he was holding his arms stiffly down, his head erect, his eyes fixed upon me as though on parade. He staggered at every blow and did not even dare to raise his hands to protect himself. That is what a man has been brought to, and that was a man beating a fellow creature! What a crime! It was as though a sharp dagger had pierced me right through. I stood as if I were struck dumb, while the sun was shining, the leaves were rejoicing and the birds were trilling the

1. Probably the Decembrist plot against the Tsar in 1825 in which the most distinguished men in Russia were concerned.

praise of God . . . I hid my face in my hands, fell on my bed, and broke into a storm of tears. And then I remembered my brother Markel and what he said on his deathbed to his servants: "My dear ones, why do you wait on me, why do you love me, am I worth your waiting on me?"

Yes, am I worth it? flashed through my mind. After all, what am I worth that another man, a fellow creature, made in the likeness and image of God, should serve me? For the first time in my life this question forced itself upon me. He had said, "Mother, my little heart, in truth we are each responsible to all for all, it's only that men don't know this. If they know it, the world would be a paradise at once."

"God, can that too be false?" I thought as I wept. "In truth, perhaps I am more than all others responsible for all, a greater sinner than all men in the world." And all at once the whole truth in its full light appeared to me: what was I going to do? I was going to kill a good, clever, noble man, who had done me no wrong, and by depriving his wife of happiness for the rest of her life, I should be torturing and killing her too. I lay thus in my bed with my face in the pillow, heedless how the time was passing. Suddenly my second, the ensign, came in with the pistols to fetch me.

"Ah," said he, "it's a good thing you are up already; it's time we were off; come along!"

I did not know what to do and hurried to and fro undecidedly; we went out to the carriage, however.

"Wait here a minute," I said to him. "I'll be back directly; I have forgotten my wallet."

And I ran back alone, straight to Afanasy's little room.

"Afanasy," I said, "I gave you two blows on the face yesterday; forgive me," I said.

He started as though he were frightened, and looked at me; and I saw that it was not enough, and on the spot, in my full officer's uniform, I dropped at his feet and bowed my head to the ground.

"Forgive me," I said.

Then he was completely aghast.

"Your honor . . . sir, what are you doing? Am I worth it?"

And he burst out crying as I had done before, hid his face in his hands, turned to the window, and shook all over with his sobs. I flew out to my comrade and jumped into the carriage.

"Ready," I cried. "Have you ever seen a conqueror?" I asked him. "Here is one before you."

I was in ecstasy, laughing and talking all the way; I don't remember what about.

He looked at me. "Well, brother, you are a plucky fellow, you'll keep up the honor of the uniform, I can see."

So we reached the place and found them there, awaiting us. We were placed twelve paces apart; he had the first shot. I stood gaily, looking him full in the face; I did not twitch an eyelash. I looked lovingly at him, for I knew what I would do. His shot just grazed my cheek and ear.

"Thank God," I cried, "no man has been killed," and I seized my pistol, turned back, and flung it far into the wood.

"That's the place for you," I cried.

I turned to my adversary.

"Forgive me, young fool that I am, sir," I said, "for my unprovoked insult to you and for forcing you to fire at me. I am ten times worse than you and more, maybe. Tell that to the person whom you hold dearest in the world."

I had no sooner said this than all three shouted at me.

"Upon my word," cried my adversary, annoyed, "if you did not want to fight, why didn't you leave me alone?"

"Yesterday I was a fool; today I know better," I answered him gaily.

"As to yesterday, I believe you, but as for today, it is difficult to agree with your opinion," said he.

"Bravo," I cried, clapping my hands. "I agree with you there too; I have deserved it!"

"Will you shoot, sir, or not?"

"No, I won't," I said, "if you like, fire at me again, but it would be better for you not to fire."

The seconds, especially mine, were shouting too: "Can you disgrace the regiment like this, facing your antagonist and begging his forgiveness! If I'd only known this!"

I stood facing them all, not laughing now.

"Gentlemen," I said, "is it really so wonderful in these days to find a man who can repent of his stupidity and publicly confess his wrong-doing?"

"But not in a duel," cried my second again.

"That's what's so strange," I said. "For I ought to have owned my fault as soon as I got here, before he had fired a shot, before leading him into a great and deadly sin; but we have made our life so grotesque, that to act in that way would have been almost impossible, for only after I have faced his shot at the distance of twelve paces could my words have any significance for him, and if I had spoken before, he would have said 'he is a coward, the sight of the pistols had frightened him, no use to listen to him.' Gentlemen," I cried suddenly, speaking straight from my heart, "look around you at the gifts of God, the clear sky, the pure air, the tender grass, the birds; nature is beautiful and sinless, and we, only we, are sinful and foolish, and we don't understand that life is heaven, for we have only to understand that and it will at once be fulfilled in all its beauty, we shall embrace each other and weep."

I would have said more but I could not; my voice broke with the sweetness and youthful gladness of it, and there was such bliss in my heart as I had never known before in my life.

"All this is rational and edifying," said my antagonist, "and in any case you are an original person."

"You may laugh," I said to him, laughing too, "but afterwards you will approve of me."

"Oh, I am ready to approve of you now," said he; "will you shake hands, for I believe you are genuinely sincere."

"No," I said, "not now; later on when I have grown worthier and deserve your esteem, then shake hands and you will do well."

We went home, my second upbraiding me all the way, while I kissed him. All my comrades heard of the affair at once and gathered together to pass judgment on me the same day.

"He has disgraced the uniform," they said; "let him resign his commission."

Some stood up for me: "He faced the shot," they said.

"Yes, but he was afraid of his other shot and begged for forgiveness."

"If he had been afraid of being shot, he would have shot his own pistol first before asking forgiveness, but he flung it loaded into the forest. No, there's something else in this, something original."

I enjoyed listening and looking at them. "My dear friends and comrades," said I, "don't worry about my resigning my commission, for I have done so already. I have sent in my papers this morning and as soon as I get my discharge, I shall go into a monastery—it's with that object I am leaving the regiment."

When I had said this every one of them burst out laughing.

"You should have told us of that first; that explains everything; we can't judge a monk."

They laughed and could not stop themselves, and not scornfully, but kindly and merrily. They all felt friendly to me at once, even those who had been sternest in their censure, and all the following month, before my discharge came, they could not make enough of me. "Ah, you monk," they would say. And everyone said something kind to me; they began trying to dissuade me, even to pity me: "What are you doing to yourself?"

"No," they would say, "he is a brave fellow, he faced fire and could have fired his own pistol too, but he had a dream the night before that he should become a monk; that's why he did it."

It was the same thing with the society of the town. Until then I had been kindly received, but had not been the object of special attention.

But now all came to know me at once and invited me; they laughed at me, but they loved me. I may mention that although everybody talked openly of our duel, the authorities took no notice of it, because my antagonist was a near relation of our general, and, as there had been no bloodshed and no serious consequences, and as I resigned my commission, they took it as a joke. And I began then to speak aloud and fearlessly, regardless of their laughter, for it was always kindly and not spiteful laughter. These conversations mostly took place in the evenings, in the company of ladies; women particularly liked listening to me then, and they made the men listen.

"But how can I possibly be responsible for all?" everyone would laugh in my face. "Can I, for instance, be responsible for you?"

"You may well not know it," I would answer, "since the whole world has long been going on a different line, since we consider the veriest lies as truth and demand the same lies from others. Here I have for once in my life acted sincerely and, well, you all look upon me as a madman. Though you are friendly to me, yet, you see, you all laugh at me."

"But how can we help being friendly to you?" said my hostess, laughing. The room was full of people. All of a sudden the young lady rose, on whose account the duel had been fought and whom only lately I had intended to be my future wife. I had not noticed her coming into the room. She got up, came to me, and held out her hand.

"Let me tell you," she said, "that I am the first not to laugh at you, but on the contrary I thank you with tears and express my respect for you and for your action then."

Her husband too came up and then they all approached me and almost kissed me. My heart was filled with joy, but my attention was especially caught by a middle-aged man who came up to me with the others. I knew him by name already, but had never made his acquaintance nor exchanged a word with him until that evening.

The mysterious visitor

He had long been an official in the town; he was in a prominent position, respected by all, rich, and with a reputation for benevolence. He subscribed considerable sums to the almshouse and the orphan asylum; he was very charitable, too, in secret, a fact which only became known after his death. He was about fifty, almost stern in appearance, and not much given to conversation. He had been married about ten years and his wife, who was still young, had borne him three children. Well, I was sitting alone in my room the following evening when my door suddenly opened and this gentleman walked in.

I must mention, by the way, that I was no longer living in my former quarters. As soon as I resigned my commission, I took rooms with an old lady, the widow of a government clerk. My landlady's servant waited upon me, for I had moved into her rooms simply because on my return from the duel I had sent Afanasy back to the regiment, as I felt ashamed to look him in the face after my last meeting with him. So prone is the man of the world to be ashamed of any righteous action.

"I have," said my visitor, "with great interest listened to you speaking in different houses the last few days, and I wanted at last to make your personal acquaintance so as to talk to you more intimately. Can you, dear sir, grant me this favor?"

"I can, with the greatest pleasure, and I shall look upon it as an honor." I said this, though I felt almost dismayed, so greatly was I impressed from the first moment by the appearance of this man. For though other people had listened to me with interest and attention, no one had come to me before with such a serious, stern, and concentrated expression. And now he had come to see me in my rooms. He sat down.

"You are, I see, a man of great strength of character," he said, "as you have dared to serve the truth, even when by doing so you risked incurring the contempt of all."

"Your praise is, perhaps, excessive," I replied.

"No, it's not excessive," he answered; "believe me, such a course of action is far more difficult than you think. It is that which has impressed me, and it is only on that account that I have come to you," he continued. "Tell me, please, that is if you are not annoyed by my perhaps unseemly curiosity, what were your exact sensations, if you can recall them, at the moment when you made up your mind to ask forgiveness at the duel? Do not think my question frivolous; on the contrary, I have in asking the question a secret motive of my own, which I will perhaps explain to you later on, if it is God's will that we should become more intimately acquainted."

All the while he was speaking, I was looking at him straight in the face, and I felt all at once a complete trust in him, and great curiosity on my side also, for I felt that there was some strange secret in his soul.

"You ask what were my exact sensations at the moment when I asked my opponent's forgiveness," I answered. "But I had better tell you from the beginning what I have not yet told anyone else." And I described all that had passed between Afanasy and me, and how I had bowed down to the ground at his feet. "From that you can see for yourself," I concluded, "that at the time of the duel it was easier for me, for I had made a beginning already at home, and when once I had started on the road, to go further along it was far from being difficult, but became a source of joy and happiness."

I liked the way he looked at me as he listened. "All that," he said, "is exceedingly interesting. I will come to see you again and again."

And from that time forth he came to see me nearly every evening. And we should have become greater friends, if only he had ever talked of himself. But about himself he scarcely ever said a word, yet continually asked me about myself. In spite of that, I became very fond of him, and spoke with perfect frankness to him about all my feelings; for, thought I, what need have I to know his secrets, since I can see without that that he is a good man. Moreover, though he is such a serious man and my senior, he comes to see a youngster like me and treats me as his equal. And I learned a great deal that was profitable from him, for he was a man of lofty mind.

"That life is heaven," he said to me suddenly, "that I have long been thinking about;" and all at once he added, "I think of nothing else indeed." He looked at me and smiled. "I am more convinced of it than you are; I will tell you later why."

I listened to him and thought that he evidently wanted to tell me something.

"Heaven," he went on, "lies hidden within all of us—here it lies hidden in me now, and if I will it, it will be revealed to me tomorrow and for all time."

I looked at him; he was speaking with great emotion and gazing mysteriously at me, as if he were questioning me.

"And that we are all responsible to all for all, apart from our own sins, you were quite right in thinking that, and it is wonderful how you could comprehend it in all its significance at once. And in very truth, so soon as men understand that, the Kingdom of Heaven will be for them not a dream, but a living reality."

"And when," I cried out to him bitterly, "when will that come to pass? And will it ever come to pass? Is it not simply a dream of ours?"

"What, then, you don't believe it?" he said. "You preach it and don't believe it yourself. Believe me; this dream, as you call it, will come to pass without doubt; it will come, but not now, for every process has its law. It's a spiritual, psychological process. To transform the world, to recreate it afresh, men must turn into another path psychologically. Until you have become really, in actual fact, a brother to everyone, brotherhood will not come to pass. No sort of scientific teaching, no kind of common interest, will ever teach men to share property and privileges with equal consideration for all. Everyone will think his share too small, and they will be always envying, complaining, and attacking one another. You ask when it will come to pass; it will come to pass, but first we have to go through the period of isolation."

"What do you mean by isolation?" I asked him.

"Why, the isolation that prevails everywhere, above all in our age—it has not fully developed, it has not reached its limit yet. For everyone strives to keep his individuality as apart as possible, wishes to secure the greatest possible fulness of life for himself; but meantime all his efforts result not in attaining fulness of life but in self-destruction, for instead of self-realization, he ends by arriving at complete solitude. All mankind in our age have split up into units; they all keep apart, each in his own groove; each one holds aloof, hides himself and hides what he has, from the rest, and he ends by being repelled by others and repelling them. He heaps up riches by himself and thinks, 'How strong I am now and how secure,' and in his madness he does not understand that the more he heaps up, the more he sinks into self-destructive impotence. For he is accustomed to rely upon himself alone and to cut himself off from the whole; he has trained himself not to believe in the help of others, in men and in humanity, and only trembles for fear he should lose his money and the privileges that he has won for himself. Everywhere in these days men have, in their mockery, ceased to understand that the true security is to be found in social solidarity rather than in isolated individual effort. But this terrible individualism must inevitably have an end, and all will suddenly understand how unnaturally they are separated from one another. It will be the spirit of the time, and people will marvel that they have sat so long in darkness without seeing the light. And then the sign of the Son of Man will be seen in the heavens. . . . But, until then, we must keep the banner flying. Sometimes even if he has to do it alone, and his conduct seems to be crazy, a man must set an example, and so draw men's souls out of their solitude, and spur them to some act of brotherly love, that the great idea may not die."

Our evenings, one after another, were spent in such stirring and fervent talk. I gave up society and visited my neighbors much less frequently. Besides, my vogue was somewhat over. I say this, not as blame, for they still loved me and treated me good-humoredly, but there's no denying that fashion is a great power in society. I began to regard my mysterious visitor with admiration, for besides enjoying his intelligence, I began to perceive that he was brooding over some plan in his heart, and was preparing himself perhaps for a great deed. Perhaps he liked my not showing curiosity about his secret, not seeking to discover it by direct question nor by insinuation. But I noticed, at last, that he seemed to show signs of wanting to tell me something. This had become quite evident, indeed, about a month after he first began to visit me.

"Do you know," he said to me once, "that people are very inquisitive about us in the town and wonder why I come to see you so often. But let them wonder, for *soon all will be explained.*"

Sometimes an extraordinary agitation would come over him, and almost always on such occasions he would get up and go away. Sometimes he would fix a long piercing look upon me, and I thought, "He will say something directly now." But he would suddenly begin talking of something ordinary and familiar. He often complained of headache too.

One day, quite unexpectedly indeed, after he had been talking with great fervor a long time, I saw him suddenly turn pale, and his face worked convulsively, while he stared persistently at me.

"What's the matter?" I said; "do you feel ill?"—he had just been complaining of a headache.

"I . . . do you know . . . I murdered someone."

He said this and smiled, with a face as white as chalk. "Why is it he is smiling?" The thought flashed through my mind before I realised anything else. I too turned pale.

"What are you saying?" I cried.

"You see," he said, with a pale smile, "how much it has cost me to say the first word. Now I have said it, I feel I've taken the first step and shall go on."

For a long while I could not believe him, and I did not believe him at that time, but only after he had been to see me three days running and told me all about it. I thought he was mad, but ended by being convinced, to my great grief and amazement. His crime was a great and terrible one.

Fourteen years before, he had murdered the widow of a landowner, a wealthy and handsome young woman who had a house in our town. He fell passionately in love with her, declared his feeling, and tried to persuade her to marry him. But she had already given her heart to another man, an officer of noble birth and high rank in the service, who was at that time away at the front, though she was expecting him soon to return. She refused his offer and begged him not to come and see her. After he had ceased to visit her, he took advantage of his knowledge of the house to enter at night through the garden by the roof, at great risk of discovery. But as often happens, a crime committed with extraordinary audacity is more successful than others.

Entering the garret through the skylight, he went down the ladder, knowing that the door at the bottom of it was sometimes, through the negligence of the servants, left unlocked. He hoped to find it so, and so it was. He made his way in the dark to her bedroom, where a light was burning. As though on purpose, both her maids had gone off to a birthday party on the same street, without asking leave. The other servants slept in the servants' quarters or in the kitchen on the ground floor. His passion flamed up at the sight of her asleep, and then vindictive, jealous anger took possession of his heart, and like a drunken man, beside himself, he thrust a knife into her heart, so that she did not even cry out. Then with devilish and criminal cunning he contrived that suspicion should fall on the servants. He was so base as to take her purse, to open her chest with keys from under her pillow, and to take some things from it, doing it all as it might have been done by an ignorant servant, leaving valuable papers and taking only money. He took some of the larger gold things, but left smaller articles that were ten times as valuable. He took with him, too, some things for himself as remembrances, but of that later. Having done this awful deed, he returned by the way he had come.

Neither the next day, when the alarm was raised, nor at any time after in his life did anyone dream of suspecting that he was the criminal. No one indeed knew of his love for her, for he was always reserved and silent and had no friend to whom he would have opened his heart. He was looked upon simply as an acquaintance, and not a very intimate one, of the murdered woman, as for the previous fortnight he had not even visited her. A serf of hers called Pyotr was at once suspected, and every circumstance confirmed the suspicion. The man knew—indeed his mistress did not conceal the fact—that having to send one of her serfs as a recruit she had decided to send him, as he had no relations and his conduct was unsatisfactory. People had heard him angrily threatening to murder her when he was drunk in a tavern. Two days before her death, he had run away, staying no one knew where in the town. The day after the murder, he was found on the road leading out of the town, dead drunk, with a knife in his pocket, and his right hand happened to be stained with blood. He declared that his nose had been bleeding, but no one believed him. The maids confessed that they had gone to a party and that the street door had been left open till they returned. And a number of similar details came to light, throwing suspicion on the innocent servant.

They arrested him, and he was tried for the murder; but a week after the arrest, the prisoner fell sick of a fever and died unconscious in the hospital. There the matter ended and the judges and the authorities and everyone in the town remained convinced that the crime had been committed by no one but the servant who had died in the hospital. And after that the punishment began.

My mysterious visitor, now my friend, told me that at first he was not in the least troubled by pangs of conscience. He was miserable a long time, but not for that reason; only from regret that he had killed the woman he loved, that she was no more, that in killing her he had killed his love, while the fire of passion was still in his veins. But of the innocent blood he had shed, of the murder of a fellow creature, he scarcely thought. The thought that his victim might have become the wife of another man was insupportable to him, and so, for a long time, he was convinced in his conscience that he could not have acted otherwise.

At first he was worried at the arrest of the servant, but his illness and death soon set his mind at rest, for the man's death was apparently (so he reflected at the time) not owing to his arrest or his fright, but a chill he had taken on the day he ran away, when he had lain all night dead drunk on the damp ground. The theft of the money and other things troubled him little, for he argued that the theft had not been committed for gain but to avert suspicion. The sum stolen was small, and he shortly afterwards subscribed the whole of it, and much more, towards the funds for maintaining an almshouse in the town. He did this on purpose to set his conscience at rest about the theft, and it's a remarkable fact that for a long time he really was at peace—he told me this himself. He entered then upon a career of great activity in the service, volunteered for a difficult and laborious duty, which occupied him two years, and being a man of strong will almost forgot the past. Whenever he recalled it, he tried not to think of it at all. He became active in philanthropy too, founded and helped to maintain many institutions in the town, did a good deal in the two capitals, and in both Moscow and Petersburg was elected a member of philanthropic societies.

At last, however, he began brooding over the past, and the strain of it was too much for him. Then he was attracted by a fine and intelligent girl and soon after married her, hoping that marriage would dispel his lonely depression, and that by entering on a new life and scrupulously doing his duty to his wife and children, he would escape from old memories altogether. But the very opposite of what he expected happened. He began, even in the first month of his marriage, to be continually fretted by the thought, "My wife loves me—but what if she knew?" When she first told him that she would soon bear him a child, he was troubled. "I am giving life, but I have taken life." Children came. "How dare I love them, teach and educate them, how can I talk to them of virtue? I have shed blood." They were splendid children; he longed to caress them. "And I can't look at their innocent candid faces, I am unworthy."

At last he began to be bitterly and ominously haunted by the blood of his murdered victim, by the young life he had destroyed, by the blood that cried out for vengeance. He had begun to have awful dreams. But being a man of fortitude, he bore his suffering a long time, thinking, "I shall expiate everything by this secret agony." But that hope too was vain; the longer it went on, the more intense was his suffering.

He was respected in society for his active benevolence, though everyone was overawed by his stern and gloomy character. But the more he was respected, the more intolerable it was for him. He confessed to me that he had thoughts of killing himself. But he began to be haunted by another idea—an idea which he had at first regarded as impossible and unthinkable, though at last it got such a hold on his heart that he could not shake it off. He dreamed of rising up, going out, and confessing in the face of all men that he had committed murder. For three years this dream had pursued him, haunting him in different forms. At last he believed with his whole heart that if he confessed his crime, he would heal his soul and would be at peace forever. But this belief filled his heart with terror, for how could he carry it out? And then came what happened at my duel.

"Looking at you, I made up my mind."

I looked at him.

"Is it possible," I cried, clasping my hands, "that such a trivial incident could give rise to such a resolution in you?"

"My resolution has been growing for the last three years," he answered, "and your story only gave the last touch to it. Looking at you, I reproached myself and envied you." He said this to me almost sullenly.

"But you won't be believed," I observed; "it's fourteen years ago."

"I have proofs, great proofs. I shall show them."

Then I cried and kissed him.

"Tell me one thing, one thing," he said (as though it all depended upon me), "my wife, my children! My wife may die of grief, and though my children won't lose their rank and property, they'll be a convict's children and forever! And what a memory, what a memory of me I shall leave in their hearts!"

I said nothing.

"And to part from them, to leave them forever? It's forever, you know, forever!"

I sat still and repeated a silent prayer. I got up at last, I felt afraid.

"Well?" He looked at me.

"Go!" said I. "Confess. Everything passes; only the truth remains. Your children will understand, when they grow up, the nobility of your resolution."

He left me that time as though he had made up his mind. Yet for more than a fortnight afterwards, he came to me every evening, still preparing himself, still unable to bring himself to the point. He made my heart ache. One day he would come determined and say fervently:

"I know it will be heaven for me, heaven, the moment I confess. Fourteen years I've been in hell. I want to suffer. I will take my punishment and begin to live. You can pass through the world doing wrong, but there's no turning back. Now I dare not love my neighbor nor even my own children. Good God, my children will understand, perhaps, what my punishment has cost me, and will not condemn me! God is not in strength but in truth."

"All will understand your sacrifice," I said to him, "if not at once, they will understand later; for you have served truth, the higher truth, not of the earth."

And he would go away seeming comforted, but the next day he would come again, bitter, pale, sarcastic.

"Every time I come to you, you look at me so inquisitively as though to say, 'He has still not confessed!' Wait a bit, don't despise me too much. It's not such an easy thing to do, as you would think. Perhaps I shall not do it at all. You won't go and inform against me, then, will you?"

And far from looking at him with indiscreet curiosity, I was afraid to look at him at all. I was quite ill from anxiety, and my heart was full of tears. I could not sleep at night.

"I have just come from my wife," he went on. "Do you understand what the word 'wife' means? When I went out, the children called to me, 'Goodbye, father, make haste back to read *The Children's Magazine* with us.' No, you don't understand that! No one is wise from another man's woe."

His eyes were glittering, his lips were twitching. Suddenly he struck the table with his fist so that everything on it danced—it was the first time he had done such a thing, he was such a mild man.

"But need I?" he exclaimed, "must I? No one has been condemned; no one has been sent to Siberia in my place; the man died of fever. And I've been punished by my sufferings for the blood I shed. And I won't be believed; they won't believe my proofs. Need I confess, need I? I am ready to go on suffering all my life for the blood I have shed, if only my wife and children may be spared. Will it be just to ruin them with me? Aren't we making a mistake? What is right in this case? And will people recognize it; will they appreciate it; will they respect it?"

"Good Lord!" I thought to myself, "he is thinking of other people's respect at such a moment!" And I felt so sorry for him then, that I believe I would have shared his fate if it could have comforted him. I saw he was beside himself. I was aghast, realizing with my heart as well as my mind what such a resolution meant.

"Decide my fate!" he exclaimed again.

"Go and confess," I whispered to him. My voice failed me, but I whispered it firmly. I took up the New Testament from the table, the Russian translation, and showed him the Gospel of St. John, chapter 12, verse 24:

"Verily, verily, I say unto you, except a corn of wheat fall into the ground and die, it abideth alone; but if it die, it bringeth forth much fruit."

I had just been reading that verse when he came in. He read it.

"That's true," he said, but he smiled bitterly. "It's terrible the things you find in those books," he said, after a pause. "It's easy enough to thrust them upon one. And who wrote them? Can they have been written by men?"

"The Holy Spirit wrote them," said I.

"It's easy for you to prate," he smiled again, this time almost with hatred.

I took the book again, opened it in another place and showed him the Epistle to the Hebrews, chapter 10, verse 31. He read:

"It is a fearful thing to fall into the hands of the living God."

He read it and simply flung down the book. He was trembling all over.

"An awful text," he said. "There's no denying you've picked out fitting ones." He rose from the chair. "Well!" he said, "Goodbye; perhaps I shan't come again . . . we shall meet in heaven. So I have been for fourteen years 'in the hands of the living God,' that's how one must think of those fourteen years. Tomorrow I will beseech those hands to let me go."

I wanted to take him in my arms and kiss him, but I did not dare—his face was contorted and sombre. He went away.

"Good God," I thought, "what has he gone to face!" I fell on my knees before the icon and wept for him before the Holy Mother of God, our swift defender and helper. I was half an hour praying in tears, and it was late, about midnight. Suddenly I saw the door open and he came in again. I was surprised.

"Where have you been?" I asked him.

"I think," he said, "I've forgotten something . . . my handkerchief, I think. . . . Well, even if I've not forgotten anything, let me stay a little."

He sat down. I stood over him.

"You sit down, too," said he.

I sat down. We sat still for two minutes; he looked intently at me and suddenly smiled—I remembered that—then he got up, embraced me warmly and kissed me.

"Remember," he said, "how I came to you a second time. Do you hear, remember it!"

And he went out.

"Tomorrow," I thought.

And so it was. I did not know that evening that the next day was his birthday. I had not been out for the last few days, so I had no chance of hearing it from anyone. On that day he always had a great gathering; everyone in the town went to it. It was the same this time. After dinner he walked into the middle of the room, with a paper in his hand—a formal declaration to the chief of his department who was present. This declaration he read aloud to the whole assembly. It contained a full account of the crime, in every detail.

"I cut myself off from men as a monster. God has visited me," he said in conclusion. "I want to suffer for my sin!"

Then he brought out and laid on the table all the things he had been keeping for fourteen years that he thought would prove his crime: the jewels belonging to the murdered woman which he had stolen to divert suspicion, a cross and locket taken from her neck with a portrait of her betrothed in the locket, her notebook, and two letters—one from her betrothed, telling her that he would soon be with her, and her unfinished answer left on the table to be sent off the next day. He carried off these two letters—what for? Why had he kept them for fourteen years afterwards instead of destroying them as evidence against him?

And this is what happened: everyone was amazed and horrified, everyone refused to believe it and thought that he was deranged, though all listened with intense curiosity. A few days later it was fully decided and agreed in every house that the unhappy man was mad. The legal authorities could not refuse to take the case up, but they too dropped it. Though the trinkets and letters made them ponder, they decided that even if they did turn out to be authentic, no charge could be based on those alone. Besides, she might have given him those things as a friend, or asked him to take care of them for her. I heard afterwards, however, that the genuineness of the things was proved by the friends and relations of the murdered woman, and that there was no doubt about them. Yet nothing was destined to come of it, after all.

Five days later, all had heard that he was ill and that his life was in danger. The nature of his illness I can't explain; they said it was an affection of the heart. But it became known that the doctors had been induced by his wife to investigate his mental condition also, and had come to the conclusion that it was a case of insanity. I betrayed nothing, though people ran to question me. But when I wanted to visit him, I was for a long while forbidden to do so, above all by his wife.

"It's you who have caused his illness," she said to me; "he was always gloomy, but for the last year people noticed that he was peculiarly excited and did strange things, and now you have been the ruin of him. Your preaching has brought him to this; for the last month he was always with you."

Indeed, not only his wife but the whole town were down on me and blamed me. "It's all your doing," they said. I was silent and indeed rejoiced at heart, for I saw plainly God's mercy to the man who had turned against himself and punished himself. I could not believe in his insanity.

They let me see him at last; he insisted upon saying goodbye to me. I went in to him and saw at once that not only his days, but his hours were numbered. He was weak, yellow; his hands trembled; he gasped for breath, but his face was full of tender and happy feeling.

"It is done!" he said. "I've long been yearning to see you; why didn't you come?"

I did not tell him that they would not let me see him.

"God has had pity on me and is calling me to Himself. I know I am dying, but I feel joy and peace for the first time after so many years. There was heaven in my heart from the moment I had done what I had to do. Now I dare to love my children and to kiss them. Neither my wife nor the judges nor anyone has believed it. My children will never believe it either. I see in that God's mercy to them. I shall die, and my name will be without a stain for them. And now I feel God near, my heart rejoices as in Heaven . . . I have done my duty."

He could not speak; he gasped for breath; he pressed my hand warmly, looking fervently at me. We did not talk for long; his wife kept peeping in at us. But he had time to whisper to me:

"Do you remember how I came back to you that second time, at midnight? I told you to remember it. You know what I came back for? I came to kill you!"

I started.

"I went out from you then into the darkness; I wandered about the streets, struggling with myself. And suddenly I hated you so that I could hardly bear it. Now, I thought, he is all that binds me, and he is my judge. I can't refuse to face my punishment tomorrow, for he knows all. It was not that I was afraid you would betray me (I never even thought of that) but I thought, 'How can I look him in the face if I don't confess?' And if you had been at the other end of the earth, but alive it would have been all the same; the thought was unendurable that you were alive knowing everything and condemning me. I hated you as though you were the cause, as though you were to blame for everything. I came back to you then, remembering that you had a dagger lying on your table. I sat down and asked you to sit down, and for a whole minute I pondered. If I had killed you, I should have been ruined by that murder even if I had not confessed the other. But I didn't think about that at all, and I didn't want to think of it at that moment. I only hated you and longed to revenge myself on you for everything. The Lord vanquished the devil in my heart. But let me tell you, you were never nearer death."

A week later he died. The whole town followed him to the grave. The chief priest made a speech full of feeling. All lamented the terrible illness that had cut short his days. But all the town was up in arms against me after the funeral, and people even refused to see me. Some, at first a few and afterwards more, began indeed to believe in the truth of his story, and they visited me and questioned me with great interest and eagerness, for man loves to see the downfall and disgrace of the righteous. But I held my tongue, and very shortly after, I left the town, and five months later by God's grace I entered upon the safe and blessed path, praising the unseen finger which had guided me so clearly to it. But I remember in my prayer to this day, the servant of God, Mihail, who suffered so greatly.

The Russian monk and his possible significance

Fathers and teachers, what is the monk? In the cultivated world, the word is nowadays pronounced by some people with a jeer, and by others it is used as a term of abuse, and this contempt for the monk is growing. It is true, alas, it is true, that there are many sluggards, gluttons, profligates, and insolent beggars among monks. Educated people point to these: "You are idlers, useless members of society; you live on the labor of others; you are shameless beggars." And yet how many meek and humble monks there are, yearning for solitude and fervent prayer in peace. These are less noticed, or passed over in silence. And how surprised men would be if I were to say that from these meek monks, who yearn for solitary prayer, the salvation of Russia will come perhaps once more. For they are in truth made ready in peace and quiet "for the day and the hour, the month and the year." Meanwhile, in their solitude, they keep the image of Christ fair and undefiled, in the purity of God's truth, from the times of the Fathers of old, the Apostles and the martyrs. And when the time comes, they will show it to the tottering creeds of the world. That is a great thought. That star will rise out of the East.

That is my view of the monk, and is it false? Is it too proud? Look at the worldly and all who set themselves up above the people of God: has not God's image and His truth been distorted in them? They have science; but in science there is nothing but what is the object of sense. The spiritual world, the higher part of man's being, is rejected altogether, dismissed with a sort of triumph, even with hatred. The world has proclaimed the reign of freedom, especially of late, but what do we see in this freedom of theirs? Nothing but slavery and self-destruction! For the world says:

"You have desires and so satisfy them, for you have the same rights as the most rich and powerful. Don't be afraid of satisfying them, and even multiply your desires." That is the modern doctrine of the world. In that they see freedom. And what follows from this right of multiplication of desires? In the rich, isolation and spiritual suicide; in the poor, envy and murder; for they have been given rights, but have not been shown the means of satisfying their wants. They maintain that the world is getting more and more united, more and more bound together in brotherly community, as it overcomes distance and sets thoughts flying through the air. Alas, put no faith in such a bond of union. Interpreting freedom as the multiplication and rapid satisfaction of desires, men distort their own nature, for many senseless and foolish desires and habits and ridiculous fancies are fostered in them. They live only for mutual envy, for luxury and ostentation. To have dinners, visits, carriages, rank, and slaves to wait on one is looked upon as a necessity, for which life, honor, and human feeling are sacrificed, and men even commit suicide if they are unable to satisfy it. We see the same thing among those who are not rich, while the poor drown their unsatisfied need and their envy in drunkenness. But soon they will drink blood instead of wine, they are being led on to it. I ask you, is such a man free? I knew one "champion of freedom" who told me himself that, when he was deprived of tobacco in prison, he was so wretched at the privation that he almost went and betrayed his cause for the sake of getting tobacco again! And such a man says, "I am fighting for the cause of humanity."

How can such a one fight; what is he fit for? He is capable perhaps of some action quickly over, but he cannot hold out long. And it's no wonder that instead of gaining freedom, they have sunk into slavery, and instead of serving the cause of brotherly love and the union of humanity, have fallen on the contrary into dissension and isolation, as my mysterious visitor and teacher said to me in my youth. And therefore the idea of the service of humanity, of brotherly love and the solidarity of mankind, is more and more dying out in the world, and indeed this idea is sometimes treated with derision. For how can a man shake off his habits, what can become of him if he is in such bondage to the habit of satisfying the innumerable desires he has created for himself? He is isolated, and what concern has he with the rest of humanity? They have succeeded in accumulating a greater mass of objects, but the joy in the world has grown less.

The monastic way is very different. Obedience, fasting, and prayer are laughed at, yet only through them lies the way to real, true freedom. I cut off my superfluous and unnecessary desires; I subdue my proud and wanton will and chastise it with obedience, and with God's help I attain freedom of spirit and with it spiritual joy. Which is most capable of conceiving a great idea and serving it—the rich man in his isolation or the man who has freed himself from the tyranny of material things and habits? The monk is reproached for his solitude: "You have secluded yourself within the walls of the monastery for your own salvation, and have forgotten the brotherly service of humanity!" But we shall see which will be most zealous in the cause of brotherly love. For it is not we, but they, who are in isolation, though they don't see that. Of old, leaders of the people came from among us, and why should they not again? The same meek and humble ascetics will rise up and go out to work for the great cause. The salvation of Russia comes from the people. And the Russian monk has always been on the side of the people. We are isolated only if the people are isolated. The people believe as we do, and an unbelieving reformer will never do anything in Russia, even if he is sincere in heart and a genius. Remember that! The people will meet the atheist and overcome him, and Russia will be one and orthodox. Take care of the peasant and guard his heart. Go on educating him quietly. That's your duty as monks, for the peasant has God in his heart.

. . .

Of prayer, of love, and of contact with other worlds

Young man, be not forgetful of prayer. Every time you pray, if your prayer is sincere, there will be new feeling and new meaning in it, which will give you fresh courage, and you will understand that prayer is an education. Remember, too, every day, and whenever you can, repeat to yourself, "Lord, have mercy on all who appear before Thee today." For every hour and every moment thousands of men leave life on this earth, and their souls appear before God. And how many of them depart in solitude, unknown, sad, dejected, that no one mourns for them or even knows whether they have lived or not. And behold, from the other end of the earth perhaps, your prayer for their rest will rise up to God, though you knew them not nor they you. How touching it must be to a soul standing in dread before the Lord to feel at that instant that, for him too, there is one to pray, that there is a fellow creature left on earth to love him too. And God will look on you both more graciously, for if you have had so much pity on him, how much more will He have pity Who is infinitely more loving and merciful than you. And He will forgive him for your sake.

Brothers, have no fear of men's sin. Love a man even in his sin, for that is the semblance of Divine Love and is the highest love on earth. Love all God's creation, the whole and every grain of sand in it. Love every leaf, every ray of God's light. Love the animals; love the plants; love everything. If you love everything, you will perceive the divine mystery in things. Once you perceive it, you will begin to comprehend it better every day. And you will come at last to love the whole world with an all-embracing love. Love the animals: God has given them the rudiments of thought and joy untroubled. Do not trouble them; don't harass them; don't deprive them of their happiness; don't work against God's intent. Man, do not pride yourself on superiority to the animals; they are without sin, and you, with your greatness, defile the earth by your appearance on it, and leave the traces of your foulness after you—alas, it is true of almost every one of us! Love children especially, for they too are sinless like the angels; they live to soften and purify our hearts and as it were to guide us. Woe to him who offends a child! Father Anfim taught me to love children. The kind, silent man used often on our wanderings to spend the coins given us on sweets and cakes for the children. He could not pass by a child without emotion, that's the nature of the man.

At some thoughts one stands perplexed, especially at the sight of men's sin, and wonders whether one should use force or humble love. Always decide to use humble love. If you resolve on that once for all, you may subdue the whole world. Loving humility is marvellously strong, the strongest of all things, and there is nothing else like it.

Every day and every hour, every minute, walk round yourself and watch yourself, and see that your image is a seemly one. You pass by a little child, you pass by, spiteful, with ugly words, with wrathful heart; you may not have noticed the child, but he has seen you, and your image, unseemly and ignoble, may remain in his defenceless heart. You don't know it, but you may have sown an evil seed in him and it may grow, and all because you were not careful before the child, because you did not foster in yourself a careful, actively benevolent love. Brothers, love is a teacher; but one must know how to acquire it, for it is hard to acquire; it is dearly bought; it is won slowly by long labor. For we must love not only occasionally, for a moment, but forever. Everyone can love occasionally; even the wicked can.

My brother asked the birds to forgive him; that sounds senseless, but it is right; for all is like an ocean, all is flowing and blending; a touch in one place sets up movement at the other end of the earth. It may be senseless to beg forgiveness of the birds, but birds would be happier at your side—a little happier, anyway—and children and all animals, if you yourself were nobler than you are now. It's all like an ocean, I tell you. Then you would pray to the birds too, consumed by an all-embracing love, in a sort of transport, and pray that they too will forgive you your sin. Treasure this ecstasy, however senseless it may seem to men.

My friends, pray to God for gladness. Be glad as children, as the birds of heaven. And let not the sin of men confound you in your doings. Fear not that it will wear away your work and hinder its being accomplished. Do not say, "Sin is mighty, wickedness is mighty, evil environment is mighty, and we are lonely and helpless, and evil environment is wearing us away and hindering our good work from being done." Fly from that dejection, children! There is only one means of salvation, then: take yourself and make yourself responsible for all men's sins; that is the truth, you know, friends, for as soon as you sincerely make yourself responsible for everything and for all men, you will see at once that it is really so, and that you are to blame for everyone and for all things. But throwing your own indolence and impotence on others, you will end by sharing the pride of Satan and murmuring against God.

Of the pride of Satan what I think is this: it is hard for us on earth to comprehend it, and therefore it is so easy to fall into error and to share it, even imagining that we are doing something grand and fine. Indeed many of the strongest feelings and movements of our nature we cannot comprehend on earth. Let not that be a stumbling block, and think not that it may serve as a justification to you for anything. For the Eternal Judge asks of you what you can comprehend and not what you cannot. You will know that yourself hereafter, for you will behold all things truly then and will not dispute them. On earth, indeed, we are as it were astray, and if it were not for the precious image of Christ before us, we should be undone and altogether lost, as was the human race before the flood. Much on earth is hidden from us, but to make up for that we have been given a precious mystic sense of our living bond with the other world, with the higher heavenly world, and the roots of our thoughts and feelings are not here but in other worlds. That is why the philosophers say that we cannot apprehend the reality of things on earth.

God took seeds from different worlds and sowed them on this earth, and His garden grew up and everything came up that could come up, but what grows lives and is alive only through the feeling of its contact with other mysterious worlds. If that feeling grows weak or is destroyed in you, the heavenly growth will die away in you. Then you will be indifferent to life and even grow to hate it. That's what I think. . . .

William James,
"The Religion of Healthy-Mindedness,"
from *The Varieties of Religious Experience*

*One of the founders of American pragmatism, William James (1842–1910)
received his primary education (with his younger brother, the novelist
Henry James) in both Europe and the United States. He went on to study
medicine at Harvard University, where he received an M.D., the only aca-
demic degree he ever obtained. From 1880 to 1907, he taught psychology
and philosophy at Harvard. The publication of his* Principles of Psychology *in 1890 brought him international recognition for his work in psychology. The Varieties of Religious Experience (1902), his study of the
psychological motivations behind religious belief, is based on the Gifford lectures he gave in Edinburgh. These studies display James's "radical empiri-
cism," his concern with collecting and presenting a rich variety of data
about what people believe without imposing any transcendental or reduction-
ist ordering principles in advance. The chapter on "The Religion of
Healthy-Mindedness" is especially interesting today given the fact that our
own turn-of-the-century malaise and "New Age" spiritual quest so closely
parallel the "self-help" movements at the end of the last century. James's
obvious respect for the spiritual aspirations of ordinary people, together with
his belief that truth is a matter of what "works" in our experience, is quite
surprising in a scientifically trained thinker.*

If we were to ask the question: "What is human life's chief concern?" one
of the answers we should receive would be: "It is happiness." How to gain,
how to keep, how to recover happiness, is in fact for most men at all times
the secret motive of all they do, and of all they are willing to endure. The
hedonistic school in ethics deduces the moral life wholly from the experiences of happiness and unhappiness which different kinds of conduct
bring; and, even more in the religious life than in the moral life, happiness
and unhappiness seem to be the poles round which the interest revolves.
We need not go so far as to say with the author whom I lately quoted that
any persistent enthusiasm is, as such, religion, nor need we call mere
laughter a religious exercise; but we must admit that any persistent enjoy-

From William James, *The Varieties of Religious Experience* (New York: Longmans,
Green & Co., 1902).

ment may *produce* the sort of religion which consists in a grateful admiration of the gift of so happy an existence; and we must also acknowledge that the more complex ways of experiencing religion are new manners of producing happiness, wonderful inner paths to a supernatural kind of happiness, when the first gift of natural existence is unhappy, as it so often proves itself to be.

With such relations between religion and happiness, it is perhaps not surprising that men come to regard the happiness which a religious belief affords as a proof of its truth. If a creed makes a man feel happy, he almost inevitably adopts it. Such a belief ought to be true; therefore it is true— such, rightly or wrongly, is one of the "immediate inferences" of the religious logic used by ordinary men.

. . .

"God has two families of children on this earth," says Francis W. Newman,[1] "*the once-born and the twice-born,*" and the once-born he describes as follows: "They see God, not as a strict Judge, not as a Glorious Potentate; but as the animating Spirit of a beautiful harmonious world, Beneficent and Kind, Merciful as well as Pure. The same characters generally have no metaphysical tendencies: they do not look back into themselves. Hence they are not distressed by their own imperfections: yet it would be absurd to call them self-righteous; for they hardly think of themselves *at all*. This childlike quality of their nature makes the opening of religion very happy to them: for they no more shrink from God, than a child from an emperor, before whom the parent trembles: in fact, they have no vivid conception of *any* of the qualities in which the severer Majesty of God consists.[2] He is to them the impersonation of Kindness and Beauty. They read his character, not in the disordered world of man, but in romantic and harmonious nature. Of human sin they know perhaps little in their own hearts and not very much in the world; and human suffering does but melt them to tenderness. Thus, when they approach God, no inward disturbance ensues; and without being as yet spiritual, they have a certain complacency and perhaps romantic sense of excitement in their simple worship."

In the Romish Church such characters find a more congenial soil to grow in than in Protestantism, whose fashions of feeling have been set by minds of a decidedly pessimistic order. But even in Protestantism they

1. *The Soul; Its Sorrows and Its Aspirations,* 3rd ed. 1852.
2. I once heard a lady describe the pleasure it gave her to think that she "could always cuddle up to God."

have been abundant enough; and in its recent "liberal" developments of Unitarianism and latitudinarianism generally, minds of this order have played and still are playing leading and constructive parts.

. . .

One can but recognize in such writers as these the presence of a temperament organically weighted on the side of cheer and fatally forbidden to linger, as those of opposite temperament linger, over the darker aspects of the universe. In some individuals optimism may become quasi-pathological. The capacity for even a transient sadness or a momentary humility seems cut off from them as by a kind of congenital anæsthesia.

. . .

Walt Whitman owes his importance in literature to the systematic expulsion from his writings of all contractile elements. The only sentiments he allowed himself to express were of the expansive order; and he expressed these in the first person, not as your mere monstrously conceited individual might so express them, but vicariously for all men, so that a passionate and mystic ontological emotion suffuses his words, and ends by persuading the reader that men and women, life and death, and all things are divinely good.

Thus it has come about that many persons to-day regard Walt Whitman as the restorer of the eternal natural religion. He has infected them with his own love of comrades, with his own gladness that he and they exist. Societies are actually formed for his cult; a periodical organ exists for its propagation, in which the lines of orthodoxy and heterodoxy are already beginning to be drawn; hymns are written by others in his peculiar prosody; and he is even explicitly compared with the founder of the Christian religion, not altogether to the advantage of the latter.

Whitman is often spoken of as a "pagan." The word nowadays means sometimes the mere natural animal man without a sense of sin; sometimes it means a Greek or Roman with his own peculiar religious consciousness. In neither of these senses does it fitly define this poet. He is more than your mere animal man who has not tasted of the tree of good and evil. He is aware enough of sin for a swagger to be present in his indifference towards it, a conscious pride in his freedom from flexions and contractions, which your genuine pagan in the first sense of the word would never show.

I could turn and live with animals, they are so placid and self-
    contained,
I stand and look at them long and long;

They do not sweat and whine about their condition.
They do not lie awake in the dark and weep for their sins.
Not one is dissatisfied, not one is demented with the mania of owning
  things,
Not one kneels to another, nor to his kind that lived thousands of years
  ago,
Not one is respectable or unhappy over the whole earth.[3]

. . .

If, then, we give the name of healthy-mindedness to the tendency which looks on all things and sees that they are good, we find that we must distinguish between a more involuntary and a more voluntary or systematic way of being healthy-minded. In its involuntary variety, healthy-mindedness is a way of feeling happy about things immediately. In its systematical variety, it is an abstract way of conceiving things as good. Every abstract way of conceiving things selects some one aspect of them as their essence for the time being, and disregards the other aspects. Systematic healthy-mindedness, conceiving good as the essential and universal aspect of being, deliberately excludes evil from its field of vision; and although, when thus nakedly stated, this might seem a difficult feat to perform for one who is intellectually sincere with himself and honest about facts, a little reflection shows that the situation is too complex to lie open to so simple a criticism.

In the first place, happiness, like every other emotional state, has blindness and insensibility to opposing facts given it as its instinctive weapon for self-protection against disturbance. When happiness is actually in possession, the thought of evil can no more acquire the feeling of reality than the thought of good can gain reality when melancholy rules. To the man actively happy, from whatever cause, evil simply cannot then and there be believed in. He must ignore it; and to the bystander he may then seem perversely to shut his eyes to it and hush it up.

But more than this: the hushing of it up may, in a perfectly candid and honest mind, grow into a deliberate religious policy, or *parti pris*. Much of what we call evil is due entirely to the way men take the phenomenon. It can so often be converted into a bracing and tonic good by a simple change of the sufferer's inner attitude from one of fear to one of fight; its sting so often departs and turns into a relish when, after vainly seeking to shun it, we agree to face about and bear it cheerfully, that a man is simply bound in honor, with reference to many of the facts that seem at first to disconcert his peace, to adopt this way of escape. Refuse to admit their badness;

3. "Song of Myself."

despise their power; ignore their presence; turn your attention the other way; and so far as you yourself are concerned at any rate, though the facts may still exist, their evil character exists no longer. Since you make them evil or good by your own thoughts about them, it is the ruling of your thoughts which proves to be your principal concern.

The deliberate adoption of an optimistic turn of mind thus makes its entrance into philosophy. And once in, it is hard to trace its lawful bounds. Not only does the human instinct for happiness, bent on self-protection by ignoring, keep working in its favor, but higher inner ideals have weighty words to say. The attitude of unhappiness is not only painful, it is mean and ugly. What can be more base and unworthy than the pining, puling, mumping mood, no matter by what outward ills it may have been engendered? What is more injurious to others? What less helpful as a way out of the difficulty? It but fastens and perpetuates the trouble which occasioned it, and increases the total evil of the situation. At all costs, then, we ought to reduce the sway of that mood; we ought to scout it in ourselves and others, and never show it tolerance. But it is impossible to carry on this discipline in the subjective sphere without zealously emphasizing the brighter and minimizing the darker aspects of the objective sphere of things at the same time. And thus our resolution not to indulge in misery, beginning at a comparatively small point within ourselves, may not stop until it has brought the entire frame of reality under a systematic conception optimistic enough to be congenial with its needs.

. . .

The systematic cultivation of healthy-mindedness as a religious attitude is therefore consonant with important currents in human nature, and is anything but absurd. In fact, we all do cultivate it more or less, even when our professed theology should in consistency forbid it. We divert our attention from disease and death as much as we can; and the slaughter-houses and indecencies without end on which our life is founded are huddled out of sight and never mentioned, so that the world we recognize officially in literature and in society is a poetic fiction far handsomer and cleaner and better than the world that really is.

The advance of liberalism, so-called, in Christianity, during the past fifty years, may fairly be called a victory of healthy-mindedness within the church over the morbidness with which the old hell-fire theology was more harmoniously related. We have now whole congregations whose preachers, far from magnifying our consciousness of sin, seem devoted rather to making little of it. They ignore, or even deny, eternal punishment, and insist on the dignity rather than on the depravity of man. They look at the continual preoccupation of the old-fashioned Christian with the salvation of his soul as something sickly and reprehensible rather than admirable; and a sanguine and "muscular" attitude, which to our fore-fathers would have seemed purely heathen, has become in their eyes an ideal element of Christian character. I am not asking whether or not they are right, I am only pointing out the change.

To my mind a current far more important and interesting religiously than that which sets in from natural science towards healthy-mindedness is that which has recently poured over America and seems to be gathering force every day—I am ignorant what foothold it may yet have acquired in Great Britain—and to which, for the sake of having a brief designation, I will give the title of the "Mind-cure movement." There are various sects of this "New Thought," to use another of the names by which it calls itself; but their agreements are so profound that their differences may be neglected for my present purpose, and I will treat the movement, without apology, as if it were a simple thing.

It is a deliberately optimistic scheme of life, with both a speculative and a practical side. In its gradual development during the last quarter of a century, it has taken up into itself a number of contributory ele-ments, and it must now be reckoned with as a genuine religious power. It has reached the stage, for example, when the demand for its literature is great enough for insincere stuff, mechanically produced for the market, to be to a certain extent supplied by publishers—a phenomenon never ob-served, I imagine, until a religion has got well past its earliest insecure beginnings.

One of the doctrinal sources of Mind-cure is the four Gospels; another is Emersonianism or New England transcendentalism; another is Ber-keleyan idealism; another is spiritism, with its messages of "law" and "progress" and "development"; another the optimistic popular science evolutionism of which I have recently spoken; and, finally, Hinduism has contributed a strain. But the most characteristic feature of the mind-cure movement is an inspiration much more direct. The leaders in this faith have had an intuitive belief in the all-saving power of healthy-minded attitudes as such, in the conquering efficacy of courage, hope, and trust, and a correlative contempt for doubt, fear, worry, and all nervously pre-cautionary states of mind.[4] Their belief has in a general way been corrobo-

4. "Cautionary Verses for Children": this title of a much used work, published early in the nineteenth century, shows how far the muse of evangelical protestant-ism in England, with her mind fixed on the idea of danger, had at last drifted away from the original gospel freedom. Mind-cure might be briefly called a reaction against all that religion of chronic anxiety which marked the earlier part of our century in the evangelical circles of England and America.

rated by the practical experience of their disciples; and this experience forms to-day a mass imposing in amount.

The blind have been made to see, the halt to walk; lifelong invalids have had their health restored. The moral fruits have been no less remarkable. The deliberate adoption of a healthy-minded attitude has proved possible to many who never supposed they had it in them; regeneration of character "has gone on on an extensive scale"; and cheerfulness has been restored to countless homes. The indirect influence of this has been great. The mind-cure principles are beginning so to pervade the air that one catches their spirit at second-hand. One hears of the "Gospel of Relaxation," of the "Don't Worry Movement," of people who repeat to themselves, "Youth, health, vigor!" when dressing in the morning, as their motto for the day. Complaints of the weather are getting to be forbidden in many households; and more and more people are recognizing it to be bad form to speak of disagreeable sensations, or to make much of the ordinary inconveniences and ailments of life. These general tonic effects on public opinion would be good even if the more striking results were non-existent. But the latter abound so that we can afford to overlook the innumerable failures and self-deceptions that are mixed in with them (for in everything human failure is a matter of course), and we can also overlook the verbiage of a good deal of the mind-cure literature, some of which is so moonstruck with optimism and so vaguely expressed that an academically trained intellect finds it almost impossible to read it at all.

. . .

To come now to a little closer quarters with their creed. The fundamental pillar on which it rests is nothing more than the general basis of all religious experience, the fact that man has a dual nature, and is connected with two spheres of thought, a shallower and a profounder sphere, in either of which he may learn to live more habitually. The shallower and lower sphere is that of the fleshly sensations, instincts, and desires, of egotism, doubt, and the lower personal interests. But whereas Christian theology has always considered *frowardness* to be the essential vice of this part of human nature, the mind-curers say that the mark of the beast in it is *fear;* and this is what gives such an entirely new religious turn to their persuasion.

"Fear," to quote a writer of the school, "has had its uses in the evolutionary process, and seems to constitute the whole of forethought in most animals; but that it should remain any part of the mental equipment of human civilized life is an absurdity. I find that the fear element of forethought is not stimulating to those more civilized persons to whom duty and attraction are the natural motives, but is weakening and deterrent. As soon as it becomes unnecessary, fear becomes a positive deterrent, and should be entirely removed, as dead flesh is removed from living tissue. To assist in the analysis of fear, and in the denunciation of its expressions, I have coined the word *fearthought* to stand for the unprofitable element of forethought, and have defined the word 'worry' as *fearthought in contradistinction to forethought.* I have also defined fearthought as *the self-imposed or self-permitted suggestion of inferiority,* in order to place it where it really belongs, in the category of harmful, unnecessary, and therefore not respectable things."[5]

. . .

Although the disciples of the mind-cure often use Christian terminology, one sees from such quotations how widely their notion of the fall of man diverges from that of ordinary Christians.

Their notion of man's higher nature is hardly less divergent, being decidedly pantheistic. The spiritual in man appears in the mind-cure philosophy as partly conscious, but chiefly subconscious; and through the subconscious part of it we are already one with the Divine without any miracle of grace, or abrupt creation of a new inner man. As this view is variously expressed by different writers, we find in it traces of Christian mysticism, of transcendental idealism, of vedantism, and of the modern psychology of the subliminal self.

. . .

Let me now pass from these abstracter statements to some more concrete accounts of experience with the mind-cure religion. I have many answers from correspondents—the only difficulty is to choose. The first two whom I shall quote are my personal friends. One of them, a woman, writing as follows, expresses well the feeling of continuity with the Infinite Power, by which all mind-cure disciples are inspired.

"The first underlying cause of all sickness, weakness, or depression is the *human sense of separateness* from that Divine Energy which we call God. The soul which can feel and affirm in serene but jubilant confidence, as did the Nazarene: 'I and my Father are one,' has no further need of healer, or of healing. This is the whole truth in a nutshell, and other foundation for wholeness can no man lay than this fact of impregnable divine union. Disease can no longer attack one whose feet are planted on this rock, who feels hourly, momently, the influx of the Deific Breath. If

---

5. Horace Fletcher, *Happiness as Found in Forethought* Minus *Fearthought, Menticulture Series,* ii. (Chicago and New York: Stone, 1897) pp. 21–25, abridged.

one with Omnipotence, how can weariness enter the consciousness, how illness assail that indomitable spark?

"This possibility of annulling forever the law of fatigue has been abundantly proven in my own case; for my earlier life bears a record of many, many years of bedridden invalidism, with spine and lower limbs paralyzed. My thoughts were no more impure than they are to-day, although my belief in the necessity of illness was dense and unenlightened; but since my resurrection in the flesh, I have worked as a healer unceasingly for fourteen years without a vacation, and can truthfully assert that I have never known a moment of fatigue or pain, although coming in touch constantly with excessive weakness, illness, and disease of all kinds. For how can a conscious part of Deity be sick?—since 'Greater is he that is *with* us than all that can strive against us.'"

. . .

On the whole, one is struck by a psychological similarity between the mind-cure movement and the Lutheran and Wesleyan movements. To the believer in moralism and works, with his anxious query, "What shall I do to be saved?" Luther and Wesley replied: "You are saved now, if you would but believe it." And the mind-curers come with precisely similar words of emancipation. They speak, it is true, to persons for whom the conception of salvation has lost its ancient theological meaning, but who labor nevertheless with the same eternal human difficulty. *Things are wrong with them;* and "What shall I do to be clear, right, sound, whole, well?" is the form of their question. And the answer is: "You *are* well, sound, and clear already, if you did but know it." "The whole matter may be summed up in one sentence," says one of the authors whom I have already quoted. "*God is well, and so are you.* You must awaken to the knowledge of your real being."

The adequacy of their message to the mental needs of a large fraction of mankind is what gave force to those earlier gospels. Exactly the same adequacy holds in the case of the mind-cure message, foolish as it may sound upon its surface; and seeing its rapid growth in influence, and its therapeutic triumphs, one is tempted to ask whether it may not be destined (probably by very reason of the crudity and extravagance of many of its manifestations) to play a part almost as great in the evolution of the popular religion of the future as did those earlier movements in their day.

. . .

Now the history of Lutheran salvation by faith, of methodistic conversions, and of what I call the mind-cure movement seems to prove the existence of numerous persons in whom—at any rate at a certain stage in their development—a change of character for the better, so far from being facilitated by the rules laid down by official moralists, will take place all the more successfully if those rules be exactly reversed. Official moralists advise us never to relax our strenuousness. "Be vigilant, day and night," they adjure us; "hold your passive tendencies in check; shrink from no effort; keep your will like a bow always bent." But the persons I speak of find that all this conscious effort leads to nothing but failure and vexation in their hands, and only makes them twofold more the children of hell they were before. The tense and voluntary attitude becomes in them an impossible fever and torment. Their machinery refuses to run at all when the bearings are made so hot and the belts so tight.

Under these circumstances the way to success, as vouched for by innumerable authentic personal narrations, is by an anti-moralistic method, by the "surrender" of which I spoke in my second lecture. Passivity, not activity; relaxation, not intentness, should be now the rule. Give up the feeling of responsibility, let go your hold, resign the care of your destiny to higher powers, be genuinely indifferent as to what becomes of it all, and you will find not only that you gain a perfect inward relief, but often also, in addition, the particular goods you sincerely thought you were renouncing. This is the salvation through self-despair, the dying to be truly born, of Lutheran theology, the passage into *nothing* of which Jacob Behmen writes. To get to it, a critical point must usually be passed, a corner turned within one. Something must give way, a native hardness must break down and liquefy; and this event (as we shall abundantly see hereafter) is frequently sudden and automatic, and leaves on the Subject an impression that he has been wrought on by an external power.

. . .

I believe that the claims of the sectarian scientist are, to say the least, premature. The experiences which we have been studying during this hour (and a great many other kinds of religious experiences are like them) plainly show the universe to be a more many-sided affair than any sect, even the scientific sect, allows for. What, in the end, are all our verifications but experiences that agree with more or less isolated systems of ideas (conceptual systems) that our minds have framed? But why in the name of common sense need we assume that only one such system of ideas can be true? The obvious outcome of our total experience is that the world can be handled according to many systems of ideas, and is so handled by different men, and will each time give some characteristic kind of profit, for which he cares, to the handler, while at the same time some other kind of profit has to be omitted or postponed. Science gives to all of us telegraphy, electric lighting, and diagnosis, and succeeds in preventing and curing a certain amount of disease. Religion in the shape of mind-cure gives to some of us serenity, moral poise, and happiness, and prevents certain forms of disease as well as science does, or even better in a certain class of persons. Evidently, then, the science and the religion are both of them genuine keys for unlocking the world's treasure-house to him who can use either of them practically. Just as evidently neither is exhaustive or exclusive of the other's simultaneous use. And why, after all, may not the world be so complex as to consist of many interpenetrating spheres of reality, which we can thus approach in alternation by using different conceptions and assuming different attitudes, just as mathematicians handle the same numerical and spatial facts by geometry, by analytical geometry, by algebra, by the calculus, or by quaternions, and each time come out right? On this view religion and science, each verified in its own way from hour to hour and from life to life, would be co-eternal. Primitive thought, with its belief in individualized personal forces, seems at any rate as far as ever from being driven by science from the field to-day. Numbers of educated people still find it the directest experimental channel by which to carry on their intercourse with reality.

11

René Descartes,
The Passions of the Soul

The French philosopher and mathematician, René Descartes (1596–1650), was a pivotal figure in the formation of our modern, scientifically based view of reality. Descartes studied Scholastic thought and classics at the College of La Flèche for nine years, and afterward spent a number of years traveling through Europe. Some vivid dreams he had while residing in a town in southern Germany in 1619 set him on the course of formulating a final, systematic account of the universe. From 1628 on he lived mostly in Holland, and there he wrote Le Monde *("The Universe"—1633),* Discourse on Method *(1637), the* Principles of Philosophy *(1644), and his best-known work,* Meditations on First Philosophy *(1641). In the late 1640s, in response to probing questions asked by Princess Elizabeth of Bohemia, he turned to questions about ethics and human psychology. The outcome of this inquiry was* The Passions of the Soul, *published in 1649, one year before his death at the age of fifty-four.*

Descartes is best known for what is called "Cartesian dualism," the view that a human being consists of two distinct substances, mind and body. On this view, the body is made up of matter, occupies space, and interacts with its physical environment according to mechanistic causal principles. The mind, in contrast, is nonmaterial: it is a spiritual substance that is not located in space and, because it exists independent of the material causal order, can act out of its own free will. Descartes's view is that these two substances are independent to the extent that each can exist without the other. A body can go on existing without being inhabited by a mind (e.g., as a corpse) and can even function in elementary ways (as animals respond to their environment even though they have not been given minds). And the mind can continue to exist even after it has been detached from the body (e.g., as a soul or ghost). Of course, so long as a person is still alive, the body and mind are tightly connected and constantly interacting.

The problem for dualism, as Descartes saw, is explaining how *the body and mind can constitute a unity. In a famous passage in the "Sixth Meditation," Descartes says he has learned from Nature through "feelings of pain, hunger, thirst, and so on that I am not only residing in my body as a pilot in his ship, but furthermore that I am intimately connected with [my body], and that the mixture is so blended, as it were, that something like a single whole is produced."* This conception of sensations and feelings as involving both body and mind led Descartes to think of "the union of soul and body" as a "primitive notion" with characteristics that embrace the entire psychophysical unity of the human being.[1] Though Descartes came up with some rather wild speculations about the relation of body and mind, his basic model of the emotions or passions bears striking similarities to our modern scientific outlook. According to this view, environmental stimuli cause events in the body, which in turn cause signals to travel up the neural pathways (Descartes thinks of this action as occurring in "animal spirits," where we would say electro-chemical discharges). These physical processes cause the mental experiences of feelings and sensations (Descartes suggests that the point of contact between physiological processes and psychological experiences is the pineal gland). Our capacity to have emotions of certain sorts is determined in advance by our God-given human nature, and so is basically good. As we grow up, these emotions are conditioned by experiences in our lives (anticipating Pavlov's theory of the conditioned reflex, Descartes says that a dog subjected to pain whenever music is played will display pain behavior whenever it hears music). Since emotions can distort our thinking and cause us to act irrationally, however, we ought to transform our emotional responses through habituation. There are interesting similarities between Descartes's view and certain ancient Greek and Roman ideas. Though Descartes was strongly influenced by the revival of Stoicism in the early modern period, he differs from the Stoics in seeing the emotions as basically good. In some ways, his final view is closer to Aristotle's ideal of instilling in oneself the kinds of habits that will lead one to feel the right way at the right times in the right situations.

1. For an excellent discussion of Descartes's later thought on the union of mind and body, see John Cottingham, *Philosophy and the Good Life: Reason and the Passions in Greek, Cartesian and Psychoanalytic Ethics* (Cambridge: Cambridge University Press, 1998), chapter 3; and Geneviève Rodis-Lewis's Introduction to Descartes's *The Passions of the Soul,* trans. Stephen H. Voss (Indianapolis: Hackett Publishing Co., 1989).

Article 1. That what is a Passion with respect to a subject is always an Action in some other respect.

The defectiveness of the sciences we inherit from the ancients is nowhere more apparent than in what they wrote about the Passions. For even though this is a topic about which knowledge has always been vigorously sought, and though it does not seem to be one of the most difficult—because, as everyone feels them in himself, one need not borrow any observation from elsewhere to discover their nature—nevertheless what the Ancients taught about them is so little, and for the most part so little believable, that I cannot hope to approach the truth unless I forsake the paths they followed. For this reason I shall be obliged to write here as though I were treating a topic which no one before me had ever described. To begin with, I take into consideration that whatever is done or happens afresh is generally called by the Philosophers a Passion with respect to the subject it happens to, and an Action with respect to what makes it happen. Thus, even though the agent and the patient are often quite different, the Action and the Passion are always a single thing, which has these two names in accordance with the two different subjects it may be referred to.

Article 2. That in order to understand the Passions of the soul we need to distinguish its functions from those of the body.

Then I also take into consideration that we notice no subject that acts more immediately upon our soul than the body it is joined to, and that consequently we ought to think that what is a Passion in the former is commonly an Action in the latter. So there is no better path for arriving at an understanding of our Passions than to examine the difference between the soul and the body, in order to understand to which of the two each of the functions within us should be attributed.

Article 3. What rule must be followed to achieve this end.

One will find no great difficulty in doing that if one bears this in mind: everything we find by experience to be in us which we see can also be in entirely inanimate bodies must be attributed to our body alone; on the other hand, everything in us which we conceive entirely incapable of belonging to a body must be attributed to our soul.

From René Descartes, *The Passions of the Soul*, trans. by Stephen H. Voss (Indianapolis: Hackett Publishing Co., 1989). Reprinted by permission of the publisher.

Article 30. That the soul is jointly united to all the parts of the body.

But in order to understand all these things more perfectly, it is necessary to know that the soul is truly joined to the whole body, and that one cannot properly say that it is in any one of its parts to the exclusion of the others, because [the body] is one, and in a way indivisible, in proportion to the disposition of its organs, which are all so related to one another that when any of them is removed this renders the whole body defective; and because [the soul] is of a nature which has no relation to extension, or to the dimensions or other properties of the stuff the body is composed of, but only to the whole collection of its organs—as becomes apparent from the fact that one cannot in any way conceive of a half or a third of a soul, or of what extension it occupies, and from the fact that [the soul] does not become smaller from some part of the body being cut off, but separates from it entirely when the collection of its organs is dissolved.

Article 31. That there is a little gland in the brain in which the soul exercises its functions in a more particular way than in the other parts.

It is also necessary to know that, even though the soul is joined to the whole body, there is nevertheless one part in [the body] in which [the soul] exercises its functions in a more particular way than in all the others. It is commonly believed that this part is the brain, or perhaps the heart—the brain because the sense organs are related thereto, and the heart because the passions are felt as if therein. But in examining the matter carefully, I seem to have plainly ascertained that the part of the body in which the soul immediately exercises its functions is in no way the heart; it is not the whole brain either, but only the innermost of its parts—a certain extremely small gland, situated in the middle of its substance, and so suspended above the duct by which the spirits of its anterior cavities are in communication with those of the posterior that its slightest movements can greatly alter the course of these spirits, and conversely the slightest changes taking place in the course of the spirits can greatly alter the movements of this gland.

Article 40. What the principal effect of the passions is.

For it is necessary to notice that the principal effect of all the passions in men is that they incite and dispose their soul to will the things for which they prepare their body, so that the sensation of fear incites it to will to flee, that of boldness to will to do battle, and so on for the rest.

Article 41. What the power of the soul is with respect to the body.

But the will is by its nature free in such a way that it can never be constrained; and of the two sorts of thoughts I have distinguished in the soul, of which the first are its actions—namely its volitions—and the others its passions—taking this word in its most general sense, which comprises all sorts of perceptions—the former are absolutely in its power and can only indirectly be altered by the body, whereas the latter depend absolutely on the actions that produce them and can only indirectly be altered by the soul, except when [the soul] is itself their cause. And the whole action of the soul consists in this: merely by willing something, it makes the little gland to which it is closely joined move in the way required to produce the effect corresponding to this volition.

Article 45. What the power of the soul is with respect to its passions.

Our passions cannot likewise be directly excited or displaced by the action of our will, but they can be indirectly by the representation of things which are usually joined with the passions we will to have and opposed to the ones we will to reject. Thus, in order to excite boldness and displace fear in oneself, it is not sufficient to have the volition to do so—one must apply oneself to attend to reasons, objects, or precedents that convince [one] that the peril is not great, that there is always more security in defense than in flight, that one will have glory and joy from having conquered, whereas one can expect only regret and shame from having fled, and similar things.

Article 46. What the reason is on account of which the soul cannot completely control its passions.

There is one particular reason why the soul cannot readily alter or check its passions, which led me to put in their definition above that they are not only caused but also maintained and strengthened by some particular movement of the spirits. This reason is that they are almost all accompanied by some excitation taking place in the heart, and consequently also throughout the blood and the spirits, so that until this excitation has ceased they remain present to our thought, in the same way as objects capable of being sensed are present to it while they are acting upon our sense organs. And as the soul, in becoming extremely attentive to something else, can keep from hearing a little noise or feeling a little pain, but cannot in the same way keep from hearing thunder or feeling the fire burning the hand, so it can easily overcome the lesser passions, but not the most vigorous and the strongest, until after the excitation of the blood and spirits has abated. The most the will can do while this excitation is in its full strength is not to consent to its effects and to restrain many of the movements to which it disposes the body. For example, if anger makes the hand rise in order to strike, the will can ordinarily restrain it; if fear incites the legs to flee, the will can stop them; and so on with the rest.

Article 47. What the struggles consist in that people customarily imagine between the lower part of the soul and the higher.

And all the struggles that people customarily imagine between the lower part of the soul, which is called sensitive, and the higher, which is rational, or between the natural appetites and the will, consist only in the opposition between the movements which the body by its spirits and the soul by its will tend to excite simultaneously in the gland. For there is only a single soul in us, and this soul has within itself no diversity of parts; the very one that is sensitive is rational, and all its appetites are volitions. The error which has been committed in having it play different characters, usually opposed to one another, arises only from the fact that its functions have not been rightly distinguished from those of the body, to which alone must be attributed everything to be found in us that is opposed to our reason. So no struggle whatever occurs here, except as follows: as the little gland in the middle of the brain is capable of being driven from one side by the soul and from the other by the animal spirits, which, as I have said above, are only bodies, it often happens that these two impulses are in opposition and the stronger one prevents the other from taking effect. Now one can distinguish two sorts of movements excited by the spirits in the gland: the first represent to the soul objects that move the senses or impressions that are met within the brain, and they make no great difference to its will; the others do make some such difference to it—namely those which cause the passions or the movements of the body that accompany them. As for the former [movements], even though they often prevent the actions of the soul or are prevented by them, yet because they are not in direct opposition we notice no struggle here. We notice [a struggle] only between the latter [movements] and the volitions that oppose them—for example, between the impetus by which the spirits impel the gland to cause in the soul the desire for some thing and that by which the soul repels [the gland] by the volition it has to shun that very thing. And what makes this struggle become noticeable for the most part is that, the will not having the power to excite the passions directly, as has already been said, it is constrained to employ artifice and apply itself to attend successively to different things. If the first of these happens to have the strength to change the course of the spirits for a moment, it may happen that the one following does not have it and that they immediately revert, because the previous disposition in the nerves, heart, and blood is unchanged—which makes the soul feel driven almost at the same time to desire and not to desire the same thing. This is what has given people occasion to imagine two powers within [the soul] which struggle against one another. All the same, a certain struggle can still be conceived, in that often the same cause which excites some passion in the soul also excites certain movements in the body, to which the soul does not contribute and which it stops or tries to stop as soon as it perceives them, as we experience when what excites fear also makes the spirits enter the muscles that move the legs to flee, and our volition to be bold stops them.

Article 48. How to tell the strength or weakness of souls; and what the misfortune of the weakest is.

Now it is by the outcome of these struggles that everyone can tell the strength or weakness of his soul. For there is no doubt that those in whom the will can naturally conquer the passions most easily and stop the accompanying movements of the body have the strongest souls. However, there are some who cannot test their strength,[1] because they never make their will do battle with its proper weapons, but only with the ones which some passions supply it in order to resist other [passions]. What I call its proper weapons are firm and decisive judgments concerning the knowledge of good and evil, which it has resolved to follow in conducting the actions of its life. And the weakest souls of all are those whose will does not decide in this way to follow certain judgments, but continually allows itself to be carried away by present passions, which, often being opposed to one another, draw [the will] by turns to their side, and, getting it to struggle against itself, put the soul in the most deplorable condition it can be in. Thus, when fear represents death as an extreme evil avoidable only by flight, if ambition from the other side represents the infamy of this flight as an evil worse than death, then these two passions agitate the will in different ways; obeying now the one and now the other, it is in continual opposition to itself, and so renders the soul enslaved and unhappy.

Article 49. That strength of the soul does not suffice without knowledge of the truth.

It is true that there are very few men so weak and irresolute that they will nothing but what their passion dictates to them. The greater part have decisive judgments which they follow in regulating a part of their actions.

1. I.e., the strength of their souls.

And though these judgments are often false, and even founded on passions by which the will has previously allowed itself to be conquered or seduced, yet, because it continues to follow them when the passion that caused them is absent, they can be regarded as its proper weapons, and souls can be thought to be stronger or weaker to the extent that they are more or less able to follow these judgments and resist the present passions opposed to them. But there is still a great difference between resolutions that proceed from some false opinion and those that rest on knowledge of the truth alone, since we are sure never to have either regret or repentance if we follow the latter, whereas we always have them upon following the former, when we discover the error therein.

Article 50. That there is no soul so weak that it cannot, when well guided, acquire an absolute power over its passions.

And here it is useful to know that—as has already been said above—although each movement of the gland seems to have been joined by nature to each of our thoughts from the beginning of our life, one can nevertheless join them to others by habituation. Experience shows this in the case of words, which excite movements in the gland which according to the institution of nature represent only their sound to the soul when they are uttered vocally, or the shape of their letters when they are written, but which nevertheless, by the disposition acquired in thinking of what they mean upon having heard their sound or seen their letters, usually make one apprehend this meaning rather than the shape of their letters or the sound of their syllables. It is also useful to know that although the movements—both of the gland and of the spirits and brain—which represent certain objects to the soul are naturally joined with those [movements] which excite certain passions in it, they can nevertheless by habituation be separated from them and joined with other quite different ones; and even that this disposition can be acquired by a single action and does not require long practice. Thus when someone unexpectedly comes upon something very foul in food he is eating with relish, the surprise of this encounter can so change the disposition of the brain that he will no longer be able to see any such food afterwards without abhorrence, whereas previously he used to eat it with pleasure. And the same thing can be observed in beasts, for even though they have no reason and perhaps no thought either, all the movements of the spirits and the gland that excite the passions in us still exist in them, and serve in them to maintain and strengthen, not the passions as in us, but the nerve and muscle movements that usually accompany them. So when a dog sees a partridge it is naturally inclined to run toward it, and when it hears a gun fired the noise naturally incites it to run away. But nevertheless setters are commonly trained so that the sight of a partridge makes them stop, and the noise they hear afterwards, when [the bird] is fired on, makes them run up to it. Now these things are useful to know in order to give everyone the courage to study the regulation of his passions. For since with a little skill one can change the movements of the brain in animals bereft of reason, it is plain that one can do it even better in men, and that even those who have the weakest souls could acquire a quite absolute dominion over all their passions if one employed enough skill in training and guiding them.[2]

Article 51. What the first causes of the passions are.

We know, from what has been said above, that the last and most proximate cause of the passions of the soul is nothing other than the agitation with which the spirits move the little gland in the middle of the brain. But this is insufficient for them to be distinguished one from another; it is necessary to seek their sources and investigate their first causes. Now though they may sometimes be caused by the action of the soul, which decides to conceive of this or that object, and also by the temperament of the body alone or by impressions haphazardly encountered in the brain, as happens when one feels sad or joyful without being able to say why, still it is apparent from what has been said that all of them can be excited as well by objects which move the senses, and that these objects are their most common and principal causes—from which it follows that, in order to find them all, it is sufficient to take into consideration all the effects of these objects.

Article 52. What their use is, and
how they can be enumerated.

Moreover, I note that objects which move the senses do not excite different passions in us in proportion to all of their diversities, but only in proportion to the different ways they can harm or profit us or, generally, be important to us; and that the use of all the passions consists in this alone: they dispose the soul to will the things nature tells us are useful and to persist in this volition, just as the same agitation of spirits that usually causes them disposes the body to the movements conducive to the execu-

2. "Them" (les) probably refers to the people, not the passions. What is striking here is that Descartes evidently envisages people coming to regulate their passions by being trained by others, Pavlov style.

tion of those things. This is why, in order to enumerate them, one needs only to investigate, in order, in how many different ways that are important to us our senses can be moved by their objects. I shall effect the enumeration of all the principal passions here according to the order in which they may thus be found.

Article 145. About those which depend only on other causes; and what Fortune is.

As for things which in no way depend on us, no matter how good they may be, one should never desire them with Passion—not only because they may fail to come about and thereby afflict us all the more, the more we have wished for them, but mainly because, in occupying our thought, they divert us from casting our affection upon other things whose acquisition does depend on us. And there are two general remedies for these vain Desires. The first is Generosity, which I shall speak about later. The second is that we should often reflect upon divine Providence, and represent to ourselves that it is impossible that anything should happen otherwise than has been determined by this Providence from all eternity; thus it is like a fate or immutable necessity which must be opposed to Fortune, in order to destroy it, as a chimera arising only from error in our understanding. For we can desire only what we consider in some way to be possible, and we can consider possible things which do not depend on us only insofar as we think they depend on Fortune—that is, insofar as we judge that they might happen and that something like them has happened at other times. Now this opinion is founded only on our failure to know all the causes that contribute to each effect. For when something we have considered to depend on Fortune does not happen, this shows that one of the causes necessary to produce it was lacking, and consequently that it was absolutely impossible, and that something like it has never happened—that is, something for the production of which a similar cause was also lacking. So if we had not been ignorant of that beforehand, we would never have considered it possible, nor consequently have desired it.

Article 146. About those which depend both on us and on others.

It is therefore necessary to reject completely the common opinion that there is a Fortune outside of us which makes things happen or fail to happen at its pleasure, and to understand that everything is directed by divine Providence, whose eternal decree is infallible and immutable in such a way that, except for the things which this same decree has willed to depend on our free will, we ought to think that from our point of view nothing happens which is not necessary and as it were fated, so that we cannot without error desire it to happen otherwise. But because most of our Desires extend to things which do not depend entirely on us or entirely on others, we should distinguish carefully within [those things] that which depends only on us, in order to limit our desire to that alone. As for what is left, even though we ought to consider its outcome entirely fated and immutable, so that our Desire may not be occupied therewith, we should not cease to attend to the reasons that make it hope to a greater or lesser extent, so that they may be instrumental in regulating our actions. So, for example, if we have business somewhere we could reach by two different routes, of which one is usually much safer than the other, then even though the decree of Providence may perhaps be such that if we go by the route considered safer we shall definitely be robbed there, while on the contrary we can take the other with no danger at all, we should not on that account be indifferent to choosing one or the other, or rest upon the immutable fatefulness of that decree; reason dictates that we should choose the route that is usually safer. And our Desire regarding it must be fulfilled once we have taken it, whatever evil may thereby have befallen us, because, this evil having been inevitable from our point of view, we had no reason to wish to be free from it but only to wish to do everything as well as our understanding could discern, as I am supposing we have done. And it is certain that when one applies oneself thus to distinguishing Fate from Fortune, one will easily accustom oneself to regulating one's Desires in such a way that they can always give us complete satisfaction, since their fulfillment depends only on us.

Article 147. About the inner Excitations of the soul.

I shall add but one further consideration here, which seems to me to be very good for keeping us from suffering any distress from the Passions: our good and our ill depend principally on inner excitations, which are excited in the soul only by the soul itself—in which respect they differ from those passions that always depend on some motion of the spirits. And although these excitations of the soul are often joined with the passions that are like them, they may also frequently be found with others, and may even originate from those that are in opposition to them. For example, when a husband mourns his dead wife, whom (as sometimes happens) he would be upset to see resuscitated, it may be that his heart is constricted by the Sadness which funeral trappings and the absence of a person to whose company he was accustomed excite in him; and it may be that some remnants of love or pity, presented to his imagination, draw genuine tears from his eyes—in spite of the fact that at the same time he feels a secret Joy in the innermost depths of his soul, whose excitation has so much power that the Sadness and tears accompanying it can diminish none of its strength. And when we read of unusual adventures in a book or see them represented on a stage, this sometimes excites Sadness in us, sometimes Joy or Love or Hatred, and in general all the Passions, according to the diversity of the objects offered to our imagination; but along with this we have the pleasure of feeling them excited in us, and this pleasure is an intellectual Joy, which can originate from Sadness as well as from any of the other Passions.

Article 148. That the exercise of virtue is a supreme remedy for the Passions.

Now, inasmuch as these inner excitations affect us more intimately and consequently have much more power over us than the Passions from which they differ but which are found with them, it is certain that, provided our soul always has what it takes to be content in its interior, none of the disturbances that come from elsewhere have any power to harm it. On the contrary, they serve to increase its joy, for in seeing that it cannot be injured by them it comes to understand its perfection. And in order that our soul may thus have what it takes to be content, it needs only to follow virtue diligently. For anyone who has lived in such a way that his conscience cannot reproach him for ever having failed to do anything he judged to be best (which is what I call following virtue here) derives a satisfaction with such power to make him happy that the most vigorous assaults of the Passions never have enough power to disturb the tranquillity of his soul.

Article 152. For what cause one may esteem oneself.

And because one of the principal parts of Wisdom is to know in what manner and for what cause anyone should esteem or scorn himself, I shall attempt to give my opinion about it here. I observe but a single thing in us which could give us just cause to esteem ourselves, namely the use of our free will and the dominion we have over our volitions. For it is only the actions that depend on that free will for which we could rightly be praised or blamed; and in making us masters of ourselves, it renders us like God in a way, provided we do not lose by laziness the rights it gives us.

Article 153. What Generosity consists in.

So I believe that true Generosity, which makes a man esteem himself as highly as he can legitimately esteem himself, consists only in this: partly in his understanding that there is nothing which truly belongs to him but this free control of his volitions, and no reason why he ought to be praised or blamed except that he uses it well or badly; and partly in his feeling within himself a firm and constant resolution to use it well, that is, never to lack the volition to undertake and execute all the things he judges to be best—which is to follow virtue perfectly.

Article 156. What the properties of Generosity are, and how it serves as a remedy for all the disorders of the Passions.

Those who are Generous in this way are naturally inclined to do great things, and yet to undertake nothing they do not feel themselves capable of. And because they esteem nothing more highly than doing good to other men and for this reason scorning their own interest, they are always perfectly courteous, affable, and of service to everyone. And along with this, they are entirely masters of their Passions—particularly Desires, Jealousy, and Envy, because there is nothing whose acquisition does not depend on them which they think is worth enough to deserve being greatly wished for; and Hatred of men, because they esteem them all; and Fear, because their confidence in their virtue reassures them; and finally Anger, because, esteeming only very little all things that depend on others, they never give their enemies such an advantage as to acknowledge being injured by them.

Article 157. About Pride.

All those who contrive a good opinion of themselves for some other cause, whatever it may be, have no true Generosity, but only a Pride which is always extremely unvirtuous—although it is the more so, the more unjust the cause is for which one esteems oneself. And the most unjust of all occurs when someone is proud without any reason—that is, when he gets that way without thinking he has any merit for which he should be appreciated, but only because he takes no account of merit, and, imagining that glory is nothing but usurpation, believes that those who attribute the most of it to themselves actually have the most. This vice is so unreasonable and so absurd that I would hardly have believed there were men who gave themselves up to it, if no one were ever praised unjustly. But flattery is everywhere so common that there is no man so deficient that he does not often see himself esteemed for things that deserve no praise, or even deserve blame—which gives the most ignorant and stupid occasion to fall into this species of Pride.

Article 161. How Generosity may be acquired.

And it must be noted that what are commonly named virtues are dispositions in the soul which dispose it to certain thoughts, so that they are different from these thoughts but can produce them and conversely be produced by them. It must also be noted that these thoughts can be produced by the soul alone, but that often some movement of the spirits happens to strengthen them, and that then they are actions of virtue and at the same time Passions of the soul. So, although there is no virtue to which good birth seems to contribute so much as that which makes one esteem oneself only at his true worth, and although it is easy to believe that all the souls God puts in our bodies are not equally noble and strong (which is the reason I have named this virtue Generosity, following the usage of our language, rather than Magnanimity, following the usage of the Schools, where [this virtue] is not well understood), it is certain nevertheless that good education is very useful for correcting deficiencies of birth, and that if one frequently occupies oneself in considering what free will is and how great the advantages are that come from a firm resolution to use it well and also, on the other hand, how vain and useless all the cares are that trouble the ambitious, one may excite in oneself the Passion and then acquire the virtue of Generosity.[3] And since this is, as it were, the key to all the other virtues, and a general remedy for all the disorders of the Passions, it seems to me that this consideration is well worth noting.

Article 211. A general remedy for the Passions.

And now that we understand [the passions], we have much less reason to fear them than we had before. For we see that they are all in their nature good, and that we have nothing to avoid but misuses or excesses of them, for which the remedies I have explained could suffice if everyone had enough interest in putting them into practice. But because I have included

3. French usage here is rooted in the etymological link between *générosité*, *génétique*, and *généalogie*, and is imbued with the ideal of noble birth; Descartes thinks it provides a better model than the use of *magnanimité* by the current schools, which do not sufficiently understand the traditional doctrine of this virtue. But while "good birth" is a natural source of generosity, anyone can be trained in its acquisition: no one is barred from the Cartesian artificial aristocracy.

among these remedies the forethought and skill by which we can correct
our constitutional deficiencies, in applying ourselves to separate within us
the movements of the blood and spirits from the thoughts to which they
are usually joined, I grant that there are few people who are sufficiently
prepared in this way against all sorts of contingencies, and that these
movements, excited in the blood by the objects of the Passions, immediately follow so swiftly from mere impressions formed in the brain and
from the disposition of the organs, even though the soul may in no way
contribute to them, that there is no human wisdom capable of withstanding them when one is insufficiently prepared for them. Thus many cannot
abstain from laughing when tickled, even though they derive no pleasure
from it. For, in spite of themselves, the impression of Joy and surprise
which previously made them laugh for the same reason, being awakened in
their fantasy, makes their lungs suddenly swell with the blood that the
heart sends there. And so those who are strongly inclined by their constitution to the excitations of Joy, Pity, Fear, or Anger cannot keep from
fainting, crying, trembling, or having their blood all stirred up just as
though they had a fever, when their fantasy is greatly affected by the object
of one of these Passions. But what can always be done on such an occasion,
and what I think I can set down here as the most general remedy for all the
excesses of the Passions and the easiest to put into practice, is this: when
one feels the blood stirred up like that, one should take warning, and recall
that everything presented to the imagination tends to deceive the soul, and
to make the reasons for favoring the object of its Passion appear to it much
stronger than they are, and those for opposing it much weaker. And when
the Passion favors only things whose execution admits of some delay, one
must abstain from making any immediate judgment about them, and
distract oneself by other thoughts until time and rest have completely
calmed the excitation in the blood. Finally, when it incites one to actions
requiring one to reach some resolution at once, the will must be inclined
above all to take into consideration and to follow the reasons opposed to
those the Passion represents, even though they appear less strong. As is
the case when one is unexpectedly attacked by some enemy, the situation does not allow one to spend any time deliberating. But what it seems
to me that those who are accustomed to reflecting on their actions can
always do is this: when they feel seized by Fear, try to divert their
thought from considering the danger, by representing to themselves the
reasons why there is much more security and honor in resistance than in
flight; on the other hand, when they feel both the Desire for vengeance
and anger inciting them to rashly pursue those attacking them, recall that
it is imprudence to lose oneself when one can save oneself without dishonor, and that if the contest is very unequal, it is better to make an

honorable retreat or beg for mercy than to expose oneself senselessly to certain death.

Article 212. That all the good and evil of this life depend on them alone.

Finally, the soul may have pleasures by itself. But as for those that are common to it and the body, they depend entirely on the Passions, so that the men they can move the most are capable of tasting the most sweetness in this life. It is true that [these men] may also find the most bitterness in it, when they do not know how to employ them well and fortune is opposed to them. But Wisdom is useful here above all: it teaches us to render ourselves such masters of them, and to manage them with such ingenuity, that the evils they cause can be easily borne, and we even derive Joy from them all.

12

Baruch Spinoza,
The Ethics

Spinoza (1632–1677) was a Sephardic Jew whose parents escaped from the Iberian Peninsula, most likely from Portugal, to the relative religious freedom of the Netherlands. Trained in Hebrew and biblical studies, he studied such Medieval philosophers as Maimonides and was no doubt familiar with the works of Descartes. But he was also influenced by a group of Amsterdam "free-thinkers" who questioned traditional Judeo-Christian dogmas and propounded a more naturalistic view of God and the world. As a result of his heterodox activities, Spinoza was excommunicated from the Jewish community in 1656 and was banished from Amsterdam. He spent the rest of his short life in Holland writing, thinking, and engaging in scientific experiments, supported most likely by a wide network of friends, though he might also have earned some income grinding lenses for optical instruments. Given the radical nature of his thought, most of his writings (including The Ethics*) were first published by his friends after his death.*

As its name implies, a primary aim of The Ethics *is to formulate an account of the good life. In order to do this, however, Spinoza must first give an account of the universe and humanity's place in it, an account that is not merely idle speculation but is rationally demonstrated using the methods of geometric proof. In one sense it is right to say that Spinoza was the first fully modern, scientific thinker: he assumes that nature (or, as he calls it, "God or Nature") is a vast, interconnected causal system in which everything occurs as the result of determining causes. In contrast to Descartes, who held a dualist view, Spinoza holds that there is only one substance in the universe, God or Nature, and this substance has infinite attributes, including being both thinking (mental) and extended (physical). Since nature, the totality of Being, is a single, all-embracing substance, all the individual things making up the universe, including human beings, are just "modes" of this one substance, place-holders in the causal order of the universe. As the totality of what is, God cannot lack anything, and so cannot have desires, and therefore cannot have a plan or purpose. This means that it is a mistake to hold that there is anything like divine purpose in reality. Moreover, since all events occur as a result of causal factors going back indefinitely into the past, there is no such thing as free will as traditionally understood. Thus, everything we humans do is determined by the causal story of the universe of which we are only tiny parts.*

The question, then, is what must be the best possible life for us, given this picture of reality. To understand Spinoza's answer to this question, we first need to be clear about his notions of goodness, activity, and knowledge. First, Spinoza argues that nothing is either good or bad in itself—things just are what they are. But we humans form an idea of goodness as meaning what is to our advantage, and we can work out an account of the life that is to our best advantage. Since whatever contributes to the self-preservation of a thing constitutes its advantage, it follows that understanding what is good for us requires that we give an account of our nature and what is to our advantage. Second, Spinoza holds that humans, like all beings, have inbuilt dispositions to ensure their own survival, what he calls their conatus *(often translated "endeavor"). This notion of a drive to self-preservation gives Spinoza a way to distinguish between active and passive ways of being: Things are "active" when they act in accord with their own nature, and they are "passive" when their behavior results from external things impinging on them. Third, Spinoza holds that there are three levels of knowledge: (1) sensory impressions, which are produced in us by bodily affections and are inadequate and confused; (2) adequate ideas, which are given clearly and distinctly to the intellect and so are known to be true; and (3) intuitive knowledge, which follows directly from knowledge of God and sees things most truly because it grasps them in terms of the ultimate causal order of the universe.*

This conception of our capacity for a higher form of understanding provides the basis for Spinoza's vision of the good life. On this view, we are in bondage when we are pushed around by our passions without having an adequate idea of what they are, and we are free if we do understand the causes of our emotions. Spinoza suggests that an adequate knowledge of our emotions involves seeing them as in some sense caused by ourselves. And since "will and intellect are one and the same thing" (II, Prop. 49, Cor.), to understand the emotions in this way is to will them to be what they are. Doing this softens their impact and leads to a more contented life. The free man, then, is one who is active rather than passive, where this means that such a person knows, and so wills, what follows inevitably from his or her own nature.

Spinoza also holds that to live according to reason is to have an intuitive knowledge of things, and that means seeing them from the point of view of eternity—to see them as God sees them. A person who can adopt a God's-eye perspective in this way is active and therefore, Spinoza argues, has power. And since "power" and "virtue" mean the same thing, such a person is "virtuous" and "free" in the only meaning of those terms that can make sense given Spinoza's vision of reality. In the end, Spinoza equates living according to reason, having full knowledge of God or nature, freedom, blessedness, and the highest goal of humans.

PART IV

OF HUMAN BONDAGE, OR THE
STRENGTH OF THE EMOTIONS

PREFACE

I assign the term "bondage" to man's lack of power to control and check the emotions. For a man at the mercy of his emotions is not his own master but is subject to fortune, in whose power he so lies that he is often compelled, although he sees the better course, to pursue the worse. In this Part I have set myself the task of demonstrating why this is so, and also what is good and what is bad in emotions. But before I begin, I should like to make a few preliminary observations on perfection and imperfection, and on good and bad.

He who has undertaken something and has brought it to completion will say that the thing is completed (perfectus = completed,—Tr.); and not only he but everyone who rightly knew, or thought he knew, the intention and aim of the author of that work. For example, if anyone sees a work (which I assume is not yet finished) and knows that the aim of the author is to build a house, he will say that the house is imperfect. On the other hand, as soon as he sees that the work has been brought to the conclusion that its author had intended to give it, he will say that it is perfect. But if anyone sees a work whose like he had never seen before, and he does not know the artificer's intention, he cannot possibly know whether the work is perfect or imperfect.

This appears to have been the original meaning of these terms. But when men began to form general ideas and to devise ideal types of houses, buildings, towers and so on, and to prefer some models to others, it came about that each called "perfect" what he saw to be in agreement with the general idea he had formed of the said thing, and 'imperfect' that which he saw at variance with his own preconceived ideal, although in the artificer's opinion it had been fully completed. There seems to be no other reason why even natural phenomena (those not made by human hand) should commonly be called perfect or imperfect. For men are wont to form general ideas both of natural phenomena and of artifacts, and these ideas they regard as models, and they believe that Nature (which they consider does nothing without an end in view) looks to these ideas and holds them

From Baruch Spinoza, *The Ethics*, from *The Ethics, Treatise on the Emendation of the Intellect, and Selected Letters*, trans. by Samuel Shirley (Indianapolis: Hackett Publishing Co., 1992). Reprinted by permission of the publisher.

before herself as models. So when they see something occurring in Nature at variance with their preconceived ideal of the thing in question, they believe that Nature has then failed or blundered and has left that thing imperfect. So we see that men are in the habit of calling natural phenomena perfect or imperfect from their own preconceptions rather than from true knowledge. For we have demonstrated that Nature does not act with an end in view; that the eternal and infinite being, whom we call God, or Nature, acts by the same necessity whereby it exists. That the necessity of his nature whereby he acts is the same as that whereby he exists has been demonstrated. So the reason or cause why God, or Nature, acts, and the reason or cause why he exists, are one and the same. Therefore, just as he does not exist for an end, so he does not act for an end; just as there is no beginning or end to his existing, so there is no beginning or end to his acting. What is termed a "final cause" is nothing but human appetite in so far as it is considered as the starting-point or primary cause of some thing. For example, when we say that being a place of habitation was the final cause of this or that house, we surely mean no more than this, that a man, from thinking of the advantages of domestic life, had an urge to build a house. Therefore, the need for a habitation in so far as it is considered as a final cause is nothing but this particular urge, which is in reality an efficient cause, and is considered as the prime cause because men are commonly ignorant of the causes of their own urges; for, as I have repeatedly said, they are conscious of their actions and appetites but unaware of the causes by which they are determined to seek something. As to the common saying that Nature sometimes fails or blunders and produces imperfect things, I count this among the fictions with which I dealt in Appendix I.

So perfection and imperfection are in reality only modes of thinking, notions which we are wont to invent from comparing individuals of the same species or kind; and it is for this reason that I previously said that by reality and perfection I mean the same thing. For we are wont to classify all the individuals in Nature under one genus which is called the highest genus, namely, the notion of Entity, which pertains to all the individuals in Nature without exception. Therefore in so far as we classify individuals in Nature under this genus and compare them with one another and find that some have more being or reality than others, to that extent we say some are more perfect than others. And in so far as we attribute to them something involving negation, such as limit, end, impotence and so on, to that extent we call them imperfect because they do not affect our minds as much as those we call perfect, and not because they lack something of their own or because Nature has blundered. For nothing belongs to the nature of any thing except that which follows from the necessity of the nature of its efficient cause; and whatever follows from the necessity of the nature of its efficient cause must necessarily be so.

As for the terms "good" and "bad," they likewise indicate nothing positive in things considered in themselves, and are nothing but modes of thinking, or notions which we form from comparing things with one another. For one and the same thing can at the same time be good and bad, and also indifferent. For example, music is good for one who is melancholy, bad for one in mourning, and neither good nor bad for the deaf. However, although this is so, these terms ought to be retained. For since we desire to form the idea of a man which we may look to as a model of human nature, we shall find it useful to keep these terms in the sense I have indicated. So in what follows I shall mean by "good" that which we certainly know to be the means for our approaching nearer to the model of human nature that we set before ourselves, and by "bad" that which we certainly know prevents us from reproducing the said model. Again, we shall say that men are more perfect or less perfect in so far as they are nearer to or further from this model. For it is important to note that when I say that somebody passes from a state of less perfection to a state of greater perfection, and vice versa, I do not mean that he changes from one essence or form to another (for example, a horse is as completely destroyed if it changes into a man as it would be if it were to change into an insect), but that we conceive his power of activity, in so far as this is understood through his nature, to be increased or diminished.

Finally, by perfection in general I shall understand reality, as I have said; that is, the essence of any thing whatsoever in as far as it exists and acts in a definite manner, without taking duration into account. For no individual thing can be said to be more perfect on the grounds that it has continued in existence over a greater period of time. The duration of things cannot be determined from their essence, for the essence of things involves no fixed and determinate period of time. But any thing whatsoever, whether it be more perfect or less perfect, will always be able to persist in existing with that same force whereby it begins to exist, so that in this respect all things are equal.

PROPOSITION 67

A free man thinks of death least of all things, and his wisdom is a meditation of life, not of death.

Proof A free man, that is, he who lives solely according to the dictates of reason, is not guided by fear of death, but directly desires the good; that is, to act, to live, to preserve his own being in accordance with the principle of seeking his own advantage. So he thinks of death least of all things, and his wisdom is a meditation upon life.

PROPOSITION 68

If men were born free, they would form no conception of good and evil so long as they were free.

Proof I have said that a free man is he who is guided solely by reason. Therefore he who is born free and remains free has only adequate ideas and thus has no conception of evil, and consequently no conception of good (for good and evil are correlative).

PROPOSITION 73

The man who is guided by reason is more free in a state where he lives under a system of law than in solitude where he obeys only himself.

Proof The man who is guided by reason is not guided to obey out of fear, but in so far as he endeavors to preserve his own being according to the dictates of reason—that is, in so far as he endeavors to live freely—he desires to take account of the life and the good of the community, and consequently to live according to the laws of the state. Therefore the man who is guided by reason desires to adhere to the laws of the state so that he may live more freely.

APPENDIX: SUMMARY OF PART IV

In this Part my exposition of the right way of living is not arranged so that it can be seen at one view. The proofs are scattered so as to meet the convenience of logical deduction one from another. So I propose to gather them together here, and arrange them under their main headings.

1. All our endeavors or desires follow from the necessity of our nature in such a way that they can be understood either through it alone as their proximate cause, or in so far as we are a part of Nature, a part that cannot be adequately conceived through itself independently of the other individual parts.
2. Desires that follow from our nature in such a way that they can be understood through it alone are those that are related to the mind in so far as the mind is conceived as consisting of adequate ideas. The other desires are related to the mind only in so far as it conceives things inadequately; and their force and increase must be defined not by human power but by the power of things external to us. So the

former are rightly called active emotions, the latter passive emotions. For the former always indicate our power, the latter our weakness and fragmentary knowledge.

3. Our active emotions, that is, those desires that are defined by man's power, that is, by reason, are always good; the other desires can be either good or evil.

4. Therefore it is of the first importance in life to perfect the intellect, or reason, as far as we can, and the highest happiness or blessedness for mankind consists in this alone. For blessedness is nothing other than that self-contentment that arises from the intuitive knowledge of God. Now to perfect the intellect is also nothing other than to understand God and the attributes and actions of God that follow from the necessity of his nature. Therefore for the man who is guided by reason, the final goal, that is, the highest Desire whereby he strives to control all the others, is that by which he is brought to an adequate conception of himself and of all things that can fall within the scope of his understanding.

5. So there is no rational life without understanding, and things are good only in so far as they assist a man to enjoy the life of the mind, which is defined by understanding. Those things only do we call evil which hinder a man's capacity to perfect reason and to enjoy a rational life.

6. But since all those things of which man is the efficient cause are necessarily good, nothing evil can befall a man except from external causes, namely, in so far as he is a part of the whole of Nature, whose laws human nature is constrained to obey, and to which it must conform in almost an infinite number of ways.

7. A man is bound to be a part of Nature and to follow its universal order; but if he dwells among individuals who are in harmony with man's nature, by that very fact his power of activity will be assisted and fostered. But if he be among individuals who are by no means in harmony with his nature, he will scarcely be able to conform to them without a great change in himself.

8. Whatsoever in nature we deem evil, that is, capable of hindering us from being able to exist and to enjoy a rational life, it is permissible for us to remove in whatever seems the safer way. On the other hand, whatever we deem good, that is, advantageous for preserving our being and for enjoying a rational life, it is permissible for us to take for our use and to use it as we please. And as an absolute rule, it is permissible by the highest natural right for everyone to do what he judges to be to his own advantage.

9. Nothing can be more in harmony with the nature of any thing than other individuals of the same species, and so (see No. 7) there is

nothing more advantageous to man for preserving his own being and enjoying a rational life than a man who is guided by reason. Again, since among particular things we know of nothing more excellent than a man who is guided by reason, nowhere can each individual display the extent of his skill and genius more than in so educating men that they come at last to live under the sway of their own reason.

10. In so far as men feel envy or some other emotion of hatred towards one another, they are contrary to one another; consequently, the more powerful they are, the more they are to be feared than other individuals of Nature.

11. Nevertheless men's hearts are conquered not by arms but by love and nobility.

12. It is of the first importance to men to establish close relationships and to bind themselves together with such ties as may most effectively unite them into one body, and, as an absolute rule, to act in such a way as serves to strengthen friendship.

13. But to this end skill and watchfulness are needed. For men are changeable (few there are who live under the direction of reason) and yet for the most part envious, and more inclined to revenge than to compassion. So it needs an unusually powerful spirit to bear with each according to his disposition and to restrain oneself from imitating their emotions. On the other hand, those whose skill is to criticise mankind and to censure vice rather than to teach virtue, and to shatter men's spirit rather than strengthen it, are a stumbling-block both to themselves and to others. Hence many men, over-impatient and with false religious zeal, have chosen to live among beasts rather than among men, just as boys or young men, unable patiently to endure the upbraidings of their parents, run away to join the army, and prefer the hardships of war and tyrannical discipline to the comfort of home and parental admonition, and suffer any burdens to be imposed on them so long as they can spite their parents.

14. So although men for the most part allow lust to govern all their actions, the advantages that follow from living in their society far exceed the disadvantages. Therefore it is better to endure their injuries with patience, and to apply oneself to such measures as promote harmony and friendship.

15. Conduct that brings about harmony is that which is related to justice, equity, and honourable dealing. For apart from resenting injustice and unfairness, men also resent what is held to be base, or contempt for the accepted customs of the state. But for winning their love the most important factors are those that are concerned with religion and piety.

16. Harmony is also commonly produced by fear, but then it is untrustworthy. Furthermore, fear arises from weakness of spirit, and therefore does not belong to the use of reason. Neither does pity, although it bears the appearance of piety.

17. Again, men are won over by generosity, especially those who do not have the wherewithal to produce what is necessary to support life. Yet it is far beyond the power and resources of a private person to come to the assistance of everyone in need. For the wealth of a private person is quite unequal to such a demand. It is also a practical impossibility for one man to establish friendship with all. Therefore the care of the poor devolves upon society as a whole, and looks only to the common good.

. . .

30. Since those things are good which assist the parts of the body to perform their function, and pleasure consists in this, that a man's power is assisted or increased in so far as he is composed of mind and body, all those things that bring pleasure are good. On the other hand, since things do not act with the object of affecting us with pleasure, and their power of acting is not adjusted to suit our needs, and, lastly, since pleasure is usually related to one part of the body in particular, the emotions of pleasure (unless one exercises reason and care), and consequently the desires that are generated from them, can be excessive. There is this further point, that from emotion we place prime importance on what is attractive in the present, and we cannot feel as strongly about the future.

31. But superstition on the other hand seems to assert that what brings pain is good and what brings pleasure is bad. But, as we have already said, nobody but the envious takes pleasure in my weakness and my misfortune. For the more we are affected with pleasure, the more we pass to a state of greater perfection, and consequently the more we participate in the divine nature. Nor can pleasure ever be evil when it is controlled by true regard for our advantage. Now he who on the other hand is guided by fear and does good in order to avoid evil is not guided by reason.

32. But human power is very limited and is infinitely surpassed by the power of external causes, and so we do not have absolute power to adapt to our purposes things external to us. However, we shall patiently bear whatever happens to us that is contrary to what is required by consideration of our own advantage, if we are conscious that we have done our duty and that our power was not extensive enough for

us to have avoided the said things, and that we are a part of the whole of Nature whose order we follow. If we clearly and distinctly understand this, that part of us which is defined by the understanding, that is, the better part of us, will be fully resigned and will endeavor to persevere in that resignation. For in so far as we understand, we can desire nothing but that which must be, nor, in an absolute sense, can we find contentment in anything but truth. And so in so far as we rightly understand these matters, the endeavor of the better part of us is in harmony with the order of the whole of Nature.

PART V

OF THE POWER OF THE INTELLECT, OR OF HUMAN FREEDOM

PREFACE

I pass on finally to that part of the *Ethics* which concerns the method, or way, leading to freedom. In this part, then, I shall be dealing with the power of reason, pointing out the degree of control reason has over the emotions, and then what is freedom of mind, or blessedness, from which we shall see how much to be preferred is the life of the wise man to the life of the ignorant man. Now we are not concerned here with the manner or way in which the intellect should be perfected, nor yet with the science of tending the body so that it may correctly perform its functions. The latter is the province of medicine, the former of logic. Here then, as I have said, I shall be dealing only with the power of the mind or reason. Above all I shall be showing the degree and nature of its command over the emotions in checking and controlling them. For I have already demonstrated that we do not have absolute command over them.

PROPOSITION 10

As long as we are not assailed by emotions that are contrary to our nature, we have the power to arrange and associate affections of the body according to the order of the intellect.

Proof Emotions that are contrary to our nature, that is, which are bad, are bad to the extent that they hinder the mind from understanding. Therefore as long as we are not assailed by emotions contrary to our nature, the power of the mind whereby it endeavors to understand things is not hindered, and thus it has the ability to form clear and distinct ideas, deducing them from one another. Consequently in this case we have the ability to arrange and associate affections of the body according to the order of the intellect.

PROPOSITION 25

The highest conatus of the mind and its highest virtue is to understand things by the third kind of knowledge.

Proof The third kind of knowledge proceeds from the adequate idea of certain of God's attributes to the adequate knowledge of the essence of things, and the more we understand things in this way, the more we understand God. Therefore the highest virtue of the mind, that is, its power or nature, or its highest conatus is to understand things by this third kind of knowledge.

PROPOSITION 26

The more apt the mind is for understanding things by the third kind of knowledge, the more it desires to understand things by this same kind of knowledge.

Proof This is evident; for in so far as we conceive the mind to be capable of understanding things by the third kind of knowledge, to that extent we conceive it as determined to understand things by that same kind of knowledge. Consequently, the more the mind is capable of this, the more it desires it.

PROPOSITION 27

From this third kind of knowledge there arises the highest possible contentment of mind.

Proof The highest virtue of the mind is to know God, that is, to understand things by the third kind of knowledge, and this virtue is all the greater the more the mind knows things by the third kind of knowledge. So he who knows things by this third kind of knowledge passes to the highest state of human perfection, and consequently is affected by the highest pleasure, this pleasure being accompanied by the idea of himself and his own virtue. Therefore, from this kind of knowledge there arises the highest possible contentment.

PROPOSITION 28

The conatus, or desire, to know things by the third kind of knowledge, cannot arise from the first kind of knowledge, but from the second.

Proof This proposition is self-evident. For whatever we understand clearly and distinctly, we understand either through itself or through something else which is conceived through itself. That is, ideas which are clear and distinct in us or which are related to the third kind of knowledge cannot follow from fragmentary or confused ideas which are related to the first kind of knowledge, but from adequate ideas, that is, from the second or third kind of knowledge. Therefore, the desire to know things by the third kind of knowledge cannot arise from the first kind of knowledge, but from the second.

PROPOSITION 29

Whatever the mind understands under a form of eternity it does not understand from the fact that it conceives the present actual existence of the body, but from the fact that it conceives the essence of the body under a form of eternity.

Proof In so far as the mind conceives the present existence of its body, to that extent it conceives a duration that can be determined by time, and only to that extent does it have the power to conceive things in relation to time. But eternity cannot be explicated through duration. Therefore to that extent the mind does not have the power to conceive things under a form of eternity. But since it is the nature of reason to conceive things under a form of eternity, and since it belongs to the nature of mind, too, to conceive the essence of the body under a form of eternity, and since there belongs to the essence of mind nothing but these two ways of conceiving, it follows that this power to conceive things under a form of eternity pertains to the mind only in so far as it conceives the essence of the body under a form of eternity.

Scholium We conceive things as actual in two ways: either in so far as we conceive them as related to a fixed time and place, or in so far as we conceive them to be contained in God and to follow from the necessity of the divine nature. Now the things that are conceived as true or real in this second way, we conceive under a form of eternity, and their ideas involve the eternal and infinite essence of God.

PROPOSITION 30

Our mind, in so far as it knows both itself and the body under a form of eternity, necessarily has a knowledge of God, and knows that it is in God and is conceived through God.

Proof Eternity is the very essence of God in so far as this essence involves necessary existence. Therefore to conceive things under a form of eternity is to conceive things in so far as they are conceived through God's essence as real entities; that is, in so far as they involve existence through God's essence. Therefore our mind, in so far as it conceives itself and the body under a form of eternity, necessarily has knowledge of God, and knows . . . etc.

PROPOSITION 33

The intellectual love of God which arises from the third kind of knowledge is eternal.

Proof The third kind of knowledge is eternal, and therefore, the love that arises from it is also necessarily eternal.

Scholium Although this love towards God has had no beginning, it yet has all the perfections of love just as if it had originated in the manner we supposed in the corollary to the preceding proposition. There is no difference, except that the mind has possessed from eternity those perfections which we then supposed to be accruing to it, accompanied by the idea of God as eternal cause. If pleasure consists in the transition to a state of greater perfection, blessedness must surely consist in this, that the mind is endowed with perfection itself.

PROPOSITION 38

The greater the number of things the mind understands by the second and third kinds of knowledge, the less subject it is to emotions that are bad, and the less it fears death.

Proof The essence of the mind consists in knowledge. Therefore the greater the number of things the mind knows by the second and third kinds of knowledge, the greater is the part of it that survives, and consequently the greater is that part of it that is not touched by emotions contrary to our nature; that is by emotions that are bad. Therefore the greater the number of things the mind understands by the second and third kinds of knowledge, the greater is that part of it that remains unimpaired, and consequently the less subject it is to emotions . . . etc.

Scholium Hence we understand that point which I touched upon and which I promised to explain in this part, namely that death is less hurtful in proportion as the mind's clear and distinct knowledge is greater, and consequently the more the mind loves God. Again, since from the third kind of knowledge there arises the highest possible contentment, hence it follows that the human mind can be of such a nature that that part of it that we have shown to perish with the body is of no account compared with that part of it that survives. But I shall be dealing with this at greater length in due course.

PROPOSITION 42

Blessedness is not the reward of virtue, but virtue itself. We do not enjoy blessedness because we keep our lusts in check. On the contrary, it is because we enjoy blessedness that we are able to keep our lusts in check.

Proof Blessedness consists in love towards God, a love that arises from the third kind of knowledge, and so this love must be related to the mind in so far as the mind is active; and therefore it is virtue itself. That is the first point. Again, the more the mind enjoys this divine love or blessedness, the more it understands; that is, the more power it has over the emotions and the less subject it is to emotions that are bad. So the mind's enjoyment of this divine love or blessedness gives it the power to check lusts. And since human power to keep lusts in check consists solely in the intellect, nobody enjoys blessedness because he has kept his emotions in check. On the contrary, the power to keep lusts in check arises from blessedness itself.

Scholium I have now completed all that I intended to demonstrate concerning the power of the mind over the emotions and concerning the freedom of the mind. This makes clear how strong the wise man is and how much he surpasses the ignorant man whose motive force is only lust. The ignorant man, besides being driven hither and thither by external causes, never possessing true contentment of spirit, lives as if he were unconscious of himself, God, and things, and as soon as he ceases to be passive, he at once ceases to be at all. On the other hand, the wise man, in so far as he is considered as such, suffers scarcely any disturbance of spirit, but being conscious, by virtue of a certain eternal necessity, of himself, of God and of things, never ceases to be, but always possesses true spiritual contentment.

If the road I have pointed out as leading to this goal seems very difficult, yet it can be found. Indeed, what is so rarely discovered is bound to be hard. For if salvation were ready to hand and could be discovered without great toil, how could it be that it is almost universally neglected? All things excellent are as difficult as they are rare.

13

Bertrand Russell,
The Conquest of Happiness

The British philosopher, mathematician, and social reformer, Bertrand Russell (1872–1970) studied at Cambridge University and later became a lecturer at that school. His most influential work was on the foundations of mathematics, especially the ground-breaking Principia Mathematica, *which he wrote with Alfred North Whitehead (three volumes, 1910–1913). A pacifist and liberal about such matters as religion and sexuality, his views were quite controversial in the early part of the century. He was dismissed from Cambridge in 1916 and spent the rest of his life living on his earnings as a writer and a lecturer. He wrote on almost every area of philosophy and made an impact on popular culture with such books as* Mysticism and Logic *(1918) and* Why I Am Not a Christian *(1957). Russell was always a zealous defender of rationality in every area of life, as is evident in his lucid and commonsensical little book,* The Conquest of Happiness *(1930). He was awarded the Nobel Prize in literature in 1950.*

What Makes People Unhappy?

Animals are happy so long as they have health and enough to eat. Human beings, one feels, ought to be, but they are not, at least in a great majority of cases. If you are unhappy yourself, you will probably be prepared to admit that you are not exceptional in this. If you are happy, ask yourself how many of your friends are so. And when you have reviewed your friends, teach yourself the art of reading faces; make yourself receptive to the moods of those whom you meet in the course of an ordinary day.

> A mark in every face I meet,
> Marks of weakness, marks of woe

says Blake. Though the kinds are different, you will find that unhappiness meets you everywhere. Stand in a busy street during working hours, or on a main thoroughfare at a week-end, or at a dance of an evening; empty your mind of your own ego and let the personalities of the strangers about you take possession of you one after another. You will find that each of these different crowds has its own trouble. In the work-hour crowd you will see anxiety, excessive concentration, dyspepsia, lack of interest in anything but the struggle, incapacity for play, unconsciousness of their fellow creatures. On a main road at the week-end, you will see men and women, all comfortably off, and some very rich, engaged in the pursuit of pleasure. This pursuit is conducted by all at a uniform pace, that of the slowest car in the procession; it is impossible to see the road for the cars, or the scenery since looking aside would cause an accident; all the occupants of all the cars are absorbed in the desire to pass other cars, which they cannot do on account of the crowd; if their minds wander from this preoccupation, as will happen occasionally to those who are not themselves driving, unutterable boredom seizes upon them and stamps their features with trivial discontent.

· · ·

These considerations lead us to the problem of the individual: what can a man or woman, here and now, in the midst of our nostalgic society, do to achieve happiness for himself or herself? In discussing this problem, I shall confine my attention to those who are not subject to any extreme cause of outward misery. I shall assume a sufficient income to secure food and shelter, sufficient health to make ordinary bodily activities possible. I shall not consider the great catastrophes, such as loss of all one's children, or public disgrace. There are things to be said about such matters, and they are important things, but they belong to a different order from the things that I wish to say. My purpose is to suggest a cure for the ordinary day-to-day unhappiness from which most people in civilized countries suffer, and which is all the more unbearable because, having no obvious external cause, it appears inescapable. I believe this unhappiness to be very largely due to mistaken views of the world, mistaken ethics, mistaken habits of life, leading to destruction of that natural zest and appetite for possible things upon which all happiness, whether of men or animals, ultimately depends. These are matters which lie within the power of the individual, and I propose to suggest the change by which his happiness, given average good fortune, may be achieved.

Perhaps the best introduction to the philosophy which I wish to advocate will be a few words of autobiography. I was not born happy. As a child, my favorite hymn was: "Weary of earth and laden with my sin." At the age of five, I reflected that, if I should live to be seventy, I had only endured, so far, a fourteenth part of my whole life, and I felt the long-spread-out boredom ahead of me to be almost unendurable. In adolescence, I hated life and was continually on the verge of suicide, from which, however, I was restrained by the desire to know more mathematics. Now, on the contrary, I enjoy life; I might almost say that with every year that passes I enjoy it more. This is due partly to having discovered what were the things that I most desired, and having gradually acquired many of these things. Partly it is due to having successfully dismissed certain objects of desire—such as the acquisition of indubitable knowledge about something or other—as essentially unattainable. But very largely it is due to a diminishing preoccupation with myself. Like others who had a Puritan education, I had the habit of meditating on my sins, follies, and shortcomings. I seemed to myself—no doubt justly—a miserable specimen. Gradually I learned to be indifferent to myself and my deficiencies; I came to center my attention increasingly upon external objects: the state of the world, various branches of knowledge, individuals for whom I felt affection. External interests, it is true, bring each its own possibility of pain: the world may be plunged in war, knowledge in some direction may be hard to achieve, friends may die. But pains of these kinds do not destroy the essential quality of life, as do those that spring from disgust with self. And every external interest inspires some activity which, so long as the interest remains alive, is a complete preventive of *ennui*. Interest in oneself, on the contrary, leads to no activity of a progressive kind. It may lead to the keeping of a diary, to getting psychoanalyzed, or perhaps to becoming a monk. But the monk will not be happy until the routine of the monastery has made him forget his own soul. The happiness which he attributes to religion he could have obtained from becoming a crossing-sweeper, provided he were compelled to remain one. External discipline is the only road to happiness for those unfortunates whose self-absorption is too profound to be cured in any other way.

Self-absorption is of various kinds. We may take the sinner, the narcissist, and the megalomaniac as three very common types.

When I speak of "the sinner," I do not mean the man who commits sins: sins are committed by every one or no one, according to our definition of the word. I mean the man who is absorbed in the consciousness of sin. This man is perpetually incurring his own disapproval, which, if he is religious, he interprets as the disapproval of God. He has an image of himself as he thinks he ought to be, which is in continual conflict with his knowledge of himself as he is. If, in his conscious thought, he has long since discarded the maxims that he was taught at his mother's knee, his sense of sin may be buried deep in his unconscious, and only emerge when he is drunk or asleep. Nevertheless it may suffice to take the savor out of everything. At bottom he still accepts all the prohibitions he was taught in infancy. Swearing is wicked; drinking is wicked; ordinary business shrewdness is wicked; above all, sex is wicked. He does not, of course, abstain from any of these pleasures, but they are all poisoned for him by the feeling that they degrade him. The one pleasure that he desires with his whole soul is that of being approvingly caressed by his mother, which he can remember having experienced in childhood. This pleasure being no longer open to him, he feels that nothing matters; since he *must* sin, he decides to sin deeply. When he falls in love, he looks for maternal tenderness, but cannot accept it, because, owing to the mother-image, he feels no respect for any woman with whom he has sexual relations. Then, in his disappointment, he becomes cruel, repents of his cruelty, and starts afresh on the dreary round of imagined sin and real remorse. This is the psychology of very many apparently hard-boiled reprobates. What drives them astray is devotion to an unattainable object (mother or mother-substitute) together with the inculcation, in early years, of a ridiculous ethical code. Liberation from the tyranny of early beliefs and affections is the first step towards happiness for these victims of maternal "virtue."

Narcissism is, in a sense, the converse of an habitual sense of sin; it consists in the habit of admiring oneself and wishing to be admired. Up to a point it is, of course, normal, and not to be deplored; it is only in its excesses that it becomes a grave evil. In many women, especially rich society women, the capacity for feeling love is completely dried up, and is replaced by a powerful desire that all men should love them. When a woman of this kind is sure that a man loves her, she has no further use for him. The same thing occurs, though less frequently, with men; the classic example is the hero of that remarkable novel "Liaisons Dangereuses," which describes the love affairs of French aristocrats just before the Revolution. When vanity is carried to this height, there is no genuine interest in any other person, and therefore no real satisfaction to be obtained from love. Other interests fail even more disastrously. A narcissist, for example, inspired by the homage paid to great painters, may become an art student; but, as painting is for him a mere means to an end, the technique never becomes interesting, and no subject can be seen except in relation to self. The result is failure and disappointment, with ridicule instead of the expected adulation. The same thing applies to those novelists whose novels always have themselves idealized as heroines. All serious success in work depends upon some genuine interest in the material with which the work is concerned. The tragedy of one successful politician after another is the gradual substitution of narcissism for an interest in the community and the measures for which he stands. The man who is only interested in himself is not admirable, and is not felt to be so. Consequently the man whose sole concern with the world is that it shall admire him is not likely to achieve his object. But even if he does, he will not be completely happy, since human instinct is never completely self-centered, and the narcissist is limiting himself artificially just as truly as is the man dominated by a sense of sin. The primitive man might be proud of being a good hunter, but he also enjoyed the activity of the chase. Vanity, when it passes beyond a point, kills pleasure in every activity for its own sake, and thus leads inevitably to listlessness and boredom. Often its source is diffidence, and its cure lies in the growth of self-respect. But this is only to be gained by successful activity inspired by objective interests.

The megalomaniac differs from the narcissist by the fact that he wishes to be powerful rather than charming, and seeks to be feared rather than loved. To this type belong many lunatics and most of the great men in history. Love of power, like vanity, is a strong element in normal human nature, and as such is to be accepted; it becomes deplorable only when it is excessive or associated with an insufficient sense of reality. Where this occurs, it makes a man unhappy or foolish, if not both. The lunatic who thinks he is a crowned head may be, in a sense, happy, but his happiness is not of a kind that any sane person would envy. Alexander the Great was psychologically of the same type as the lunatic, though he possessed the talent to achieve the lunatic's dream. He could not, however, achieve his own dream, which enlarged its scope as his achievement grew. When it became clear that he was the greatest conqueror known to fame, he decided that he was a god. Was he a happy man? His drunkenness, his furious rages, his indifference to women, and his claim to divinity, suggest that he was not. There is no ultimate satisfaction in the cultivation of one element of human nature at the expense of all the others, nor in viewing all the world as raw material for the magnificence of one's own ego. Usually the megalomaniac, whether insane or nominally sane, is the product of some excessive humiliation. Napoleon suffered at school from inferiority to his schoolfellows, who were rich aristocrats, while he was a penurious scholarship boy. When he allowed the return of the *émigrés*, he had the satisfaction of seeing his former schoolfellows bowing down before him. What bliss! Yet it led to the wish to obtain a similar satisfaction at the expense of the Czar, and this led to Saint Helena. Since no man can be omnipotent, a life dominated wholly by love of power can hardly fail, sooner or later, to meet with obstacles that cannot be overcome. The knowledge that this is so can be prevented from obtruding on consciousness only by some form of lunacy, though if a man is sufficiently great he can imprison or execute those who point this out to him. Repressions in the political and in the psychoanalytic sense thus go hand in hand. And wherever psychoanalytic repression in any marked form takes place, there is no genuine happiness. Power kept within its proper bounds may add greatly to happiness, but as the sole end of life it leads to disaster, inwardly if not outwardly.

The psychological causes of unhappiness, it is clear, are many and various. But all have something in common. The typical unhappy man is one who, having been deprived in youth of some normal satisfaction, has come to value this one kind of satisfaction more than any other, and has therefore given to his life a one-sided direction, together with a quite undue emphasis upon the achievement as opposed to the activities connected with it. There is, however, a further development which is very common in the present day. A man may feel so completely thwarted that he seeks no form of satisfaction, but only distraction and oblivion. He then becomes a devotee of "pleasure." That is to say, he seeks to make life bearable by becoming less alive. Drunkenness, for example, is temporary suicide: the happiness that it brings is merely negative, a momentary cessation of unhappiness. The narcissist and the megalomaniac believe that happiness is possible, though they may adopt mistaken means of achieving it; but the man who seeks intoxication, in whatever form, has given up hope except in oblivion. In his case, the first thing to be done is to persuade him that happiness is desirable. Men who are unhappy, like men who sleep badly, are always proud of the fact. Perhaps their pride is like that of the fox who had lost his tail; if so, the way to cure it is to point out to them how they can grow a new tail. Very few men, I believe, will deliberately choose unhappiness if they see a way of being happy. I do not deny that such men exist, but they are not sufficiently numerous to be important. I shall therefore assume that the reader would rather be happy than unhappy. Whether I can help him to realize this wish, I do not know; but at any rate the attempt can do no harm.

. . .

The Happy Man

Happiness, as is evident, depends partly upon external circumstances and partly upon oneself. We have been concerned in this volume with the part which depends upon oneself, and we have been led to the view that so far as this part is concerned the recipe for happiness is a very simple one. It is thought by many that happiness is impossible without a creed of a more or less religious kind. It is thought by many who are themselves unhappy that their sorrows have complicated and highly intellectualized sources. I do not believe that such things are genuine causes of either happiness or unhappiness; I think they are only symptoms. The man who is unhappy will, as a rule, adopt an unhappy creed, while the man who is happy will adopt a happy creed; each may attribute his happiness or unhappiness to his beliefs, while the real causation is the other way round. Certain things are indispensable to the happiness of most men, but these are simple things: food and shelter, health, love, successful work and the respect of one's own herd. To some people parenthood also is essential. Where these things are lacking, only the exceptional man can achieve happiness; but where they are enjoyed, or can be obtained by well-directed effort, the man who is still unhappy is suffering from some psychological maladjustment which, if it is very grave, may need the services of a psychiatrist, but can in ordinary cases be cured by the patient himself, provided he sets about the matter in the right way. Where outward circumstances are not definitely unfortunate, a man should be able to achieve happiness, provided that his passions and interests are directed outward, not inward. It should be our endeavor, therefore, both in education and in attempts to adjust ourselves to the world, to aim at avoiding self-centered passions and at acquiring those affections and those interests which will prevent our thoughts from dwelling perpetually upon ourselves. It is not the nature of most men to be happy in a prison, and the passions which shut us up in ourselves constitute one of the worst kinds of prisons. Among such passions some of the commonest are fear, envy, the sense of sin, self-pity and self-admiration. In all these our desires are centered upon ourselves: there is no genuine interest in the outer world, but only a concern lest it should in some way injure us or fail to feed our ego. Fear is the principal reason why men are so unwilling to admit facts and so anxious to wrap themselves round in a warm garment of myth. But the thorns tear the warm garment and the cold blasts penetrate through the rents, and the man who has become accustomed to its warmth suffers far more from these blasts than a man who has hardened himself to them from the first. Moreover, those who deceive themselves generally know at bottom that they are doing so, and live in a state of apprehension lest some untoward event should force unwelcome realizations upon them.

One of the great drawbacks to self-centered passions is that they afford so little variety in life. The man who loves only himself cannot, it is true, be accused of promiscuity in his affections, but he is bound in the end to suffer intolerable boredom from the invariable sameness of the object of his devotion. The man who suffers from a sense of sin is suffering from a particular kind of self-love. In all this vast universe the thing that appears to him of most importance is that he himself should be virtuous. It is a grave defect in certain forms of traditional religion that they have encouraged this particular kind of self-absorption.

The happy man is the man who lives objectively, who has free affections and wide interests, who secures his happiness through these interests and affections and through the fact that they, in turn, make him an object of interest and affection to many others. To be the recipient of affection is a potent cause of happiness, but the man who demands affection is not the man upon whom it is bestowed. The man who receives affection is, speaking broadly, the man who gives it. But it is useless to attempt to give it as a calculation, in the way in which one might lend money at interest, for a calculated affection is not genuine and is not felt to be so by the recipient.

What then can a man do who is unhappy because he is encased in self? So long as he continues to think about the causes of his unhappiness, he continues to be self-centered and therefore does not get outside the vicious circle; if he is to get outside it, it must be by genuine interests, not by simulated interests adopted merely as a medicine. Although this difficulty is real, there is nevertheless much that he can do if he has rightly diagnosed his trouble. If, for example, his trouble is due to a sense of sin, conscious or unconscious, he can first persuade his conscious mind that he has no reason to feel sinful, and then proceed, by the kind of technique that we have considered in earlier chapters, to plant this rational conviction in his unconscious mind, concerning himself meanwhile with some more or less neutral activity. If he succeeds in dispelling the sense of sin, it is probable that genuinely objective interests will arise spontaneously. If his trouble is self-pity, he can deal with it in the same manner after first persuading himself that there is nothing extraordinarily unfortunate in his circumstances. If fear is his trouble, let him practice exercises designed to give courage. Courage in war has been recognized from time immemorial as an important virtue, and a great part of the training of boys and young men has been devoted to producing a type of character capable of fearlessness in battle. But moral courage and intellectual courage have been much less studied; they also, however, have their technique. Admit to yourself every day at least one painful truth; you will find this quite as useful as the Boy Scout's daily kind action. Teach yourself to feel that life would still be worth living even if you were not, as of course you are, immeasurably superior to all your friends in virtue and in intelligence. Exercises of this sort prolonged through several years will at last enable you to admit facts without flinching, and will, in so doing, free you from the empire of fear over a very large field.

What the objective interests are to be that will arise in you when you have overcome the disease of self-absorption must be left to the spontaneous workings of your nature and of external circumstances. Do not say to yourself in advance, "I should be happy if I could become absorbed in stamp-collecting," and thereupon set to work to collect stamps, for it may well happen that you will fail altogether to find stamp-collecting interesting. Only what genuinely interests you can be of any use to you, but you may be pretty sure that genuine objective interests will grow up as soon as you have learnt not to be immersed in self.

The happy life is to an extraordinary extent the same as the good life.

Professional moralists have made too much of self-denial, and in so doing have put the emphasis in the wrong place. Conscious self-denial leaves a man self-absorbed and vividly aware of what he has sacrificed; in consequence it fails often of its immediate object and almost always of its ultimate purpose. What is needed is not self-denial, but that kind of direction of interest outward which will lead spontaneously and naturally to the same acts that a person absorbed in the pursuit of his own virtue could only perform by means of conscious self-denial. I have written in this book as a hedonist, that is to say, as one who regards happiness as the good, but the acts to be recommended from the point of view of the hedonist are on the whole the same as those to be recommended by the sane moralist. The moralist, however, is too apt, though this is not, of course, universally true, to stress the act rather than the state of mind. The effects of an act upon the agent will be widely different, according to his state of mind at the moment. If you see a child drowning and save it as the result of a direct impulse to bring help, you will emerge none the worse morally. If, on the other hand, you say to yourself, "It is the part of virtue to succor the helpless, and I wish to be a virtuous man, therefore I must save this child," you will be an even worse man afterwards than you were before. What applies in this extreme case, applies in many other instances that are less obvious.

There is another difference, somewhat more subtle, between the attitude towards life that I have been recommending and that which is recommended by the traditional moralists. The traditional moralist, for example, will say that love should be unselfish. In a certain sense he is right, that is to say, it should not be selfish beyond a point, but it should undoubtedly be of such a nature that one's own happiness is bound up in its success. If a man were to invite a lady to marry him on the ground that he ardently desired her happiness and at the same time considered that she would afford him ideal opportunities of self-abnegation, I think it may be doubted whether she would be altogether pleased. Undoubtedly we should desire the happiness of those whom we love, but not as an alternative to our own. In fact the whole antithesis between self and the rest of the world, which is implied in the doctrine of self-denial, disappears as soon as we have any genuine interest in persons or things outside ourselves. Through such interests a man comes to feel himself part of the stream of life, not a hard separate entity like a billiard ball, which can have no relation with other such entities except that of collision. All unhappiness depends upon some kind of disintegration or lack of integration; there is disintegration within the self through lack of coordination between the conscious and the unconscious mind; there is lack of integration between the self and society, where the two are not knit together by the force of objective interests and affections. The happy man is the man who does not suffer from either of these failures of unity, whose personality is neither divided against itself nor pitted against the world. Such a man feels himself a citizen of the universe, enjoying freely the spectacle that it offers and the joys that it affords, untroubled by the thought of death because he feels himself not really separate from those who will come after him. It is in such profound instinctive union with the stream of life that the greatest joy is to be found.

14

Michel de Montaigne, "Of Experience," from the *Essays*

A nobleman whose estate was not far from Bordeaux, Montaigne (1533–1592) served as mayor of Bordeaux and was an advisor to both the Catholic and Protestant factions in the brutal wars of religion sweeping through France. At the age of thirty-eight, he retired from his law practice to spend his time writing what he called essais, *the French word for "trial" or "attempt," a new literary form invented by Montaigne. These essays, generally rambling and inconclusive reflections on various topics, build on Montaigne's knowledge of classical Stoic, Epicurean, and Skeptical authors. From the Pyrrhonian skeptics he learned that all things are changing, that one's beliefs are determined by one's cultural and historical context, and that it is best to seek quietude rather than certainty. The more he worked and reworked his essays, the more Montaigne was convinced that there is no way to arrive at definite answers about the most important questions in life. "I do not portray being," he wrote; "I portray passing."*

What emerges from the Essays *is an awareness of the mutability, uncertainty, and fragility of the human condition. Montaigne took as his motto the words "Que sais-je?"—"What do I know?" His late essay, "Of Experience," displays his open-ended and playful form of investigation. Studying oneself is an endless task, but if you are honest about what shows up in the flow of experience, you can arrive at some tentative conclusions about your own nature, and you can dedicate your life to being true to that nature. Montaigne's image of self-exploration stands in stark contrast to the preoccupation with self-mastery and total clarity found in most Western inquiries into the good life. The* Essays, *consisting of winding, unstructured attempts at self-discovery, lead to an ideal of tolerance and self-acceptance, and to a willingness to embrace life on its own terms.*

Men do not know the natural infirmity of their mind: it does nothing but ferret and quest, and keeps incessantly whirling around, building up and becoming entangled in its own work, like our silkworms, and is suffocated in it. *A mouse in a pitch barrel* [Erasmus]. It thinks it notices from a distance some sort of glimmer of imaginary light and truth; but while running toward it, it is crossed by so many difficulties and obstacles, and diverted by so many new quests, that it strays from the road, bewildered. Not very different from what happened to Aesop's dogs, who, discovering something that looked like a dead body floating in the sea, and being unable to approach it, attempted to drink up the water and dry up the passage, and choked in the attempt. To which may be joined what a certain Crates said of the writings of Heraclitus, that they needed a good swimmer for a reader, so that the depth and weight of Heraclitus' learning should not sink him and drown him.

It is only personal weakness that makes us content with what others or we ourselves have found out in this hunt for knowledge. An abler man will not rest content with it. There is always room for a successor, yes, and for ourselves, and a road in another direction. There is no end to our researches; our end is in the other world. It is a sign of contraction of the mind when it is content, or of weariness. A spirited mind never stops within itself; it is always aspiring and going beyond its strength; it has impulses beyond its powers of achievement. If it does not advance and press forward and stand at bay and clash, it is only half alive. Its pursuits are boundless and without form; its food is wonder, the chase, ambiguity. Apollo revealed this clearly enough, always speaking to us equivocally, obscurely, and obliquely, not satisfying us, but keeping our minds interested and busy. It is an irregular, perpetual motion, without model and without aim. Its inventions excite, pursue, and produce one another.

> So in a running stream one wave we see
> After another roll incessantly,
> And line by line, each does eternally
> Pursue the other, each the other flee.
> By this one, that one ever on is sped,
> And this one by the other ever led;
> The water still does into water go,
> Still the same brook, but different waters flow.
>
> LA BOÉTIE

From Michel de Montaigne, *Selections from the Essays*, edited and translated by Donald M. Frame. Copyright 1943, 1973. Reprinted by permission of Harlan Davidson, Inc.

It is more of a job to interpret the interpretations than to interpret the things, and there are more books about books than about any other subject: we do nothing but write glosses about each other. The world is swarming with commentaries; of authors there is a great scarcity.

Is it not the chief and most reputed learning of our times to learn to understand the learned? Is that not the common and ultimate end of all studies?

Our opinions are grafted upon one another. The first serves as a stock for the second, the second for the third. Thus we scale the ladder, step by step. And thence it happens that he who has mounted highest has often more honor than merit; for he has only mounted one speck higher on the shoulders of the next last.

How often and perhaps how stupidly have I extended my book to make it speak of itself! Stupidly, if only for this reason, that I should have remembered what I say of others who do the same: that these frequent sheep's eyes at their own work testify that their heart thrills with love for it, and that even the rough, disdainful blows with which they beat it are only the love taps and affectations of maternal fondness; in keeping with Aristotle, to whom self-appreciation and self-depreciation often spring from the same sort of arrogance. For as for my excuse, that I ought to have more liberty in this than others, precisely because I write of myself and my writings as of my other actions, because my theme turns in upon itself—I do not know whether everyone will accept it.

. . .

I study myself more than any other subject. That is my metaphysics, that is my physics.

> By what art God our home, the world, controls;
> Whence the moon rises, where she sets, how rolls
> Her horns together monthly, and again
> Grows full; whence come the winds that rule the main;
> Where Eurus' blast holds sway; whence springs the rain
> That ever fills the clouds; whether some day
> The citadels of the world will pass away.
>
> PROPERTIUS

> Inquire, you who the laboring world survey.
>
> LUCAN

In this universe of things I ignorantly and negligently let myself be guided by the general law of the world. I shall know it well enough when I feel it. My knowledge could not make it change its path; it will not modify itself for me. It is folly to hope it, and greater folly to be troubled about it, since it is necessarily uniform, public, and common. The goodness and capacity of the governor should free us absolutely and fully from worrying about his government.

Philosophical inquiries and meditations serve only as food for our curiosity. The philosophers with much reason refer us to the rules of Nature: but these have no concern with such sublime knowledge. The philosophers falsify them and show us the face of Nature painted in too high a color, and too sophisticated, whence spring so many varied portraits of so uniform a subject. As she has furnished us with feet to walk with, so she has given us wisdom to guide us in life: a wisdom not so ingenious, robust, and pompous as that of their invention, but correspondingly easy and salutary, performing very well what the other talks about, in a man who has the good fortune to know how to occupy himself simply and in an orderly way, that is to say naturally. The more simply we trust to Nature, the more wisely we trust to her. Oh, what a sweet and soft and healthy pillow is ignorance and incuriosity, to rest a well-made head!

I would rather be an authority on myself than on Cicero.[1] In the experience I have of myself I find enough to make me wise, if I were a good scholar. He who calls back to mind the excess of his past anger, and how far this fever carried him away, sees the ugliness of this passion better than in Aristotle, and conceives a more justified hatred for it. He who remembers the evils he has undergone, and those that have threatened him, and the slight causes that have changed him from one state to another, prepares himself in that way for future changes and for recognizing his condition. The life of Caesar has no more to show us than our own; an emperor's or an ordinary man's, it is still a life subject to all human accidents. Let us only listen: we tell ourselves all we most need.

He who remembers having been mistaken so many, many times in his own judgment, is he not a fool if he does not distrust it forever after? When I find myself convicted of a false opinion by another man's reasoning, I do not so much learn what new thing he has told me and this particular bit of ignorance—that would be small gain—as I learn my weakness in general, and the treachery of my understanding; whence I derive the reformation of the whole mass. With all my other errors I do the same, and I feel that this rule is very useful for my life. I do not regard the species and the individual, like a stone I have stumbled on; I learn to mistrust my gait throughout, and I strive to regulate it. To learn that we

1. The 1588 edition read: "than on Plato."

have said or done a foolish thing, that is nothing; we must learn that we are nothing but fools, a far broader and more important lesson.

The slips that my memory has made so often, even when it reassures me most about itself, are not vainly lost on me; there is no use in her swearing to me now and assuring me, I shake my ears. The first opposition offered to her testimony puts me in suspense, and I would not dare trust her in any weighty matter, or guarantee her in another person's affairs. And were it not that what I do for lack of memory, others do still more often for lack of good faith, I should always accept the truth in matters of fact from another man's mouth rather than from my own.

If each man watched closely the effects and circumstances of the passions that dominate him, as I have done with the ones I have fallen prey to, he would see them coming and would check their impetuosity and course a bit. They do not always leap at our throats at a single bound; there are threats and degrees.

> As when a rising wind makes white waves fly,
> The sea heaves slowly, raises billows high,
> And surges from the depths to meet the sky.
>
> VIRGIL

Judgment holds in me a magisterial seat, at least it carefully tries to. It lets my feelings go their way, both hatred and friendship, even the friendship I bear myself, without being changed and corrupted by them. If it cannot reform the other parts according to itself, at least it does not let itself be deformed to match them; it plays its game apart.

The advice to everyone to know himself must have an important effect, since the god of learning and light had it planted on the front of his temple, as comprising all the counsel he had to give us. Plato also says that wisdom is nothing else but the execution of this command, and Socrates, in Xenophon, verifies it in detail.

The difficulties and obscurity in any science are perceived only by those who have access to it. For a man needs at least some degree of intelligence to be able to notice that he does not know; and we must push against a door to know that it is closed to us. Whence arises this Platonic subtlety, that neither those who know need inquire, since they know, nor those who do not know, since in order to inquire they must know what they are inquiring about. Thus in this matter of knowing oneself, the fact that everyone is seen to be so cocksure and self-satisfied, that everyone thinks he understands enough about himself, signifies that everyone understands nothing about it, as Socrates teaches Euthydemus in Xenophon.

I, who make no other profession, find in me such infinite depth and variety, that what I have learned bears no other fruit than to make me realize how much I still have to learn. To my weakness, so often recognized, I owe the inclination I have to modesty, obedience to the beliefs that are prescribed me, a constant coolness and moderation in my opinions, and my hatred for that aggressive and quarrelsome arrogance that believes and trusts wholly in itself, a mortal enemy of discipline and truth. Hear them laying down the law: the first stupidities that they advance are in the style in which men establish religions and laws. *Nothing is more discreditable than to have assertion and proof precede knowledge and perception* [Cicero].

Aristarchus used to say that in former times there were scarcely seven wise men in the world, and that in his time there were scarcely seven ignorant men. Would we not have more reason than he to say that in our time? Affirmation and opinionativeness are express signs of stupidity. This man must have fallen on his nose a hundred times in one day; there he stands on his "ergos,"[2] as positive and unshaken as before. You would think that someone had since infused in him some sort of new soul and intellectual vigor, and that he was like that ancient son of the earth, who renewed his courage and strength by his fall:

> Whose limbs, however tired,
> By touching Mother Earth, with energy were fired.
>   LUCAN

Does not this headstrong incorrigible think that he picks up a new mind by picking up a new argument?

It is from my experience that I affirm human ignorance, which is, in my opinion, the most certain fact in the school of the world. Those who will not conclude their own ignorance from so vain an example as mine, or as theirs, let them recognize it through Socrates, the master of masters. For the philosopher Antisthenes used to say to his pupils: "Let us go, you and I, to hear Socrates; there I shall be a pupil with you." And, maintaining this doctrine of his Stoic sect, that virtue was enough to make a life fully happy and free from need of anything whatever, he would add: "Excepting the strength of Socrates."

This long attention that I devote to studying myself trains me also to judge passably of others, and there are few things of which I speak more felicitously and excusably. It often happens that I see and distinguish the

---

2. Montaigne's word, *ergots*, means the spurs or hackles of a gamecock. But it also may mean *ergos* or *ergotisms*, the quibbling use of Latin *ergo* (therefore) by a choplogic (see Rabelais, *Pantagruel*, chap. 10).

characters of my friends more exactly than they do themselves. I have astonished at least one by the pertinence of my description, and have given him information about himself.

. . .

Experience has further taught me this, that we ruin ourselves by impatience. Troubles have their life and their limits, their illnesses and their health.

The constitution of diseases is patterned after the constitution of animals. They have their destiny, limited from their birth, and their days. He who tries to cut them short imperiously by force, in the midst of their course, prolongs and multiplies them, and stimulates them instead of appeasing them. I agree with Crantor, that we must neither obstinately and heedlessly oppose evils nor weakly succumb to them, but give way to them naturally, according to their condition and our own. We should give free passage to diseases; and I find that they do not stay so long with me, who let them go ahead; and some of those that are considered most stubborn and tenacious, I have shaken off by their own decadence, without help and without art, and against the rules of medicine. Let us give Nature a chance; she knows her business better than we do. "But so-and-so died of it." So will you, if not of that disease, of some other. And how many have not failed to die of it, with three doctors at their backsides? Example is a hazy mirror, reflecting all things in all ways. If it is a pleasant medicine, take it; it is always that much present gain. I shall never balk at the name or the color, if it is delicious and appetizing. Pleasure is one of the principal kinds of profit.

I have allowed colds, gouty discharges, looseness, palpitations of the heart, migraines, and other ailments to grow old and die a natural death within me; I lost them when I had half trained myself to harbor them. They are conjured better by courtesy than by defiance. We must meekly suffer the laws of our condition. We are born to grow old, to grow weak, to be sick, in spite of all medicine. That is the first lesson that the Mexicans give their children, when, as soon as they come out of their mother's womb, they greet them thus: "Child, you have come into the world to endure; endure, suffer, and keep quiet."

It is unjust to complain that what may happen to anyone has happened to someone. *Complain if anything has been unjustly decreed against you alone* [Seneca]. Look at an old man praying God to keep him in entire and vigorous health, that is to say, to restore his youth.

Fool, why aspire in vain with childish prayers?
OVID

Is it not madness? His condition does not allow it. The gout, the stone, indigestion, are symptoms of length of years, as are heat, rains, and winds of long journeys. Plato does not believe that Aesculapius was at any pains to attempt by treatment to prolong life in a wasted and feeble body, useless to its country, useless to its calling and for producing healthy, robust children; and he does not consider such concern consistent with divine justice and forethought, which should guide all things toward utility. My good man, it is all over. No one can put you on your feet again; at most they will plaster and prop you up a bit, and prolong your misery an hour or so:

> Like one who, wishing to support a while
> A tottering building, props the creaking pile,
> Until one day the house, the props, and all
> Together with a dreadful havoc fall.
>   MAXIMIANUS

We must learn to endure what we cannot avoid. Our life is composed, like the harmony of the world, of contrary things, also of different tones, sweet and harsh, sharp and flat, soft and loud. If a musician liked only one kind, what would he have to say? He must know how to use them together and blend them. And so must we do with good and evil, which are consubstantial with our life. Our existence is impossible without this mixture, and one element is no less necessary for it than the other. To try to kick against natural necessity is to imitate the folly of Ctesiphon, who undertook a kicking match with his mule.

· · ·

But you do not die of being sick, you die of being alive. Death kills you well enough without the help of illness. And illnesses have put off death for some, who have lived longer for thinking that they were on their way out and dying. Furthermore, there are diseases, as there are wounds, that are medicinal and salutary.

The stone is often no less fond of life than you. We see men in whom it has continued from their childhood up to their extreme old age; and if they had not deserted it, it was ready to accompany them still further. You kill it more often than it kills you; and even if it set before you the picture of imminent death, would it not be a kind service for a man of that age to bring him home to meditations upon his end?

And what is worse, you have no reason left for being cured. In any case, the common fate will call you any day. Consider how artfully and gently the stone weans you from life and detaches you from the world; not forcing you with tyrannical subjections, like so many other afflictions that you see in old people, which keep them continually hobbled and without relief from infirmities and pains, but by warnings and instructions repeated at intervals, intermingled with long pauses for rest, as if to give you a chance to meditate and repeat its lesson at your leisure. To give you a chance to form a sound judgment and make up your mind to it like a brave man, it sets before you the lot that is your condition, the good and also the bad, and a life that on the same day is now very joyous, now unbearable. If you do not embrace death, at least you shake hands with it once a month. Whereby you have the further hope that it will catch you some day without a threat, and that, being so often led to the port, confident that you are still within the accustomed limits, some morning you and your confidence will have crossed the water unawares. We have no cause for complaint about illnesses that divide the time fairly with health.

I am obliged to Fortune for assailing me so often with the same kind of weapons. She fashions and trains me against them by use, hardens and accustoms me. Henceforth I know just about at what cost I shall be quit of them.

. . .

I, who boast of embracing the pleasures of life so assiduously and so particularly, find in them, when I look at them thus minutely, virtually nothing but wind. But what of it? We are all wind. And even the wind, more wisely than we, loves to make a noise and move about, and is content with its own functions, without wishing for stability and solidity, qualities that do not belong to it.

The pure pleasures of imagination, as well as the pains, some say, are the greatest, as the scales of Critolaus expressed it. No wonder; it composes them to its liking and cuts them out of whole cloth. I see signal, and perhaps desirable, examples of this every day. But I, being of a mixed constitution, and coarse, am unable to cling so completely to this single and simple object as to keep myself from grossly pursuing the present pleasures of the general human law—intellectually sensual, sensually intellectual. The Cyrenaic philosophers hold that the bodily pleasures, like the pains, are the more powerful, as being both twofold and more equitable.

There are some who from savage stupidity, as Aristotle says, are disgusted with them; I know some who are that way from ambition. Why do they not also give up breathing? Why do they not live on their own air, and refuse light, because it is free and costs them neither invention nor vigor? Let Mars, or Pallas, or Mercury give them sustenance, instead of Venus, Ceres, and Bacchus, just to see what happens. Won't they try to square the circle while perched on their wives! I hate to have people order us to keep our minds in the clouds while our bodies are at table. I would not have the mind nailed down to it nor wallowing at it, but attending to it; sitting at it, not lying down at it.

Aristippus defended the body alone, as if we had no soul; Zeno embraced only the soul, as if we had no body. Both were wrong. Pythagoras, they say, followed a philosophy that was all contemplation, Socrates one that was all conduct and action; Plato found the balance between the two. But they say so to make a good story, and the true balance is found in Socrates, and Plato is much more Socratic than Pythagorean, and it becomes him better.

When I dance, I dance; when I sleep, I sleep; yes, and when I walk alone in a beautiful orchard, if my thoughts have been dwelling on extraneous incidents for some part of the time, for some other part I bring them back to the walk, to the orchard, to the sweetness of this solitude, and to me. Nature has observed this principle like a mother, that the actions she has enjoined on us for our need should also give us pleasure; and she invites us to them not only through reason, but also through appetite. It is unjust to infringe her laws.

When I see both Caesar and Alexander, in the thick of their great tasks, so fully enjoying natural and therefore necessary and just pleasures, I do not say that that is relaxing their souls, I say that it is toughening them, subordinating these violent occupations and laborious thoughts, by the vigor of their spirits, to the practice of everyday life: wise men, had they believed that this was their ordinary occupation, the other the extraordinary.

We are great fools. "He has spent his life in idleness," we say; "I have done nothing today." What, have you not lived? That is not only the fundamental but the most illustrious of your occupations. "If I had been placed in a position to manage great affairs, I would have shown what I could do." Have you been able to think out and manage your own life? You have done the greatest task of all. To show and exploit her resources Nature has no need of fortune; she shows herself equally on all levels and behind a curtain as well as without one. To compose our character is our duty, not to compose books, and to win, not battles and provinces, but order and tranquillity in our conduct. Our great and glorious masterpiece is to live appropriately. All other things, ruling, hoarding, building, are only little appendages and props, at most.

. . .

Popular opinion is wrong: it is much easier to go along the sides, where the outer edge serves as a limit and a guide, than by the middle way, wide and open, and to go by art than by nature; but it is also much less noble and less commendable. Greatness of soul is not so much pressing upward and forward as knowing how to set oneself in order and circumscribe oneself. It regards as great whatever is adequate, and shows its elevation by liking moderate things better than eminent ones. There is nothing so beautiful and legitimate as to play the man well and properly, no knowledge so hard to acquire as the knowledge of how to live this life well and naturally; and the most barbarous of our maladies is to despise our being.

He who wants to detach his soul, let him do it boldly, if he can, when his body is ill, to free it from the contagion; at other times, on the contrary, let the soul assist and favor the body and not refuse to take part in its natural pleasures and enjoy them conjugally, bringing to them moderation, if it is the wiser of the two, for fear that through lack of discretion they may merge into pain. Intemperance is the plague of sensual pleasure; and temperance is not its scourge, it is its seasoning. Eudoxus, who made pleasure the supreme good, and his fellows, who raised it to such high value, savored it in its most charming sweetness by means of temperance, which they possessed in singular and exemplary degree.

I order my soul to look upon both pain and pleasure with a gaze equally self-controlled—*for it is as wrong for the soul to overflow from joy as to contract in sorrow* [Cicero]—and equally firm, but gaily at the one, at the other severely, and, according to its ability, as anxious to extinguish the one as to extend the other. Viewing good things sanely implies viewing bad things sanely. And pain has something not to be avoided in its mild beginning, and pleasure something to be avoided in its excessive ending. Plato couples them together and claims that it is equally the function of fortitude to fight against pain and against the immoderate and bewitching blandishments of pleasure. They are two fountains: whoever draws the right amount from the right one at the right time, whether city, man, or beast, is very fortunate. The first we must take as a necessary medicine, but more sparingly; the other for thirst, but not to the point of drunkenness. Pain, pleasure, love, hatred, are the first things a child feels; if when reason comes they cling to her, that is virtue.

I have a vocabulary all my own. I "pass the time," when it is rainy and disagreeable; when it is good, I do not want to pass it; I savor it, I cling to it. We must run through the bad and settle on the good. This ordinary expression "pastime" or "pass the time" represents the habit of those wise folk who think they can make no better use of their life than to let it slip by and escape it, pass it by, sidestep it, and, as far as in them lies, ignore it and run away from it, as something irksome and contemptible. But I know it to be otherwise and find it both agreeable and worth prizing, even in its last decline, in which I now possess it; and nature has placed it in our hands adorned with such favorable conditions that we have only ourselves to blame if it weighs on us and if it escapes us unprofitably. *The life of the fool is joyless, full of trepidation, given over wholly to the future* [Seneca]. However, I am reconciling myself to the thought of losing it, without regret, but as something that by its nature must be lost; not as something annoying and troublesome. Then too, not to dislike dying is properly becoming only to those who like living. It takes management to enjoy life. I enjoy it twice as much as others, for the measure of enjoyment depends on the greater or lesser attention that we lend it. Especially at this moment, when I perceive that mine is so brief in time, I try to increase it in weight; I try to arrest the speed of its flight by the speed with which I grasp it, and to compensate for the haste of its ebb by my vigor in using it. The shorter my possession of life, the deeper and fuller I must make it.

Others feel the sweetness of some satisfaction and of prosperity; I feel it as they do, but it is not in passing and slipping by. Instead we must study it, savor it, and ruminate it, to give proper thanks for it to him who grants it to us. They enjoy the other pleasures as they do that of sleep, without being conscious of them. To the end that sleep itself should not escape me thus stupidly, at one time I saw fit to have mine disturbed, so that I might gain a glimpse of it. I meditate on any satisfaction; I do not skim over it, I sound it, and bend my reason, now grown peevish and hard to please, to welcome it. Do I find myself in some tranquil state? Is there some voluptuous pleasure that tickles me? I do not let my senses pilfer it, I bring my soul into it, not to implicate herself, but to enjoy herself, not to lose herself but to find herself. And I set her, for her part, to admire herself in this prosperous estate, to weigh and appreciate and amplify the happiness of it. She measures the extent of her debt to God for being at peace with her conscience and free from other inner passions, for having her body in its natural condition, enjoying controlledly and adequately the agreeable and pleasant functions with which he is pleased to compensate by his grace for the pains with which his justice chastises us in its turn; how much it is worth to her to be lodged at such a point that wherever she casts her eyes, the sky is calm around her: no desire, no fear or doubt to disturb the air for her, no difficulty, past, present, or future, over which her imagination may not pass without hurt.

This consideration gains great luster by comparison between my condition and that of others. Thus I set before me in a thousand forms those who are carried away and tossed about by fortune or their own error, and also those, closer to my way, who accept their good fortune so languidly and indifferently. They are the people who really "pass their time"; they pass over the present and what they possess, to be the slaves of hope, and for shadows and vain images that fancy dangles before them—

> Like ghosts that after death are said to flit,
> Or visions that delude the slumbering wit
>
> VIRGIL

—which hasten and prolong their flight the more they are pursued. The fruit and goal of their pursuit is to pursue, as Alexander said that the purpose of his work was to work,

> Believing nothing done while aught was left to do.
>
> LUCAN

As for me, then, I love life and cultivate it just as God has been pleased to grant it to us. I do not go about wishing that it should lack the need to eat and drink, and it would seem to me no less excusable a failing to wish that need to be doubled. *The wise man is the keenest searcher for natural treasures* [Seneca]. Nor do I wish that we should sustain ourselves by merely putting into our mouths a little of that drug by which Epimenides took away his appetite and kept himself alive; nor that we should beget children insensibly with our fingers or our heels, but rather, with due respect, that we could also beget them voluptuously with our fingers and heels; nor that the body should be without desire and without titillation. Those are ungrateful and unfair complaints. I accept with all my heart and with gratitude what nature has done for me, and I am pleased with myself and proud of myself that I do. We wrong that great and all-powerful Giver by refusing his gift, nullifying it, and disfiguring it. Himself all good, he has made all things good. *All things that are according to nature are worthy of esteem* [Cicero].

Of the opinions of philosophy I most gladly embrace those that are most solid, that is to say, most human and most our own; my opinions, in conformity with my conduct, are low and humble. Philosophy is very childish, to my mind, when she gets up on her hind legs and preaches to us that it is a barbarous alliance to marry the divine with the earthly, the reasonable with the unreasonable, the severe with the indulgent, the honorable with the dishonorable; that sensual pleasure is a brutish thing unworthy of being enjoyed by the wise man; that the only pleasure he derives from the enjoyment of a beautiful young wife is the pleasure of his consciousness of doing the right thing, like putting on his boots for a useful ride. May her followers have no more right and sinews and sap in deflowering their wives than her lessons have!

That is not what Socrates says, her tutor and ours. He prizes bodily pleasure as he should, but he prefers that of the mind, as having more power, constancy, ease, variety, and dignity. The latter by no means goes alone, according to him—he is not so fanciful—but only comes first. For him temperance is the moderator, not the adversary, of pleasures.

Nature is a gentle guide, but no more gentle than wise and just. *We must penetrate into the nature of things and clearly see exactly what it demands* [Cicero]. I seek her footprints everywhere. We have confused them with artificial tracks, and for that reason the sovereign good of the Academics and the Peripatetics, which is "to live according to nature," becomes hard to limit and express; also that of the Stoics, a neighbor to the other, which is "to consent to nature."

Is it not an error to consider some actions less worthy because they are necessary? No, they will not knock it out of my head that the marriage of pleasure with necessity, with whom, says an ancient, the gods always conspire, is a very suitable one. To what purpose do we dismember by divorce a structure made up of such close and brotherly correspondence? On the contrary, let us bind it together again by mutual services. Let the mind arouse and quicken the heaviness of the body, and the body check and make fast the lightness of the mind. *He who praises the nature of the soul as the sovereign good and condemns the nature of the flesh as evil, truly both carnally desires the soul and carnally shuns the flesh; for his feeling is inspired by human vanity, not by divine truth* [Saint Augustine].

There is no part unworthy of our care in this gift that God has given us; we are accountable for it even to a single hair. And it is not a perfunctory charge to man to guide man according to his nature; it is express, simple, and of prime importance, and the creator has given it to us seriously and sternly. Authority alone has power over common intelligences, and has more weight in a foreign language. Let us renew the charge here. *Who would not say that it is the essence of folly to do lazily and rebelliously what has to be done, to impel the body one way and the soul another, to be split between the most conflicting motions?* [Seneca.]

Come on now, just to see, some day get some man to tell you the absorbing thoughts and fancies that he takes into his head, and for the sake of which he turns his mind from a good meal and laments the time he spends on feeding himself. You will find there is nothing so insipid in all the dishes on your table as this fine entertainment of his mind (most of the time we should do better to go to sleep completely than to stay awake for what we do stay awake for); and you will find that his ideas and aspirations are not worth your stew. Even if they were the transports of Archimedes himself, what of it? I am not here touching on, or mixing up with that brattish rabble of men that we are, or with the vanity of the desires and musings that distract us, those venerable souls, exalted by ardent piety and religion to constant and conscientious meditation on divine things, who, anticipating, by dint of keen and vehement hope, the enjoyment of eternal food, final goal and ultimate limit of Christian desires, sole constant and incorruptible pleasure, scorn to give their attention to our beggarly, watery, and ambiguous comforts, and readily resign to the body the concern and enjoyment of sensual and temporal fodder. That is a privileged study. Between ourselves, these are two things that I have always observed to be in singular accord: supercelestial thoughts and subterranean conduct.

Aesop, that great man, saw his master pissing as he walked. "What next?" he said. "Shall we have to shit as we run?" Let us manage our time; we shall still have a lot left idle and ill spent. Our mind likes to think it has not enough leisure hours to do its own business unless it dissociates itself from the body for the little time that the body really needs it.

They want to get out of themselves and escape from the man. That is madness: instead of changing into angels, they change into beasts; instead of raising themselves, they lower themselves. These transcendental humors frighten me, like lofty and inaccessible places; and nothing is so hard for me to stomach in the life of Socrates as his ecstasies and possessions by his daemon, nothing is so human in Plato as the qualities for which they say he is called divine. And of our sciences, those seem to me most terrestrial and low which have risen the highest. And I find nothing so humble and so mortal in the life of Alexander as his fancies about his immortalization. Philotas stung him wittily by his answer. He congratulated him by letter on the oracle of Jupiter Ammon which had lodged him among the gods: "As far as you are concerned, I am very glad of it; but there is reason to pity the men who will have to live with and obey a man who exceeds and is not content with a man's proportions."

> Since you obey the gods, you rule the world.
> HORACE

The nice inscription with which the Athenians honored the entry of Pompey into their city is in accord with my meaning.

> You are as much a god as you will own
> That you are nothing but a man alone.
> AMYOT'S PLUTARCH

It is an absolute perfection and virtually divine to know how to enjoy our being rightfully. We seek other conditions because we do not understand the use of our own, and go outside of ourselves because we do not know what it is like inside. Yet there is no use our mounting on stilts, for on stilts we must still walk on our own legs. And on the loftiest throne in the world we are still sitting only on our own rump.

The most beautiful lives, to my mind, are those that conform to the common human pattern, with order, but without miracle and without eccentricity. Now old age needs to be treated a little more tenderly. Let us commend it to that god who is the protector of health and wisdom, but gay and sociable wisdom:

> Grant me but health, Latona's son,
> And to enjoy the wealth I've won,
> And honored age, with mind entire
> And not unsolaced by the lyre.
>
> HORACE

15

Blaise Pascal,
Pensées

A brilliant mathematician, physicist, and inventor, Pascal's (1623–1662) life was transformed by a profound religious experience on November 23, 1654, a "night of fire" in which he had a direct vision of "the living God." After that experience, he involved himself in supporting the Augustinian renewal led by the Jansenists, defending their emphasis on God's grace and predestination against Jesuit attacks. He is best known for the polished style and depth of the thoughts, or pensées, *he was working on at the time of his death at the age of thirty-nine.*

Pascal offers us a powerful description of everyday life as shot through with self-deception and inauthenticity. Much of our life is thrown into "diversion," the attempt to keep ourselves busy and distracted with scintillating preoccupations. As a result, our lives are characterized by "inconstancy, boredom, and anxiety." Pascal's aim is to pull us back from this frenzy of activity in order to get us to reflect on what life is all about. In his view, human existence involves a fundamental paradox. On the one hand, we are basically animals, part of the material realm, engrossed in sensual desires; on the other, we are thinking beings who can rise above our animal nature and strive to be like God. Because of this dual nature, we are torn apart and miserable, swinging between grandiosity and depression, with no basis for happiness and stability. The solution, in Pascal's view, is to give ourselves over to the "God-man," to God made incarnate in Christ. As Pascal sums it up, "Wretchedness of man without God, Happiness of man with God." The divine truth is known neither through sensory observations nor reason, but through the heart—our capacity for direct, intuitive knowledge of higher things. Pascal's deep-felt explorations of the inner self, together with his recognition of the fundamental paradox of human existence, makes him a precursor of the later existentialists.

. . . Let man then contemplate the whole of nature in her full and lofty majesty, let him turn his gaze away from the lowly objects around him; let him behold the dazzling light set like an eternal lamp to light up the universe, let him see the earth as a mere speck compared to the vast orbit described by this star, and let him marvel at finding this vast orbit itself to

199

Reprinted from Blaise Pascal, *Pensées*, trans. by A. J. Krailsheimer (London: Penguin Books, 1995). Reprinted with permission.

be no more than the tiniest point compared to that described by the stars revolving in the firmament. But if our eyes stop there, let our imagination proceed further; it will grow weary of conceiving things before nature tires of producing them. The whole visible world is only an imperceptible dot in nature's ample bosom. No idea comes near it; it is no good inflating our conceptions beyond imaginable space, we only bring forth atoms compared to the reality of things. Nature is an infinite sphere whose centre is everywhere and circumference nowhere. In short it is the greatest perceptible mark of God's omnipotence that our imagination should lose itself in that thought.

Let man, returning to himself, consider what he is in comparison with what exists; let him regard himself as lost, and from this little dungeon, in which he finds himself lodged, I mean the universe, let him learn to take the earth, its realms, its cities, its houses and himself at their proper value.

What is a man in the infinite?

. . .

I want to show him a new abyss. I want to depict to him not only the visible universe, but all the conceivable immensity of nature enclosed in this miniature atom. Let him see there an infinity of universes, each with its firmament, its planets, its earth, in the same proportions as in the visible world, and on that earth animals, and finally mites, in which he will find again the same results as in the first; and finding the same thing yet again in the others without end or respite, he will be lost in such wonders, as astounding in their minuteness as the others in their amplitude. For who will not marvel that our body, a moment ago imperceptible in a universe, itself imperceptible in the bosom of the whole, should now be a colossus, a world, or rather a whole, compared to the nothingness beyond our reach? Anyone who considers himself in this way will be terrified at himself, and, seeing his mass, as given him by nature, supporting him between these two abysses of infinity and nothingness, will tremble at these marvels. I believe that with his curiosity changing into wonder he will be more disposed to contemplate them in silence than investigate them with presumption.

For, after all, what is man in nature? A nothing compared to the infinite, a whole compared to the nothing, a middle point between all and nothing, infinitely remote from an understanding of the extremes; the end of things and their principles are unattainably hidden from him in impenetrable secrecy.

Equally incapable of seeing the nothingness from which he emerges and the infinity in which he is engulfed.

What else can he do, then, but perceive some semblance of the middle of things, eternally hopeless of knowing either their principles or their end? All things have come out of nothingness and are carried onwards to infinity. Who can follow these astonishing processes? The author of these wonders understands them: no one else can.

Because they failed to contemplate these infinities, men have rashly undertaken to probe into nature as if there were some proportion between themselves and her.

Strangely enough they wanted to know the principles of things and go on from there to know everything, inspired by a presumption as infinite as their object. For there can be no doubt that such a plan could not be conceived without infinite presumption or a capacity as infinite as that of nature.

. . .

Let us then realize our limitations. We are something and we are not everything. Such being as we have conceals from us the knowledge of first principles, which arise from nothingness, and the smallness of our being hides infinity from our sight.

Our intelligence occupies the same rank in the order of intellect as our body in the whole range of nature.

Limited in every respect, we find this intermediate state between two extremes reflected in all our faculties. Our senses can perceive nothing extreme; too much noise deafens us, too much light dazzles; when we are too far or too close we cannot see properly; an argument is obscured by being too long or too short; too much truth bewilders us.

. . .

In a word, extremes are as if they did not exist for us nor we for them; they escape us or we escape them.

Such is our true state. That is what makes us incapable of certain knowledge or absolute ignorance. We are floating in a medium of vast extent, always drifting uncertainly, blown to and fro; whenever we think we have a fixed point to which we can cling and make fast, it shifts and leaves us behind; if we follow it, it eludes our grasp, slips away, and flees eternally before us. Nothing stands still for us. This is our natural state and yet the state most contrary to our inclinations. We burn with desire to find a firm footing, an ultimate, lasting base on which to build a tower rising up to infinity, but our whole foundation cracks and the earth opens up into the depth of the abyss.

Let us then seek neither assurance nor stability; our reason is always deceived by the inconsistency of appearances; nothing can fix the finite between the two infinites which enclose and evade it.

Once that is clearly understood, I think that each of us can stay quietly in the state in which nature has placed him. Since the middle station allotted to us is always far from the extremes, what does it matter if someone else has a slightly better understanding of things? If he has, and if he takes them a little further, is he not still infinitely remote from the goal? Is not our span of life equally infinitesimal in eternity, even if it is extended by ten years?

. . .

And what makes our inability to know things absolute is that they are simple in themselves, while we are composed of two opposing natures of different kinds, soul and body. For it is impossible for the part of us which reasons to be anything but spiritual, and even if it were claimed that we are simply corporeal, that would still more preclude us from knowing things, since there is nothing so inconceivable as the idea that matter knows itself. We cannot possibly know how it could know itself.

Thus, if we are simply material, we can know nothing at all, and, if we are composed of mind and matter, we cannot have perfect knowledge of things which are simply spiritual or corporeal.

That is why nearly all philosophers confuse their ideas of things, and speak spiritually of corporeal things and corporeally of spiritual ones, for they boldly assert that bodies tend to fall, that they aspire towards their centre, that they flee from destruction, that they fear a void, that they have inclinations, sympathies, antipathies, all things pertaining only to things spiritual. And when they speak of minds, they consider them as being in a place, and attribute to them movement from one place to another, which are things pertaining only to bodies.

Instead of receiving ideas of these things in their purity, we colour them with our qualities and stamp our own composite being on all the simple things we contemplate. . . .

200   Man is only a reed, the weakest in nature, but he is a thinking reed. There is no need for the whole universe to take up arms to crush him: a vapour, a drop of water is enough to kill him. But even if the universe were to crush him, man would still be nobler than his slayer, because he knows that he is dying and the advantage the universe has over him. The universe knows none of this.

Thus all our dignity consists in thought. It is on thought that we must depend for our recovery, not on space and time, which we could never fill. Let us then strive to think well; that is the basic principle of morality.

201   The eternal silence of these infinite spaces fills me with dread.

The heart has its reasons of which reason knows nothing: we know this in   *423*
countless ways.

I say that it is natural for the heart to love the universal being or itself,
according to its allegiance, and it hardens itself against either as it chooses.
You have rejected one and kept the other. Is it reason that makes you love
yourself?

It is the heart which perceives God and not the reason. That is what faith   *424*
is: God perceived by the heart, not by the reason.

This is what I see and what troubles me. I look around in every direction   *429*
and all I see is darkness. Nature has nothing to offer me that does not give
rise to doubt and anxiety. If I saw no sign there of a Divinity I should
decide on a negative solution: if I saw signs of a Creator everywhere I
should peacefully settle down in the faith. But, seeing too much to deny
and not enough to affirm, I am in a pitiful state. . . .

The nature of self-love and of this human self is to love only self and   *978*
consider only self. But what is it to do? It cannot prevent the object of its
love from being full of faults and wretchedness: it wants to be great and
sees that it is small; it wants to be happy and sees that it is wretched; it
wants to be perfect and sees that it is full of imperfections; it wants to be
the object of men's love and esteem and sees that its faults deserve only
their dislike and contempt.

. . .

Thus human life is nothing but a perpetual illusion; there is nothing but
mutual deception and flattery. No one talks about us in our presence as he
would in our absence. Human relations are only based on this mutual
deception; and few friendships would survive if everyone knew what his
friend said about him behind his back, even though he spoke sincerely and
dispassionately.

Man is therefore nothing but disguise, falsehood and hypocrisy, both in
himself and with regard to others. He does not want to be told the truth.
He avoids telling it to others, and all these tendencies, so remote from
justice and reason, are naturally rooted in his heart.

16

Jean-Jacques Rousseau,
Emile

Immensely popular during his lifetime, the Swiss-born French philosopher Rousseau (1712–1778) had a profound effect on both the Enlightenment (especially on Immanuel Kant) and on nineteenth-century Romanticism. He is best known for his theory of the "natural man," the pre-socialized human who is noble and in touch with nature, and who first becomes corrupt through the influence of society. The novel Emile *(1762) argues that education should not be a matter of instilling knowledge in the child's mind, but rather of drawing out the spontaneous goodness and insight already lying within the child. Rousseau's vision of the child's inborn wisdom and the harm done through socialization has had a profound effect on the philosophy of education and seems as relevant today as it did two centuries ago.*

Absolute good and evil are unknown to us. In this life they are blended together; we never enjoy any perfectly pure feeling, nor do we remain for more than a moment in the same state. The feelings of our minds, like the changes in our bodies, are in a continual flux. Good and ill are common to all, but in varying proportions. The happiest is he who suffers least; the most miserable is he who enjoys least. Ever more sorrow than joy—this is the lot of all of us. Man's happiness in this world is but a negative state; it must be reckoned by the fewness of his ills.

Every feeling of hardship is inseparable from the desire to escape from it; every idea of pleasure from the desire to enjoy it. All desire implies a want, and all wants are painful; hence our wretchedness consists in the disproportion between our desires and our powers. A conscious being whose powers were equal to his desires would be perfectly happy.

What then is human wisdom? Where is the path of true happiness? The mere limitation of our desires is not enough, for if they were less than our powers, part of our faculties would be idle, and we should not enjoy our whole being; neither is the mere extension of our powers enough, for if our desires were also increased we should only be the more miserable. True happiness consists in decreasing the difference between our desires and our powers, in establishing a perfect equilibrium between the power and

From Jean-Jacques Rousseau, *Emile*, trans. by Barbara Foxley (London: J. M. Dent & Sons Ltd., 1911).

the will. Then only, when all its forces are employed, will the soul be at rest and man will find himself in his true position.

In this condition, nature, who does everything for the best, has placed him from the first. To begin with, she gives him only such desires as are necessary for self-preservation and such powers as are sufficient for their satisfaction. All the rest she has stored in his mind as a sort of reserve, to be drawn upon at need. It is only in this primitive condition that we find the equilibrium between desire and power, and then alone man is not unhappy. As soon as his potential powers of mind begin to function, imagination, more powerful than all the rest, awakes, and precedes all the rest. It is imagination which enlarges the bounds of possibility for us, whether for good or ill, and therefore stimulates and feeds desires by the hope of satisfying them. But the object which seemed within our grasp flies quicker than we can follow; when we think we have grasped it, it transforms itself and is again far ahead of us. We no longer perceive the country we have traversed, and we think nothing of it; that which lies before us becomes vaster and stretches still before us. Thus we exhaust our strength, yet never reach our goal, and the nearer we are to pleasure, the further we are from happiness.

On the other hand, the more nearly a man's condition approximates to this state of nature the less difference is there between his desires and his powers, and happiness is therefore less remote. Lacking everything, he is never less miserable; for misery consists, not in the lack of things, but in the needs which they inspire.

· · ·

Is it nature that carries men so far from their real selves? Is it her will that each should learn his fate from others and even be the last to learn it; so that a man dies happy or miserable before he knows what he is about. There is a healthy, cheerful, strong, and vigorous man; it does me good to see him; his eyes tell of content and well-being; he is the picture of happiness. A letter comes by post; the happy man glances at it, it is addressed to him, he opens it and reads it. In a moment he is changed, he turns pale and falls into a swoon. When he comes to himself he weeps, laments, and groans, he tears his hair, and his shrieks re-echo through the air. You would say he was in convulsions. Fool, what harm has this bit of paper done you? What limb has it torn away? What crime has it made you commit? What change has it wrought in you to reduce you to this state of misery?

· · ·

Let us lay it down as an incontrovertible rule that the first impulses of nature are always right; there is no original sin in the human heart, the how and why of the entrance of every vice can be traced. The only natural passion is self-love or selfishness taken in a wider sense. This selfishness is good in itself and in relation to ourselves; and as the child has no necessary relations to other people he is naturally indifferent to them; his self-love only becomes good or bad by the use made of it and the relations established by its means. Until the time is ripe for the appearance of reason, that guide of selfishness, the main thing is that the child shall do nothing because you are watching him or listening to him; in a word, nothing because of other people, but only what nature asks of him; then he will never do wrong.

I do not mean to say that he will never do any mischief, never hurt himself, never break a costly ornament if you leave it within his reach. He might do much damage without doing wrong, since wrong-doing depends on the harmful intention which will never be his. If once he meant to do harm, his whole education would be ruined; he would be almost hopelessly bad.

. . .

Our first duties are to ourselves; our first feelings are centred on self; all our instincts are at first directed to our own preservation and our own welfare. Thus the first notion of justice springs not from what we owe to others, but from what is due to us. Here is another error in popular methods of education. If you talk to children of their duties, and not of their rights, you are beginning at the wrong end, and telling them what they cannot understand, what cannot be of any interest to them.

. . .

According to this principle, any one who wanted to consider himself as an isolated individual, self-sufficing and independent of others, could only be utterly wretched. He could not even continue to exist, for finding the whole earth appropriated by others while he had only himself, how could he get the means of subsistence? When we leave the state of nature we compel others to do the same; no one can remain in a state of nature in spite of his fellow-creatures, and to try to remain in it when it is no longer practicable, would really be to leave it, for self-preservation is nature's first law.

Thus the idea of social relations is gradually developed in the child's mind, before he can really be an active member of human society. Emile sees that to get tools for his own use, other people must have theirs, and that he can get in exchange what he needs and they possess. I easily bring him to feel the need of such exchange and to take advantage of it.

. . .

Self-love is always good, always in accordance with the order of nature. The preservation of our own life is specially entrusted to each one of us, and our first care is, and must be, to watch over our own life; and how can we continually watch over it, if we do not take the greatest interest in it?

Self-preservation requires, therefore, that we shall love ourselves; we must love ourselves above everything, and it follows directly from this that we love what contributes to our preservation. Every child becomes fond of its nurse; Romulus must have loved the she-wolf who suckled him. At first this attachment is quite unconscious; the individual is attracted to that which contributes to his welfare and repelled by that which is harmful; this is merely blind instinct. What transforms this instinct into feeling, the liking into love, the aversion into hatred, is the evident intention of helping or hurting us. We do not become passionately attached to objects without feeling, which only follow the direction given them; but those from which we expect benefit or injury from their internal disposition, from their will. Those we see acting freely for or against us, inspire us with like feelings to those they exhibit towards us. Something does us good, we seek after it; but we love the person who does us good; something harms us and we shrink from it, but we hate the person who tries to hurt us.

. . .

But remember, in the first place, that when I want to train a natural man, I do not want to make him a savage and to send him back to the woods, but that living in the whirl of social life it is enough that he should not let himself be carried away by the passions and prejudices of men; let him see with his eyes and feel with his heart, let him own no sway but that of reason.

. . .

The morality of our actions consists entirely in the judgments we ourselves form with regard to them. If good is good, it must be good in the depth of our heart as well as in our actions; and the first reward of justice is the consciousness that we are acting justly. If moral goodness is in accordance with our nature, man can only be healthy in mind and body when he is good. If it is not so, and if man is by nature evil, he cannot cease to be evil without corrupting his nature, and goodness in him is a crime against nature. If he is made to do harm to his fellow-creatures, as the wolf is made to devour his prey, a humane man would be as depraved a creature as a pitiful wolf; and virtue alone would cause remorse.

My young friend, let us look within, let us set aside all personal prejudices and see whither our inclinations lead us. Do we take more pleasure in the sight of the sufferings of others or their joys? Is it pleasanter to do a kind action or an unkind action, and which leaves the more delightful memory behind it? Why do you enjoy the theatre? Do you delight in the crimes you behold? Do you weep over the punishment which overtakes the criminal? They say we are indifferent to everything but self-interest; yet we find our consolation in our sufferings in the charms of friendship and humanity, and even in our pleasures we should be too lonely and miserable if we had no one to share them with us. If there is no such thing as morality in man's heart, what is the source of his rapturous admiration of noble deeds, his passionate devotion to great men? What connection is there between self-interest and this enthusiasm for virtue? Why should I choose to be Cato dying by his own hand, rather than Caesar in his triumphs? Take from our hearts this love of what is noble and you rob us of the joy of life. The mean-spirited man in whom these delicious feelings have been stifled among vile passions, who by thinking of no one but himself comes at last to love no one but himself, this man feels no raptures, his cold heart no longer throbs with joy, and his eyes no longer fill with the sweet tears of sympathy, he delights in nothing; the wretch has neither life nor feeling, he is already dead.

There are many bad men in this world, but there are few of these dead souls, alive only to self-interest, and insensible to all that is right and good. We only delight in injustice so long as it is to our own advantage: in every other case we wish the innocent to be protected. If we see some act of violence or injustice in town or country, our hearts are at once stirred to their depths by an instinctive anger and wrath, which bids us go to the help of the oppressed: but we are restrained by a stronger duty, and the law deprives us of our right to protect the innocent. On the other hand, if some deed of mercy or generosity meets our eye, what reverence and love does it inspire! Do we not say to ourselves, "I should like to have done that myself"? What does it matter to us that two thousand years ago a man was just or unjust? and yet we take the same interest in ancient history as if it happened yesterday. What are the crimes of Cataline to me? I shall not be his victim. Why then have I the same horror of his crimes as if he were living now? We do not hate the wicked merely because of the harm they do to ourselves, but because they are wicked. Not only do we wish to be happy ourselves, we wish others to be happy too, and if this happiness does not interfere with our own happiness, it increases it. In conclusion, whether we will or not, we pity the unfortunate: when we see their suffering we suffer too. Even the most depraved are not wholly without this instinct, and it often leads them to self-contradiction. The highwayman who robs the traveller, clothes the nakedness of the poor; the fiercest murderer supports a fainting man.

Men speak of the voice of remorse, the secret punishment of hidden crimes, by which such are often brought to light. Alas! who does not know its unwelcome voice? We speak from experience, and we would gladly stifle this imperious feeling which causes us such agony. Let us obey the call of nature; we shall see that her yoke is easy and that when we give heed to her voice we find a joy in the answer of a good conscience. The wicked fears and flees from her; he delights to escape from himself; his anxious eyes look around him for some object of diversion; without bitter satire and rude mockery he would always be sorrowful; the scornful laugh is his one pleasure. Not so the just man, who finds his peace within himself; there is joy not malice in his laughter, a joy which springs from his own heart; he is as cheerful alone as in company, his satisfaction does not depend on those who approach him; it includes them.

. . .

It is no part of my scheme to enter at present into metaphysical discussions which neither you nor I can understand, discussions which really lead nowhere. I have told you already that I do not wish to philosophise with you, but to help you to consult your own heart. If all the philosophers in the world should prove that I am wrong, and you feel that I am right, that is all I ask.

For this purpose it is enough to lead you to distinguish between our acquired ideas and our natural feelings; for feeling precedes knowledge; and since we do not learn to seek what is good for us and avoid what is bad for us, but get this desire from nature, in the same way the love of good and the hatred of evil are as natural to us as our self-love. The decrees of conscience are not judgments but feelings. Although all our ideas come from without, the feelings by which they are weighed are within us, and it is by these feelings alone that we perceive fitness or unfitness of things in relation to ourselves, which leads us to seek or shun these things.

To exist is to feel; our feeling is undoubtedly earlier than our intelligence, and we had feelings before we had ideas.[1] Whatever may be the

---

1. In some respects ideas are feelings and feelings are ideas. Both terms are appropriate to any perception with which we are concerned, appropriate both to the object of that perception and to ourselves who are affected by it; it is merely the order in which we are affected which decides the appropriate term. When we are chiefly concerned with the object and only think of ourselves as it were by reflec-

cause of our being, it has provided for our preservation by giving us feelings suited to our nature; and no one can deny that these at least are innate. These feelings, so far as the individual is concerned, are self-love, fear, pain, the dread of death, the desire for comfort. Again, if, as it is impossible to doubt, man is by nature sociable, or at least fitted to become sociable, he can only be so by means of other innate feelings, relative to his kind; for if only physical well-being were considered, men would certainly be scattered rather than brought together. But the motive power of conscience is derived from the moral system formed through this twofold relation to himself and to his fellow-men. To know good is not to love it; this knowledge is not innate in man; but as soon as his reason leads him to perceive it, his conscience impels him to love it; it is this feeling which is innate.

So I do not think, my young friend, that it is impossible to explain the immediate force of conscience as a result of our own nature, independent of reason itself. And even should it be impossible, it is unnecessary; for those who deny this principle, admitted and received by everybody else in the world, do not prove that there is no such thing; they are content to affirm, and when we affirm its existence we have quite as good grounds as they, while we have moreover the witness within us, the voice of conscience, which speaks on its own behalf. If the first beams of judgment dazzle us and confuse the objects we behold, let us wait till our feeble sight grows clear and strong, and in the light of reason we shall soon behold these very objects as nature has already showed them to us. Or rather let us be simpler and less pretentious; let us be content with the first feelings we experience in ourselves, since science always brings us back to these, unless it has led us astray.

Conscience! Conscience! Divine instinct, immortal voice from heaven; sure guide for a creature ignorant and finite indeed, yet intelligent and free; infallible judge of good and evil, making man like to God! In thee consists the excellence of man's nature and the morality of his actions; apart from thee, I find nothing in myself to raise me above the beasts— nothing but the sad privilege of wandering from one error to another, by the help of an unbridled understanding and a reason which knows no principle.

---

tion, that is an idea; when, on the other hand, the impression received excites our chief attention and we only think in the second place of the object which caused it, it is a feeling.

17

Ralph Waldo Emerson, "Self-Reliance"

The essays of Ralph Waldo Emerson (1803–1882) have been immensely influential in shaping the contemporary American mind. Emerson graduated from Harvard in 1820 and spent several years as a teacher before becoming a Unitarian minister in 1826. He resigned from his pastorate in 1832 and traveled in Europe, where he met Coleridge, Wordsworth, and Carlyle. Returning to the United States, Emerson became a public lecturer, living on what he earned through his writings and annual lecture tours. He is best known for the two volumes of Essays *(1841, 1844) he developed from his lectures.*

Emerson's philosophy, called "transcendentalism," was influenced by Coleridge and the nature poets, Plato, Eastern philosophy, and Swedenborg. It holds that the world we see around us is an appearance or manifestation of a more genuine reality, the divine inner life, which is the source of Nature and the unifying principle in all things. This inner reality is present in each human and is known through intuition. The belief in a "universal soul within or behind [each] individual life" (Nature, 1836) provides the basis for Emerson's claim that each individual should strive to grasp and be true to the truth he or she finds within. In "Self-Reliance," he suggests that we should turn away from custom, convention, and tradition, and try to live according to the insights we discover within ourselves. If we can get in touch with the greater reality within us, we will free ourselves from the conformism of the crowd and realize our unique, inherent potential.

"Ne te quaesiveris extra."[1]

Man is his own star; and the soul that can
Render an honest and a perfect man,
Commands all light, all influence, all fate;
Nothing to him falls early or too late.
Our acts our angels are, or good or ill,
Our fatal shadows that walk by us still.

EPILOGUE TO BEAUMONT AND FLETCHER'S
HONEST MAN'S FORTUNE

1. "Do not seek yourself outside yourself."

From *Complete Works of Ralph Waldo Emerson* (Boston: Houghton Mifflin & Co., 1903–4).

> Cast the bantling on the rocks,
> Suckle him with the she-wolf's teat,
> Wintered with the hawk and fox,
> Power and speed be hands and feet.

I read the other day some verses written by an eminent painter which were original and not conventional. The soul always hears an admonition in such lines, let the subject be what it may. The sentiment they instil is of more value than any thought they may contain. To believe your own thought, to believe that what is true for you in your private heart is true for all men,—that is genius. Speak your latent conviction, and it shall be the universal sense; for the inmost in due time becomes the outmost, and our first thought is rendered back to us by the trumpets of the Last Judgment. Familiar as the voice of the mind is to each, the highest merit we ascribe to Moses, Plato and Milton is that they set at naught books and traditions, and spoke not what men, but what *they* thought. A man should learn to detect and watch that gleam of light which flashes across his mind from within, more than the lustre of the firmament of bards and sages. Yet he dismisses without notice his thought, because it is his. In every work of genius we recognize our own rejected thoughts; they come back to us with a certain alienated majesty. Great works of art have no more affecting lesson for us than this. They teach us to abide by our spontaneous impression with good-humored inflexibility then most when the whole cry of voices is on the other side. Else to-morrow a stranger will say with masterly good sense precisely what we have thought and felt all the time, and we shall be forced to take with shame our own opinion from another.

There is a time in every man's education when he arrives at the conviction that envy is ignorance; that imitation is suicide; that he must take himself for better for worse as his portion; that though the wide universe is full of good, no kernel of nourishing corn can come to him but through his toil bestowed on that plot of ground which is given to him to till. The power which resides in him is new in nature, and none but he knows what that is which he can do, nor does he know until he has tried. Not for nothing one face, one character, one fact, makes much impression on him, and another none. This sculpture in the memory is not without preëstablished harmony. The eye was placed where one ray should fall, that it might testify of that particular ray. We but half express ourselves, and are ashamed of that divine idea which each of us represents. It may be safely trusted as proportionate and of good issues, so it be faithfully imparted, but God will not have his work made manifest by cowards. A man is relieved and gay when he has put his heart into his work and done his best; but what he has said or done otherwise shall give him no peace. It is a deliverance which does not deliver. In the attempt his genius deserts him; no muse befriends; no invention, no hope.

Trust thyself: every heart vibrates to that iron string. Accept the place the divine providence has found for you, the society of your contemporaries, the connection of events. Great men have always done so, and confided themselves childlike to the genius of their age, betraying their perception that the absolutely trustworthy was seated at their heart, working through their hands, predominating in all their being. And we are now men, and must accept in the highest mind the same transcendent destiny; and not minors and invalids in a protected corner, not cowards fleeing before a revolution, but guides, redeemers and benefactors, obeying the Almighty effort and advancing on Chaos and the Dark.

What pretty oracles nature yields us on this text in the face and behavior of children, babes, and even brutes! That divided and rebel mind, that distrust of a sentiment because our arithmetic has computed the strength and means opposed to our purpose, these have not. Their mind being whole, their eye is as yet unconquered, and when we look in their faces we are disconcerted. Infancy conforms to nobody; all conform to it; so that one babe commonly makes four or five out of the adults who prattle and play to it. So God has armed youth and puberty and manhood no less with its own piquancy and charm, and made it enviable and gracious and its claims not to be put by, if it will stand by itself. Do not think the youth has no force, because he cannot speak to you and me. Hark! in the next room his voice is sufficiently clear and emphatic. It seems he knows how to speak to his contemporaries. Bashful or bold then, he will know how to make us seniors very unnecessary.

The nonchalance of boys who are sure of a dinner, and would disdain as much as a lord to do or say aught to conciliate one, is the healthy attitude of human nature. A boy is in the parlor what the pit is in the playhouse; independent, irresponsible, looking out from his corner on such people and facts as pass by, he tries and sentences them on their merits, in the swift, summary way of boys, as good, bad, interesting, silly, eloquent, troublesome. He cumbers himself never about consequences, about interests; he gives an independent, genuine verdict. You must court him; he does not court you. But the man is as it were clapped into jail by his consciousness. As soon as he has once acted or spoken with *éclat* he is a committed person, watched by the sympathy or the hatred of hundreds, whose affections must now enter into his account. There is no Lethe for this. Ah, that he could pass again into his neutrality! Who can thus avoid all pledges and, having observed, observe again from the same unaffected, unbiased, unbribable, unaffrighted innocence,—must always be formidable. He would utter opinions on all passing affairs, which being seen to be not private but necessary, would sink like darts into the ear of men, and put them in fear.

These are the voices which we hear in solitude, but they grow faint and inaudible as we enter into the world. Society everywhere is in conspiracy against the manhood of every one of its members. Society is a joint-stock company, in which the members agree, for the better securing of his bread to each shareholder, to surrender the liberty and culture of the eater. The virtue in most request is conformity. Self-reliance is its aversion. It loves not realities and creators, but names and customs.

Whoso would be a man, must be a nonconformist. He who would gather immortal palms must not be hindered by the name of goodness, but must explore if it be goodness. Nothing is at last sacred but the integrity of your own mind. Absolve you to yourself, and you shall have the suffrage of the world. I remember an answer which when quite young I was prompted to make to a valued adviser who was wont to importune me with the dear old doctrines of the church. On my saying, "What have I to do with the sacredness of traditions, if I live wholly from within?" my friend suggested,—"But these impulses may be from below, not from above." I replied, "They do not seem to me to be such; but if I am the Devil's child, I will live then from the Devil." No law can be sacred to me but that of my nature. Good and bad are but names very readily transferable to that or this; the only right is what is after my constitution; the only wrong what is against it. A man is to carry himself in the presence of all opposition as if every thing were titular and ephemeral but he. I am ashamed to think how easily we capitulate to badges and names, to large societies and dead institutions. Every decent and well-spoken individual affects and sways me more than is right. I ought to go upright and vital, and speak the rude truth in all ways. If malice and vanity wear the coat of philanthropy, shall that pass? If an angry bigot assumes this bountiful cause of Abolition, and comes to me with his last news from Barbadoes, why should I not say to him, "Go love thy infant; love thy wood-chopper; be good-natured and modest; have that grace; and never varnish your hard, uncharitable ambition with this incredible tenderness for black folk a thousand miles off. Thy love afar is spite at home." Rough and graceless would be such greeting, but truth is handsomer than the affectation of love. Your goodness must have some edge to it,—else it is none. The doctrine of hatred must be preached, as the counteraction of the doctrine of love, when that pules and whines. I shun father and mother and wife and brother when my genius calls me. I would write on the lintels of the door-post, *Whim.* I hope it is somewhat better than whim at last, but we cannot spend the day in explanation. Expect me not to show cause why I seek or why I exclude company. Then again, do not tell me, as a good man did to-day, of my obligation to put all poor men in good situations. Are they *my* poor? I tell thee, thou foolish philanthropist, that I grudge the dollar, the dime, the cent I give to such men as do not belong to me and to whom I do not belong. There is a class of persons to whom by all spiritual affinity I am bought and sold; for them I will go to prison if need be; but your miscellaneous popular charities; the education at college of fools; the building of meeting-houses to the vain end to which many now stand; alms to sots, and the thousand-fold Relief Societies;—though I confess with shame I sometimes succumb and give the dollar, it is a wicked dollar, which by and by I shall have the manhood to withhold.

Virtues are, in the popular estimate, rather the exception than the rule. There is the man *and* his virtues. Men do what is called a good action, as some piece of courage or charity, much as they would pay a fine in expiation of daily non-appearance on parade. Their works are done as an apology or extenuation of their living in the world,—as invalids and the insane pay a high board. Their virtues are penances. I do not wish to expiate, but to live. My life is for itself and not for a spectacle. I much prefer that it should be of a lower strain, so it be genuine and equal, than that it should be glittering and unsteady. I wish it to be sound and sweet, and not to need diet and bleeding. I ask primary evidence that you are a man, and refuse this appeal from the man to his actions. I know that for myself it makes no difference whether I do or forbear those actions which are reckoned excellent. I cannot consent to pay for a privilege where I have intrinsic right. Few and mean as my gifts may be, I actually am, and do not need for my own assurance or the assurance of my fellows any secondary testimony.

What I must do is all that concerns me, not what the people think. This rule, equally arduous in actual and in intellectual life, may serve for the whole distinction between greatness and meanness. It is the harder because you will always find those who think they know what is your duty better than you know it. It is easy in the world to live after the world's opinion; it is easy in solitude to live after our own; but the great man is he who in the midst of the crowd keeps with perfect sweetness the independence of solitude.

The objection to conforming to usages that have become dead to you is that it scatters your force. It loses your time and blurs the impression of your character. If you maintain a dead church, contribute to a dead Bible-society, vote with a great party either for the government or against it, spread your table like base housekeepers,—under all these screens I have difficulty to detect the precise man you are: and of course so much force is withdrawn from your proper life. But do your work, and I shall know you. Do your work, and you shall reinforce yourself. A man must consider what a blind-man's-bluff is this game of conformity. If I know your sect I anticipate your argument. I hear a preacher announce for his text and topic the expediency of one of the institutions of his church. Do I not know beforehand that not possibly can he say a new and spontaneous word? Do I not know that with all this ostentation of examining the grounds of the institution he will do no such thing? Do I not know that he is pledged to himself not to look but at one side, the permitted side, not as a man, but as a parish minister? He is a retained attorney, and these airs of the bench are the emptiest affectation. Well, most men have bound their eyes with one or another handkerchief, and attached themselves to some one of these communities of opinion. This conformity makes them not false in a few particulars, authors of a few lies, but false in all particulars. Their every truth is not quite true. Their two is not the real two, their four not the real four; so that every word they say chagrins us and we know not where to begin to set them right. Meantime nature is not slow to equip us in the prison-uniform of the party to which we adhere. We come to wear one cut of face and figure, and acquire by degrees the gentlest asinine expression. There is a mortifying experience in particular, which does not fail to wreak itself also in the general history; I mean "the foolish face of praise," the forced smile which we put on in company where we do not feel at ease, in answer to conversation which does not interest us. The muscles, not spontaneously moved but moved by a low usurping wilfulness, grow tight about the outline of the face, with the most disagreeable sensation.

For nonconformity the world whips you with its displeasure. And therefore a man must know how to estimate a sour face. The by-standers look askance on him in the public street or in the friend's parlor. If this aversion had its origin in contempt and resistance like his own he might well go home with a sad countenance; but the sour faces of the multitude, like their sweet faces, have no deep cause, but are put on and off as the wind blows and a newspaper directs. Yet is the discontent of the multitude more formidable than that of the senate and the college. It is easy enough for a firm man who knows the world to brook the rage of the cultivated classes. Their rage is decorous and prudent, for they are timid, as being very vulnerable themselves. But when to their feminine rage the indignation of the people is added, when the ignorant and the poor are aroused, when the unintelligent brute force that lies at the bottom of society is made to growl and mow, it needs the habit of magnanimity and religion to treat it godlike as a trifle of no concernment.

The other terror that scares us from self-trust is our consistency; a reverence for our past act or word because the eyes of others have no other data for computing our orbit than our past acts, and we are loth to disappoint them.

But why should you keep your head over your shoulder? Why drag about this corpse of your memory, lest you contradict somewhat you have stated in this or that public place? Suppose you should contradict yourself; what then? It seems to be a rule of wisdom never to rely on your memory alone, scarcely even in acts of pure memory, but to bring the past for judgment into the thousand-eyed present, and live ever in a new day. In your metaphysics you have denied personality to the Deity, yet when the devout motions of the soul come, yield to them heart and life, though they should clothe God with shape and color. Leave your theory, as Joseph his coat in the hand of the harlot, and flee.

A foolish consistency is the hobgoblin of little minds, adored by little statesmen and philosophers and divines. With consistency a great soul has simply nothing to do. He may as well concern himself with his shadow on the wall. Speak what you think now in hard words and to-morrow speak what to-morrow thinks in hard words again, though it contradict every thing you said to-day.— "Ah, so you shall be sure to be misunderstood."— Is it so bad then to be misunderstood? Pythagoras was misunderstood, and Socrates, and Jesus, and Luther, and Copernicus, and Galileo, and Newton, and every pure and wise spirit that ever took flesh. To be great is to be misunderstood.

I suppose no man can violate his nature. All the sallies of his will are rounded in by the law of his being, as the inequalities of Andes and Himmaleh are insignificant in the curve of the sphere. Nor does it matter how you gauge and try him. A character is like an acrostic or Alexandrian stanza;—read it forward, backward, or across, it still spells the same thing. In this pleasing contrite wood-life which God allows me, let me record day by day my honest thought without prospect or retrospect, and, I cannot doubt, it will be found symmetrical, though I mean it not and see it not. My book should smell of pines and resound with the hum of insects. The swallow over my window should interweave that thread or straw he carries in his bill into my web also. We pass for what we are. Character teaches above our wills. Men imagine that they communicate their virtue or vice only by overt actions, and do not see that virtue or vice emit a breath every moment.

There will be an agreement in whatever variety of actions, so they be each honest and natural in their hour. For of one will, the actions will be harmonious, however unlike they seem. These varieties are lost sight of at a little distance, at a little height of thought. One tendency unites them all. The voyage of the best ship is a zigzag line of a hundred tacks. See the line from a sufficient distance, and it straightens itself to the average tendency. Your genuine action will explain itself and will explain your other genuine actions. Your conformity explains nothing. Act singly, and what you have

already done singly will justify you now. Greatness appeals to the future. If
I can be firm enough to-day to do right and scorn eyes, I must have done so
much right before as to defend me now. Be it how it will, do right now.
Always scorn appearances and you always may. The force of character is
cumulative. All the foregone days of virtue work their health into this.
What makes the majesty of the heroes of the senate and the field, which so
fills the imagination? The consciousness of a train of great days and
victories behind. They shed a united light on the advancing actor. He is
attended as by a visible escort of angels. That is it which throws thunder
into Chatham's voice, and dignity into Washington's port, and America
into Adams's eye. Honor is venerable to us because it is no ephemera. It is
always ancient virtue. We worship it to-day because it is not of to-day. We
love it and pay it homage because it is not a trap for our love and homage,
but is self-dependent, self-derived, and therefore of an old immaculate
pedigree, even if shown in a young person.

I hope in these days we have heard the last of conformity and consistency. Let the words be gazetted and ridiculous henceforward. Instead
of the gong for dinner, let us hear a whistle from the Spartan fife. Let us
never bow and apologize more. A great man is coming to eat at my house. I
do not wish to please him; I wish that he should wish to please me. I will
stand here for humanity, and though I would make it kind, I would make it
true. Let us affront and reprimand the smooth mediocrity and squalid
contentment of the times, and hurl in the face of custom and trade and
office, the fact which is the upshot of all history, that there is a great
responsible Thinker and Actor working wherever a man works; that a true
man belongs to no other time or place, but is the centre of things. Where
he is, there is nature. He measures you and all men and all events. Ordinarily, every body in society reminds us of somewhat else, or of some
other person. Character, reality, reminds you of nothing else; it takes place
of the whole creation. The man must be so much that he must make all
circumstances indifferent. Every true man is a cause, a country, and an
age; requires infinite spaces and numbers and time fully to accomplish his
design;—and posterity seem to follow his steps as a train of clients. A man
Caesar is born, and for ages after we have a Roman Empire. Christ is born,
and millions of minds so grow and cleave to his genius that he is con-
founded with virtue and the possible of man. An institution is the length-
ened shadow of one man; as, Monachism, of the Hermit Antony; the
Reformation, of Luther; Quakerism, of Fox; Methodism, of Wesley; Abolition, of Clarkson. Scipio, Milton called "the height of Rome"; and all
history resolves itself very easily into the biography of a few stout and
earnest persons.

Let a man then know his worth, and keep things under his feet. Let him not peep or steal, or skulk up and down with the air of a charity-boy, a bastard, or an interloper in the world which exists for him. But the man in the street, finding no worth in himself which corresponds to the force which built a tower or sculptured a marble god, feels poor when he looks on these.

. . .

The world has been instructed by its kings, who have so magnetized the eyes of nations. It has been taught by this colossal symbol the mutual reverence that is due from man to man. The joyful loyalty with which men have everywhere suffered the king, the noble, or the great proprietor to walk among them by a law of his own, make his own scale of men and things and reverse theirs, pay for benefits not with money but with honor, and represent the law in his person, was the hieroglyphic by which they obscurely signified their consciousness of their own right and comeliness, the right of every man.

The magnetism which all original action exerts is explained when we inquire the reason of self-trust. Who is the Trustee? What is the aboriginal Self, on which a universal reliance may be grounded? What is the nature and power of that science-baffling star, without parallax, without calculable elements, which shoots a ray of beauty even into trivial and impure actions, if the least mark of independence appear? The inquiry leads us to that source, at once the essence of genius, of virtue, and of life, which we call Spontaneity or Instinct. We denote this primary wisdom as Intuition, whilst all later teachings are tuitions. In that deep force, the last fact behind which analysis cannot go, all things find their common origin. For the sense of being which in calm hours rises, we know not how, in the soul, is not diverse from things, from space, from light, from time, from man, but one with them and proceeds obviously from the same source whence their life and being also proceed. We first share the life by which things exist and afterwards see them as appearances in nature and forget that we have shared their cause. Here is the fountain of action and of thought. Here are the lungs of that inspiration which giveth man wisdom and which cannot be denied without impiety and atheism. We lie in the lap of immense intelligence, which makes us receivers of its truth and organs of its activity. When we discern justice, when we discern truth, we do nothing of ourselves, but allow a passage to its beams. If we ask whence this comes, if we seek to pry into the soul that causes, all philosophy is at fault. Its presence or its absence is all we can affirm. Every man discriminates between the voluntary acts of his mind and his involuntary perceptions, and knows that to his involuntary perceptions a perfect faith is due. He may err in the expression of them, but he knows that these things are so, like day and night, not to be disputed. My wilful actions and acquisitions are but roving;—the idlest reverie, the faintest native emotion, command my curiosity and respect. Thoughtless people contradict as readily the statement of perceptions as of opinions, or rather much more readily; for they do not distinguish between perception and notion. They fancy that I choose to see this or that thing. But perception is not whimsical, but fatal. If I see a trait, my children will see it after me, and in course of time all mankind,—although it may chance that no one has seen it before me. For my perception of it is as much a fact as the sun.

The relations of the soul to the divine spirit are so pure that it is profane to seek to interpose helps. It must be that when God speaketh he should communicate, not one thing, but all things; should fill the world with his voice; should scatter forth light, nature, time, souls, from the centre of the present thought; and new date and new create the whole. Whenever a mind is simple and receives a divine wisdom, old things pass away,— means, teachers, texts, temples fall; it lives now, and absorbs past and future into the present hour. All things are made sacred by relation to it,— one as much as another. All things are dissolved to their centre by their cause, and in the universal miracle petty and particular miracles disappear. If therefore a man claims to know and speak of God and carries you backward to the phraseology of some old mouldered nation in another country, in another world, believe him not. Is the acorn better than the oak which is its fulness and completion? Is the parent better than the child into whom he has cast his ripened being? Whence then this worship of the past? The centuries are conspirators against the sanity and authority of the soul. Time and space are but physiological colors which the eye makes, but the soul is light: where it is, is day; where it was, is night; and history is an impertinence and an injury if it be any thing more than a cheerful apologue or parable of my being and becoming.

Man is timid and apologetic; he is no longer upright; he dares not say "I think," "I am," but quotes some saint or sage. He is ashamed before the blade of grass or the blowing rose. These roses under my window make no reference to former roses or to better ones; they are for what they are; they exist with God to-day. There is no time to them. There is simply the rose; it is perfect in every moment of its existence. Before a leaf-bud has burst, its whole life acts; in the full-blown flower there is no more; in the leafless root there is no less. Its nature is satisfied and it satisfies nature in all moments alike. But man postpones or remembers; he does not live in the present, but with reverted eye laments the past, or, heedless of the riches that surround him, stands on tiptoe to foresee the future. He cannot be happy and strong until he too lives with nature in the present, above time.

This should be plain enough. Yet see what strong intellects dare not yet hear God himself unless he speak the phraseology of I know not what David, or Jeremiah, or Paul. We shall not always set so great a price on a few texts, on a few lives. We are like children who repeat by rote the sentences of grandames and tutors, and, as they grow older, of the men of talents and character they chance to see,—painfully recollecting the exact word they spoke; afterwards, when they come into the point of view which those had who uttered these sayings, they understand them and are willing to let the words go; for at any time they can use words as good when occasion comes. If we live truly, we shall see truly. It is as easy for the strong man to be strong, as it is for the weak to be weak. When we have new perception, we shall gladly disburden the memory of its hoarded treasures as old rubbish. When a man lives with God, his voice shall be as sweet as the murmur of the brook and the rustle of the corn.

And now at last the highest truth on this subject remains unsaid; probably cannot be said; for all that we say is the far-off remembering of the intuition. That thought by what I can now nearest approach to say it, is this. When good is near you, when you have life in yourself, it is not by any known or accustomed way; you shall not discern the footprints of any other; you shall not see the face of man; you shall not hear any name;—the way, the thought, the good, shall be wholly strange and new. It shall exclude example and experience. You take the way from man, not to man. All persons that ever existed are its forgotten ministers. Fear and hope are alike beneath it. There is somewhat low even in hope. In the hour of vision there is nothing that can be called gratitude, nor properly joy. The soul raised over passion beholds identity and eternal causation, perceives the self-existence of Truth and Right, and calms itself with knowing that all things go well. Vast spaces of nature, the Atlantic Ocean, the South Sea; long intervals of time, years, centuries, are of no account. This which I think and feel underlay every former state of life and circumstances, as it does underlie my present, and what is called life and what is called death.

Life only avails, not the having lived. Power ceases in the instant of repose; it resides in the moment of transition from a past to a new state, in the shooting of the gulf, in the darting to an aim. This one fact the world hates; that the soul *becomes;* for that forever degrades the past, turns all riches to poverty, all reputation to a shame, confounds the saint with the rogue, shoves Jesus and Judas equally aside. Why then do we prate of self-reliance? Inasmuch as the soul is present there will be power not confident but agent. To talk of reliance is a poor external way of speaking. Speak rather of that which relies because it works and is. Who has more obedience than I masters me, though he should not raise his finger. Round him I must revolve by the gravitation of spirits. We fancy it rhetoric when we speak of eminent virtue. We do not yet see that virtue is Height, and that a man or a company of men, plastic and permeable to principles, by the law of nature must overpower and ride all cities, nations, kings, rich men, poets, who are not.

This is the ultimate fact which we so quickly reach on this, as on every topic, the resolution of all into the ever-blessed ONE. Self-existence is the attribute of the Supreme Cause, and it constitutes the measure of good by the degree in which it enters into all lower forms. All things real are so by so much virtue as they contain. Commerce, husbandry, hunting, whaling, war, eloquence, personal weight, are somewhat, and engage my respect as examples of its presence and impure action. I see the same law working in nature for conservation and growth. Power is, in nature, the essential measure of right. Nature suffers nothing to remain in her kingdoms which cannot help itself. The genesis and maturation of a planet, its poise and orbit, the bended tree recovering itself from the strong wind, the vital resources of every animal and vegetable, are demonstrations of the self-sufficing and therefore self-relying soul.

Thus all concentrates: let us not rove; let us sit at home with the cause. Let us stun and astonish the intruding rabble of men and books and institutions by a simple declaration of the divine fact. Bid the invaders take the shoes from off their feet, for God is here within. Let our simplicity judge them, and our docility to our own law demonstrate the poverty of nature and fortune beside our native riches.

. . .

If we cannot at once rise to the sanctities of obedience and faith, let us at least resist our temptations; let us enter into the state of war and wake Thor and Woden, courage and constancy, in our Saxon breasts. This is to be done in our smooth times by speaking the truth. Check this lying hospitality and lying affection. Live no longer to the expectation of these deceived and deceiving people with whom we converse. Say to them, "O father, O mother, O wife, O brother, O friend, I have lived with you after appearances hitherto. Henceforward I am the truth's. Be it known unto you that henceforward I obey no law less than the eternal law. I will have no covenants but proximities. I shall endeavor to nourish my parents, to support my family, to be the chaste husband of one wife,—but these relations I must fill after a new and unprecedented way. I appeal from you customs. I must be myself. I cannot break myself any longer for you, or you. If you can love me for what I am, we shall be the happier. If you cannot, I will still seek to deserve that you should. I will not hide my tastes or aversions. I will so trust that what is deep is holy, that I will do strongly before the sun and moon whatever inly rejoices me and the heart appoints. If you are noble, I will love you; if you are not, I will not hurt you and myself by hypocritical attentions. If you are true, but not in the same truth with me, cleave to your companions; I will seek my own. I do this not selfishly but humbly and truly. It is alike your interest, and mine, and all men's, however long we have dwelt in lies, to live in truth. Does this sound harsh to-day? You will soon love what is dictated by your nature as well as mine, and if we follow the truth it will bring us out safe at last."—But so may you give these friends pain. Yes, but I cannot sell my liberty and my power, to save their sensibility. Besides, all persons have their moments of reason, when they look out into the region of absolute truth; then will they justify me and do the same thing.

The populace think that your rejection of popular standards is a rejection of all standard, and mere antinomianism; and the bold sensualist will use the name of philosophy to gild his crimes. But the law of consciousness abides. There are two confessionals, in one or the other of which we must be shriven. You may fulfil your round of duties by clearing yourself in the *direct*, or in the *reflex* way. Consider whether you have satisfied your relations to father, mother, cousin, neighbor, town, cat and dog—whether any of these can upbraid you. But I may also neglect this reflex standard and absolve me to myself. I have my own stern claims and perfect circle. It denies the name of duty to many offices that are called duties. But if I can discharge its debts it enables me to dispense with the popular code. If any one imagines that this law is lax, let him keep its commandment one day.

And truly it demands something godlike in him who has cast off the common motives of humanity and has ventured to trust himself for a taskmaster. High be his heart, faithful his will, clear his sight, that he may in good earnest be doctrine, society, law, to himself, that a simple purpose may be to him as strong as iron necessity is to others!

If any man consider the present aspects of what is called by distinction *society*, he will see the need of these ethics. The sinew and heart of man seem to be drawn out, and we are become timorous, desponding whimperers. We are afraid of truth, afraid of fortune, afraid of death, and afraid of each other. Our age yields no great and perfect persons. We want men and women who shall renovate life and our social state, but we see that most natures are insolvent, cannot satisfy their own wants, have an ambition out of all proportion to their practical force and do lean and beg day and night continually. Our housekeeping is mendicant, our arts, our occupations, our marriages, our religion we have not chosen, but society has chosen for us. We are parlor soldiers. We shun the rugged battle of fate, where strength is born.

If our young men miscarry in their first enterprises they lose all heart. If the young merchant fails, men say he is *ruined*. If the finest genius studies at one of our colleges and is not installed in an office within one year afterwards in the cities or suburbs of Boston or New York, it seems to his friends and to himself that he is right in being disheartened and in complaining the rest of his life. A sturdy lad from New Hampshire or Vermont, who in turn tries all the professions, who *teams it, farms it, peddles,* keeps a school, preaches, edits a newspaper, goes to Congress, buys a township, and so forth, in successive years, and always like a cat falls on his feet, is worth a hundred of these city dolls. He walks abreast with his days and feels no shame in not "studying a profession," for he does not postpone his life, but lives already. He has not one chance, but a hundred chances. Let a Stoic open the resources of man and tell men they are not leaning willows, but can and must detach themselves; that with the exercise of self-trust, new powers shall appear; that a man is the word made flesh, born to shed healing to the nations; that he should be ashamed of our compassion, and that the moment he acts from himself, tossing the laws, the books, idolatries and customs out of the window, we pity him no more but thank and revere him;—and that teacher shall restore the life of man to splendor and make his name dear to all history.

. . .

Insist on yourself; never imitate. Your own gift you can present every moment with the cumulative force of a whole life's cultivation; but of the adopted talent of another you have only an extemporaneous half possession. That which each can do best, none but his Maker can teach him. No man yet knows what it is, nor can, till that person has exhibited it. Where is the master who could have taught Shakspeare? Where is the master who could have instructed Franklin, or Washington, or Bacon, or Newton? Every great man is a unique. The Scipionism of Scipio is precisely that part he could not borrow. Shakspeare will never be made by the study of Shakspeare. Do that which is assigned you, and you cannot hope too much or dare too much. There is at this moment for you an utterance brave and grand as that of the colossal chisel of Phidias, or trowel of the Egyptians, or the pen of Moses or Dante, but different from all these. Not possibly will the soul, all rich, all eloquent, with thousand-cloven tongue, deign to repeat itself; but if you can hear what these patriarchs say, surely you can reply to them in the same pitch of voice; for the ear and the tongue are two organs of one nature. Abide in the simple and noble regions of thy life, obey thy heart, and thou shalt reproduce the Foreworld again.

. . .

Society is a wave. The wave moves onward, but the water of which it is composed does not. The same particle does not rise from the valley to the

ridge. Its unity is only phenomenal. The persons who make up a nation to-
day, next year die, and their experience dies with them.

And so the reliance on Property, including the reliance on governments
which protect it, is the want of self-reliance. Men have looked away from
themselves and at things so long that they have come to esteem the
religious, learned and civil institutions as guards of property, and they
deprecate assaults on these, because they feel them to be assaults on
property. They measure their esteem of each other by what each has, and
not by what each is. But a cultivated man becomes ashamed of his property, out of new respect for his nature. Especially he hates what he has if he
see that it is accidental,—came to him by inheritance, or gift, or crime;
then he feels that it is not having; it does not belong to him, has no root in
him and merely lies there because no revolution or no robber takes it away.
But that which a man is, does always by necessity acquire; and what the
man acquires, is living property, which does not wait the beck of rulers, or
mobs, or revolutions, or fire, or storm, or bankruptcies, but perpetually
renews itself wherever the man breathes. "Thy lot or portion of life," said
the Caliph Ali, "is seeking after thee; therefore be at rest from seeking
after it." Our dependence on these foreign goods leads us to our slavish
respect for numbers. The political parties meet in numerous conventions;
the greater the concourse and with each new uproar of announcement,
The delegation from Essex! The Democrats from New Hampshire! The
Whigs of Maine! the young patriot feels himself stronger than before by a
new thousand of eyes and arms. In like manner the reformers summon
conventions and vote and resolve in multitude. Not so, O friends! will the
God deign to enter and inhabit you, but by a method precisely the reverse.
It is only as a man puts off all foreign support and stands alone that I see
him to be strong and to prevail. He is weaker by every recruit to his
banner. Is not a man better than a town? Ask nothing of men, and, in the
endless mutation, thou only firm column must presently appear the up-
holder of all that surrounds thee. He who knows that power is inborn, that
he is weak because he has looked for good out of him and elsewhere, and,
so perceiving throws himself unhesitatingly on his thought, instantly
rights himself, stands in the erect position, commands his limbs, works
miracles; just as a man who stands on his feet is stronger than a man who
stands on his head.

So use all that is called Fortune. Most men gamble with her, and gain
all, and lose all, as her wheel rolls. But do thou leave as unlawful these
winnings, and deal with Cause and Effect, the chancellors of God. In the
Will work and acquire, and thou hast chained the wheel of Chance, and
shall sit hereafter out of fear from her rotations. A political victory, a rise of

rents, the recovery of your sick or the return of your absent friend, or some other favorable event raises your spirits, and you think good days are preparing for you. Do not believe it. Nothing can bring you peace but yourself. Nothing can bring you peace but the triumph of principles.

18

Friedrich Nietzsche,
The Gay Science

*Raised in a religious household in Prussia, Friedrich Nietzsche (1844–
1900) was a professor of classical philology at the University of Basel until
he was forced to resign in 1879 due to chronic illness. For the next ten years
he wrote extensively, producing such works as* The Gay Science *(1882, ex-
panded in 1887),* Beyond Good and Evil *(1886),* On the Genealogy of
Morals *(1887), and* Twilight of the Idols *(1889). In 1888 he suffered a
complete mental collapse and remained an invalid until his death. Nietzsche
was a vehement critic of both classical models of the good life, especially
what he called "Platonism," and the Judeo-Christian conception of personal
salvation. All these conceptions presuppose what he calls the "ascetic ideal,"
the assumption that we need to discipline and restrain ourselves in order to
achieve some higher good dictated by nature or God or reason or whatever
seems like an absolute at the time. In his view, such asceticism is groundless,
since there are no absolutes or higher sources of value we must obey—this is
what it means to say that "God is dead." If we have nowhere to turn but
ourselves, we might as well liberate ourselves from the craving for metaphysical comfort—from the search for big, transcendent god-terms that tell
us how to live—and instead take over the task of defining our own lives as
we see fit. Such a project of self-fashioning calls for us to embrace life on its
own terms—to "love our fate" (amor fati)—and then shape our lives in
terms of our own vision of what we are and should be. This ideal of creating
one's own life as a work of art has been highly influential in the recent
movement called "postmodernism," with its conception of the good life as involving creativity, playfulness, and an openness to new possibilities.*

58

Only as creators!—This has given me the greatest difficulty and goes on
being my greatest difficulty: to recognize that unspeakably more depends
on *what things are called* than on what they are. The fame, name, and

From Friedrich Nietzsche, *The Gay Science*, trans. by Richard Polt (Hackett Publishing Co., 1995). Reprinted by permission of the publisher.

appearance of a thing, what it counts as, its customary measure and weight—which in the beginning is an arbitrary error for the most part, thrown over things like a garment and alien to their essence, even to their skin—due to the continuous growth of belief in it from generation to generation, this gradually grows, as it were, onto and into the thing, and turns into its very body. The initial appearance almost always becomes the essence in the end and *acts* as essence! But only a fool would think it was enough to point to this beginning and to this misty mantle of illusion in order to *destroy* the world that counts as essential, so-called "*reality!*" Only as creators can we destroy! But we also should not forget this: creating new names and assessments and apparent truths is eventually enough to create new "things."

120

Health of the soul.—The beloved medical formula for morality (whose originator is Ariston of Chios[1]), "Virtue is the health of the soul," would at least, in order to be serviceable, have to be changed into: "Your virtue is the health of your soul." For there is no health in itself, and all attempts to define such a thing have failed lamentably. It all depends on your aim, your horizon, your strengths, your inclinations, your errors, and especially on the ideals and phantasms of your soul—this is what determines *what*, even for your *body*, health must mean. Hence there are countless healths of the body. And the more one allows the individual and the incomparable to raise its head again—the more one unlearns the dogma of "human equality"—the more our medical doctors will have to abandon the concept of a normal health, as well as a normal diet and the normal course of a sickness. And only then could it be time to reflect on the health and sickness of the *soul* and to find each person's special virtue in the health of the soul—which could certainly look in one person like the opposite of health in another. In the end, there would still remain open the great question of whether we could *do without* getting sick, even in the development of our virtue, and whether specifically our thirst for knowledge and self-knowledge does not require the sick soul as much as the healthy one—in short, whether the exclusive will to health is not a prejudice, a cowardice, and perhaps a piece of highly delicate barbarism and backwardness.

124

In the horizon of the infinite.—We have left the land behind and boarded the ship! We have burned our bridges—more than that, we have de-

1. A prominent Stoic philosopher in Athens around 250 B.C.E.

molished the land behind us! Now, little ship, watch out! By your side lies the ocean; true, it does not always roar, and sometimes it lies there like silk and gold and daydreams of kindness. But the hours are coming when you will recognize that it is infinite, and that there is nothing more terrifying than infinity. Oh, the poor bird that felt itself free and now collides with the walls of this cage! Alas, when homesickness for the land comes over you, as if there had been more *freedom* there—and there is no longer any "land!"

125

The madman.—Haven't you heard of that madman who lit a lantern in the bright morning, ran to the marketplace, and shouted unceasingly: "I seek God! I seek God!"? Since many of those who did not believe in God happened to be standing around there, he was the cause of great laughter. "Did he get lost, then?" said one. "Has he lost his way like a child?" said another. "Or is he hiding? Is he scared of us? Did he go for a boat ride? Did he emigrate?" They all shouted and laughed together.

The madman sprang into their midst and transfixed them with his gaze. "Where has God gone?" he cried, "I'll tell you where! *We've killed him—* you and I! We are all his murderers! But how have we done this? How could we have drunk up the sea? Who gave us the sponge to erase the whole horizon? What were we doing when we unchained this Earth from its sun? Now where is it going? Where are we moving? Away from all suns? Aren't we falling constantly? Backwards, sideways, forwards, in every direction? Is there still an above and a below? Aren't we wandering as if through an endless nothing? Isn't empty space breathing upon us? Hasn't it gotten colder? Isn't night and more night continuously coming upon us? Don't lanterns have to be lit in the morning? Don't we yet hear the noise of the gravediggers who are burying God? Don't we yet smell the divine rot?—For gods rot too! God is dead! God remains dead! And we have killed him! . . .

270

What does your conscience say?—"You shall become who you are."

276

For the new year.—Still I live, still I think; I must still live, for I must still think. *Sum, ergo cogito; cogito, ergo sum.*[2] On this day, all allow themselves to express their wish and their most beloved thought. So I too want to say what I wished for from myself today, and what thought first ran across my heart this year—what thought shall be for me the ground, guarantee, and sweetness of all further life! I want to learn more and more to see as beautiful what is necessary in things—in this way I will be one of those who make things beautiful. *Amor fati* [love of fate]: let that be my love from now on! I do not want to wage any war against what is ugly. I do not want to accuse; I do not even want to accuse the accusers. Let *looking away* be my only negation! And all in all, to sum it up: some day I want to be only a Yes-sayer!

283

Preparatory human beings.—I welcome all the signs that a more virile, a more warlike age is upon us, an age that above all will return bravery to its place of honor! For this age shall prepare the way for a still higher age, and gather the strength that that age will someday need—an age that will bring heroism into knowledge and *wage wars* for the sake of thoughts and their consequences.

For now, this requires many preparatory, brave human beings, who certainly cannot arise from nothing—any more than from the sand and slime of today's civilization and big-city culture; human beings who understand how to be satisfied with constant, invisible activity—silent, solitary, and resolute; human beings who have an inner penchant for seeking in all things what is *to be overcome* in them; human beings to whom cheerfulness, patience, simplicity, and contempt for the great vanities belong as much as do magnanimity in victory and indulgence for the small vanities of all the defeated; human beings with a sharp and free judgment about all victors, and about the role played by chance in all victory and fame; human beings with their own holidays, their own workdays, their own periods of mourning, who are used to command and sure in commanding, and are no less prepared to obey when it is appropriate, equally proud in one and in the other case, equally serving their own interests; more endangered human beings, more fruitful human beings, happier human beings!

2. I am, therefore I think; I think, therefore I am. "I think, therefore I am" is the first principle of the philosophy of Descartes (*Discourse on Method*, Part 4).

For, believe me, the secret to reaping the greatest fruitfulness and the greatest enjoyment from existence is *to live dangerously!* Build your cities by Vesuvius! Send your ships into unexplored seas! Live at war with your fellows and with yourselves! Be robbers and conquerors, as long as you cannot be rulers and possessors, you knowing ones! The time is nearly gone when it could be enough for you to live hidden in the woods like shy deer! At last knowledge will reach out its hand for what is due to it—it will want to *rule* and *possess*, and you will too, along with it!

290

One thing is needful.—"Giving style" to one's character—a great and rare art! It is practiced by those who survey everything that their nature offers in the way of strengths and weaknesses, and then fit them all into an artistic plan, until each thing appears as art and reason, and even the weakness charms the eye. Here a great mass of second nature has been added, there a piece of first nature has been removed—in both cases, through long practice and daily work. Here the ugliness that resists removal has been hidden, there it has been reinterpreted into the sublime. Much that is vague and resists formation has been saved up and used for views from afar—it is meant to signal in the direction of the distant and immeasurable. Finally, when the work is complete, it becomes clear how it was the compulsion of a single taste that was ruling and forming, in things both great and small. Whether the taste was a good or a bad one means less than one thinks—it is enough that it is *one* taste!

It will be the strong, domineering natures who, in such a compulsion, in such a constraint and completion under their own laws, will savor their most refined joy. The passion of their formidable wills is relieved by the contemplation of all stylized nature, all conquered nature in a position of service; if they have to build palaces and lay out gardens, it also goes against their grain to set nature free.—In contrast, it is the weak characters, lacking power over themselves, who *hate* the constraint of style; they feel that if this grievous compulsion were imposed on them, they would have to be *debased* by it; they become slaves as soon as they serve, they hate service. Such spirits, who can be spirits of the first rank, are always out to fashion or explain themselves and their surroundings as *free* nature—wild, arbitrary, fantastic, disordered, and surprising. And this is good for them to do, for only thus can they do themselves good!

For one thing is needful: that human beings *attain* satisfaction with themselves—be it through this or that poetry and art—for only then can one stand to look at human beings! Those who are dissatisfied with themselves are constantly ready to take revenge for this; the rest of us will be their victims, if only by always having to stand the ugly sight of them. For the sight of the ugly makes one bad and somber.

335

Hurray for physics!— . . . All who still judge, "everyone would have to act this way in this case," have not yet progressed five steps in self-knowledge. Otherwise they would know that identical actions neither exist nor can exist—that every action that has been done, was done in a completely unique and irretrievable way, and that the same will hold of every future action; that all prescriptions for action relate only to the crass exterior (even the most interior and subtle prescriptions of all moralities up to now); that with these prescriptions, we may well attain an appearance of sameness, *but only an appearance;* that *every* action, whether you look into it or look back at it, is and remains an impenetrable thing; that our opinions about "good," "noble," "great," can never be *proved* by our actions, because every action is unknowable; that certainly our opinions, valuations, and tables of goods are among the most powerful gears in the clockwork of our actions, but that in every particular case the law of their mechanism is unprovable.

Let us *confine* ourselves, then, to purifying our opinions and valuations, and to *creating our own new tables of goods*—but we no longer want to brood over the "moral value of our actions!" Yes, my friends! As regards all the moral blather of some people about others, it's time to feel sick. Sitting in moral judgment should be contrary to our taste! Let's leave this blather and this bad taste to those who have nothing else to do except drag the past a bit farther through time, and who themselves are never the present—in other words, the many, the majority! We, however, *want to become who we are*—the new, the unique, the incomparable, those who give themselves the law, those who create themselves! And for this, we must become the best learners and discoverers of everything lawful and necessary in the world; we must be *physicists* so that we can be *creators* in this sense—while up to now, all valuations and ideals were built on *ignorance* of physics or in *contradiction* to it. And thus: hurray for physics! And a still bigger cheer for what *forces* us to it—our honesty!

341

The heaviest weight.—What if one day or one night a demon slinked after you into your loneliest loneliness and said to you: "This life, as you live it now and as you have lived it, you will have to live once more and countless times more. And there will be nothing new about it, but every pain and every pleasure, and every thought and sigh, and everything unspeakably small and great in your life must come back to you, and all in the same series and sequence—and likewise this spider and this moonlight between the trees, and likewise this moment and I myself. The eternal hourglass of existence is turned over again and again—and you with it, you mote of dust!"

Wouldn't you throw yourself down and gnash your teeth and damn the demon who spoke this way? Or have you ever experienced a prodigious moment in which you would answer him: "You are a god and I have never heard anything more godlike!" If that thought took control of you, it would change you as you are, and maybe shatter you. The question in each and every thing, "Do you will this once more and countless times more?" would lie as the heaviest weight upon your acts! Or how benevolent would you have to become toward yourself and toward life in order to *long for nothing more ardently* than for this ultimate eternal sanction and seal?

343

What our cheerfulness means.—The greatest recent event—that "God is dead," that the belief in the Christian God has become unbelievable— already begins to cast its first shadows on Europe. At least for the few whose eye, the *suspicion* in whose eye is strong and keen enough for this spectacle, some sun seems to have gone down, some deep old trust seems to have turned into doubt. To them, our old world has to seem duskier, more distrustful, more alien, "older" from day to day. For the most part, however, we may assert that the event is far too great, too distant, too removed from most people's capacity to comprehend, for us even to say that the news of it has *arrived* yet—much less that many know yet *what* has really taken place here, and what must all collapse now, once this belief has been undermined, because it was built on it, leaning on it, grown into it— for instance, our entire European morality. This long profusion and procession of breakdown, destruction, decline, and upheaval that now stands before us—who today has yet guessed enough of this to have to serve as the teacher and harbinger of this tremendous logic of terror, the prophet of a gloom and an eclipse of the sun, the like of which has probably never yet happened on earth?

Even we born riddle-solvers who wait, as it were, on the mountaintops, stationed between today and tomorrow, and suspended in the contradiction between today and tomorrow, we firstborns and premature births of the coming century, into whose sight the shadows that must soon envelop Europe *should* really have already come—how is it that even we await the arrival of this gloom without truly being wrapped up in it, and above all,

without care and fear for *ourselves?* Are we perhaps still too concerned
with the *immediate consequences* of this event? After all, these immediate
consequences, its consequences for *us*, are, contrary to what one might
expect, not at all sad and gloomy, but rather like a new kind of light that is
hard to describe, a new kind of happiness, alleviation, cheering, encouragement, and dawn. In fact, when we hear the news that the "old God is
dead," we philosophers and "free spirits" feel as if we were struck by the
rays of a new dawn; at this news, our heart overflows with thankfulness,
wonder, presentiment, expectation. At last the horizon appears free to us
again, even granted that it is not bright. At last our ships may set out again,
set out towards every danger. Every daring act of the knower is allowed
again. The sea, *our* sea lies open there again; maybe there was never before
such an "open sea."

349

The origin of scholars once again.—Wanting to preserve oneself expresses a
situation of emergency, a constriction of the real, fundamental drive of
life, which aims at *extending its power*, and in this willing, often enough
puts self-preservation into question and sacrifices it. One should take it as
symptomatic if particular philosophers, such as the consumptive Spinoza
for example, saw the decisive point precisely in the so-called drive for self-
preservation, had to see it there—for they were people in situations of
emergency. The fact that our modern natural sciences have entangled
themselves to such an extent in the Spinozistic dogma (finally and most
crudely in Darwinism, with its unbelievably one-sided doctrine of the
"struggle for existence") is probably a result of the ancestry of most
natural scientists: in this respect they belong to the "people"; their ances-
tors were poor and humble folks who were all too familiar with the
difficulty of surviving. There hovers over the whole of English Darwinism
something like the stale air of English overpopulation, reeking of small
people and their cramped needs. But as a natural scientist, one should
emerge from one's human corner. And in nature what *rules* is not emergency situations, but overflow, superfluity, even to the point of absurdity.
The struggle for existence is only an *exception*, a temporary restriction of
the will to live; everywhere the struggle, both great and small, revolves
around supremacy, around growth and expansion, around power, in accordance with the will to power, which is precisely the will of life.

356

How things will get more and more "artistic" in Europe.—The need to make
a living still forces upon nearly all male Europeans a *role*, their so-called

profession—even today, in our time of transition, when so much is ceasing to force things upon us. Some retain the freedom, an apparent freedom, to choose this role themselves; most have it chosen for them. The result is strange enough: nearly all Europeans confuse themselves with their role when they reach a more advanced age. They themselves are the victims of their "good acting"; they themselves have forgotten to what extent chance, moods, and whims controlled them when their "profession" was decided—and how many other roles they perhaps *could* have played, for now it is too late! Viewed more deeply, the role has really *become* character; and art, nature.

There have been ages in which one believed with solid confidence, in fact with piety, that one was predestined for precisely this business, precisely this way of earning one's bread, and simply did not want to recognize the element of chance, role, arbitrariness. Classes, guilds, and hereditary trade privileges brought about, with the help of this belief, those enormous social hierarchies that characterize the Middle Ages and which one has to credit with one thing at least: durability (and duration is, on earth, a value of the highest rank!).

But there are opposite ages, the really democratic ages, when people turn more and more against this belief, and a certain cheeky belief and contrary point of view comes to the fore—that belief of the Athenians, which was first noticed in the age of Pericles, that belief of the Americans today, which increasingly wants to become the belief of the Europeans. In such ages, individuals are convinced that they can do practically anything, *can handle practically any role;* they all experiment with themselves, improvise, experiment again, take pleasure in experimenting; all nature ceases and becomes art. Once the Greeks had adopted this *role-faith*—an artist's faith, if you will—they underwent step by step, as is well known, an amazing transformation, which is not in every respect worthy of imitation: *they really became actors.* As actors, they worked their magic on the whole world and conquered it, finally including even the "conqueror of the world" (for the *Graeculus histrio*[3] defeated Rome, and *not* Greek culture, as innocents usually say).

But what I fear, what today we can already grasp with our hands if we feel like doing so, is that we modern human beings are already on the same path; in every case where human beings begin to discover to what extent they are playing a role and to what extent they *can* be actors, they *become* actors. With this, there emerges a new human flora and fauna, of a type which cannot develop in more stable and confined ages—or is left "beneath," beneath the ban and suspicion of dishonor. With this, there always

3. Latin: "little Greek actor," with a contemptuous tone.

emerge the most interesting and craziest ages of history, in which the "actors," *all* sorts of actors, are the real masters. By the same token, another class of human beings is put at an ever greater disadvantage, and is finally made impossible—above all, the great "architects"; constructive energy is paralyzed; the courage to make plans for the long run is discouraged; the organizational geniuses begin to be rare; who dares anymore to undertake works for whose completion one would have to *count on millennia?* For that basic faith is dying out on which one can count in that way, the faith on the basis of which one can make promises, anticipate the future in a plan, sacrifice the future to one's plan: namely, the faith that human beings have value, have meaning, only in so far as they are *stones in a great construction*—for which purpose they must first of all be *stable,* "stones," and above all not actors!

Briefly put—ah, it will still be kept silent long enough!—what from now on will no longer be constructed, no longer *can* be constructed, is a *society* in the old sense of the word; we are lacking everything to build this construction—above all, the material. *None of us is material for a society anymore*—there's a truth that is timely! It makes no difference to me that meanwhile the most short-sighted, perhaps most honest, and in any case the noisiest kind of human being that there is today, our friends the socialists, believe, hope for, dream, and above all scream and scribble roughly the opposite—for one can already read their watchword for the future, "free society," on every table and wall. Free society? Yes, yes! But you know, gentlemen, don't you, what such a thing is built of? Wooden iron! The famous wooden iron! And this wooden iron isn't even wooden.[4]

370

What is romanticism?— . . . What is romanticism? Every art, every philosophy, may be seen as a means of health and assistance in the service of growing, struggling life; they always presuppose suffering and sufferers. But there are two kinds of sufferers: on the one hand, those who suffer from the *over-fullness of life,* who want a Dionysian art, and thus a tragic view and insight into life, and on the other hand, those who suffer from the *impoverishment of life,* who seek calm, stillness, smooth seas, salvation from themselves through art and knowledge, or else intoxication, convulsions, numbing and insanity. To the double needs of the *latter* type there corresponds all romanticism in arts and knowledge; to them there corresponded (and corresponds) Schopenhauer just as much as Richard

4. "Wooden iron" is a proverbial German example of an oxymoron, such as "square circle."

Wagner, to name the most famous and marked romantics whom at that time I *misunderstood*—*not* to their disadvantage, by the way, as one may concede to me in all fairness. Those who are richest in the fullness of life, the Dionysian god and human being, can permit themselves not only the sight of the terrible and questionable, but even the terrible deed, and the luxury of destruction, disintegration, negation. With them, what is evil, senseless, and ugly seems to be allowed, as it were, as a result of an overflow of engendering, impregnating forces that can create a bountiful orchard from any wasteland. In contrast, those who suffer the most and are poorest in life would most need mildness, peacefulness, kindness in thought and action, and if possible, a god that is really a god for the sick, a "savior." They would equally need logic, the conceptual intelligibility of existence—for logic calms one, makes one confident—and in short, a certain warm, fear-dispelling narrowness and enclosure within optimistic horizons.

Thus I gradually learned to comprehend Epicurus, the opposite of a Dionysian pessimist, and likewise the "Christian," who in fact is just a kind of Epicurean and, like the Epicurean, is essentially a romantic. My sight grew ever sharper for that most difficult and dangerous form of *backward inference* in which the most mistakes are made: the backward inference from the work to the author, from the deed to the doer, from the ideal to the one who finds it *necessary*, from every way of thinking and valuing to the *need* that is in command behind it.

With regard to all aesthetic values, I now make use of this main distinction: I ask in every individual case, "Is it hunger or overflow that has become creative here?" Another distinction would seem to recommend itself more to begin with—it is more obvious by far—namely, paying attention to whether the longing for fixation, externalization, *being*, is the cause of the creation, or whether it is the longing for destruction, change, the new, the future, *becoming*. But both forms of longing, considered more deeply, still prove to be ambiguous, and in fact they can be interpreted in terms of the previously mentioned and, as it seems to me, preferable scheme. The longing for *destruction*, change, becoming can be the expression of the over-full force pregnant with the future (my term for this is, as is known, the word "Dionysian"), but it can also be the hatred of the misfits, the destitute, and the hapless, who destroy, *must* destroy, because what endures, in fact all endurance, all being itself, irritates and incites them—in order to understand this emotion, take a close look at our anarchists.

The will to *eternalize* likewise requires a twofold interpretation. It can, on the one hand, come from gratitude and love; an art with this origin will always be an art of apotheosis, perhaps dithyrambic with Rubens, or blissfully playful with Hafiz, clear and kindly with Goethe, and shedding a Homeric light and glory upon all things. But this can also be that tyrannic will of one who is suffering severely, is struggling and tortured, and would like to forge what is most personal, individual, narrow, and really idiosyncratic in this suffering into a binding law and compulsion; who takes revenge, as it were, on all things by imprinting, branding, and forcing upon them *his* image, the image of *his* torture. The latter is *romantic pessimism* in its most explicit form, be it Schopenhauerian philosophy of will, or Wagnerian music—romantic pessimism, the last *great* event in the destiny of our culture.

(That there *could* still be a quite different pessimism, a classical pessimism—this premonition and vision belongs to me, as inseparable from me, as my *proprium* and *ipsissimum* [my own and most proper possession]; it's just that the word "classical" offends my ears; it is overused by far and has become too blunt and unrecognizable. I call this pessimism of the future—for it is coming, I see it coming!—*Dionysian* pessimism.)

374

Our new "infinite."—How far the perspectival character of existence reaches, or even whether existence has any other character; whether an existence without interpretation, without "sense," becomes precisely "nonsense"; whether, on the other hand, all existence is not essentially an *interpreting* existence—this cannot be figured out, and rightfully so, even by the most diligent and painfully conscientious analysis and self-examination of the intellect, since in this analysis the human intellect cannot help seeing itself under its own perspectival forms, and *only* in them. We cannot see around our own corner. It is hopeless curiosity to want to know what other sorts of intellect and perspective there *could* be—for instance, whether any beings can perceive time backwards, or alternately forwards and backwards (which would entail a different direction of life, and a different concept of cause and effect).

But I think that today we are at least far from the laughable presumption of decreeing from our corner that one is *allowed* to have perspectives only from this corner. Rather, the world has once more become "infinite" for us—inasmuch as we cannot exclude the possibility that it *contains infinite interpretations*. Once again the great horror takes hold of us—but who would want directly to deify *this* monster of an unknown world in the old style again? And, as it were, to worship the *unknown* from now on as "the *Unknown One?*" Ah, there are too many *ungodly* possibilities of interpretation comprised in this unknown, too much devilry, stupidity, folly of interpretation—our own human, all too human interpretation itself, which we know. . . .

375

Why we seem to be Epicureans.—We are wary, we moderns, of all ultimate convictions; our mistrust lies in wait for the enchantments and trickeries of conscience that lie in every strong belief, in every unconditional Yes and No; how is this to be explained? Perhaps one may see in this, to a large extent, the caution of the "burned child," the disappointed idealist. But the other and better factor is the rejoicing curiosity of an erstwhile corner-dweller who has been brought by his corner to the point of despair, and now revels and delights in the opposite of the corner, in the unlimited, in the "free in itself." Thus there develops a nearly Epicurean craving for knowledge which does not want to let the questionable character of things get by it easily; likewise, an aversion to big moral words and moral attitudes, a taste that rejects all crass, foursquare oppositions, and is proudly aware of its practiced restraint. For *that* is what constitutes our pride, this easy tightening of the reins in our headlong urge for certainty, this self-control of the rider in his wildest riding. For now, as before, we have mad and fiery beasts beneath us, and if we hesitate, it is danger least of all that makes us hesitate.

382

The great health.—We new, nameless, hardly intelligible, premature births of a yet unproven future—for a new end, we also need a new means, namely a new health, a stronger, shrewder, tougher, bolder, gladder health than any health has been up to now. Whoever has a soul that thirsts to have experienced the entire range of values and desirables up to now, and to have sailed around all the coasts of this ideal "Mediterranean"; whoever wants to know from the adventures of one's ownmost experience how it feels to be a conqueror and discoverer of the ideal, and likewise an artist, a saint, a lawmaker, a sage, a scholar, a devotee, a soothsayer, a divine loner in the old style—requires one thing above all for this, *the great health*—a health such as one does not simply have, but also constantly acquires and must acquire, because one is giving it up again and again, and must do so!

And now, after having been on our way like this for a long time, we Argonauts of the ideal, braver perhaps than is prudent, and having been shipwrecked often enough and brought to grief, but healthier, as I said, than one would like to let us be, dangerously healthy, healthy ever again—now it would seem to us as if, as a reward for this, we have a yet-undiscovered land before us, whose boundaries no one has yet discerned, a Beyond to all lands and corners of the ideal up to now, a world so over-rich in what is beautiful, strange, questionable, terrible and divine, that our curiosity as well as our thirst for possession is beside itself—alas, nothing will satisfy us anymore!

How could we, after such views and with such a burning hunger in our conscience and our science, still be content *with the human beings of the present?* This is too bad, but it is unavoidable that when we look at their worthiest goals and hopes it is hard for us to keep a straight face, and maybe we will just not look at them anymore. A different ideal runs ahead of us, an odd, seductive, perilous ideal which we would not like to per-suade anyone to follow, because we do not so easily grant anyone *the right to do so:* the ideal of a spirit that plays naively, that is, not deliberately but from overflowing fullness and power, with all that up to now was called holy, good, untouchable, divine; for whom the highest thing in which the common people find their fair standard of value would just amount to danger, decline, and debasement, or at least, rest, blindness, and tempo-rary self-forgetfulness; the ideal of a human and superhuman well-being and goodwill that will often enough appear *inhuman,* for instance when beside all earthly seriousness up to now, beside every sort of solemnity in gesture, word, sound, look, morality and task, it presents itself as their most personified, involuntary parody—but with which, nonetheless, per-haps *the great seriousness* first begins, the real question mark is first posed, the destiny of the soul takes a turn, the clock's hand moves, the tragedy *begins.* . . .

19

Jean-Paul Sartre,
Being and Nothingness

Author of plays and novels as well as philosophical works, Jean-Paul Sartre (1905–1980) was one of the greatest intellectuals in twentieth-century France. In 1929 he graduated from the prestigious École Normale and met his lifelong companion and coworker, Simone de Beauvoir. In the 1940s he wrote such literary works as No Exit, The Flies, *and* The Age of Reason, *as well as his most important philosophical work,* Being and Nothingness *(1943). Sartre was a staunch supporter of movements for social justice and peace throughout his life. In 1964 he refused to accept the Nobel Prize in literature as a protest against the way such prizes turn authors into institutions.*

Sartre's writings were a primary source of the worldwide interest in existentialism in the fifties and sixties. Existentialism is a philosophy which focuses on the concrete existence of the individual, describing our actual lives and pointing toward a more authentic way of life. The basic claim of Sartrean existentialism is that human beings have free will, that is, they are free to define their own lives and can therefore break with their past at any moment and set out in a radically new direction. To support this conception of human freedom, Sartre argues as follows. Each of us has certain fixed traits that have taken a determinate shape over the course of his or her life. These "given" factors (a particular body-type, a specific circle of friends and family, a "situation," etc.) make up the person's "facticity," what Sartre calls the "in itself," which that person has to come to terms with in living out his or her life. At the same time, however, we also have the ability to reflect on our facticity and make a decision about what we are going to do with it in undertaking projects into the future. This ability to seize on possibilities and take a stand into the future is called our "transcendence." As reflective, or "for itself," we can transcend or surpass what we have been so far by deciding to act in specific ways. For example, if you have a cowardly disposition and tend to run away from frightening situations, you can always choose to change yourself by deciding to stand firm in some particular situation. And if you stand firm over and over again, you will begin to become a brave person. Thus, on Sartre's view, if you go on being cowardly, it is not because of any factors outside your control; it is because you are choosing to be a coward—you could always change if you wanted to. It follows, then, that all of us are creating our own lives through our choices. Human beings are self-creating or self-fashioning beings.

Sartre's conception of humans as consisting of both facticity and transcendence implies that what is most unique about humans is that they have a certain "lack" or "nothingness" at the core of their being. If I am always more than the sum total of what I have been up to this moment—if I have the ability to say "no" to my inherent tendencies and change myself through my free choices—then I can never completely be anything once and for all. Sartre says that humans can never be something in the way a cabbage can be a cabbage, for, as capable of reflection and self-transformation, we always stand out into an open realm of possibilities that transcend our "in itself." The fact that a human being is characterized by both facticity and transcendence implies that humans are capable of self-deception or bad faith. We can deny one of the aspects that make us up, thinking of ourselves as all transcendence—pure spirits capable of anything, with no real attachments to the world—or as pure facticity—as brute objects controlled by the causal order of the material universe. Either way, this is bad faith. In Sartre's view, bad faith pervades much of our everyday life. It lies at the root of the bourgeoisie's "spirit of seriousness," the complacent assurance that there is a human nature or higher absolute which dictates what we really are and how we ought to live. In Sartre's view, it is bad faith to think that there is anything outside us or fixed within us that dictates what we are and should be.

Sartre also holds that humans are driven by a desire to close up or heal the tension at the core of their being. Humans want to actually be something once and for all—they want to be both "in itself" and "for itself," to be both complete and free, as God is supposed to be. But such a goal can never be achieved, for as long as you are alive, you are free, and so you have the ability to overthrow what you have done up to now and start out on a new track. But this means, as we have already seen, that there is a lack or gap in a human being: you can never ultimately realize or fulfill yourself in the sense of giving yourself a stable, finished identity. Thus, Sartre concludes Being and Nothingness *by saying "Man is a useless passion." To be human is to be constantly driven forward by the desire to be complete, but such a completion is ultimately never possible so long as we are still alive.*

Bad Faith and Falsehood

. . . In our Introduction we defined consciousness as "a being such that in its being, its being is in question in so far as this being implies a being other than itself." But now that we have examined the meaning of "the question," we can at present also write the formula thus: "Consciousness is a being, the nature of which is to be conscious of the nothingness of its being." In a prohibition or a veto, for example, the human being denies a future transcendence. But this negation is not explicative. My consciousness is not restricted to *envisioning a négatité*. It constitutes itself in its own flesh as the nihilation of a possibility which another human reality projects as *its* possibility. For that reason it must arise in the world as a *Not;* it is as a Not that the slave first apprehends the master, or that the prisoner who is trying to escape sees the guard who is watching him. There are even men (*e.g.,* caretakers, overseers, gaolers,) whose social reality is uniquely that of the Not, who will live and die, having forever been only a Not upon the earth. Others so as to make the Not a part of their very subjectivity, establish their human personality as a perpetual negation. This is the meaning and function of what Scheler calls "the man of resentment"—in reality, the Not. But there exist more subtle behaviors, the description of which will lead us further into the inwardness of consciousness. Irony is one of these. In irony a man annihilates what he posits within one and the same act; he leads us to believe in order not to be believed; he affirms to deny and denies to affirm; he creates a positive object but it has no being other than its nothingness. Thus attitudes of negation toward the self permit us to raise a new question: What are we to say is the being of man who has the possibility of denying himself? But it is out of the question to discuss the attitude of "self-negation" in its universality. The kinds of behavior which can be ranked under this heading are too diverse; we risk retaining only the abstract form of them. It is best to choose and to examine one determined attitude which is essential to human reality and which is such that consciousness instead of directing its negation outward turns it toward itself. This attitude, it seems to me, is *bad faith* (*mauvaise foi*).

Frequently this is identified with falsehood. We say indifferently of a person that he shows signs of bad faith or that he lies to himself. We shall willingly grant that bad faith is a lie to oneself, on condition that we distinguish the lie to oneself from lying in general. Lying is a negative attitude, we will agree to that. But this negation does not bear on con-

From *Essays in Existentialism,* edited by Wade Baskin. Copyright © 1965 by Philosophical Library, Inc. Published by arrangement with Carol Publishing Group. A Citadel Press Book.

sciousness itself; it aims only at the transcendent. The essence of the lie implies in fact that the liar actually is in complete possession of the truth which he is hiding. A man does not lie about what he is ignorant of; he does not lie when he spreads an error of which he himself is the dupe; he does not lie when he is mistaken. The ideal description of the liar would be a cynical consciousness, affirming truth within himself, denying it in his *words,* and denying that negation as such. Now this doubly negative attitude rests on the transcendent; the fact expressed is transcendent since it do.s not exist, and the original negation rests on a *truth;* that is, on a particular type of transcendence. As for the inner negation which I effect correlatively with the affirmation for myself of the truth, this rests on *words;* that is, on an event in the world. Furthermore the inner disposition of the liar is positive; it could be the object of an affirmative judgment. The liar intends to deceive and he does not seek to hide this intention from himself nor to disguise the translucency of consciousness; on the contrary, he has recourse to it when there is a question of deciding secondary behavior. It explicitly exercises a regulatory control over all attitudes. As for his flaunted intention of telling the truth ("I'd never want to deceive you! This is true! I swear it!")—all this, of course, is the object of an inner negation, but also it is not recognized by the liar as *his* intention. It is played, imitated, it is the intention of the character which he plays in the eyes of his questioner, but this character, precisely because he does *not exist,* is a transcendent. Thus the lie does not put into the play the inner structure of present consciousness; all the negations which constitute it bear on objects which by this fact are removed from consciousness. The lie then does not require special ontological foundation, and the explanations which the existence of negation in general requires are valid without change in the case of deceit. Of course we have described the ideal lie; doubtless it happens often enough that the liar is more or less the victim of his lie, that he half persuades himself of it. But these common, popular forms of the lie are also degenerate aspects of it; they represent intermediaries between falsehood and bad faith. The lie is a behavior of transcendence.

The lie is also a normal phenomenon of what Heidegger calls the "*Mitsein.*"[1] It presupposes my existence, the existence of the Other, my existence *for* the Other, and the existence of the Other *for* me. Thus there is no difficulty in holding that the liar must make the project of the lie in entire clarity and that he must possess a complete comprehension of the lie and of the truth which he is altering. It is sufficient that an over-all opacity hide his intentions from the *Other;* it is sufficient that the Other can take

1. A "being-with" others in the world. Tr.

the lie for truth. By the lie consciousness affirms that it exists by nature as *hidden from the Other;* it utilizes for its own profit the ontological duality of myself and myself in the eyes of the Other.

The situation cannot be the same for bad faith if this, as we have said, is indeed a lie to oneself. To be sure, the one who practices bad faith is hiding a displeasing truth or presenting as truth a pleasing untruth. Bad faith then has in appearance the structure of falsehood. Only what changes everything is the fact that in bad faith it is from myself that I am hiding the truth. Thus the duality of the deceiver and the deceived does not exist here. Bad faith on the contrary implies in essence the unity of a *single* consciousness. This does not mean that it cannot be conditioned by the *Mit-sein* like all other phenomena of human reality, but the *Mit-sein* can call forth bad faith only by presenting itself as a *situation* which bad faith permits surpassing; bad faith does not come from outside to human reality. One does not undergo his bad faith; one is not infected with it; it is not a *state.* But consciousness affects itself with bad faith. There must be an original intention and a project of bad faith; this project implies a comprehension of bad faith as such and a pre-reflective apprehension (of) consciousness as affecting itself with bad faith. It follows first that the one to whom the lie is told and the one who lies are one and the same person, which means that I must know in my capacity as deceiver the truth which is hidden from me in my capacity as the one deceived. Better yet I must know the truth very exactly *in order* to conceal it more carefully—and this not at two different moments, which at a pinch would allow us to re-establish a semblance of duality—but in the unitary structure of a single project. How then can the lie subsist if the duality which conditions it is suppressed?

To this difficulty is added another which is derived from the total translucency of consciousness. That which affects itself with bad faith must be conscious (of) its bad faith since the being of consciousness is consciousness of being. It appears then that I must be in good faith, at least to the extent that I am conscious of my bad faith. But then this whole psychic system is annihilated. We must agree in fact that if I deliberately and cynically attempt to lie to myself, I fail completely in this undertaking; the lie falls back and collapses beneath my look; it is ruined *from behind* by the very consciousness of lying to myself which pitilessly constitutes itself well within my project as its very condition. We have here an *evanescent* phenomenon which exists only in and through its own differentiation. To be sure, these phenomena are frequent and we shall see that there is in fact an "evanescence" of bad faith, which, it is evident, vacillates continually between good faith and cynicism: Even though the existence of bad faith is very precarious, and though it belongs to the kind of psychic structures which we might call "metastable,"[2] it presents nonetheless an autonomous and durable form. It can even be the normal aspect of life for a very great number of people. A person can *live* in bad faith, which does not mean that he does not have abrupt awakenings to cynicism or to good faith, but which implies a constant and particular style of life. Our embarrassment then appears extreme since we can neither reject nor comprehend bad faith. . . .

Patterns of Bad Faith

If we wish to get out of this difficulty, we should examine more closely the patterns of bad faith and attempt a description of them. This description will permit us perhaps to fix more exactly the conditions for the possibility of bad faith; that is, to reply to the question we raised at the outset: "What must be the being of man if he is to be capable of bad faith?"

Take the example of a woman who has consented to go out with a particular man for the first time. She knows very well the intentions which the man who is speaking to her cherishes regarding her. She knows also that it will be necessary sooner or later for her to make a decision. But she does not want to realize the urgency; she concerns herself only with what is respectful and discreet in the attitude of her companion. She does not apprehend this conduct as an attempt to achieve what we call "the first approach"; that is, she does not want to see possibilities of temporal development which his conduct presents. She restricts this behavior to what is in the present; she does not wish to read in the phrases which he addresses to her anything other than their explicit meaning. If he says to her, "I find you so attractive!" she disarms this phrase of its sexual background; she attaches to the conversation and to the behavior of the speaker, the immediate meanings, which she imagines as objective qualities. The man who is speaking to her appears to her sincere and respectful as the table is round or square, as the wall coloring is blue or gray. The qualities thus attached to the person she is listening to are in this way fixed in a permanence like that of things, which is no other than the projection of the strict present of the qualities into the temporal flux. This is because she does not quite know what she wants. She is profoundly aware of the desire which she inspires, but the desire cruel and naked would humiliate and horrify her. Yet she would find no charm in a respect which would be only respect. In order to satisfy her, there must be a feeling which is addressed wholly to her *personality*—i.e., to her full freedom—and which would be a recognition of her freedom. But at the same time this feeling

2. A word meaning subject to sudden changes or transitions. Tr.

must be wholly desire; that is, it must address itself to her body as object. This time then she refuses to apprehend the desire for what it is; she does not even give it a name; she recognizes it only to the extent that it transcends itself toward admiration, esteem, respect and that it is wholly absorbed in the more refined forms which it produces, to the extent of no longer figuring anymore as a sort of warmth and density. But then suppose he takes her hand. This act of her companion risks changing the situation by calling for an immediate decision. To leave the hand there is to consent in herself to flirt, to engage herself. To withdraw it is to break the troubled and unstable harmony which gives the hour its charm. The aim is to postpone the moment of decision as long as possible. We know what happens next; the young woman leaves her hand there, but she *does not notice* that she is leaving it. She does not notice because it happens by chance that she is at this moment all intellect. She draws her companion up to the most lofty regions of sentimental speculation; she speaks of Life, of her life, she shows herself in her essential aspect—a personality, a consciousness. And during this time the divorce of the body from the soul is accomplished; the hand rests inert between the warm hands of her companion—neither consenting nor resisting—a thing.

We shall say that this woman is in bad faith. But we see immediately that she uses various procedures in order to maintain herself in this bad faith. She has disarmed the actions of her companion by reducing them to being only what they are; that is, to existing in the mode of the in-itself. But she permits herself to enjoy his desire, to the extent that she will apprehend it as not being what it is, will recognize its transcendence. Finally while sensing profoundly the presence of her own body—to the degree of being disturbed perhaps—she realizes herself as *not being* her own body, and she contemplates it as though from above as a passive object to which events can *happen* but which can neither provoke them nor avoid them because all its possibilities are outside of it. What unity do we find in these various aspects of bad faith? It is a certain art of forming contradictory concepts which unite in themselves both an idea and the negation of that idea. The basic concept which is thus engendered, utilizes the double property of the human being, who is at once a *facticity* and a *transcendence*. These two aspects of human reality are and ought to be capable of a valid coordination. But bad faith does not wish either to coordinate them nor to surmount them in a synthesis. Bad faith seeks to affirm their identity while preserving their differences. It must affirm facticity as *being* transcendence and transcendence as *being* facticity, in such a way that at the instant when a person apprehends the one, he can find himself abruptly faced with the other.

We can find the prototype of formulae of bad faith in certain famous expressions which have been rightly conceived to produce their whole effect in a spirit of bad faith. Take for example, the title of a work by Jacques Chardonne, *Love Is Much More than Love.* We see here how unity is established between *present* love in its facticity—"the contact of two skins," sensuality, egoism, Proust's mechanism of jealousy, Adler's battle of the *sexes,* etc.—and love as transcendence—Mauriac's "river of fire," the longing for the infinite, Plato's *eros,* Lawrence's deep cosmic intuition, etc. Here we leave facticity to find ourselves suddenly beyond the present and the factual condition of man, beyond the psychological, in the heart of metaphysics. On the other hand, the title of a play by Sarment, *I Am Too Great for Myself,* which also presents characters in bad faith, throws us first into full transcendence in order suddenly to imprison us within the narrow limits of our factual essence. We will discover this structure again in the famous sentence: "He has become what he was" or in its no less famous opposite: "Eternity at last changes each man into himself." It is well understood that these various formulae have only the appearance of bad faith; they have been conceived in this paradoxical form explicitly to shock the mind and discountenance it by an enigma. But it is precisely this appearance which is of concern to us. What counts here is that the formulae do not constitute new, solidly structured ideas; on the contrary, they are formed so as to remain in perpetual disintegration and so that we may slide at any time from naturalistic present to transcendence and vice versa.

We can see the use which bad faith can make of these judgments which all aim at establishing that I am not what I am. If I were only what I *am,* I could, for example, seriously consider an adverse criticism which someone makes of me, question myself scrupulously, and perhaps be compelled to recognize the truth in it. But thanks to transcendence, I am not subject to all that I am. I do not even have to discuss the justice of the reproach. As Suzanne says to Figaro, "To prove that I am right would be to recognize that I can be wrong." I am on a plane where no reproach can touch me since what I really am is my transcendence. I flee from myself, I escape myself, I leave my tattered garment in the hands of the fault-finder. But the ambiguity necessary for bad faith comes from the fact that I affirm here that I *am* my transcendence in the mode of being of a thing. It is only thus, in fact, that I can feel that I escape all reproaches. It is in the sense that our young woman purifies the desire of anything humiliating by being willing to consider it only as pure transcendence, which she avoids even naming. But inversely "I Am Too Great for Myself," while showing our transcendence changed into facticity, is the source of an infinity of excuses for our failures or our weaknesses. Similarly the young coquette maintains transcendence to the extent that the respect, the esteem manifested by the actions of her admirer are already on the plane of the transcendent. But she arrests this transcendence, she glues it down with all the facticity of the present; respect is nothing other than respect, it is an arrested surpassing which no longer surpasses itself toward anything.

But although this *metastable* concept of "transcendence-facticity" is one of the most basic instruments of bad faith, it is not the only one of its kind. We can equally well use another kind of duplicity derived from human reality which we will express roughly by saying that its being-for-itself implies complementarily a being-for-others. Upon any one of my conducts it is always possible to converge two looks, mine and that of the Other. The conduct will not present exactly the same structure in each case. But as we shall see later, as each look perceives it, there is between these two aspects of my being, no difference between appearance and being—as if I were to my self the truth of myself and as if the Other possessed only a deformed image of me. The equal dignity of being possessed by my being-for-others and by my being-for-myself permits a perpetually disintegrating synthesis and a perpetual game of escape from the for-itself to the for-others and from the for-others to the for-itself. We have seen also the use which our young lady made of our being-in-the-midst-of-the-world—i.e., of our inert presence as a passive object among other objects—in order to relieve herself suddenly from the functions of her being-in-the-world—that is, from the being which causes there to be a world by projecting itself beyond the world toward its own possibilities. Let us note finally the confusing syntheses which play on the nihilating ambiguity of these temporal ekstases, affirming at once that I am what I have been (the man who deliberately *arrests himself* at one period in his life and refuses to take into consideration the later changes) and that I am not what I have been (the man who in the face of reproaches or rancor dissociates himself from his past by insisting on his freedom and on his perpetual re-creation). In all these concepts, which have only a transitive role in the reasoning and which are eliminated from the conclusion, (like hypochondriacs in the calculations of physicians), we find again the same structure. We have to deal with human reality as a being which is what it is not and which is not what it is.

But what exactly is necessary in order for these concepts of disintegration to be able to receive even a pretence of existence, in order for them to be able to appear for an instant to consciousness, even in a process of evanescence? A quick examination of the idea of sincerity, the antithesis of bad faith, will be very instructive in this connection. Actually sincerity presents itself as a demand and consequently is not a *state*. Now what is the ideal to be attained in this case? It is necessary that a man be *for himself* only what he *is*. But is this not precisely the definition of the in-itself—or if you prefer—the principle of identity? To posit as an ideal the being of things, is this not to assert by the same stroke that this being does not belong to human reality and that the principle of identity, far from being a universal axiom universally applied, is only a synthetic principle enjoying a merely regional universality? Thus in order that the concepts of bad faith can put us under illusion at least for an instant, in order that the candor of "pure hearts" (*cf.* Gide, Kessel) can have validity for human reality as an ideal, the principle of identity must not represent a constitutive principle of human reality and human reality must not be necessarily what it is but must be able to be what it is not. What does this mean?

If man is what he is, bad faith is for ever impossible and candor ceases to be his ideal and becomes instead his being. But is man what he is? And more generally, how can he *be* what he is when he exists as consciousness of being? If candor or sincerity is a universal value, it is evident that the maxim "one must be what one is" does not serve solely as a regulating principle for judgments and concepts by which I express what I am. It posits not merely an ideal of knowing but an ideal of *being;* it proposes for us an absolute equivalence of being with itself as a prototype of being. In this sense it is necessary that *we make ourselves* what we are. But what are we then if we have the constant obligation to make ourselves what we are, if our mode of being is having the obligation to be what we are?

Let us consider this waiter in the café. His movement is quick and forward, a little too precise, a little too rapid. He comes toward the patrons with a step a little too quick. He bends forward a little too eagerly; his voice, his eyes express an interest a little too solicitous for the order of the customer. Finally there he returns, trying to imitate in his walk the inflexible stiffness of some kind of automaton while carrying his tray with the recklessness of a tight-rope-walker by putting it in a perpetually unstable, perpetually broken equilibrium which he perpetually reestablishes by a light movement of the arm and hand. All his behavior seems to us a game. He applies himself to chaining his movements as if they were mechanisms, the one regulating the other; his gestures and even his voice seem to be mechanisms; he gives himself the quickness and pitiless rapidity of things. He is playing, he is amusing himself. But what is he playing? We need not watch long before we can explain it: he is playing *at being* a waiter in a café. There is nothing there to surprise us. The game is a kind of marking out and investigation. The child plays with his body in order to explore it, to take inventory of it; the waiter in the café plays with his condition in order to *realize* it. This obligation is not different from that which is imposed on all tradesmen. Their condition is wholly one of ceremony. The public demands of them that they realize it as a ceremony; there is the dance of the grocer, of the tailor, of the auctioneer, by which they endeavour to persuade their clientele that they are nothing but a grocer, an auctioneer, a tailor. A grocer who dreams is offensive to the buyer, because such a grocer is not wholly a grocer. Society demands that he limit himself to his function as a grocer, just as the soldier at attention makes himself into a soldier-thing with a direct regard which does not see at all, which is no longer meant to see, since it is the rule and not the interest of the moment which determines the point he must fix his eyes on (the sight "fixed at ten paces"). There are indeed many precautions to imprison a man in what he is, as if we lived in perpetual fear that he might escape from it, that he might break away and suddenly elude his condition.

In a parallel situation, from within, the waiter in the café cannot be immediately a café waiter in the sense that this inkwell *is* an inkwell, or the glass is a glass. It is by no means that he cannot form reflective judgments or concepts concerning his condition. He knows well what it "means": the obligation of getting up at five o'clock, of sweeping the floor of the shop before the restaurant opens, of starting the coffee pot going, *etc.* He knows the rights which it allows: the right to the tips, the right to belong to a union, etc. But all these concepts, all these judgments refer to the transcendent. It is a matter of abstract possibilities, of rights and duties conferred on a "person possessing rights." And it is precisely this person *who I have to be* (if I am the waiter in question) and who I am not. It is not that I do not wish to be this person or that I want this person to be different. But rather there is no common measure between his being and mine. It is a "representation" for others and for myself, which means that I can be he only in *representation*. But if I represent myself as him, I am not he; I am separated from him as the object from the subject, separated *by nothing,* but this nothing isolates me from him. I cannot be he, I can only play *at being* him; that is, imagine to myself that I am he. And thereby I affect him with nothingness. In vain do I fulfill the functions of a café waiter. I can be he only in the neutralized mode, as the actor is Hamlet, by mechanically making the *typical gestures* of my state and by aiming at myself as an imaginary café waiter through those gestures taken as an "analogue." What I attempt to realize is a being-in-itself of the café waiter, as if it were not just in my power to confer their value and their urgency upon my duties and the rights of my position, as if it were not my free choice to get up each morning at five o'clock or to remain in bed, even though it meant getting fired. As if from the very fact that I sustain this role in existence I did not transcend it on every side, as if I did not constitute myself as one *beyond* my condition. Yet there is no doubt that I *am* in a sense a café waiter—otherwise could I not just as well call myself a diplomat or a reporter? But if I am one, this cannot be in the mode of being in-itself. I am a waiter in the mode of *being what I am not.*

Furthermore we are dealing with more than mere social positions; I am

Self-Realization

never any one of my attitudes, any one of my actions. The good speaker is the one who *plays* at speaking, because he cannot *be speaking*. The attentive pupil who wishes to *be* attentive, his eyes riveted on the teacher, his ears open wide, so exhausts himself in playing the attentive role that he ends up by no longer hearing anything. Perpetually absent to my body, to my acts, I am despite myself that "divine absence" of which Valéry speaks. I cannot say either that I *am* here or that I *am* not here, in the sense that we say "that box of matches *is* on the table"; this would be to confuse my "being-in-the-world" with a "being-in the midst of the world." Nor that I *am* standing, nor that I *am* seated; this would be to confuse my body with the idiosyncratic totality of which it is only one of the structures. On all sides I escape being and yet—I am.

But take a mode of being which concerns only myself: I am sad. One might think that surely I am the sadness in the mode of being what I am. What is the sadness, however, if not the intentional unity which comes to reassemble and animate the totality of my conduct? It is the meaning of this dull look with which I view the world, of my bowed shoulders, of my lowered head, of the listlessness in my whole body. But at the very moment when I adopt each of these attitudes, do I not know that I shall not be able to hold on to it? Let a stranger suddenly appear and I will lift up my head, I will assume a lively cheerfulness. What will remain of my sadness except that I obligingly promise it an appointment for later after the departure of the visitor? Moreover is not this sadness itself a *conduct?* Is it not consciousness which affects itself with sadness as a magical recource against a situation too urgent?[3] And in this case even, should we not say that being sad means first to make oneself sad? That may be, someone will say, but after all doesn't giving oneself the being of sadness mean to *receive* this being? It makes no difference from where I receive it. The fact is that a consciousness which affects itself with sadness *is* sad precisely for this reason. But it is difficult to comprehend the nature of consciousness; the being-sad is not a ready-made being which I give to myself as I can give this book to my friend. I do not possess the property of *affecting myself with being.* If I make myself sad, I must continue to make myself sad from beginning to end. I cannot treat my sadness as an impulse finally achieved and put it on file without recreating it, nor can I carry it in the manner of an inert body which continues its movement after the initial shock. There is no inertia in consciousness. If I make myself sad, it is because I *am* not sad—the being of the sadness escapes me by and in the very act by which I affect myself with it. The being-in-itself of sadness perpetually haunts my

3. *Esquisse d'une théorie des émotions*, Hermann Paul. In English, *The Emotions. Outline of a Theory* (Philosophical Library, 1948).

consciousness (of) being sad, but it is as a value which I cannot realize; it stands as a regulative meaning of my sadness, not as its constitutive modality.

. . .

But bad faith is not restricted to denying the qualities which I possess, to not seeing the being which I am. It attempts also to constitute myself as being what I am not. It apprehends me positively as courageous when I am not so. And that is possible, once again, only if I am what I am not; that is, if non-being in me does not have being even as non-being. Of course necessarily I *am not* courageous; otherwise bad faith would not be *bad* faith. But in addition my effort in bad faith must include the ontological comprehension that even in my usual being what I *am*, I am not it really and that there is no such difference between the being of "being-sad," for example—which I *am* in the mode of not being what I am—and the "non-being" of not-being-courageous which I wish to hide from myself. Moreover it is particularly requisite that the very negation of being should be itself the object of a perpetual nihilation, that the very meaning of "non-being" be perpetually in question in human reality. If I *were not* courageous in the way in which this inkwell is not a table; that is, if I were isolated in my cowardice, propped firmly against it, incapable of putting it in relation to its opposite, if I were not capable of *determining* myself as cowardly—that is, to deny courage to myself and thereby to escape my cowardice in the very moment that I posit it—if it were not on principle *impossible* for me to coincide with my *not-being-courageous* as well as with my being-courageous—then any project of bad faith would be prohibited me. Thus in order for bad faith to be possible, sincerity itself must be in bad faith. The condition of the possibility for bad faith is that human reality, in its most immediate being, in the intrastructure of the pre-reflective *cogito*, must be what it is not and not be what it is.

. . .

Freedom and Responsibility

Although the considerations which are about to follow are of interest primarily to the ethicist, it may nevertheless be worthwhile after these descriptions and arguments to return to the freedom of the for-itself and to try to understand what the fact of this freedom represents for human destiny.

The essential consequence of our earlier remarks is that man being condemned to be free carries the weight of the whole world on his shoulders; he is responsible for the world and for himself as a way of being.

We are taking the word "responsibility" in its ordinary sense as "consciousness (of) being the incontestable author of an event or of an object." In this sense the responsibility of the for-itself is overwhelming since he[4] is the one by whom it happens that *there is* a world; since he is also the one who makes himself be, then whatever may be the situation in which he finds himself, the for-itself must wholly assume this situation with its peculiar coefficient of adversity, even though it be insupportable. He must assume the situation with the proud consciousness of being the author of it, for the very worst disadvantages or the worst threats which can endanger my person have meaning only in and through my project; and it is on the ground of the engagement which I am that they appear. It is therefore senseless to think of complaining since nothing foreign has decided what we feel, what we live, or what we are.

Furthermore this absolute responsibility is not resignation; it is simply the logical requirement of the consequences of our freedom. What happens to me happens through me, and I can neither affect myself with it nor revolt against it nor resign myself to it. Moreover everything which happens to me is *mine*. By this we must understand first of all that I am always equal to what happens to me *qua* man, for what happens to a man through other men and through himself can be only human. The most terrible situations of war, the worst tortures do not create a non-human state of things; there is no non-human situation. It is only through fear, flight, and recourse to magical types of conduct that I shall decide on the non-human, but this decision is human, and I shall carry the entire responsibility for it. But in addition the situation is *mine* because it is the image of my free choice of myself, and everything which it presents to me is *mine* in that this represents me and symbolizes me. Is it not I who decide the coefficient of adversity in things and even their unpredictability by deciding myself?

Thus there are no *accidents* in a life; a community event which suddenly bursts forth and involves me in it does not come from the outside. If I am mobilized in a war, this war is *my* war; it is in my image and I deserve it. I deserve it first because I could always get out of it by suicide or by desertion; these ultimate possibles are those which must always be present for us when there is a question of envisaging a situation. For lack of getting out of it, I have *chosen* it. This can be due to inertia, to cowardice in the face of public opinion, or because I prefer certain other values to the value

---

4. I am shifting to the personal pronoun here since Sartre is describing the for-itself in concrete personal terms rather than as a metaphysical entity. Strictly speaking, of course, this is his position throughout, and the French "*il*" is indifferently "he" or "it." Tr.

of the refusal to join in the war (the good opinion of my relatives, the honor of my family, etc.). Anyway you look at it, it is a matter of a choice. This choice will be repeated later on again and again without a break until the end of the war. Therefore we must agree with the statement by J. Romains, "In war there are no innocent victims." If therefore I have preferred war to death or to dishonor, everything takes place as if I bore the entire responsibility for this war. Of course others have declared it, and one might be tempted perhaps to consider me as a simple accomplice. But this notion of complicity has only a juridical sense, and it does not hold here. For it depended on me that for me and by me this war should not exist, and I have decided that it does exist. There was no compulsion here, for the compulsion could have got no hold on a freedom. I did not have any excuse; for as we have said repeatedly in this book, the peculiar character of human-reality is that it is without excuse. Therefore it remains for me only to lay claim to this war.

But in addition the war is *mine* because by the sole fact that it arises in a situation which I cause to be and that I can discover it there only by engaging myself for or against it, I can no longer distinguish at present the choice which I make of myself from the choice which I make of the war. To live this war is to choose myself through it and to choose it through my choice of myself. There can be no question of considering it as "four years of vacation" or as a "reprieve," as a "recess," the essential part of my responsibilities being elsewhere in my married, family, or professional life. In this war which I have chosen I choose myself from day to day, and I make it mine by making myself. If it is going to be four empty years, then it is I who bear the responsibility for this.

Finally, as we pointed out earlier, each person is an absolute choice of self from the standpoint of a world of knowledges and of techniques which this choice both assumes and illumines; each person is an absolute upsurge at an absolute date and is perfectly unthinkable at another date. It is therefore a waste of time to ask what I should have been if this war had not broken out, for I have chosen myself as one of the possible meanings of the epoch which imperceptibly led to war. I am not distinct from this same epoch; I could not be transported to another epoch without contradiction. Thus *I am* this war which restricts and limits and makes comprehensible the period which preceded it. In this sense we may define more precisely the responsibility of the for-itself if to the earlier quoted statement, "There are no innocent victims," we add the words, "We have the war we deserve." Thus, totally free, undistinguishable from the period for which I have chosen to be the meaning, as profoundly responsible for the war as if I had myself declared it, unable to live without integrating it in *my* situation, engaging myself in it wholly and stamping it with my seal, I must be without remorse or regrets as I am without excuse; for from the instant of my upsurge into being, I carry the weight of the world by myself alone without anything or any person being able to lighten it.

Yet this responsibility is of a very particular type. Someone will say, "I did not ask to be born." This is a naive way of throwing greater emphasis on our facticity. I am responsible for everything, in fact, except for my very responsibility, for I am not the foundation of my being. Therefore everything takes place as if I were compelled to be responsible. I am *abandoned* in the world, not in the sense that I might remain abandoned and passive in a hostile universe like a board floating on the water, but rather in the sense that I find myself suddenly alone and without help, engaged in a world for which I bear the whole responsibility without being able, whatever I do, to tear myself away from this responsibility for an instant. For I am responsible for my very desire of fleeing responsibilities. To make myself passive in the world, to refuse to act upon things and upon Others is still to choose myself, and suicide is one mode among others of being-in-the-world. Yet I find an absolute responsibility for the fact that my facticity (here the fact of my birth) is directly inapprehensible and even inconceivable, for this fact of my birth never appears as a brute fact but always across a projective reconstruction of my for-itself. I am ashamed of being born or I am astonished at it or I rejoice over it, or in attempting to get rid of my life I affirm that I live and I assume this life as bad. Thus in a certain sense I *choose* being born. This choice itself is integrally affected with facticity since I am not able not to choose, but this facticity in turn will appear only in so far as I surpass it toward my ends. Thus facticity is everywhere but inapprehensible; I never encounter anything except my responsibility. That is why I cannot ask, "*Why* was I born?" or curse the day of my birth or declare that I did not ask to be born, for these various attitudes toward my birth—i.e., toward the *fact* that I realize a presence in the world—are absolutely nothing else but ways of assuming this birth in full responsibility and of making it *mine*. Here again I encounter only myself and my projects so that finally my abandonment—i.e., my facticity—consists simply in the fact that I am condemned to be wholly responsible for myself. I am the being which *is* in such a way that in its being its being is in question. And this "is" of my being *is* as present and inapprehensible.

Under these conditions since every event in the world can be revealed to me only as an *opportunity* (an opportunity made use of, lacked, neglected, etc.), or better yet since everything which happens to us can be considered as a *chance* (i.e., can appear to us only as a way of realizing this being which is in question in our being) and since others as transcendences-transcended are themselves only *opportunities* and *chances*, the responsibility of the for-itself extends to the entire world as a peopled-world. It is precisely thus that the for-itself apprehends itself in anguish; that is, as a being which is neither the foundation of its own being nor of the Other's being nor of the in-itselfs which form the world, but a being which is compelled to decide the meaning of being—within it and everywhere outside of it. The one who realizes in anguish his condition as *being* thrown into a responsibility which extends to his very abandonment has no longer either remorse or regret or excuse; he is no longer anything but a freedom which perfectly reveals itself and whose being resides in this very revelation. But as we pointed out at the beginning of this work, most of the time we flee anguish in bad faith.

. . .

The Desire to Be God

. . . The most discerning ethicists have shown how a desire reaches beyond itself. Pascal believed that he could discover in hunting, for example, or tennis, or in a hundred other occupations, the need of being diverted. He revealed that in an activity which would be absurd if reduced to itself, there was a meaning which transcended it; that is, an indication which referred to the reality of man in general and to his condition. Similarly Stendhal in spite of his attachment to ideologists, and Proust in spite of his intellectualistic and analytical tendencies, have shown that love and jealousy can not be reduced to the strict desire of possessing a *particular* woman, but that these emotions aim at laying hold of the world in its entirety through the woman. This is the meaning of Stendhal's crystallization, and it is precisely for this reason that love as Stendhal describes it appears as a mode of being in the world. Love is a fundamental relation of the for-itself to the world and to itself (selfness) through a particular woman; the woman represents only a conducting body which is placed in the circuit. These analyses may be inexact or only partially true; nevertheless they make us suspect a method other than pure analytical description. In the same way Catholic novelists immediately see in carnal love its surpassing toward God—in Don Juan, "the eternally unsatisfied," in sin, "the place empty of God." There is no question here of finding again an abstract behind the concrete; the impulse toward God is no *less concrete* than the impulse toward a particular woman. On the contrary, it is a matter of rediscovering under the partial and incomplete aspects of the subject the veritable concreteness which can be only the totality of his impulse toward being, his original relation to himself, to the world, and to the Other, in the unity of internal relations and of a fundamental project. This impulse can be only purely individual and unique. Far from estranging us from the person, as Bourget's analysis, for example, does in constituting the individual by means of a summation of general maxims, this impulse will not lead us to find in the need of writing—and of writing particular books—the need of activity in general. On the contrary, rejecting equally the theory of malleable clay and that of the bundle of drives, we will discover the individual person in the initial project which constitutes him. It is for this reason that the irreducibility of the result attained will be revealed as self-evident, not because it is the poorest and the most abstract but because it is the richest. The intuition here will be accompanied by an individual fullness.

. . .

Thus the best way to conceive of the fundamental project of human reality is to say that man is the being whose project is to be God. Whatever may be the myths and rites of the religion considered, God is first "sensible to the heart" of man as the one who identifies and defines him in his ultimate and fundamental project. If man possesses a pre-ontological comprehension of the being of God, it is not the great wonders of nature nor the power of society which have conferred it upon him. God, value and supreme end of transcendence, represents the permanent limit in terms of which man makes known to himself what he is. To be man means to reach toward being God. Or if you prefer, man fundamentally is the desire to be God.

It may be asked, if man on coming into the world is borne toward God as toward his limit, if he can choose only to be God, what becomes of freedom? For freedom is nothing other than a choice which creates for itself its own possibilities, but it appears here that the initial project of being God, which "defines" man, comes close to being the same as a human "nature" or an "essence." The answer is that while the *meaning* of the desire is ultimately the project of being God, the desire is never *constituted* by this meaning; on the contrary, it always represents a particular discovery of its ends. These ends in fact are pursued in terms of a particular empirical situation, and it is this very pursuit which constitutes the surroundings as a *situation*. The desire of being is always realized as the desire of a mode of being. And this desire of a mode of being expresses itself in turn as the meaning of the myriads of concrete desires which constitute the web of our conscious life. Thus we find ourselves before very complex symbolic structures which have *at least* three stories. In empirical desire I can discern a symbolization of a fundamental concrete desire which is the person himself and which represents the mode in which he has decided that being would be in question in his being. This fundamental desire in turn expresses concretely in the world within the particular situation enveloping the individual, an abstract meaningful structure which is the desire of being in general; it must be considered as human reality in the person, and it brings about his community with others, thus making it possible to state that there is a truth concerning man and not only concerning individuals who cannot be compared. Absolute concreteness, completion, existence as a totality belong then to the free and fundamental desire which is the unique person. Empirical desire is only a symbolization of this; it refers to this and derives its meaning from it while remaining partial and reducible, for the empirical desire can not be conceived in isolation. On the other hand, the desire of being in its abstract purity is the *truth* of the concrete fundamental desire, but it does not exist by virtue of reality. Thus the fundamental project, the person, the free realization of human truth is everywhere in all desires. . . . It is never apprehended except through desires—as we can apprehend space only through bodies which shape it for us, though space is a specific reality and not a concept. Or, if you like, it is like the object of Husserl, which reveals itself only by *Abschattungen,* and which nevertheless does not allow itself to be absorbed by any one *Abschattung.* We can understand after these remarks that the abstract, ontological "desire to be" is unable to represent the fundamental, *human* structure of the individual; it cannot be an obstacle to his freedom. Freedom in fact . . . is strictly identified with nihilation. The only being which can be called free is the being which nihilates its being. Moreover we know that nihilation is *lack of being* and can not be otherwise. Freedom is precisely the being which makes itself a lack of being. But since desire, as we have established, is identical with lack of being, freedom can arise only as being which makes itself a desire of being; that is, as the project-for-itself of being in-itself-for-itself. Here we have arrived at an abstract structure which can by no means be considered as the nature or essence of freedom. Freedom is existence, and in it existence precedes essence. The upsurge of freedom is immediate and concrete and is not to be distinguished from its choice; that is, from the person himself. But the structure under consideration can be called the *truth* of freedom; that is, it is the human meaning of freedom.

It should be possible to establish the human truth of the person, as we have attempted to do by an ontological phenomenology. The catalogue of empirical desires ought to be made the object of appropriate psychological investigations, observation and induction and, as needed, experience can serve to draw up this list. They will indicate to the philosopher the comprehensible relations which can unite to each other various desires and various patterns of behaviors, and will bring to light certain concrete connections between the subject of experience and "situations" experientially defined (which at bottom originate only from limitations applied in the name of positivity to the fundamental situation of the subject in the world). But in establishing and classifying fundamental desires of *individual persons* neither of these methods is appropriate. Actually there can be no question of determining *a priori* and ontologically what appears in all the unpredictability of a free act. . . . The very fact that we can subject any man whatsoever to such an investigation—that is what belongs to human reality in general. Or, if you prefer, this is what can be established by an ontology. But the inquiry itself and its results are on principle wholly outside the possibilities of an ontology.

Simone de Beauvoir,
The Ethics of Ambiguity

Simone de Beauvoir (1908–1986) received her degree in philosophy at the Sorbonne in 1929 and taught at lycées (roughly the equivalent of high schools) until 1942, when she devoted herself to the life of a writer and lecturer. Her monumental book on the condition of women, The Second Sex *(1949–50), remains one of the classics of feminist thought. A lifelong companion of Sartre, she described the lives of many of the French existentialists and intellectuals in her best-known novel,* The Mandarins *(1954).*

Beginning with the view of the human condition worked out by Sartre in Being and Nothingness, *Beauvoir tries to see what sort of ethics follows from existentialism. Like Sartre, and drawing on Montaigne and Pascal, she portrays the human condition as characterized by a deep-seated tension or ambiguity. On the one hand, humans are mortal creatures, part of the natural order and so under the sway of the laws of nature. On the other hand, we are thinking beings who can reflect on our lives and can make choices about who and what we are going to be. Though as objects we are not much different than other physical things, our being as subjects means that we are free and have sovereignty over our own lives. As in Sartre, this ambiguity at the core of our being implies a fundamental lack or gap within us—we can never fully be anything once and for all—but we can embrace this ambiguity, assume the tension that we are, and live with integrity, clarity, and a commitment to insuring the freedom of others.*

To point the way to her conception of the good life, Beauvoir presents a rogues' gallery of inauthentic types—the serious man, the nihilist, the passionate man—showing for each why that way of life is incomplete and characterized by bad faith. In the course of her study of the ethical consequences of existentialism, she tries to show that realizing one's own freedom entails respecting the freedom of others, so that achieving personal fulfillment is inseparable from caring for the well-being of other people in a shared world.

"The continuous work of our life," says Montaigne, "is to build death." He quotes the Latin poets: *Prima, quae vitam dedit, hora corpsit.* And again: *Nascentes morimur.*[1] Man knows and thinks this tragic ambivalence which the animal and the plant merely undergo. A new paradox is thereby introduced into his destiny. "Rational animal," "thinking reed," he escapes from his natural condition without, however, freeing himself from it. He is still a part of this world of which he is a consciousness. He asserts himself as a pure internality against which no external power can take hold, and he also experiences himself as a thing crushed by the dark weight of other things. At every moment he can grasp the non-temporal truth of his existence. But between the past which no longer is and the future which is not yet, this moment when he exists is nothing. This privilege, which he alone possesses, of being a sovereign and unique subject amidst a universe of objects, is what he shares with all his fellow-men. In turn an object for others, he is nothing more than an individual in the collectivity on which he depends.

As long as there have been men and they have lived, they have all felt this tragic ambiguity of their condition, but as long as there have been philosophers and they have thought, most of them have tried to mask it. They have striven to reduce mind to matter, or to reabsorb matter into mind, or to merge them within a single substance. Those who have accepted the dualism have established a hierarchy between body and soul which permits of considering as negligible the part of the self which cannot be saved. They have denied death, either by integrating it with life or by promising to man immortality. Or, again they have denied life, considering it as a veil of illusion beneath which is hidden the truth of Nirvana.

And the ethics which they have proposed to their disciples has always pursued the same goal. It has been a matter of eliminating the ambiguity by making oneself pure inwardness or pure externality, by escaping from the sensible world or by being engulfed in it, by yielding to eternity or enclosing oneself in the pure moment.

. . .

From the very beginning, existentialism defined itself as a philosophy of ambiguity. It was by affirming the irreducible character of ambiguity that

---

1. Reading *carpsit* for *corpsit*, the first quote means, "The hour that first gives us life also plucks it away"; the second means, "As soon as we are born, we begin to die."—Ed.

From *The Ethics of Ambiguity*, by Simone de Beauvoir, translated by Bernard Frechtman. Copyright © 1948, 1976 by Philosophical Library. Published by arrangement with Carol Publishing Group. A Citadel Press Book.

Kierkegaard opposed himself to Hegel, and it is by ambiguity that, in our own generation, Sartre, in *Being and Nothingness*, fundamentally defined man, that being whose being is not to be, that subjectivity which realizes itself only as a presence in the world, that engaged freedom, that surging of the for-oneself which is immediately given for others. But it is also claimed that existentialism is a philosophy of the absurd and of despair. It encloses man in a sterile anguish, in an empty subjectivity. It is incapable of furnishing him with any principle for making choices. Let him do as he pleases. In any case, the game is lost. Does not Sartre declare, in effect, that man is a "useless passion," that he tries in vain to realize the synthesis of the for-oneself and the in-oneself, to make himself God?

. . .

Man's passion is useless; he has no means for becoming the being that he is not. That too is true. And it is also true that in *Being and Nothingness* Sartre has insisted above all on the abortive aspect of the human adventure. It is only in the last pages that he opens up the perspective for an ethics. However, if we reflect upon his descriptions of existence, we perceive that they are far from condemning man without recourse.

The failure described in *Being and Nothingness* is definitive, but it is also ambiguous. Man, Sartre tells us, is "a being who *makes himself* a lack of being *in order that there might be* being." That means, first of all, that his passion is not inflicted upon him from without. He chooses it. It is his very being and, as such, does not imply the idea of unhappiness. If this choice is considered as useless, it is because there exists no absolute value before the passion of man, outside of it, in relation to which one might distinguish the useless from the useful.

. . .

Man makes himself a lack, but he can deny the lack as lack and affirm himself as a positive existence. He then assumes the failure. And the condemned action, insofar as it is an effort to be, finds its validity insofar as it is a manifestation of existence. However, rather than being a Hegelian act of surpassing, it is a matter of a conversion. For in Hegel the surpassed terms are preserved only as abstract moments, whereas we consider that existence still remains a negativity in the positive affirmation of itself. And it does not appear, in its turn, as the term of a further synthesis. The failure is not surpassed, but assumed. Existence asserts itself as an absolute which must seek its justification within itself and not suppress itself, even though it may be lost by preserving itself. To attain his truth, man must not attempt to dispel the ambiguity of his being but, on the contrary, accept the task of realizing it. He rejoins himself only to the extent that he agrees to remain at a distance from himself. This conversion is sharply distinguished from the Stoic conversion in that it does not claim to oppose to the sensible universe a formal freedom which is without content. To exist genuinely is not to deny this spontaneous movement of my transcendence, but only to refuse to lose myself in it. Existentialist conversion should rather be compared to Husserlian reduction: let man put his will to be "in parentheses" and he will thereby be brought to the consciousness of his true condition. And just as phenomenological reduction prevents the errors of dogmatism by suspending all affirmation concerning the mode of reality of the external world, whose flesh and bone presence the reduction does not, however, contest, so existentialist conversion does not suppress my instincts, desires, plans, and passions. It merely prevents any possibility of failure by refusing to set up as absolutes the ends toward which my transcendence thrusts itself, and by considering them in their connection with the freedom which projects them.

The first implication of such an attitude is that the genuine man will not agree to recognize any foreign absolute. When a man projects into an ideal heaven that impossible synthesis of the for-itself and the in-itself that is called God, it is because he wishes the regard of this existing Being to change his existence into being; but if he agrees not to be in order to exist genuinely, he will abandon the dream of an inhuman objectivity. He will understand that it is not a matter of being right in the eyes of a God, but of being right in his own eyes. Renouncing the thought of seeking the guarantee for his existence outside of himself, he will also refuse to believe in unconditioned values which would set themselves up athwart his freedom like things. Value is this lacking-being of which freedom *makes itself* a lack; and it is because the latter makes itself a lack that value appears. It is desire which creates the desirable, and the project which sets up the end. It is human existence which makes values spring up in the world on the basis of which it will be able to judge the enterprise in which it will be engaged. But first it locates itself beyond any pessimism, as beyond any optimism, for the fact of its original springing forth is a pure contingency. Before existence there is no more reason to exist than not to exist. The lack of existence can not be evaluated since it is the fact on the basis of which all evaluation is defined. It can not be compared to anything for there is nothing outside of it to serve as a term of comparison. This rejection of any extrinsic justification also confirms the rejection of an original pessimism which we posited at the beginning. Since it is unjustifiable from without, to declare from without that it is unjustifiable is not to condemn it. And the truth is that outside of existence there is nobody. Man exists. For him it is not a question of wondering whether his presence in the world is useful, whether life is worth the trouble of being lived. These questions make no sense. It is a matter of knowing whether he wants to live and under what conditions.

But if man is free to define for himself the conditions of a life which is valid in his own eyes, can he not choose whatever he likes and act however he likes? Dostoievsky asserted, "If God does not exist, everything is permitted." Today's believers use this formula for their own advantage. To reestablish man at the heart of his destiny is, they claim, to repudiate all ethics. However, far from God's absence authorizing all license, the contrary is the case, because man is abandoned on the earth, because his acts are definitive, absolute engagements. He bears the responsibility for a world which is not the work of a strange power, but of himself, where his defeats are inscribed, and his victories as well.

. . .

As for us, whatever the case may be, we believe in freedom. Is it true that this belief must lead us to despair? Must we grant this curious paradox: that from the moment a man recognizes himself as free, he is prohibited from wishing for anything?

On the contrary, it appears to us that by turning toward this freedom we are going to discover a principle of action whose range will be universal. The characteristic feature of all ethics is to consider human life as a game that can be won or lost and to teach man the means of winning. Now, we have seen that the original scheme of man is ambiguous: he wants to be, and to the extent that he coincides with this wish, he fails. All the plans in which this will to be is actualized are condemned; and the ends circumscribed by these plans remain mirages. Human transcendence is vainly engulfed in those miscarried attempts. But man also wills himself to be a disclosure of being, and if he coincides with this wish, he wins, for the fact is that the world becomes present by his presence in it. But the disclosure implies a perpetual tension to keep being at a certain distance, to tear oneself from the world, and to assert oneself as a freedom. To wish for the disclosure of the world and to assert oneself as freedom are one and the same movement. Freedom is the source from which all significations and all values spring. It is the original condition of all justification of existence. The man who seeks to justify his life must want freedom itself absolutely and above everything else.

. . .

Every man casts himself into the world by making himself a lack of being; he thereby contributes to reinvesting it with human signification. He discloses it. And in this movement even the most outcast sometimes feel the joy of existing. They then manifest existence as a happiness and the world as a source of joy. But it is up to each one to make himself a lack of more or less various, profound, and rich aspects of being. What is called vitality, sensitivity, and intelligence are not ready-made qualities, but a way of casting oneself into the world and of disclosing being. Doubtless, every one casts himself into it on the basis of his physiological possibilities, but the body itself is not a brute fact. It expresses our relationship to the world, and that is why it is an object of sympathy or repulsion. And on the other hand, it *determines* no behavior. There is vitality only by means of free generosity. Intelligence supposes good will, and, inversely, a man is never stupid if he adapts his language and his behavior to his capacities, and sensitivity is nothing else but the presence which is attentive to the world and to itself. The reward for these spontaneous qualities issues from the fact that they make significances and goals appear in the world. They discover reasons for existing. They confirm us in the pride and joy of our destiny as man. To the extent that they subsist in an individual they still arouse sympathy, even if he has made himself hateful by the meaning which he has given to his life. I have heard it said that at the Nuremberg trial Goering exerted a certain seductive power on his judges because of the vitality which emanated from him.

· · ·

After Hegel, Kierkegaard and Nietzsche also railed at the deceitful stupidity of the serious man and his universe. And *Being and Nothingness* is in large part a description of the serious man and his universe. The serious man gets rid of his freedom by claiming to subordinate it to values which would be unconditioned. He imagines that the accession to these values likewise permanently confers value upon himself. Shielded with "rights," he fulfills himself as a *being* who is escaping from the stress of existence. The serious is not defined by the nature of the ends pursued. A frivolous lady of fashion can have this mentality of the serious as well as an engineer. There is the serious from the moment that freedom denies itself to the advantage of ends which one claims are absolute.

· · ·

The serious man's dishonesty issues from his being obliged ceaselessly to renew the denial of this freedom. He chooses to live in an infantile world, but to the child the values are really given. The serious man must mask the movement by which he gives them to himself, like the mythomaniac who while reading a love-letter pretends to forget that she has sent it to herself. We have already pointed out that certain adults can live in the universe of the serious in all honesty, for example, those who are denied all instruments of escape, those who are enslaved or who are mystified. The less economic and social circumstances allow an individual to act upon the world, the more this world appears to him as given. This is the case of women who inherit a long tradition of submission and of those who are called "the humble." There is often laziness and timidity in their resignation; their honesty is not quite complete; but to the extent that it exists, their freedom remains available, it is not denied.

. . .

This failure of the serious sometimes brings about a radical disorder. Conscious of being unable to be anything, man then decides to be nothing. We shall call this attitude nihilistic. The nihilist is close to the spirit of seriousness, for instead of realizing his negativity as a living movement, he conceives his annihilation in a substantial way. He wants to *be* nothing, and this nothing that he dreams of is still another sort of being, the exact Hegelian antithesis of being, a stationary datum. Nihilism is disappointed seriousness which has turned back upon itself. A choice of this kind is not encountered among those who, feeling the joy of existence, assume its gratuity.

. . .

The nihilist attitude manifests a certain truth. In this attitude one experiences the ambiguity of the human condition. But the mistake is that it defines man not as the positive existence of a lack, but as a lack at the heart of existence, whereas the truth is that existence is not a lack as such. And if freedom is experienced in this case in the form of rejection, it is not genuinely fulfilled. The nihilist is right in thinking that the world *possesses* no justification and that he himself *is* nothing. But he forgets that it is up to him to justify the world and to make himself exist validly. Instead of integrating death into life, he sees in it the only truth of the life which appears to him as a disguised death. However, there is life, and the nihilist knows that he is alive. That's where his failure lies. He rejects existence without managing to eliminate it. He denies any meaning to his transcendence, and yet he transcends himself. A man who delights in freedom can find an ally in the nihilist because they contest the serious world together, but he also sees in him an enemy insofar as the nihilist is a systematic rejection of the world and man, and if this rejection ends up in a positive desire for destruction, it then establishes a tyranny which freedom must stand up against.

. . .

What characterizes the passionate man is that he sets up the object as an absolute, not, like the serious man, as a thing detached from himself, but as a thing disclosed by his subjectivity.

. . .

Nothing exists outside of his stubborn project; therefore nothing can induce him to modify his choices. And having involved his whole life with an external object which can continually escape him, he tragically feels his dependence. Even if it does not definitely disappear, the object never gives itself. The passionate man makes himself a lack of being not that there might *be* being, but in order to be. And he remains at a distance; he is never fulfilled.

That is why though the passionate man inspires a certain admiration, he also inspires a kind of horror at the same time. One admires the pride of a subjectivity which chooses its end without bending itself to any foreign law and the precious brilliance of the object revealed by the force of this assertion. But one also considers the solitude in which this subjectivity encloses itself as injurious.

· · ·

There is no way for a man to escape from this world. It is in this world that—avoiding the pitfalls we have just pointed out—he must realize himself morally. Freedom must project itself toward its own reality through a content whose value it establishes. An end is valid only by a return to the freedom which established it and which willed itself through this end. But this will implies that freedom is not to be engulfed in any goal; neither is it to dissipate itself vainly without aiming at a goal. It is not necessary for the subject to seek to be, but it must desire that there *be* being. To will oneself free and to will that there be *being* are one and the same choice, the choice that man makes of himself as a presence in the world. We can neither say that the free man wants freedom in order to desire being, nor that he wants the disclosure of being by freedom. These are two aspects of a single reality. And whichever be the one under consideration, they both imply the bond of each man with all others.

This bond does not immediately reveal itself to everybody. A young man wills himself free. He wills that there be being. This spontaneous liberality which casts him ardently into the world can ally itself to what is commonly called egoism. Often the young man perceives only that aspect of his relationship to others whereby others appear as enemies. In the preface to *The Inner Experience* Georges Bataille emphasizes very forcefully that each individual wants to be All. He sees in every other man and particularly in those whose existence is asserted with most brilliance, a limit, a condemnation of himself. "Each consciousness," said Hegel, "seeks the death of the other." And indeed at every moment others are stealing the whole world away from me. The first movement is to hate them. But this hatred is naive, and the desire immediately struggles against itself. If I were really everything there would be nothing beside me;

the world would be empty. There would be nothing to possess, and I myself would be nothing. If he is reasonable, the young man immediately understands that by taking the world away from me, others also give it to me, since a thing is given to me only by the movement which snatches it from me. To will that there be being is also to will that there be men by and for whom the world is endowed with human significations. One can reveal the world only on a basis revealed by other men. No project can be defined except by its interference with other projects. To make being "be" is to communicate with others by means of being.

This truth is found in another form when we say that freedom can not will itself without aiming at an open future. The ends which it gives itself must be unable to be transcended by any reflection, but only the freedom of other men can extend them beyond our life. I have tried to show in *Pyrrhus and Cineas* that every man needs the freedom of other men and, in a sense, always wants it, even though he may be a tyrant; the only thing he fails to do is to assume honestly the consequences of such a wish. Only the freedom of others keeps each one of us from hardening in the absurdity of facticity. And if we are to believe the Christian myth of creation, God himself was in agreement on this point with the existentialist doctrine since, in the words of an anti-fascist priest, "He had such respect for man that He created him free."

Thus, it can be seen to what an extent those people are mistaken—or are lying—who try to make of existentialism a solipsism, like Nietzsche, would exalt the bare will to power. According to this interpretation, as widespread as it is erroneous, the individual, knowing himself and choosing himself as the creator of his own values, would seek to impose them on others. The result would be a conflict of opposed wills enclosed in their solitude. But we have seen that, on the contrary, to the extent that passion, pride, and the spirit of adventure lead to this tyranny and its conflicts, existentialist ethics condems them; and it does so not in the name of an abstract law, but because, if it is true that every project emanates from subjectivity, it is also true that this subjective movement establishes by itself a surpassing of subjectivity. Man can find a justification of his own existence only in the existence of other men. Now, he needs such a justification; there is no escaping it. Moral anxiety does not come to man from without; he finds within himself the anxious question, "What's the use?" Or, to put it better, he himself is this urgent interrogation. He flees it only by fleeing himself, and as soon as he exists he answers. It may perhaps be said that it is for *himself* that he is moral, and that such an attitude is egotistical. But there is no ethics against which this charge, which immediately destroys itself, can not be leveled; for how can I worry about what does not concern me? I concern others and they concern me. There we have an irreducible truth. The me-others relationship is as indissoluble as the subject-object relationship.

At the same time the other charge which is often directed at existentialism also collapses: of being a formal doctrine, incapable of proposing any content to the freedom which it wants engaged. To will oneself free is also to will others free. This will is not an abstract formula. It points out to each person concrete action to be achieved.

21

Karl Marx,
"Alienated Labor,"
from the *Economic and Philosophic*
Manuscripts of 1844

Karl Marx (1818–1883), social philosopher and economic theorist, is the author (with Frederick Engels) of The Communist Manifesto *(1848), one of the founding documents of modern socialism and communism. He obtained his degree in philosophy with a dissertation on Epicurus and worked for several years as a journalist in Germany, France, and Belgium. After the Revolutions of 1848, he was expelled from Europe and spent the rest of his life in London. There, earning some money writing for the* New York Tribune *but mainly supported by Engels, he wrote his monumental* Capital *(three volumes, 1867–1894).*

Marx's early manuscripts, though harshly critical of Hegel (1770–1831—the dominant German philosopher in the early nineteenth century), made use of Hegel's concepts of human existence and alienation in developing a "materialist" account of economic and social relations in capitalist society. Following Hegel, Marx holds that human beings are not self-contained entities who also happen to work. On the contrary, a person's work—his or her creative activity—makes that person the person he or she is. For example, the craftsperson working with clay in her studio realizes and defines herself as a craftsperson of a particular sort through the ways she forms the clay. Her very being as a human of a particular sort is shaped and given content through the way she expresses herself in the world. Seen from this standpoint, nature is not just raw material on hand for our use; instead, nature is the medium through which we realize our identity as humans. Moreover, Marx holds that an essential feature of humans is their species-being: they are social beings who understand their work as contributing to the wider human community. And this means that the craftsperson is not just creating for herself; she creates for others, and only finds her creative activity meaningful to the extent she sees it as for others. What this view of human creativity shows is that humans fulfill and realize their hu-

manity through meaningful work which is experienced as contributing to the good of all.

Now in capitalist society, these features of human nature are inverted and perverted. Instead of finding fulfillment in his work, the laborer encounters the product of his labor as an inhuman, external thing whose sole function is to make money. Instead of feeling herself at one with nature, she feels alienated from the medium of her activity. And instead of contributing to the public good, he sees his work as a mere means to his own personal survival. As a result, people in capitalist society begin to feel as if they are in a "war of all against all" struggling for scarce resources and, worse still, they feel that this is a natural state. No longer finding their humanity in their work, laborers feel dehumanized and degraded, pawns in the capitalists' game, slaves to the drudgery of meaningless work. Marx's proposed solution seems quite idealistic by our standards: a communal system of production based on cooperation rather than acquisitiveness and self-interest.

Alienated Labor

We have proceeded from the presuppositions of political economy. We have accepted its language and its laws. We presupposed private property, the separation of labor, capital and land, hence of wages, profit of capital and rent, likewise the division of labor, competition, the concept of exchange value, etc. From political economy itself, in its own words, we have shown that the worker sinks to the level of a commodity, the most miserable commodity; that the misery of the worker is inversely proportional to the power and volume of his production; that the necessary result of competition is the accumulation of capital in a few hands and thus the revival of monopoly in a more frightful form; and finally that the distinction between capitalist and landowner, between agricultural laborer and industrial worker, disappears and the whole society must divide into the two classes of *proprietors* and propertyless *workers*.

Political economy proceeds from the fact of private property. It does not explain private property. It grasps the actual, *material* process of private property in abstract and general formulae which it then takes as *laws*. It does not *comprehend* these laws, that is, does not prove them as proceeding from the nature of private property. Political economy does not disclose the reason for the division between capital and labor, between capital and land. When, for example, the relation of wages to profits is determined,

From *Writings of the Young Marx on Philosophy and Society*, trans. and ed. by Loyd D. Easton and Kurt H. Guddat (Indianapolis: Hackett Publishing Co., 1997). Reprinted with permission.

the ultimate basis is taken to be the interest of the capitalists; that is, political economy assumes what it should develop. Similarly, competition is referred to at every point and explained from external circumstances. Political economy teaches us nothing about the extent to which these external, apparently accidental circumstances are simply the expression of a necessary development. We have seen how political economy regards exchange itself as an accidental fact. The only wheels which political economy puts in motion are *greed* and the *war among the greedy, competition.*

Just because political economy does not grasp the interconnections within the movement, the doctrine of competition could stand opposed to the doctrine of monopoly, the doctrine of freedom of craft to that of the guild, the doctrine of the division of landed property to that of the great estate. Competition, freedom of craft, and division of landed property were developed and conceived only as accidental, deliberate, forced consequences of monopoly, the guild, and feudal property, rather than necessary, inevitable, natural consequences.

We now have to grasp the essential connection among private property, greed, division of labor, capital and landownership, and the connection of exchange with competition, of value with the devaluation of men, of monopoly with competition, etc., and of this whole alienation with the *money*-system.

Let us not put ourselves in a fictitious primordial state like a political economist trying to clarify things. Such a primordial state clarifies nothing. It merely pushes the issue into a gray, misty distance. It acknowledges as a fact or event what it should deduce, namely, the necessary relation between two things for example, between division of labor and exchange. In such a manner theology explains the origin of evil by the fall of man. That is, it asserts as a fact in the form of history what it should explain.

We proceed from a *present* fact of political economy.

The worker becomes poorer the more wealth he produces, the more his production increases in power and extent. The worker becomes a cheaper commodity the more commodities he produces. The *increase in value* of the world of things is directly proportional to the *decrease in value* of the human world. Labor not only produces commodities. It also produces itself and the worker as a *commodity,* and indeed in the same proportion as it produces commodities in general.

This fact simply indicates that the object which labor produces, its product, stands opposed to it as an *alien thing,* as a *power independent* of the producer. The product of labor is labor embodied and made objective in a thing. It is the *objectification* of labor. The realization of labor is its objectification. In the viewpoint of political economy this realization of labor appears as the *diminution* of the worker, the objectification as the *loss of and subservience to the object*, and the appropriation as *alienation* [*Entfremdung*], as externalization [*Entäusserung*].

So much does the realization of labor appear as diminution that the worker is diminished to the point of starvation. So much does objectification appear as loss of the object that the worker is robbed of the most essential objects not only of life but also of work. Indeed, work itself becomes a thing of which he can take possession only with the greatest effort and with the most unpredictable interruptions. So much does the appropriation of the object appear as alienation that the more objects the worker produces, the fewer he can own and the more he falls under the domination of his product, of capital.

All these consequences follow from the fact that the worker is related to the *product of his labor* as to an *alien* object. For it is clear according to this premise: The more the worker exerts himself, the more powerful becomes the alien objective world which he fashions against himself, the poorer he and his inner world become, the less there is that belongs to him. It is the same in religion. The more man attributes to God, the less he retains in himself. The worker puts his life into the object; then it no longer belongs to him but to the object. The greater this activity, the poorer is the worker. What the product of his work is, he is not. The greater this product is, the smaller he is himself. The *externalization* of the worker in his product means not only that his work becomes an object, an *external* existence, but also that it exists *outside him* independently, alien, an autonomous power, opposed to him. The life he has given to the object confronts him as hostile and alien.

Let us now consider more closely the *objectification*, the worker's production and with it the *alienation* and *loss* of the object, his product.

The worker can make nothing without *nature*, without the *sensuous external world*. It is the material wherein his labor realizes itself, wherein it is active, out of which and by means of which it produces.

But as nature furnishes to labor the *means of life* in the sense that labor cannot *live* without objects upon which labor is exercised, nature also furnishes the *means of life* in the narrower sense, namely, the means of physical subsistence of the *worker* himself.

The more the worker *appropriates* the external world and sensuous nature through his labor, the more he deprives himself of the *means of life* in two respects: first, that the sensuous external world gradually ceases to be an object belonging to his labor, a *means of life* of his work; secondly, that it gradually ceases to be a *means of life* in the immediate sense, a means of physical subsistence of the worker.

In these two respects, therefore, the worker becomes a slave to his objects; first, in that he receives an *object of labor,* that is, he receives *labor,* and secondly that he receives the *means of subsistence.* The first enables him to exist as a *worker* and the second as a *physical subject.* The terminus of this slavery is that he can only maintain himself as a *physical subject* so far as he is a *worker,* and only as a *physical subject* is he a worker.

(The alienation of the worker in his object is expressed according to the laws of political economy as follows: the more the worker produces, the less he has to consume; the more values he creates the more worthless and unworthy he becomes; the better shaped his product, the more misshapen is he; the more civilized his product, the more barbaric is the worker; the more powerful the work, the more powerless becomes the worker; the more intelligence the work has, the more witless is the worker and the more he becomes a slave of nature.)

Political economy conceals the alienation in the nature of labor by ignoring the direct relationship between the worker (labor) *and production.* To be sure, labor produces marvels for the wealthy but it produces deprivation for the worker. It produces palaces, but hovels for the worker. It produces beauty, but mutilation for the worker. It displaces labor through machines, but it throws some workers back into barbarous labor and turns others into machines. It produces intelligence, but for the worker it produces imbecility and cretinism.

The direct relationship of labor to its products is the relationship of the worker to the objects of his production. The relationship of the rich to the objects of production and to production itself is only a *consequence* of this first relationship and confirms it. Later we shall observe the latter aspect.

Thus, when we ask, What is the essential relationship of labor? we ask about the relationship of the *worker* to production.

Up to now we have considered the alienation, the externalization of the worker only from one side: his *relationship to the products of his labor.* But alienation is shown not only in the result but also in the *process of production,* in the *producing activity* itself. How could the worker stand in an alien relationship to the product of his activity if he did not alienate himself from himself in the very act of production? After all, the product is only the résumé of activity, of production. If the product of work is externalization, production itself must be active externalization, externalization of activity, activity of externalization. Only alienation—and externalization in the activity of labor itself—is summarized in the alienation of the object of labor.

What constitutes the externalization of labor?

First is the fact that labor is *external* to the laborer—that is, it is not part of his nature—and that the worker does not affirm himself in his work but denies himself, feels miserable and unhappy, develops no free physical and mental energy but mortifies his flesh and ruins his mind. The worker, therefore feels at ease only outside work, and during work he is outside himself. He is at home when he is not working and when he is working he is not at home. His work, therefore, is not voluntary, but coerced, *forced labor*. It is not the satisfaction of a need but only a *means* to satisfy other needs. Its alien character is obvious from the fact that as soon as no physical or other pressure exists, labor is avoided like the plague. External labor, labor in which man is externalized, is labor of self-sacrifice, of penance. Finally, the external nature of work for the worker appears in the fact that it is not his own but another person's, that in work he does not belong to himself but to someone else. In religion the spontaneity of human imagination, the spontaneity of the human brain and heart, acts independently of the individual as an alien, divine or devilish activity. Similarly, the activity of the worker is not his own spontaneous activity. It belongs to another. It is the loss of his own self.

The result, therefore, is that man (the worker) feels that he is acting freely only in his animal functions—eating, drinking, and procreating, or at most in his shelter and finery—while in his human functions he feels only like an animal. The animalistic becomes the human and the human the animalistic.

To be sure, eating, drinking, and procreation are genuine human functions. In abstraction, however, and separated from the remaining sphere of human activities and turned into final and sole ends, they are animal functions.

We have considered labor, the act of alienation of practical human activity, in two aspects: (1) the relationship of the worker to the *product of labor* as an alien object dominating him. This relationship is at the same time the relationship to the sensuous external world, to natural objects as an alien world hostile to him; (2) the relationship of labor to the *act of production* in *labor*. This relationship is that of the worker to his own activity as alien and not belonging to him, activity as passivity, power as weakness, procreation as emasculation, the worker's *own* physical and spiritual energy, his personal life—for what else is life but activity—as an activity turned against him, independent of him, and not belonging to him. *Self-alienation*, as against the alienation of the *object*, stated above.

We have now to derive a third aspect of *alienated labor* from the two previous ones.

Man is a species-being [*Gattungswesen*] not only in that he practically and theoretically makes his own species as well as that of other things his object, but also—and this is only another expression for the same thing— in that as present and living species he considers himself to be a *universal* and consequently free being.

The life of the species in man as in animals is physical in that man, (like the animal) lives by inorganic nature. And as man is more universal than the animal, the realm of inorganic nature by which he lives is more universal. As plants, animals, minerals, air, light, etc., in theory form a part of human consciousness, partly as objects of natural science, partly as objects of art—his spiritual inorganic nature or spiritual means of life which he first must prepare for enjoyment and assimilation—so they also form in practice a part of human life and human activity. Man lives physically only by these products of nature; they may appear in the form of food, heat, clothing, housing, etc. The universality of man appears in practice in the universality which makes the whole of nature his *inorganic* body: (1) as a direct means of life, and (2) as the matter, object, and instrument of his life activity. Nature is the *inorganic body* of man, that is, nature insofar as it is not the human body. Man *lives* by nature. This means that nature is his *body* with which he must remain in perpetual process in order not to die. That the physical and spiritual life of man is tied up with nature is another way of saying that nature is linked to itself, for man is a part of nature.

In alienating (1) nature from man, and (2) man from himself, his own active function, his life activity, alienated labor also alienates the *species* from him; it makes *species-life* the means of individual life. In the first place it alienates species-life and the individual life, and secondly it turns the latter in its abstraction into the purpose of the former, also in its abstract and alienated form.

For labor, *life activity,* and *productive life* appear to man at first only as a *means* to satisfy a need, the need to maintain physical existence. Productive life, however, is species-life. It is life begetting life. In the mode of life activity lies the entire character of a species, its species-character; and free conscious activity is the species-character of man. Life itself appears only as a *means of life.*

The animal is immediately one with its life activity, not distinct from it. The animal is *its life activity.* Man makes his life activity itself into an object of will and consciousness. He has conscious life activity. It is not a determination with which he immediately identifies. Conscious life activity distinguishes man immediately from the life activity of the animal. Only thereby is he a species-being. Or rather, he is only a conscious being—that is, his own life is an object for him—since he is a species-being. Only on that account is his activity free activity. Alienated labor reverses the relationship in that man, since he is a conscious being, makes his life activity, his *essence,* only a means for his *existence.*

The practical creation of an *objective world,* the *treatment* of inorganic nature, is proof that man is a conscious species-being, that is, a being which is related to its species as to its own essence or is related to itself as a species-being. To be sure animals also produce. They build themselves nests, dwelling places, like the bees, beavers, ants, etc. But the animal produces only what is immediately necessary for itself or its young. It produces in a one-sided way while man produces universally. The animal produces under the domination of immediate physical need while man produces free of physical need and only genuinely so in freedom from such need. The animal only produces itself while man reproduces the whole of nature. The animal's product belongs immediately to its physical body while man is free when he confronts his product. The animal builds only according to the standard and need of the species to which it belongs while man knows how to produce according to the standard of any species and at all times knows how to apply an intrinsic standard to the object. Thus man creates also according to the laws of beauty.

In the treatment of the objective world, therefore, man proves himself to be genuinely a *species-being*. This production is his active species-life. Through it nature appears as *his* work and his actuality. The object of labor is thus the *objectification of man's species-life:* he produces himself not only intellectually, as in consciousness, but also actively in a real sense and sees himself in a world he made. In taking from man the object of his production, alienated labor takes from his *species-life,* his actual and objective existence as a species. It changes his superiority to the animal to inferiority, since he is deprived of nature, his inorganic body.

By degrading free spontaneous activity to the level of a means, alienated labor makes the species-life of man a means of his physical existence.

The consciousness which man has from his species is altered through alienation, so that species-life becomes a means for him.

(3) Alienated labor hence turns the *species-existence of man,* and also nature as his mental species-capacity, into an existence *alien* to him, into the *means* of his *individual existence.* It alienates his spiritual nature, his *human essence,* from his own body and likewise from nature outside him.

(4) A direct consequence of man's alienation from the product of his work, from his life activity, and from his species-existence, is the *alienation of man* from *man.* When man confronts himself, he confronts *other* men. What holds true of man's relationship to his work, to the product of his work, and to himself, also holds true of man's relationship to other men, to their labor, and the object of their labor.

In general, the statement that man is alienated from his species-existence means that one man is alienated from another just as each man is alienated from human nature.

The alienation of man, the relation of man to himself, is realized and expressed in the relation between man and other men.

Thus in the relation of alienated labor every man sees the others according to the standard and the relation in which he finds himself as a worker.

We began with an economic fact, the alienation of the worker and his product. We have given expression to the concept of this fact: *alienated, externalized* labor. We have analyzed this concept and have thus analyzed merely a fact of political economy.

Let us now see further how the concept of alienated, externalized labor must express and represent itself in actuality.

If the product of labor is alien to me, confronts me as an alien power, to whom then does it belong?

If my own activity does not belong to me, if it is an alien and forced activity, to whom then does it belong?

To a being *other* than myself.

Who is this being?

Gods? To be sure, in early times the main production, for example, the building of temples in Egypt, India, and Mexico, appears to be in the service of the gods, just as the product belongs to the gods. But gods alone were never workmasters. The same is true of *nature.* And what a contradiction it would be if the more man subjugates nature through his work and the more the miracles of gods are rendered superfluous by the marvels of industry, man should renounce his joy in producing and the enjoyment of his product for love of these powers.

The *alien* being who owns labor and the product of labor, whom labor serves and whom the product of labor satisfies can only be *man* himself.

That the product of labor does not belong to the worker and an alien power confronts him is possible only because this product belongs to *a man other than the worker.* If his activity is torment for him, it must be the *pleasure* and the life-enjoyment for another. Not gods, not nature, but only man himself can be this alien power over man.

Let us consider the statement previously made, that the relationship of man to himself is *objective* and *actual* to him only through his relationship to other men. If man is related to the product of his labor, to his objectified labor, as to an *alien,* hostile, powerful object independent of him, he is so related that another alien, hostile, powerful man independent of him is the lord of this object. If he is unfree in relation to his own activity, he is related to it as bonded activity, activity under the domination, coercion, and yoke of another man.

Every self-alienation of man, from himself and from nature, appears in the relationship which he postulates between other men and himself and nature. Thus religious self-alienation appears necessarily in the relation of laity to priest, or also to a mediator, since we are here now concerned with the spiritual world. In the practical real world self-alienation can appear only in the practical real relationships to other men. The means whereby the alienation proceeds is a *practical* means. Through alienated labor man thus not only produces his relationship to the object and to the act of production as an alien man at enmity with him. He also creates the relation in which other men stand to his production and product, and the relation in which he stands to these other men. Just as he begets his own production as loss of his reality, as his punishment; just as he begets his own product as a loss, a product not belonging to him, so he begets the domination of the non-producer over production and over product. As he alienates his own activity from himself, he confers upon the stranger an activity which is not his own.

Up to this point, we have investigated the relationship only from the side of the worker and will later investigate it also from the side of the non-worker.

Thus through *alienated externalized labor* does the worker create the relation to this work of man alienated to labor and standing outside it. The relation of the worker to labor produces the relation of the capitalist to labor, or whatever one wishes to call the lord of labor. *Private property* is thus product, result, and necessary consequence of *externalized labor,* of the external relation of the worker to nature and to himself.

Private property thus is derived, through analysis, from the concept of *externalized labor,* that is, *externalized man,* alienated labor, alienated life, and *alienated* man.

We have obtained the concept of *externalized labor* (*externalized life*) from political economy as a result of the *movement of private property.* But the analysis of this idea shows that though private property appears to be the ground and cause of externalized labor, it is rather a consequence of externalized labor, just as gods are *originally* not the cause but the effect of an aberration of the human mind. Later this relationship reverses.

Only at the final culmination of the development of private property does this, its secret, reappear—namely, that on the one hand it is the *product* of externalized labor and that secondly it is the *means* through which labor externalizes itself, the *realization of this externalization.*

W. E. B. Du Bois, "Of Our Spiritual Strivings," from *The Souls of Black Folk: Essays and Sketches*

Over the course of his long life, African-American sociologist, writer, and reformer W. E. B. Du Bois (1868–1963) was one of the most eloquent spokesmen against racial injustice. He received his Ph.D. from Harvard University in 1895 and taught economics and history at Atlanta University for twenty-five years. One of the cofounders of what was to become the National Association for the Advancement of Colored People (NAACP), Du Bois edited that association's magazine, Crisis, *until 1932. In his later years, he worked for pan-Africanism, becoming increasingly discouraged with racial progress in the United States. In 1961, he joined the Communist Party and moved to Ghana, where he died in self-imposed exile. This early essay conveys a powerful sense of the impact of racism on people and the need for a commitment to racial justice.*

Of Our Spiritual Strivings

Between me and the other world there is ever an unasked question: unasked by some through feelings of delicacy; by others through the difficulty of rightly framing it. All, nevertheless, flutter round it. They approach me in a half-hesitant sort of way, eye me curiously or compassionately, and then, instead of saying directly, How does it feel to be a problem? they say, I know an excellent colored man in my town; or, I fought at Mechanicsville; or, Do not these Southern outrages make your blood boil? At these I smile, or am interested, or reduce the boiling to a simmer, as the occasion may require. To the real question, How does it feel to be a problem? I answer seldom a word.

And yet, being a problem is a strange experience,—peculiar even for one who has never been anything else, save perhaps in babyhood and in Europe. It is in the early days of rollicking boyhood that the revelation first bursts upon one, all in a day, as it were. I remember well when the shadow

From W. E. B. Du Bois, *The Souls of Black Folk: Essays and Sketches* (Chicago: A. C. McClurg, 1903).

swept across me. I was a little thing, away up in the hills of New England, where the dark Housatonic winds between Hoosac and Taghkanic to the sea. In a wee wooden schoolhouse, something put it into the boys' and girls' heads to buy gorgeous visiting-cards—ten cents a package—and exchange. The exchange was merry, till one girl, a tall newcomer, refused my card,—refused it peremptorily, with a glance. Then it dawned upon me with a certain suddenness that I was different from the others; or like, mayhap, in heart and life and longing, but shut out from their world by a vast veil. I had thereafter no desire to tear down that veil, to creep through; I held all beyond it in common contempt, and lived above it in a region of blue sky and great wandering shadows. That sky was bluest when I could beat my mates at examination-time, or beat them at a foot-race, or even beat their stringy heads. Alas, with the years all this fine contempt began to fade; for the words I longed for, and all their dazzling opportunities, were theirs, not mine. But they should not keep these prizes, I said; some, all, I would wrest from them. Just how I would do it I could never decide: by reading law, by healing the sick, by telling the wonderful tales that swam in my head,—some way. With other black boys the strife was not so fiercely sunny: their youth shrunk into tasteless sycophancy, or into silent hatred of the pale world about them and mocking distrust of everything white; or wasted itself in a bitter cry, Why did God make me an outcast and a stranger in mine own house? The shades of the prison-house closed round about us all: walls strait and stubborn to the whitest, but relentlessly narrow, tall, and unscalable to sons of night who must plod darkly on in resignation, or beat unavailing palms against the stone, or steadily, half hopelessly, watch the streak of blue above.

After the Egyptian and Indian, the Greek and Roman, the Teuton and Mongolian, the Negro is a sort of seventh son, born with a veil, and gifted with second-sight in this American world,—a world which yields him no true self-consciousness, but only lets him see himself through the revelation of the other world. It is a peculiar sensation, this double-consciousness, this sense of always looking at one's self through the eyes of others, of measuring one's soul by the tape of a world that looks on in amused contempt and pity. One ever feels his twoness,—an American, a Negro; two souls, two thoughts, two unreconciled strivings; two warring ideals in one dark body, whose dogged strength alone keeps it from being torn asunder.

The history of the American Negro is the history of this strife,—this longing to attain self-conscious manhood, to merge his double self into a better and truer self. In this merging he wishes neither of the older selves to be lost. He would not Africanize America, for America has too much to teach the world and Africa. He would not bleach his Negro soul in a flood of white Americanism, for he knows that Negro blood has a message for the world. He simply wishes to make it possible for a man to be both a Negro and an American, without being cursed and spit upon by his fellows, without having the doors of Opportunity closed roughly in his face.

This, then, is the end of his striving: to be a co-worker in the kingdom of culture, to escape both death and isolation, to husband and use his best powers and his latent genius. These powers of body and mind have in the past been strangely wasted, dispersed, or forgotten. The shadow of a mighty Negro past flits through the tale of Ethiopia the Shadowy and of Egypt the Sphinx. Through history, the powers of single black men flash here and there like falling stars, and die sometimes before the world has rightly gauged their brightness. Here in America, in the few days since Emancipation, the black man's turning hither and thither in hesitant and doubtful striving has often made his very strength to lose effectiveness, to seem like absence of power, like weakness. And yet it is not weakness,—it is the contradiction of double aims. The double-aimed struggle of the black artisan—on the one hand to escape white contempt for a nation of mere hewers of wood and drawers of water, and on the other hand to plough and nail and dig for a poverty-stricken horde—could only result in making him a poor craftsman, for he had but half a heart in either cause. By the poverty and ignorance of his people, the Negro minister or doctor was tempted toward quackery and demagogy; and by the criticism of the other world, toward ideals that made him ashamed of his lowly tasks. The would-be black *savant* was confronted by the paradox that the knowledge his people needed was a twice-told tale to his white neighbors, while the knowledge which would teach the white world was Greek to his own flesh and blood. The innate love of harmony and beauty that set the ruder souls of his people a-dancing and a-singing raised but confusion and doubt in the soul of the black artist; for the beauty revealed to him was the soul-beauty of a race which his larger audience despised, and he could not articulate the message of another people. This waste of double aims, this seeking to satisfy two unreconciled ideals, has wrought sad havoc with the courage and faith and deeds of ten thousand thousand people,—has sent them often wooing false gods and invoking false means of salvation, and at times has even seemed about to make them ashamed of themselves.

Away back in the days of bondage they thought to see in one divine event the end of all doubt and disappointment; few men ever worshipped Freedom with half such unquestioning faith as did the American Negro for two centuries. To him, so far as he thought and dreamed, slavery was indeed the sum of all villanies, the cause of all sorrow, the root of all prejudice; Emancipation was the key to a promised land of sweeter beauty

than ever stretched before the eyes of wearied Israelites. In song and
exhortation swelled one refrain—Liberty; in his tears and curses the God
he implored had Freedom in his right hand. At last it came,—suddenly,
fearfully, like a dream. With one wild carnival of blood and passion came
the message in his own plaintive cadences:—

"Shout, O children!
Shout, you're free!
For God has bought your liberty!"

Years have passed away since then,—ten, twenty, forty; forty years of
national life, forty years of renewal and development, and yet the swarthy
spectre sits in its accustomed seat at the Nation's feast. In vain do we cry to
this our vastest social problem:—

"Take any shape but that, and my firm nerves
Shall never tremble!"

The Nation has not yet found peace from its sins; the freedman has not yet
found in freedom his promised land. Whatever of good may have come in
these years of change, the shadow of a deep disappointment rests upon the
Negro people,—a disappointment all the more bitter because the unattained ideal was unbounded save by the simple ignorance of a lowly
people.

The first decade was merely a prolongation of the vain search for
freedom, the boon that seemed ever barely to elude their grasp,—like a
tantalizing will-o'-the-wisp, maddening and misleading the headless host.
The holocaust of war, the terrors of the Ku-Klux Klan, the lies of carpet-
baggers, the disorganization of industry, and the contradictory advice of
friends and foes, left the bewildered serf with no new watchword beyond
the old cry for freedom. As the time flew, however, he began to grasp a new
idea. The ideal of liberty demanded for its attainment powerful means,
and these the Fifteenth Amendment gave him. The ballot, which before
he had looked upon as a visible sign of freedom, he now regarded as the
chief means of gaining and perfecting the liberty with which war had
partially endowed him. And why not? Had not votes made war and eman-
cipated millions? Had not votes enfranchised the freedmen? Was anything
impossible to a power that had done all this? A million black men started
with renewed zeal to vote themselves into the kingdom. So the decade
flew away, the revolution of 1876 came, and left the half-free serf weary,
wondering, but still inspired. Slowly but steadily, in the following years, a
new vision began gradually to replace the dream of political power,—a

powerful movement, the rise of another ideal to guide the unguided, another pillar of fire by night after a clouded day. It was the ideal of "book-learning"; the curiosity, born of compulsory ignorance, to know and test the power of the cabalistic letters of the white man, the longing to know. Here at last seemed to have been discovered the mountain path to Canaan; longer than the highway of Emancipation and law, steep and rugged, but straight, leading to heights high enough to overlook life.

Up the new path the advance guard toiled, slowly, heavily, doggedly; only those who have watched and guided the faltering feet, the misty minds, the dull understandings, of the dark pupils of these schools know how faithfully, how piteously, this people strove to learn. It was weary work. The cold statistician wrote down the inches of progress here and there, noted also where here and there a foot had slipped or some one had fallen. To the tired climbers, the horizon was ever dark, the mists were often cold, the Canaan was always dim and far away. If, however, the vistas disclosed as yet no goal, no resting-place, little but flattery and criticism, the journey at least gave leisure for reflection and self-examination; it changed the child of Emancipation to the youth with dawning self-consciousness, self-realization, self-respect. In those sombre forests of his striving his own soul rose before him, and he saw himself,—darkly as through a veil; and yet he saw in himself some faint revelation of his power, of his mission. He began to have a dim feeling that, to attain his place in the world, he must be himself, and not another. For the first time he sought to analyze the burden he bore upon his back, that dead-weight of social degradation partially masked behind a half-named Negro problem. He felt his poverty; without a cent, without a home, without land, tools, or savings, he had entered into competition with rich, landed, skilled neighbors. To be a poor man is hard, but to be a poor race in a land of dollars is the very bottom of hardships. He felt the weight of his ignorance,—not simply of letters, but of life, of business, of the humanities; the accumulated sloth and shirking and awkwardness of decades and centuries shackled his hands and feet. Nor was his burden all poverty and ignorance. The red stain of bastardy, which two centuries of systematic legal defilement of Negro women had stamped upon his race, meant not only the loss of ancient African chastity, but also the hereditary weight of a mass of corruption from white adulterers, threatening almost the obliteration of the Negro home.

A people thus handicapped ought not to be asked to race with the world, but rather allowed to give all its time and thought to its own social problems. But alas! while sociologists gleefully count his bastards and his prostitutes, the very soul of the toiling, sweating black man is darkened by the shadow of a vast despair. Men call the shadow prejudice, and learnedly explain it as the natural defence of culture against barbarism, learning against ignorance, purity against crime, the "higher" against the "lower" races. To which the Negro cries Amen! and swears that to so much of this strange prejudice as is founded on just homage to civilization, culture, righteousness, and progress, he humbly bows and meekly does obeisance. But before that nameless prejudice that leaps beyond all this he stands helpless, dismayed, and well-nigh speechless; before that personal disrespect and mockery, the ridicule and systematic humiliation, the distortion of fact and wanton license of fancy, the cynical ignoring of the better and the boisterous welcoming of the worse, the all-pervading desire to inculcate disdain for everything black, from Toussaint to the devil,— before this there rises a sickening despair that would disarm and discourage any nation save that black host to whom "discouragement" is an unwritten word.

But the facing of so vast a prejudice could not but bring the inevitable self-questioning, self-disparagement, and lowering of ideals which ever accompany repression and breed in an atmosphere of contempt and hate. Whisperings and portents came borne upon the four winds: Lo! we are diseased and dying, cried the dark hosts; we cannot write, our voting is vain; what need of education, since we must always cook and serve? And the Nation echoed and enforced this self-criticism, saying: Be content to be servants, and nothing more; what need of higher culture for half-men? Away with the black man's ballot, by force or fraud,—and behold the suicide of a race! Nevertheless, out of the evil came something of good,— the more careful adjustment of education to real life, the clearer perception of the Negroes' social responsibilities, and the sobering realization of the meaning of progress.

So dawned the time of *Sturm und Drang:* storm and stress to-day rocks our little boat on the mad waters of the world-sea; there is within and without the sound of conflict, the burning of body and rending of soul; inspiration strives with doubt, and faith with vain questionings. The bright ideals of the past,—physical freedom, political power, the training of brains and the training of hands,—all these in turn have waxed and waned, until even the last grows dim and overcast. Are they all wrong,— all false? No, not that, but each alone was over-simple and incomplete,— the dreams of a credulous race-childhood, or the fond imaginings of the other world which does not know and does not want to know our power. To be really true, all these ideals must be melted and welded into one. The training of the schools we need to-day more than ever,—the training of deft hands, quick eyes and ears, and above all the broader, deeper, higher culture of gifted minds and pure hearts. The power of the ballot we need in sheer self-defence,—else what shall save us from a second slavery?

Freedom, too, the long-sought, we still seek,—the freedom of life and limb, the freedom to work and think, the freedom to love and aspire. Work, culture, liberty,—all these we need, not singly but together, not successively but together, each growing and aiding each, and all striving toward that vaster ideal that swims before the Negro people, the ideal of human brotherhood, gained through the unifying ideal of Race; the ideal of fostering and developing the traits and talents of the Negro, not in opposition to or contempt for other races, but rather in large conformity to the greater ideals of the American Republic, in order that some day on American soil two world-races may give each to each those characteristics both so sadly lack. We the darker ones come even now not altogether empty-handed: there are to-day no truer exponents of the pure human spirit of the Declaration of Independence than the American Negroes; there is no true American music but the wild sweet melodies of the Negro slave; the American fairy tales and folklore are Indian and African; and, all in all, we black men seem the sole oasis of simple faith and reverence in a dusty desert of dollars and smartness. Will America be poorer if she replace her brutal dyspeptic blundering with light-hearted but determined Negro humility? or her coarse and cruel wit with loving jovial good-humor? or her vulgar music with the soul of the Sorrow Songs?

Merely a concrete test of the underlying principles of the great republic is the Negro Problem, and the spiritual striving of the freedmen's sons is the travail of souls whose burden is almost beyond the measure of their strength, but who bear it in the name of an historic race, in the name of this the land of their fathers' fathers, and in the name of human opportunity.

23

Martin Buber,
"The Way of Man, According to the
Teachings of Hasidism,"
from *Hasidism and Modern Man*

The philosopher and theologian Martin Buber (1878–1965) taught Jewish philosophy and religion in Germany until he was forced to leave in 1938, and thereafter lived and wrote in Jerusalem. His thought, bringing together the insights of Hasidism with the ideas of the existentialists, produced one of the most influential visions of the human's relation to others and to God of our time. His best-known work, I and Thou (1923), emphasizes the way reality is something that emerges in the dialogical interaction between people. The most fundamental relationship, the I-Thou relation, is one in which people relate to each other in a way characterized by openness, reciprocity, and personal commitment. In Buber's view, when we look at things in terms of this relationship, we will see that it is an illusion to suppose that the self is, at the most basic level, an isolated individual driven solely by self-interest. Instead, what is most basic is the world that arises between humans as they encounter each other and influence each other.

The study called "The Way of Man" (1948) lays out the Hasidic vision of life as always embedded within a shared life-world, and as dedicated to transforming the world in order to offer it up to God. As Buber writes in the Introduction to the study, "The task of man, of every man, according to Hasidic teaching, is to affirm for God's sake the world and himself and by this very means to transform both." As the passages in this selection reveal, this means starting out from oneself, but that does not mean being egoistically involved in one's own selfish concerns, for one acts for the sake of the world and others, and ultimately for God. In this respect Buber's thought expands on the well-known words of Rabbi Hillel: "If I am not for myself, who will be for me? If I am only for myself, what am I?"

IV. Beginning with Oneself

Once when Rabbi Yitzhak of Vorki was playing host to certain prominent men of Israel, they discussed the value to a household of an honest and efficient servant. They said that a good servant made for good management and cited Joseph at whose hands everything prospered. Rabbi Yitzhak objected. "I once thought that too," he said. "But then my teacher showed me that everything depends on the master of the house. You see, in my youth my wife gave me a great deal of trouble and, though I myself put up with her as best I could, I was sorry for the servants. So I went to my teacher, Rabbi David of Lelov, and asked him whether I should oppose my wife. All he said was: 'Why do you speak to me? Speak to yourself!' I thought over these words for quite a while before I understood them. But I did understand them when I recalled a certain saying of the Baal-Shem: 'There is thought, speech and action. Thought corresponds to one's wife, speech to one's children, and action to one's servants. Whoever straightens himself out in regard to all three will find that everything prospers at his hands.' Then I understood what my teacher had meant: everything depended on myself."

This story touches upon one of the deepest and most difficult problems of our life: the true origin of conflict between man and man.

Manifestations of conflict are usually explained either by the motives of which the quarreling parties are conscious as the occasion of their quarrel, and by the objective situations and processes which underlie these motives and in which both parties are involved; or, proceeding analytically, we try to explore the unconscious complexes to which these motives relate like mere symptoms of an illness to the organic disturbances themselves. Hasidic teaching coincides with this conception in that it, too, derives the problematics of external from that of internal life. But it differs in two essential points, one fundamental and one practical, the latter of which is even more important than the former.

The fundamental difference is that Hasidic teaching is not concerned with the exploration of particular psychical complications, but envisages man as a whole. This is, however, by no means a quantitative difference. For the Hasidic conception springs from the realization that the isolation of elements and partial processes from the whole hinders the comprehension of the whole, and that real transformation, real restoration, at first of the single person and subsequently of the relationship between him and his fellow men, can only be achieved by the comprehension of the whole as a

From Martin Buber, *Hasidism and Modern Man*, trans. by M. Friedman (Atlantic Highlands, NJ: Humanities Press International, 1958, 1988). Reprinted with permission.

whole. (Putting it paradoxically: the search for the center of gravity shifts it and thereby frustrates the whole attempt at overcoming the problematics involved.) This is not to say that there is no need to consider all the phenomena of the soul; but no one of them should be made so much the center of attention as if everything else could be derived from it; rather, they shall all be made starting points—not singly but in their vital connection.

The practical difference is that in Hasidism man is not treated as an object of examination but is called upon to "straighten himself out." At first, a man should himself realize that conflict-situations between himself and others are nothing but the effects of conflict-situations in his own soul; then he should try to overcome this inner conflict, so that afterwards he may go out to his fellow men and enter into new, transformed relationships with them.

Man naturally tries to avoid this decisive reversal—extremely repugnant to him in his accustomed relationship to the world—by referring him who thus appeals to him, or his own soul, if it is his soul that makes the appeal, to the fact that every conflict involves two parties and that, if he is expected to turn his attention from the external to his own internal conflict, his opponent should be expected to do the same. But just this perspective, in which a man sees himself only as an individual contrasted with other individuals, and not as a genuine person, whose transformation helps toward the transformation of the world, contains the fundamental error which Hasidic teaching denounces. The essential thing is to begin with oneself, and at this moment a man has nothing in the world to care about other than this beginning. Any other attitude would distract him from what he is about to begin, weaken his initiative, and thus frustrate the entire bold undertaking.

Rabbi Bunam taught:

"Our sages say: 'Seek peace in your own place.' You cannot find peace anywhere save in your own self. In the psalm we read: 'There is no peace in my bones because of my sin.' When a man has made peace within himself, he will be able to make peace in the whole world."

However, the story from which I started does not confine itself to pointing out the true origin of external conflicts, i.e., the internal conflict, in a general way. The quoted saying of the Baal-Shem states exactly in what the decisive inner conflict consists. It is the conflict between three principles in man's being and life, the principle of thought, the principle of speech, and the principle of action. The origin of all conflict between me and my fellow men is that I do not say what I mean, and that I do not do what I say. For this confuses and poisons, again and again and in increasing measure, the situation between myself and the other man, and I, in my internal disintegration, am no longer able to master it but, contrary to all my illusions, have become its slave. By our contradiction, our lie, we foster conflict-situations and give them power over us until they enslave us. From here, there is no way out but by the crucial realization: Everything depends on myself; and the crucial decision: I will straighten myself out.

But in order that a man may be capable of this great feat, he must first find his way from the casual, accessory elements of his existence to his own self; he must find his own self, not the trivial ego of the egotistic individual, but the deeper self of the person living in a relationship to the world. And that is also contrary to everything we are accustomed to.

I will close this chapter with an old jest as retold by a zaddik.

Rabbi Hanokh told this story:

> There was once a man who was very stupid. When he got up in the morning it was so hard for him to find his clothes that at night he almost hesitated to go to bed for thinking of the trouble he would have on waking. One evening he finally made a great effort, took paper and pencil and as he undressed noted down exactly where he put everything he had on. The next morning, very well pleased with himself, he took the slip of paper in his hand and read: "cap"—there it was, he set it on his head; "pants"—there they lay, he got into them; and so it went until he was fully dressed. "That's all very well, but now where am I myself?" he asked in great consternation. "Where in the world am I?" He looked and looked, but it was a vain search; he could not find himself. "And that is how it is with us," said the rabbi.

V. Not to Be Preoccupied with Oneself

Rabbi Hayyim of Zans[1] had married his son to the daughter of Rabbi Eliezer. The day after the wedding he visited the father of the bride and said: "Now that we are related I feel close to you and can tell you what is eating at my heart. Look! My hair and beard have grown white, and I have not yet atoned!"

"O my friend," replied Rabbi Eliezer, "you are thinking only of yourself. How about forgetting yourself and thinking of the world?"

What is said here seems to contradict everything I have hitherto reported of the teachings of Hasidism. We have heard that everyone should search his own heart, choose his particular way, bring about the unity of his being, begin with himself; and now we are told that man should forget himself. But, if we examine this injunction more closely, we find that it is not only consistent with the others but fits into the whole as a necessary link, as a necessary stage, in its particular place. One need only ask one question: "What for?" What am I to choose my particular way for? What

1. Nowy Sacz in Western Galicia.

am I to unify my being for? The reply is: Not for my own sake. This is why the previous injunction was: to *begin* with oneself. To begin with oneself, but not to end with oneself; to start from oneself, but not to aim at oneself; to comprehend oneself, but not to be preoccupied with oneself.

We see a zaddik, a wise, pious, kindly man, reproach himself in his old age for not yet having performed the true turning. The reply given him is apparently prompted by the opinion that he greatly overrates his sins and greatly underrates the penance he has already done. But what Rabbi Eliezer says goes beyond this. He says, in quite a general sense: "Do not keep worrying about what you have done wrong, but apply the soul-power you are now wasting on self-reproach to such active relationship to the world as you are destined for. You should not be occupied with yourself but with the world."

First of all, we should properly understand what is said here about turning. It is known that turning stands in the center of the Jewish conception of the way of man. Turning is capable of renewing a man from within and changing his position in God's world, so that he who turns is seen standing above the perfect zaddik who does not know the abyss of sin. But turning means here something much greater than repentance and acts of penance; it means that, by a reversal of his whole being, a man who had been lost in the maze of selfishness, where he had always set himself as his goal, finds a way to God, that is, a way to the fulfillment of the particular task for which he, this particular man, has been destined by God. Repentance can only be an incentive to such active reversal; he who goes on fretting himself with repentance, he who tortures himself with the idea that his acts of penance are not sufficient, withholds his best energies from the work of reversal. In a sermon on the Day of Atonement, the Rabbi of Ger warned against self-torture:

"He who has done ill and talks about it and thinks about it all the time does not cast the base thing he did out of his thoughts, and whatever one thinks therein one is, one's soul is wholly and utterly in what one thinks, and so he dwells in baseness. He will certainly not be able to turn, for his spirit will grow coarse and his heart stubborn, and in addition to this he may be overcome by gloom. What would you? Rake the muck this way, rake the muck that way—it will always be muck. Have I sinned, or have I not sinned—what does Heaven get out of it? In the time I am brooding over it I could be stringing pearls for the delight of Heaven. That is why it is written: 'Depart from evil and do good'—turn wholly away from evil, do not dwell upon it, and do good. You have done wrong? Then counteract it by doing right."

But the significance of our story goes beyond this. He who tortures himself incessantly with the idea that he has not yet sufficiently atoned is essentially concerned with the salvation of his soul, with his personal fate in eternity. By rejecting this aim, Hasidism merely draws a conclusion from the teachings of Judaism generally. One of the main points in which Christianity differs from Judaism is that it makes each man's salvation his highest aim. Judaism regards each man's soul as a serving member of God's Creation which, by man's work, is to become the Kingdom of God; thus no soul has its object in itself, in its own salvation. True, each is to know itself, purify itself, perfect itself, but not for its own sake—neither for the sake of its temporal happiness nor for that of its eternal bliss—but for the sake of the work which it is destined to perform upon the world.

The pursuit of one's own salvation is here regarded merely as the sublimest form of self-intending. Self-intending is what Hasidism rejects most emphatically, and quite especially in the case of the man who has found and developed his own self. Rabbi Bunam said: "It is written: 'Now Korah took.' What did he take? He wanted to take himself—therefore, nothing he did could be of any worth." This is why Bunam contrasted the eternal Korah with the eternal Moses, the "humble" man, whose doings are not aimed at himself. Rabbi Bunam taught: "In every generation the soul of Moses and the soul of Korah return. But if once, in days to come, the soul of Korah is willing to subject itself to the soul of Moses, Korah will be redeemed."

Rabbi Bunam thus sees, as it were, the history of mankind on its road to redemption as a process involving two kinds of men, the proud who, if sometimes in the sublimest form, think of themselves, and the humble, who in all matters think of the world. Only when pride subjects itself to humility can it be redeemed; and only when it is redeemed can the world be redeemed.

After Rabbi Bunam's death, one of his disciples—the aforementioned Rabbi of Ger, from whose sermon on the Day of Atonement I quoted a few sentences—remarked: "Rabbi Bunam had the keys to all the firmaments. And why not? A man who does not think of himself is given all the keys."

The greatest of Rabbi Bunam's disciples, a truly tragic figure among the zaddikim, Rabbi Mendel of Kotzk, once said to his congregation: "What, after all, do I demand of you? Only three things: not to look furtively outside yourself, not to look furtively into others, and not to aim at yourselves." That is to say: firstly, everyone should preserve and hallow his own soul in its own particularity and in its own place and not envy the particularity and place of others; secondly, everyone should respect the secret in the soul of his fellow man and not, with brazen curiosity, intrude upon it and take advantage of it; and thirdly, everyone, in his relationship to the world, should be careful not to set himself as his aim.

24

Alasdair MacIntyre,
"The Virtues, the Unity of a Human Life and the Concept of a Tradition,"
from *After Virtue*

Alasdair MacIntyre (b. 1929) currently teaches at Duke University. He has written books on ethics, Freudian theory, Marxism, and contemporary culture. After Virtue (1981) begins with the claim that moral debates in the modern world are often intractable and interminable, in part because our contemporary framework of moral understanding has lost some of the basic concepts needed to really make sense of moral issues. Much of the book then (1) shows how the rather thin framework of moral understanding in contemporary life arose, and (2) tries to recover older ways of thinking about life that existed in earlier times. In trying to recover the conception of virtues from ancient Greek thought, MacIntyre makes it clear he is drawing on ideas that were formulated by Aristotle more than two millennia ago. In MacIntyre's view, the notions of virtue, personal identity, and narrative are tightly connected. The image of a unified, cohesive life story guided by core virtues that is found here provides a powerful antidote to our current tendency to think of life as a matter of just getting by from day to day.

Any contemporary attempt to envisage each human life as a whole, as a unity, whose character provides the virtues with an adequate *telos* encounters two different kinds of obstacle, one social and one philosophical. The social obstacles derive from the way in which modernity partitions each human life into a variety of segments, each with its own norms and modes of behaviour. So work is divided from leisure, private life from public, the corporate from the personal. So both childhood and old age have been wrenched away from the rest of human life and made over into distinct realms. And all these separations have been achieved so that it is the distinctiveness of each and not the unity of the life of the individual who passes through those parts in terms of which we are taught to think and to feel.

The philosophical obstacles derive from two distinct tendencies, one chiefly, though not only, domesticated in analytical philosophy and one at home in both sociological theory and in existentialism. The former is the tendency to think atomistically about human action and to analyse complex actions and transactions in terms of simple components. Hence the recurrence in more than one context of the notion of "a basic action." That particular actions derive their character as parts of larger wholes is a point of view alien to our dominant ways of thinking and yet one which it is necessary at least to consider if we are to begin to understand how a life may be more than a sequence of individual actions and episodes.

Equally the unity of a human life becomes invisible to us when a sharp separation is made either between the individual and the roles that he or she plays—a separation characteristic not only of Sartre's existentialism, but also of the sociological theory of Ralf Dahrendorf—or between the different role- and quasi-role-enactments of an individual life so that life comes to appear as nothing but a series of unconnected episodes—a liquidation of the self characteristic, as I noticed earlier, of Goffman's sociological theory. I already also suggested that both the Sartrian and the Goffmanesque conceptions of selfhood are highly characteristic of the modes of thought and practice of modernity. It is perhaps therefore unsurprising to realize that the self as thus conceived cannot be envisaged as a bearer of the Aristotelian virtues.

For a self separated from its roles in the Sartrian mode loses that arena of social relationships in which the Aristotelian virtues function if they function at all. The patterns of a virtuous life would fall under those condemnations of conventionality which Sartre put into a mouth of Antoine Roquentin in *La Nausée* and which he uttered in his own person in *L'Etre et le néant*. Indeed the self's refusal of the inauthenticity of conventionalized social relationships becomes what integrity is diminished into in Sartre's account.

At the same time the liquidation of the self into a set of demarcated areas of role-playing allows no scope for the exercise of dispositions which could genuinely be accounted virtues in any sense remotely Aristotelian. For a virtue is not a disposition that makes for success only in some one particular type of situation. What are spoken of as the virtues of a good committee man or of a good administrator or of a gambler or a pool hustler are professional skills professionally deployed in those situations where they can be effective, not virtues. Someone who genuinely possesses a virtue can be expected to manifest it in very different types of situation, many of them situations where the practice of a virtue cannot be expected to be effective in the way that we expect a professional skill to be. Hector exhibited one and the same courage in his parting from Andromache and on the battlefield with Achilles; Eleanor Marx exhibited one and the same compassion in her relationship with her father, in her work with trade unionists and in her entanglement with Aveling. And the unity of a virtue in someone's life is intelligible only as a characteristic of a unitary life, a life that can be conceived and evaluated as a whole. Hence just as in the discussion of the changes in and fragmentation of morality which accompanied the rise of modernity in the earlier parts of this book, each stage in the emergence of the characteristically modern views of the moral judgement was accompanied by a corresponding stage in the emergence of the characteristically modern conceptions of selfhood; so now, in defining the particular pre-modern concept of the virtues with which I have been preoccupied, it has become necessary to say something of the concomitant concept of selfhood, a concept of a self whose unity resides in the unity of a narrative which links birth to life to death as narrative beginning to middle to end.

Such a conception of the self is perhaps less unfamiliar than it may appear at first sight. Just because it has played a key part in the cultures which are historically the predecessors of our own, it would not be surprising if it turned out to be still an unacknowledged presence in many of our ways of thinking and acting. Hence it is not inappropriate to begin by scrutinizing some of our most taken-for-granted, but clearly correct conceptual insights about human actions and selfhood in order to show how natural it is to think of the self in a narrative mode.

It is a conceptual commonplace, both for philosophers and for ordinary agents, that one and the same segment of human behaviour may be correctly characterized in a number of different ways. To the question "What is he doing?" the answers may with equal truth and appropriateness be "Digging," "Gardening," "Taking exercise," "Preparing for winter" or "Pleasing his wife." Some of these answers will characterize the agent's intentions, others unintended consequences of his actions, and of these unintended consequences some may be such that the agent is aware of them and others not. What is important to notice immediately is that any answer to the questions of how we are to understand or to explain a given segment of behaviour will presuppose some prior answer to the question of how these different correct answers to the question 'What is he doing?' are related to each other. For if someone's primary intention is to put the garden in order before the winter and it is only incidentally the case that in so doing he is taking exercise and pleasing his wife, we have one type of behaviour to be explained; but if the agent's primary intention is to please his wife by taking exercise, we have quite another type of behaviour to be explained and we will have to look in a different direction for understanding and explanation.

In the first place the episode has been situated in an annual cycle of domestic activity, and the behaviour embodies an intention which presupposes a particular type of household-cum-garden setting with the peculiar narrative history of that setting in which this segment of behaviour now becomes an episode. In the second instance the episode has been situated in the narrative history of a marriage, a very different, even if related, social setting. We cannot, that is to say, characterize behaviour independently of intentions, and we cannot characterize intentions independently of the settings which make those intentions intelligible both to agents themselves and to others.

I use the word "setting" here as a relatively inclusive term. A social setting may be an institution, it may be what I have called a practice, or it may be a milieu of some other human kind. But it is central to the notion of a setting as I am going to understand it that a setting has a history, a history within which the histories of individual agents not only are, but have to be, situated, just because without the setting and its changes through time the history of the individual agent and his changes through time will be unintelligible. Of course one and the same piece of behaviour may belong to more than one setting. There are at least two different ways in which this may be so.

In my earlier example the agent's activity may be part of the history both of the cycle of household activity and of his marriage, two histories which have happened to intersect. The household may have its own history stretching back through hundreds of years, as do the histories of some European farms, where the farm has had a life of its own, even though different families have in different periods inhabited it; and the marriage will certainly have its own history, a history which itself presupposes that a particular point has been reached in the history of the institution of marriage. If we are to relate some particular segment of behaviour in any precise way to an agent's intentions and thus to the settings which that agent inhabits, we shall have to understand in a precise way how the variety of correct characterizations of the agent's behaviour relate to each other first by identifying which characteristics refer us to an intention and which do not and then by classifying further the items in both categories.

Where intentions are concerned, we need to know which intention or intentions were primary, that is to say, of which it is the case that, had the agent intended otherwise, he would not have performed that action. Thus if we know that a man is gardening with the self-avowed purposes of healthful exercise and of pleasing his wife, we do not yet know how to understand what he is doing until we know the answer to such questions as whether he would continue gardening if he continued to believe that gardening was healthful exercise, but discovered that his gardening no longer pleased his wife, *and* whether he would continue gardening, if he ceased to believe that gardening was healthful exercise, but continued to believe that it pleased his wife, *and* whether he would continue gardening if he changed his beliefs on both points. That is to say, we need to know both what certain of his beliefs are and which of them are causally effective; and, that is to say, we need to know whether certain contrary-to-fact hypothetical statements are true or false. And until we know this, we shall not know how to characterize correctly what the agent is doing.

Consider another equally trivial example of a set of compatibly correct answers to the question "What is he doing?" "Writing a sentence"; "Finishing his book"; "Contributing to the debate on the theory of action"; "Trying to get tenure." Here the intentions can be ordered in terms of the stretch of time to which reference is made. Each of the shorter-term intentions is, and can only be made, intelligible by reference to some longer-term intentions; and the characterization of the behaviour in terms of the longer-term intentions can only be correct if some of the characterizations in terms of shorter-term intentions are also correct. Hence the behaviour is only characterized adequately when we know what the longer and longest-term intentions invoked are and how the shorter-term intentions are related to the longer. Once again we are involved in writing a narrative history.

Intentions thus need to be ordered both causally and temporally and both orderings will make references to settings, references already made obliquely by such elementary terms as "gardening," "wife," "book" and "tenure." Moreover the correct identification of the agent's beliefs will be an essential constituent of this task; failure at this point would mean failure in the whole enterprise. (The conclusion may seem obvious; but it already entails one important consequence. There is no such thing as "behaviour," to be identified prior to and independently of intentions, beliefs and settings. Hence the project of a science of behaviour takes on a mysterious and somewhat outré character. It is not that such a science is impossible; but there is nothing for it to be but a science of uninterpreted physical movement such as B. F. Skinner aspires to. It is no part of my task here to examine Skinner's problems; but it is worth noticing that it is not at all clear what a scientific experiment could be, if one were a Skinnerian; since the conception of an experiment is certainly one of intention- and belief-informed behaviour. And what would be utterly doomed to failure would be the project of a science of, say, *political* behaviour, detached from a study of intentions, beliefs and settings. It is perhaps worth noting that when the expression "the behavioural sciences" was given its first influential use in a Ford Foundation Report of 1953, the term "behaviour" was defined so as to include what were called "such subjective behaviour as attitudes, beliefs, expectations, motivations and aspirations" as well as "overt acts." But what the Report's wording seems to imply is that it is cataloguing two distinct sets of items, available for independent study. If the argument so far is correct, then there is only one set of items.)

Consider what the argument so far implies about the interrelationships of the intentional, the social and the historical. We identify a particular action only by invoking two kinds of context, implicitly if not explicitly. We place the agent's intentions, I have suggested, in causal and temporal order with reference to their role in his or her history; and we also place them with reference to their role in the history of the setting or settings to which they belong. In doing this, in determining what causal efficacy the agent's intentions had in one or more directions, and how his short-term intentions succeeded or failed to be constitutive of long-term intentions, we ourselves write a further part of these histories. Narrative history of a certain kind turns out to be the basic and essential genre for the characterization of human actions.

It is important to be clear how different the standpoint presupposed by the argument so far is from that of those analytical philosophers who have constructed accounts of human actions which make central the notion of "a" human action. A course of human events is then seen as a complex sequence of individual actions, and a natural question is: How do we individuate human actions? Now there are contexts in which such notions are at home. In the recipes of a cookery book for instance actions are individuated in just the way that some analytical philosophers have supposed to be possible of all actions. "Take six eggs. Then break them into a bowl. Add flour, salt, sugar, etc." But the point about such sequences is that each element in them is intelligible as an action only as a–possible–element–in–a–sequence. Moreover even such a sequence requires a context to be intelligible. If in the middle of my lecture on Kant's ethics I suddenly broke six eggs into a bowl and added flour and sugar, proceeding all the while with my Kantian exegesis, I have *not*, simply in virtue of the fact that I was following a sequence prescribed by Fanny Farmer, performed an intelligible action.

To this it might be related that I certainly performed an action or a set of actions, if not an intelligible action. But to this I want to reply that the concept of an intelligible action is a more fundamental concept than that of an action as such. Unintelligible actions are failed candidates for the status of intelligible action; and to lump unintelligible actions and intelligible actions together in a single class of actions and then to characterize action in terms of what items of both sets have in common is to make the mistake of ignoring this. It is also to neglect the central importance of the concept of intelligibility.

The importance of the concept of intelligibility is closely related to the fact that the most basic distinction of all embedded in our discourse and our practice in this area is that between human beings and other beings. Human beings can be held to account for that of which they are the authors; other beings cannot. To identify an occurrence as an action is in the paradigmatic instances to identify it under a type of description which enables us to see that occurrence as flowing intelligibly from a human agent's intentions, motives, passions and purposes. It is therefore to understand an action as something for which someone is accountable, about which it is always appropriate to ask the agent for an intelligible account. When an occurrence is apparently the intended action of a human agent, but nonetheless we cannot so identify it, we are both intellectually and practically baffled. We do not know how to respond; we do not know how to explain; we do not even know how to characterize minimally as an intelligible action; our distinction between the humanly accountable and the merely natural seems to have broken down. And this kind of bafflement does indeed occur in a number of different kinds of situation; when we enter alien cultures or even alien social structures within our own culture, in our encounters with certain types of neurotic or psychotic patient (it is indeed the unintelligibility of such patient's actions that leads to their being treated as patients; actions unintelligible to the agent as well as to everyone else are understood—rightly—as a kind of suffering), but also in everyday situations. Consider an example.

I am standing waiting for a bus and the young man standing next to me suddenly says: "The name of the common wild duck is *Histrionicus histrionicus histrionicus.*" There is no problem as to the meaning of the sentence he uttered: the problem is, how to answer the question, what was he doing in uttering it? Suppose he just uttered such sentences at random intervals; this would be one possible form of madness. We would render his act of utterance intelligible if one of the following turned out to be true. He has mistaken me for someone who yesterday had approached him in the library and asked: "Do you by any chance know the Latin name of the common wild duck?" *Or* he has just come from a session with his psychotherapist who has urged him to break down his shyness by talking to strangers. "But what shall I say?" "Oh, anything at all." *Or* he is a Soviet spy waiting at a prearranged rendezvous and uttering the ill-chosen code sentence which will identify him to his contact. In each case the act of utterance becomes intelligible by finding its place in a narrative.

To this it may be replied that the supplying of a narrative is not necessary to make such an act intelligible. All that is required is that we can identify the relevant type of speech-act (e.g., "He was answering a question") or some purpose served by his utterance (e.g., "He was trying to attract your attention"). But speech-acts and purposes too can be intelligible or unintelligible. Suppose that the man at the bus stop explains his act of utterance by saying "I was answering a question." I reply: "But I never asked you any question to which that could have been the answer." He says, "Oh, I know *that.*" Once again his action becomes unintelligible. And a parallel example could easily be constructed to show that the mere fact that an action serves some purpose of a recognized type is not sufficient to render an action intelligible. Both purposes and speech-acts require contexts.

The most familiar type of context in and by reference to which speech-acts and purposes are rendered intelligible is the conversation. Conversation is so all-pervasive a feature of the human world that it tends to escape philosophical attention. Yet remove conversation from human life and what would be left? Consider then what is involved in following a conversation and finding it intelligible or unintelligible. (To find a conversation intelligible is not the same as to understand it; for a conversation which I overhear may be intelligible, but I may fail to understand it.) If I listen to a conversation between two other people my ability to grasp the thread of the conversation will involve an ability to bring it under some one out of a set of descriptions in which the degree and kind of coherence in the conversation is brought out: "a drunken, rambling quarrel," "a serious intellectual disagreement," "a tragic misunderstanding of each other," "a comic, even farcical misconstrual of each other's motives," "a penetrating interchange of views," "a struggle to dominate each other," "a trivial exchange of gossip."

The use of words such as "tragic," "comic," and "farcical" is not marginal to such evaluations. We allocate conversations to genres, just as we do literary narratives. Indeed a conversation is a dramatic work, even if a very short one, in which the participants are not only the actors, but also the joint authors, working out in agreement or disagreement the mode of their production. For it is not just that conversations belong to genres in just the way that plays and novels do; but they have beginnings, middles and endings just as do literary works. They embody reversals and recognitions; they move towards and away from climaxes. There may within a longer conversation be digressions and subplots, indeed digressions within digressions and subplots within subplots.

But if this is true of conversations, it is true also *mutatis mutandis* of battles, chess games, courtships, philosophy seminars, families at the dinner table, businessmen negotiating contracts—that is, of human transactions in general. For conversation, understood widely enough, is the form of human transactions in general. Conversational behaviour is not a special sort or aspect of human behaviour, even though the forms of language-using and of human life are such that the deeds of others speak for them as much as do their words. For that is possible only because they are the deeds of those who have words.

I am presenting both convervations in particular then and human actions in general as enacted narratives. Narrative is not the work of poets, dramatists and novelists reflecting upon events which had no narrative order before one was imposed by the singer or the writer; narrative form is neither disguise nor decoration. Barbara Hardy has written that "we dream in narrative, day-dream in narrative, remember, anticipate, hope, despair, believe, doubt, plan, revise, criticise, construct, gossip, learn, hate and love by narrative" in arguing the same point.[1]

At the beginning of this chapter I argued that in successfully identifying and understanding what someone else is doing we always move towards placing a particular episode in the context of a set of narrative histories, histories both of the individuals concerned and of the settings in which they act and suffer. It is now becoming clear that we render the actions of others intelligible in this way because action itself has a basically historical character. It is because we all live out narratives in our lives and because we understand our own lives in terms of the narratives that we live out that the form of narrative is appropriate for understanding the actions of others. Stories are lived before they are told—except in the case of fiction.

This has of course been denied in recent debates. Louis O. Mink, quarrelling with Barbara Hardy's view, has asserted: "Stories are not lived but told. Life has no beginnings, middles, or ends; there are meetings, but the start of an affair belongs to the story we tell ourselves later, and there are partings, but final partings only in the story. There are hopes, plans, battles and ideas, but only in retrospective stories are hopes unfulfilled, plans miscarried, battles decisive, and ideas seminal. Only in the story is it America which Columbus discovers and only in the story is the kingdom lost for want of a nail."[2]

What are we to say to this? Certainly we must agree that it is only retrospectively that hopes can be characterized as unfulfilled or battles as decisive and so on. But we so characterize them in life as much as in art. And to someone who says that in life there are no endings, or that final partings take place only in stories, one is tempted to reply, "But have you never heard of death?" Homer did not have to tell the tale of Hector before Andromache could lament unfulfilled hope and final parting. There are

1. Barbara Hardy, "Towards a Poetics of Fiction: An Approach through Narrative," *Novel*, 2, 1968: 5–14, p. 5.

2. Louis O. Mink, "History and Fiction as Modes of Comprehension," *New Literary History*, 1, 1970: 541–558, pp. 557–8.

countless Hectors and countless Andromaches whose lives embodied the
form of their Homeric namesakes, but who never came to the attention of
any poet. What is true is that in taking an event as a beginning or an ending
we bestow a significance upon it which may be debatable. Did the Roman
republic end with the death of Julius Caesar, or at Philippi, or with the
founding of the principate? The answer is surely that, like Charles II, it
was a long time a-dying; but this answer implies the reality of its ending as
much as do any of the former. There is a crucial sense in which the
principate of Augustus, or the taking of the oath in the tennis court, or the
decision to construct an atomic bomb at Los Alamos constitute beginnings; the peace of 404 B.C., the abolition of the Scottish Parliament and
the battle of Waterloo equally constitute endings; while there are many
events which are both endings and beginnings.

As with beginnings, middles and endings, so also with genres and with
the phenomenon of embedding. Consider the question of to what genre
the life of Thomas Becket belongs, a question which has to be asked and
answered before we can decide how it is to be written. (On Mink's paradoxical view this question could not be asked until *after* the life had been
written.) In some of the medieval versions, Thomas's career is presented
in terms of the canons of medieval hagiography. In the Icelandic *Thomas
Saga* he is presented as a saga hero. In Dom David Knowles's modern
biography the story is a tragedy, the tragic relationship of Thomas and
Henry II, each of whom satisfies Aristotle's demand that the hero be a
great man with a fatal flaw. Now it clearly makes sense to ask who is right,
if anyone: the monk William of Canterbury, the author of the saga, or the
Cambridge Regius Professor Emeritus? The answer appears to be clearly
the last. The true genre of the life is neither hagiography nor saga, but
tragedy. So of such modern narrative subjects as the life of Trotsky or that
of Lenin, of the history of the Soviet Communist Party or the American
presidency, we may also ask: To what genre does their history belong? And
this is the same question as: What type of account of their history will be
both true and intelligible?

Or consider again how one narrative may be embedded in another. In
both plays and novels there are well-known examples: the play within the
play in *Hamlet*, Wandering Willie's Tale in *Redgauntlet*, Aeneas' narrative
to Dido in book 2 of the *Aeneid*, and so on. But there are equally well-
known examples in real life. Consider again the way in which the career of
Becket as archbishop and chancellor is embedded within the reign of
Henry II, or the way in which the tragic life of Mary Stuart is embedded in
that of Elizabeth I, or the history of the Confederacy within the history of
the United States. Someone may discover (or not discover) that he or she
is a character in a number of narratives at the same time, some of them

embedded in others. Or again, what seemed to be an intelligible narrative in which one was playing a part may be transformed wholly or partly into a story of unintelligible episodes. This last is what happened to Kafka's character K. in both *The Trial* and *The Castle.* (It is no accident that Kafka could not end his novels, for the notion of an ending like that of a beginning has its sense only in terms of intelligible narrative.)

I spoke earlier of the agent as not only an actor, but an author. Now I must emphasize that what the agent is able to do and say intelligibly as an actor is deeply affected by the fact that we are never more (and sometimes less) than the co-authors of our own narratives. Only in fantasy do we live what story we please. In life, as both Aristotle and Engels noted, we are always under certain constraints. We enter upon a stage which we did not design and we find ourselves part of an action that was not of our making. Each of us being a main character in his own drama plays subordinate parts in the dramas of others, and each drama constrains the others. In my drama, perhaps, I am Hamlet or Iago or at least the swineherd who may yet become a prince, but to you I am only A Gentleman or at best Second Murderer, while you are my Polonius or my Gravedigger, but your own hero. Each of our dramas exerts constraints on each other's, making the whole different from the parts, but still dramatic.

It is considerations as complex as these which are involved in making the notion of intelligibility the conceptual connecting link between the notion of action and that of narrative. Once we have understood its importance the claim that the concept of an action is secondary to that of an intelligible action will perhaps appear less bizarre and so too will the claim that the notion of "an" action, while of the highest practical importance, is always a potentially misleading abstraction. An action is a moment in a possible or actual history or in a number of such histories. The notion of a history is as fundamental a notion as the notion of an action. Each requires the other. But I cannot say this without noticing that it is precisely this that Sartre denies—as indeed his whole theory of the self, which captures so well the spirit of modernity, requires that he should. In *La Nausée,* Sartre makes Antoine Roquentin argue not just what Mink argues, that narrative is very different from life, but that to present human life in the form of a narrative is always to falsify it. There are not and there cannot be any true stories. Human life is composed of discrete actions which lead nowhere, which have no order; the story-teller imposes on human events retrospectively an order which they did not have while they were lived. Clearly if Sartre/Roquentin is right—I speak of Sartre/Roquentin to distinguish him from such other well-known characters as Sartre/Heidegger and Sartre/Marx—my central contention must be mistaken. There is nonetheless an important point of agreement between my thesis and that of

Sartre/Roquentin. We agree in identifying the intelligibility of an action with its place in a narrative sequence. Only Sartre/Roquentin takes it that human actions are as such unintelligible occurrences: it is to a realization of the metaphysical implications of this that Roquentin is brought in the course of the novel and the practical effect upon him is to bring to an end his own project of writing an historical biography. This project no longer makes sense. Either he will write what is true or he will write an intelligible history, but the one possibility excludes the other. Is Sartre/Roquentin right?

We can discover what is wrong with Sartre's thesis in either of two ways. One is to ask: what would human actions deprived of any falsifying narrative order be like? Sartre himself never answers this question; it is striking that in order to show that there are no true narratives, he himself writes a narrative albeit a fictional one. But the only picture that I find myself able to form of human nature *an-sich*, prior to the alleged misinterpretation by narrative is the kind of dislocated sequence which Dr. Johnson offers us in his notes of his travels in France: "There we waited on the ladies— Morville's.—Spain. Country towns all beggars. At Dijon he could not find the way to Orleans.—Cross roads of France very bad.—Five soldiers.—Women.—Soldiers escaped.—The Colonel would not lose five men for the sake of one woman.—The magistrate cannot seize a soldier but by the Colonel's permission, etc., etc."[3] What this suggests is what I take to be true, namely that the characterization of actions allegedly prior to any narrative form being imposed upon them will always turn out to be the presentation of what are plainly the disjointed parts of some possible narrative.

We can also approach the question in another way. What I have called a history is an enacted dramatic narrative in which the characters are also the authors. The characters of course never start literally *ab initio;* they plunge *in medias res*, the beginnings of their story already made for them by what and who has gone before. But when Julian Grenfell or Edward Thomas went off to France in the 1914–18 war they no less enacted a narrative than did Menelaus or Odysseus when *they* went off. The difference between imaginary characters and real ones is not in the narrative form of what they do; it is in the degree of their authorship of that form and of their own deeds. Of course just as they do not begin where they please, they cannot go on exactly as they please either; each character is constrained by the actions of others and by the social settings presup-

3. Philip Hobsbaum, *A Reader's Guide to Charles Dickens* (New York: Farrar, Straus and Giroux, 1973), p. 32.

posed in his and their actions, a point forcibly made by Marx in the classical, if not entirely satisfactory account of human life as enacted dramatic narrative, *The Eighteenth Brumaire of Louis Bonaparte*.

I call Marx's account less than satisfactory partly because he wishes to present the narrative of human social life in a way that will be compatible with a view of that life as law-governed and predictable in a particular way. But it is crucial that at any given point in an enacted dramatic narrative we do not know what will happen next. The kind of unpredictability for which I argued [in chapter 8, *After Virtue*] is required by the narrative structure of human life, and the empirical generalizations and explorations which social scientists discover provide a kind of understanding of human life which is perfectly compatible with that structure.

This unpredictability coexists with a second crucial characteristic of all lived narratives, a certain teleological character. We live out our lives, both individually and in our relationships with each other, in the light of certain conceptions of a possible shared future, a future in which certain possibilities beckon us forward and others repel us, some seem already foreclosed and others perhaps inevitable. There is no present which is not informed by some image of some future and an image of the future which always presents itself in the form of a *telos*—or of a variety of ends or goals—towards which we are either moving or failing to move in the present. Unpredictability and teleology therefore coexist as part of our lives; like characters in a fictional narrative we do not know what will happen next, but none the less our lives have a certain form which projects itself towards our future. Thus the narratives which we live out have both an unpredictable and a partially teleological character. If the narrative of our individual and social lives is to continue intelligibly—and either type of narrative may lapse into unintelligibility—it is always both the case that there are constraints on how the story can continue *and* that within those constraints there are indefinitely many ways that it can continue.

A central thesis then begins to emerge: man is in his actions and practice, as well as in his fictions, essentially a story-telling animal. He is not essentially, but becomes through his history, a teller of stories that aspire to truth. But the key question for men is not about their own authorship; I can only answer the question "What am I to do?" if I can answer the prior question "Of what story or stories do I find myself a part?" We enter human society, that is, with one or more imputed characters—roles into which we have been drafted—and we have to learn what they are in order to be able to understand how others respond to us and how our responses to them are apt to be construed. It is through hearing stories about wicked stepmothers, lost children, good but misguided kings, wolves that suckle twin boys, youngest sons who receive no inheritance but must make their own way in the world and eldest sons who waste their inheritance on riotous living and go into exile to live with the swine, that children learn or mislearn both what a child and what a parent is, what the cast of characters may be in the drama into which they have been born and what the ways of the world are. Deprive children of stories and you leave them unscripted, anxious stutterers in their actions as in their words. Hence there is no way to give us an understanding of any society, including our own, except through the stock of stories which constitute its initial dramatic resources. Mythology, in its original sense, is at the heart of things. Vico was right and so was Joyce. And so too of course is that moral tradition from heroic society to its medieval heirs according to which the telling of stories has a key part in educating us into the virtues.

I suggested earlier that "an" action is always an episode in a possible history: I would now like to make a related suggestion about another concept, that of personal identity. Derek Parfit and others have recently drawn our attention to the contrast between the criteria of strict identity, which is an all-or-nothing matter (*either* the Tichborne claimant *is* the last Tichborne heir; *either* all the properties of the last heir belong to the claimant *or* the claimant is not the heir—Leibniz's Law applies) and the psychological continuities of personality which are a matter of more or less. (Am I the same man at fifty I was at forty in respect of memory, intellectual powers, critical responses? More or less.) But what is crucial to human beings as characters in enacted narratives is that, possessing only the resources of psychological continuity, we have to be able to respond to the imputation of strict identity. I am forever whatever I have been at any time for others—and I may at any time be called upon to answer for it— no matter how changed I may be now. There is no way of *founding* my identity—or lack of it—on the psychological continuity or discontinuity of the self. The self inhabits a character whose unity is given as the unity of a character. Once again there is a crucial disagreement with empiricist or analytical philosophers on the one hand and with existentialists on the other.

Empiricists, such as Locke or Hume, tried to give an account of personal identity solely in terms of psychological states or events. Analytical philosophers, in so many ways their heirs as well as their critics, have wrestled with the connection between those states and events and strict identity understood in terms of Leibniz's Law. Both have failed to see that a background has been omitted, the lack of which makes the problems insoluble. That background is provided by the concept of a story and of that kind of unity of character which a story requires. Just as a history is not a sequence of actions, but the concept of an action is that of a moment in an actual or possible history abstracted for some purpose from that history, so the characters in a history are not a collection of persons, but the concept of a person is that of a character abstracted from a history.

What the narrative concept of selfhood requires is thus twofold. On the one hand, I am what I may justifiably be taken by others to be in the course of living out a story that runs from my birth to my death; I am the *subject* of a history that is my own and no one else's, that has its own peculiar meaning. When someone complains—as do some of those who attempt or commit suicide—that his or her life is meaningless, he or she is often and perhaps characteristically complaining that the narrative of their life has become unintelligible to them, that it lacks any point, any movement towards a climax or a *telos*. Hence the point of doing any one thing rather than another at crucial junctures in their lives seems to such a person to have been lost.

To be the subject of a narrative that runs from one's birth to one's death is, I remarked earlier, to be accountable for the actions and experiences which compose a narratable life. It is, that is, to be open to being asked to give a certain kind of account of what one did or what happened to one or what one witnessed at any earlier point in one's life the time at which the question is posed. Of course someone may have forgotten or suffered brain damage or simply not attended sufficiently at the relevant times to be able to give the relevant account. But to say of someone under some one description ("The prisoner of the Château d'If") that he is the same person as someone characterized quite differently ("The Count of Monte Cristo") is precisely to say that it makes sense to ask him to give an intelligible narrative account enabling us to understand how he could at different times and different places be one and the same person and yet be so differently characterized. Thus personal identity is just that identity presupposed by the unity of the character which the unity of a narrative requires. Without such unity there would not be subjects of whom stories could be told.

The other aspect of narrative selfhood is correlative: I am not only accountable, I am one who can always ask others for an account, who can put others to the question. I am part of their story, as they are part of mine. The narrative of any one life is part of an interlocking set of narratives. Moreover this asking for and giving of accounts itself plays an important part in constituting narratives. Asking you what you did and why, saying what I did and why, pondering the differences between your account of what I did and my account of what I did, and vice versa, these are essential constituents of all but the very simplest and barest of narratives. Thus without the accountability of the self those trains of events that constitute all but the simplest and barest of narratives could not occur; and without that same accountability narratives would lack that continuity required to make both them and the actions that constitute them intelligible.

It is important to notice that I am not arguing that the concepts of narrative or of intelligibility or of accountability are *more* fundamental than that of personal identity. The concepts of narrative, intelligibility and accountability presuppose the applicability of the concept of personal identity, just as it presupposes their applicability and just as indeed each of these three presupposes the applicability of the two others. The relationship is one of mutual presupposition. It does follow of course that all attempts to elucidate the notion of personal identity independently of and in isolation from the notions of narrative, intelligibility and accountability are bound to fail. As all such attempts have.

It is now possible to return to the question from which this enquiry into the nature of human action and identity started: In what does the unity of an individual life consist? The answer is that its unity is the unity of a narrative embodied in a single life. To ask "What is the good for me?" is to ask how best I might live out that unity and bring it to completion. To ask "What is the good for man?" is to ask what all answers to the former question must have in common. But now it is important to emphasize that it is the systematic asking of these two questions and the attempt to answer them in deed as well as in word which provide the moral life with its unity. The unity of a human life is the unity of a narrative quest. Quests sometimes fail, are frustrated, abandoned or dissipated into distractions; and human lives may in all these ways also fail. But the only criteria for success or failure in a human life as a whole are the criteria of success or failure in a narrated or to-be-narrated quest. A quest for what?

Two key features of the medieval conception of a quest need to be recalled. The first is that without some at least partly determinate conception of the final *telos* there could not be any beginning to a quest. Some conception of the good for man is required. Whence is such a conception to be drawn? Precisely from those questions which led us to attempt to transcend that limited conception of the virtues which is available in and through practices. It is in looking for a conception of *the* good which will enable us to order other goods, for a conception of *the* good which will enable us to extend our understanding of the purpose and content of the virtues, for a conception of *the* good which will enable us to understand the place of integrity and constancy in life, that we initially define the kind of life which is a quest for the good. But secondly it is clear the medieval conception of a quest is not at all that of a search for something already adequately characterized, as miners search for gold or geologists for oil. It is in the course of the quest and only through encountering and coping with the various particular harms, dangers, temptations and distractions which provide any quest with its episodes and incidents that the goal of the quest is finally to be understood. A quest is always an education both as to the character of that which is sought and in self-knowledge.

The virtues therefore are to be understood as those dispositions which will not only sustain practices and enable us to achieve the goods internal to practices, but which will also sustain us in the relevant kind of quest for the good, by enabling us to overcome the harms, dangers, temptations and distractions which we encounter, and which will furnish us with increasing self-knowledge and increasing knowledge of the good. The catalogue of the virtues will therefore include the virtues required to sustain the kind of households and the kind of political communities in which men and women can seek for the good together and the virtues necessary for philosophical enquiry about the character of the good. We have then arrived at a provisional conclusion about the good life for man: the good life for man is the life spent in seeking for the good life for man, and the virtues necessary for the seeking are those which will enable us to understand what more and what else the good life for man is. We have also completed the second stage in our account of the virtues, by situating them in relation to the good life for man and not only in relation to practices. But our enquiry requires a third stage.

For I am never able to seek for the good or exercise the virtues only *qua* individual. This is partly because what it is to live the good life concretely varies from circumstance to circumstances even when it is one and the same conception of the good life and one and the same set of virtues which are being embodied in a human life. What the good life is for a fifth-century Athenian general will not be the same as what it was for a medieval nun or a seventeenth-century farmer. But it is not just that different individuals live in different social circumstances; it is also that we all approach our own circumstances as bearers of a particular social identity. I am someone's son or daughter, someone else's cousin or uncle; I am a citizen of this or that city, a member of this or that guild or profession; I belong to this clan, that tribe, this nation. Hence what is good for me has to be the good for one who inhabits these roles. As such, I inherit from the past of my family, my city, my tribe, my nation, a variety of debts, inheritances, rightful expectations and obligations. These constitute the given of my life, my moral starting point. This is in part what gives my life its own moral particularity.

This thought is likely to appear alien and even surprising from the standpoint of modern individualism. From the standpoint of individualism I am what I myself choose to be. I can always, if I wish to, put in question what are taken to be the merely contingent social features of my existence. I may biologically be my father's son; but I cannot be held responsible for what he did unless I choose implicitly or explicitly to assume such responsibility. I may legally be a citizen of a certain country; but I cannot be held responsible for what my country does or has done unless I choose implicitly or explicitly to assume such responsibility. Such individualism is expressed by those modern Americans who deny any responsibility for the effects of slavery upon black Americans, saying "I never owned any slaves." It is more subtly the standpoint of those other modern Americans who accept a nicely calculated responsibility for such effects measured precisely by the benefits they themselves as individuals have indirectly received from slavery. In both cases "being an American" is not in itself taken to be part of the moral identity of the individual. And of course there is nothing peculiar to modern Americans in this attitude: the Englishman who says, "*I* never did any wrong to Ireland; why bring up that old history as though it had something to do with *me?*" or the young German who believes that being born after 1945 means that what Nazis did to Jews has no moral relevance to his relationship to his Jewish contemporaries, exhibit the same attitude, that according to which the self is detachable from its social and historical roles and statuses. And the self so detached is of course a self very much at home in either Sartre's or Goffman's perspective, a self that can have no history. The contrast with the narrative view of the self is clear. For the story of my life is always embedded in the story of those communities from which I derive my identity. I am born with a past; and to try to cut myself off from that past, in the individualist mode, is to deform my present relationships. The possession of an historical identity and the possession of a social identity coincide. Notice that rebellion against my identity is always one possible mode of expressing it.

Notice also that the fact that the self has to find its moral identity in and through its membership in communities such as those of the family, the neighbourhood, the city and the tribe does not entail that the self has to accept the moral *limitations* of the particularity of those forms of community. Without those moral particularities to begin from there would never be anywhere to begin; but it is in moving forward from such particularity that the search for the good, for the universal, consists. Yet particularity can never be simply left behind or obliterated. The notion of escaping from it into a realm of entirely universal maxims which belong to man as such, whether in its eighteenth-century Kantian form or in the presentation of some modern analytical moral philosophies, is an illusion and an illusion with painful consequences. When men and women identify what are in fact their partial and particular causes too easily and too completely with the cause of some universal principle, they usually behave worse than they would otherwise do.

What I am, therefore, is in key part what I inherit, a specific past that is present to some degree in my present. I find myself part of a history and that is generally to say, whether I like it or not, whether I recognize it or not, one of the bearers of a tradition. It was important when I characterized the concept of a practice to notice that practices always have histories and that at any given moment what a practice is depends on a mode of understanding it which has been transmitted often through many generations. And thus, insofar as the virtues sustain the relationships required for practices, they have to sustain relationships to the past—and to the future—as well as in the present. But the traditions through which particular practices are transmitted and reshaped never exist in isolation for larger social traditions. What constitutes such traditions?

We are apt to be misled here by the ideological uses to which the concept of a tradition has been put by conservative political theorists. Characteristically such theorists have followed Burke in contrasting tradition with reason and the stability of tradition with conflict. Both contrasts obfuscate. For all reasoning takes place within the context of some traditional mode of thought, transcending through criticism and invention the limitations of what had hitherto been reasoned in that tradition; this is as true of modern physics as of medieval logic. Moreover when a tradition is in good order it is always partially constituted by an argument about the goods the pursuit of which gives to that tradition its particular point and purpose.

So when an institution—a university, say, or a farm, or a hospital—is the bearer of a tradition of practice or practices, its common life will be partly, but in a centrally important way, constituted by a continuous argument as to what a university is and ought to be or what good farming is or what good medicine is. Traditions, when vital, embody continuities of conflict. Indeed when a tradition becomes Burkean, it is always dying or dead.

The individualism of modernity could of course find no use for the notion of tradition within its own conceptual scheme except as an adversary notion; it therefore all too willingly abandoned it to the Burkeans, who, faithful to Burke's own allegiance, tried to combine adherence in politics to a conception of tradition which would vindicate the oligarchical revolution of property of 1688 and adherence in economics to the doctrine and institutions of the free market. The theoretical incoherence of this mismatch did not deprive it of ideological usefulness. But the outcome has been that modern conservatives are for the most part engaged in conserving only older rather than later versions of liberal individualism. Their own core doctrine is as liberal and as individualist as that of self-avowed liberals.

A living tradition then is an historically extended, socially embodied argument, and an argument precisely in part about the goods which constitute that tradition. Within a tradition the pursuit of goods extends through generations, sometimes through many generations. Hence the individual's search for his or her good is generally and characteristically conducted within a context defined by those traditions of which the individual's life is a part, and this is true both of those goods which are internal to practices and of the goods of a single life. Once again the narrative phenomenon of embedding is crucial: the history of a practice in our time is generally and characteristically embedded in and made intelligible in terms of the larger and longer history of the tradition through which the practice in its present form was conveyed to us; the history of each of our own lives is generally and characteristically embedded in and made intelligible in terms of the larger and longer histories of a number of traditions. I have to say "generally and characteristically" rather than "always," for traditions decay, disintegrate and disappear. What then sustains and strengthens traditions? What weakens and destroys them?

The answer in key part is: the exercise or the lack of exercise of the relevant virtues. The virtues find their point and purpose not only in sustaining those relationships necessary if the variety of goods internal to practices are to be achieved and not only in sustaining the form of an individual life in which that individual may seek out his or her good as the good of his or her whole life, but also in sustaining those traditions which provide both practices and individual lives with their necessary historical context. Lack of justice, lack of truthfulness, lack of courage, lack of the relevant intellectual virtues—these corrupt traditions, just as they do those institutions and practices which derive their life from the traditions of which they are the contemporary embodiments. To recognize this is of course also to recognize the existence of an additional virtue, one whose importance is perhaps most obvious when it is least present, the virtue of having an adequate sense of the traditions to which one belongs or which confront one. This virtue is not to be confused with any form of conservative antiquarianism; I am not praising those who choose the conventional conservative role of *laudator temporis acti*. It is rather the case that an adequate sense of tradition manifests itself in a grasp of those future possibilities which the past has made available to the present. Living traditions, just because they continue a not-yet-completed narrative, confront a future whose determinate and determinable character, so far as it possesses any, derives from the past.

In practical reasoning the possession of this virtue is not manifested so much in the knowledge of a set of generalizations or maxims which may provide our practical inferences with major premises; its presence or

absence rather appears on the kind of capacity for judgement which the
agent possesses in knowing how to select among the relevant stack of
maxims and how to apply them in particular situations. Cardinal Pole
possessed it, Mary Tudor did not; Montrose possessed it, Charles I did
not. What Cardinal Pole and the Marquis of Montrose possessed were in
fact those virtues which enable their possessors to pursue both their own
good and the good of the tradition of which they are the bearers even in
situations defined by the necessity of tragic, dilemmatic choice.

It has often been suggested—by J. L. Austin, for example—that *either*
we can admit the existence of rival and contingently incompatible goods
which make incompatible claims to our practical allegiance *or* we can
believe in some determinate conception of *the* good life for man, but that
these are mutually exclusive alternatives. No one can consistently hold
both these views. What this contention is blind to is that there may be
better or worse ways for individuals to live through the tragic confronta-
tion of good with good. And that to know what the good life for man is
may require knowing what are the better and what are the worse ways of
living in and through such situations. Nothing *a priori* rules out this
possibility; and this suggests that within a view such as Austin's there is
concealed an unacknowledged empirical premise about the character of
tragic situations.

One way in which the choice between rival goods in a tragic situation
differs from the modern choice between incommensurable moral premises
is that *both* of the alternative courses of action which confront the individual have to be recognized as leading to some authentic and substantial
good. By choosing one I do nothing to diminish or derogate from the
claims upon me of the other; and therefore, whatever I do, I shall have left
undone what I ought to have done. The tragic protagonist, unlike the
moral agent as depicted by Sartre or Hare, is not choosing between allegiance to one moral principle rather than another, nor is he or she deciding
upon some principle of priority between moral principles. Hence the
"ought" involved has a different meaning and force from that of the
"ought" in moral principles understood in a modern way. For the tragic
protagonist cannot do everything that he or she ought to do. This
"ought," unlike Kant's, does not imply "can." Moreover any attempt to
map the logic of such "ought" assertions on to some modal calculus so as
to produce a version of deontic logic has to fail.[4]

Yet it is clear that the moral task of the tragic protagonist may be
performed better or worse, independently of the choice between alterna-

4. Bas C. Van Fraasen, "Values and the Heart's Command," *Journal of Philosophy*,
70, 1973: 5–19.

tives that he or she makes—*ex hypothesi* he or she has no *right* choice to make. The tragic protagonist may behave heroically or unheroically, generously or ungenerously, gracefully or gracelessly, prudently or imprudently. To perform his or her task better rather than worse will be to do both what is better for him or her *qua* individual or *qua* parent or child or *qua* citizen or member of a profession, or perhaps *qua* some or all of these. The existence of tragic dilemmas casts no doubt upon and provides no counterexamples to the thesis that assertions of the form "To do this in this way would be better for X and/or for his or her family, city or profession" are susceptible of objective truth and falsity, any more than the existence of alternative and contingently incompatible forms of medical treatment casts doubt on the thesis that assertions of the form "To undergo this medical treatment in this way would be better for X and/or his or her family" are susceptible of objective truth and falsity.[5]

The presupposition of this objectivity is of course that we can understand the notion of "good for X" and cognate notions in terms of some conception of the unity of X's life. What is better or worse for X depends upon the character of that intelligible narrative which provides X's life with its unity. Unsurprisingly it is the lack of any such unifying conception of a human life which underlies modern denials of the factual character of moral judgements and more especially of those judgements which ascribe virtues or vices to individuals.

I argued earlier that every moral philosophy has some particular sociology as its counterpart. What I have tried to spell out here is the kind of understanding of social life which the tradition of the virtues requires, a kind of understanding very different from those dominant in the culture of bureaucratic individualism. Within that culture conceptions of the virtues become marginal and the tradition of the virtues remains central only in the lives of social groups whose existence is on the margins of the central culture. Within the central culture of liberal or bureaucratic individualism new conceptions of the virtues emerge and the concept of a virtue is itself transformed.

5. See, from a different point of view, the illuminating discussion in Samuel Guttenplan, "Moral Realism and Moral Dilemmas," *Proceedings of the Aristotelian Society*, 1979–80: 61–80.

25

Nel Noddings,
Caring: A Feminine Approach to Ethics and
Moral Education

Nel Noddings (b. 1929), a professor in the School of Education at Stanford University, has written extensively on education, but is perhaps best known for her original and insightful reflections on women's understanding of life and morality. Her Women and Evil *(1989) presents an overview of the different ways men and women have understood evil. Her immensely influential earlier book,* Caring *(1981), formulates an eloquent account of the distinctive, caring way women tend to relate to others.*

The focus of our attention will be upon how to meet the other morally. Ethical caring, the relation in which we do meet the other morally, will be described as arising out of natural caring—that relation in which we respond as one-caring out of love or natural inclination. The relation of natural caring will be identified as the human condition that we, consciously or unconsciously, perceive as "good." It is that condition toward which we long and strive, and it is our longing for caring—to be in that special relation—that provides the motivation for us to be moral. We want to be *moral* in order to remain in the caring relation and to enhance the ideal of ourselves as one-caring.

It is this ethical ideal, this realistic picture of ourselves as one-caring, that guides us as we strive to meet the other morally. Everything depends upon the nature and strength of this ideal, for we shall not have absolute principles to guide us. Indeed, I shall reject ethics of principle as ambiguous and unstable. Wherever there is a principle, there is implied its exception and, too often, principles function to separate us from each other. We may become dangerously self-righteous when we perceive ourselves as holding a precious principle not held by the other. The other may then be devalued and treated "differently." Our ethic of caring will not permit this to happen. We recognize that in fear, anger, or hatred we will treat the other differently, but this treatment is never conducted ethically.

Hence, when we must use violence or strategies on the other, we are already diminished ethically. Our efforts must, then, be directed to the maintenance of conditions that will permit caring to flourish. Along with the rejection of principles and rules as the major guide to ethical behavior, I shall also reject the notion of universalizability. Many of those writing and thinking about ethics insist that any ethical judgment—by virtue of its *being* an ethical judgment—must be universalizable; that is, it must be the case that, if under conditions X you are required to do A, then under sufficiently similar conditions, I too am required to do A. I shall reject this emphatically. First, my attention is not on judgment and not on the particular acts we perform but on how we meet the other morally. Second, in recognition of the feminine approach to meeting the other morally— our insistence on caring for the other—I shall want to preserve the uniqueness of human encounters. Since so much depends on the subjective experience of those involved in ethical encounters, conditions are rarely "sufficiently similar" for me to declare that you must do what I must do. There is, however, a fundamental universality in our ethic, as there must be to escape relativism. The caring attitude, that attitude which expresses our earliest memories of being cared for and our growing store of memories of both caring and being cared for, is universally accessible. Since caring and the commitment to sustain it form the universal heart of the ethic, we must establish a convincing and comprehensive picture of caring at the outset.

. . .

Problems Arising in the Analysis of One-Caring

As I think about how I feel when I care, about what my frame of mind is, I see that my caring is always characterized by a move away from self. Yet not all instances of caring are alike even from the view of one-caring. Conditions change, and the time spanned by caring varies. While I care for my children throughout our mutual lifetimes, I may care only momentarily for a stranger in need. The intensity varies. I care deeply for those in my inner circles and more lightly for those farther removed from my personal life. Even with those close to me, the intensity of caring varies; it may be calm and steady most of the time and desperately anxious in emergencies.

The acts performed out of caring vary with both situational conditions and type of relationship. It may bother me briefly, as a teacher, to learn that students in general are not doing well with the subject I teach, but I cannot really be said to care for each of the students having difficulty. And if I have not taken up a serious study of the difficulties themselves, I cannot be said to care about the problem qua problem. But if one of my own students is having difficulty, I may experience the engrossment and motivational displacement of caring. Does this caring spring out of the relationship I have formed with the student? Or, is it possible that I cared in some meaningful way before I even met the particular student?

The problems arising here involve time spans, intensity, and certain formal aspects of caring. Later, I shall explore the concept of chains of caring in which certain formal links to known cared-fors bind us to the possibility of caring. The construction of such formal chains places us in a state of readiness to care. Because my future students are related (formally, *as* students) to present, actual students for whom I do care, I am prepared to care for them also.

As we become aware of the problems involving time, intensity, and formal relationships, we may be led to reconsider the requirement of engrossment. We might instead describe caring of different sorts, on different levels and at varying degrees of intensity. Although I understand why several writers have chosen to speak of special kinds of caring appropriate to particular relationships, I shall claim that these efforts obscure the fundamental truth. At bottom, all caring involves engrossment. The engrossment need not be intense nor need it be pervasive in the life of the one-caring, but it must occur. This requirement does not force caring into the model of romantic love, as some critics fear, for our engrossment may be latent for long periods. We may say of caring as Martin Buber says of love, "it endures, but only in the alternation of actuality and latency." The difference that this approach makes is significant. Whatever roles I assume in life, I may be described in constant terms as one-caring. My first and unending obligation is to meet the other as one-caring. Formal constraints may be added to the fundamental requirement, but they do not replace or weaken it. When we discuss pedagogical caring, for example, we shall develop it from the analysis of caring itself and not from the formal requirements of teaching as a profession.

Another problem arises when we consider situations in which we do not naturally care. Responding to my own child crying in the night may require a physical effort, but it does not usually require what might be called an ethical effort. I naturally want to relieve my child's distress. But receiving the other as he feels and trying to do so are qualitatively different modes. In the first, I am already "with" the other. My motivational energies are flowing toward him and, perhaps, toward his ends. In the second, I may dimly or dramatically perceive a reality that is a repugnant possibility for me. Dwelling in it may bring self-revulsion and disgust. Then I must withdraw. I do not "care" for this person. I may hate him, but I need not. If I do something in his behalf—defend his legal rights or confirm a statement he makes—it is because I care about my own ethical self. In caring for my ethical self, I grapple with the question: Must I try to care? When and for whom? A description of the ethical ideal and its construction will be essential in trying to answer these questions.

There are other limitations in caring. Not only are there those for whom I do not naturally care—situations in which engrossment brings revulsion and motivational displacement is unthinkable—but there are, also, many beyond the reach of my caring. I shall reject the notion of universal caring—that is, caring for everyone—on the grounds that it is impossible to actualize and leads us to substitute abstract problem solving and mere talk for genuine caring. Many of us think that it is not only possible to care for everyone but morally obligatory that we should do so. We can, in a sense that will need elaboration, "care about" everyone; that is, we can maintain an internal state of readiness to try to care for whoever crosses our path. But this is different from the caring-for to which we refer when we use the word "caring." If we are thoughtful persons, we know that the difference is great, and we may even deliberately restrict our contacts so that the caring-for of which we are capable does not deteriorate to mere verbal caring-about. I shall not try to maintain this linguistic distinction, because it seems somewhat unnatural, but we should keep in mind the real distinction we are pointing at: in one sense, "caring" refers to an actuality; in the other, it refers to a verbal commitment to the possibility of caring.

We may add both guilt and conflict to our growing list of problems in connection with the analysis of caring. Conflict arises when our engrossment is divided, and several cared-fors demand incompatible decisions from us. Another sort of conflict occurs when what the cared-for wants is not what we think would be best for him, and still another sort arises when we become overburdened and our caring turns into "cares and burdens." Any of these conflicts may induce guilt. Further, we may feel guilty when we fall short of doing what the cared-for wants us to do or when we bring about outcomes we ourselves did not intend to bring about. Conflict and guilt are inescapable risks of caring, and their consideration will suggest an exploration of courage.

The one-caring is, however, not alone in the caring relationship. Sometimes caring turns inward—as for Mr. Smith in his description of worries and burdens—because conditions are intolerable or because the cared-for is singularly difficult. Clearly, we need also to analyze the role of the cared-for.

· · ·

Caring and Acting

Let's return briefly to the issue of action. Perhaps, with a better notion of what constitutes the first- and second-person aspects of caring, we can now say something more determinate about acts of caring. Our motivation in caring is directed toward the welfare, protection, or enhancement of the cared-for. When we care, we should, ideally, be able to present reasons for our action/inaction which would persuade a reasonable, disinterested observer that we have acted in behalf of the cared-for. This does not mean that all such observers have to agree that they would have behaved exactly as we did in a particular caring situation. They may, on the contrary, see preferred alternatives. They may experience the very conflicts that caused us anxiety and still suggest a different course of action; or they may proceed in a purely rational-objective way and suggest the same or a different course. But, frequently, and especially in the case of inaction, we are not willing to supply reasons to an actual observer; our ideal observer is, and remains, an abstraction. The reasons we would give, those we give to ourselves in honest subjective thinking, should be so well connected to the objective elements of the problem that our course of action clearly either stands a chance of succeeding in behalf of the cared-for, or can have been engaged in only with the hope of effecting something for the cared-for.

Caring involves stepping out of one's own personal frame of reference into the other's. When we care, we consider the other's point of view, his objective needs, and what he expects of us. Our attention, our mental engrossment is on the cared-for, not on ourselves. Our reasons for acting, then, have to do both with the other's wants and desires and with the objective elements of his problematic situation. If the stray cat is healthy and relatively safe, we do not whisk it off to the county shelter; instead, we provide food and water and encourage freedom. Why condemn it to death when it might enjoy a vagabond freedom? If our minds are on ourselves, however—if we have never really left our own a priori frame of reference—our reasons for acting point back at us and not outward to the cared-for. When we want to be thought of as caring, we often act routinely in a way that may easily secure that credit for us.

This gives us, as outsiders to the relation, a way, not infallible to be sure, to judge caretaking for signs of real caring. To care is to act not by fixed rule but by affection and regard. It seems likely, then, that the actions of one-caring will be varied rather than rule-bound; that is, her actions, while predictable in a global sense, will be unpredictable in detail. Variation is to be expected if the one claiming to care really cares, for her engrossment is in the variable and never fully understood other, in the particular other, in a particular set of circumstances. Rule-bound responses in the name of caring lead us to suspect that the claimant wants most to be credited with caring.

To act as one-caring, then, is to act with special regard for the particular person in a concrete situation. We act not to achieve for ourselves a commendation but to protect or enhance the welfare of the cared-for. Because we are inclined toward the cared-for, we want to act in a way that will please him. But we wish to please him for his sake and not for the promise of his grateful response to our generosity. Even this motivation—to act so that the happiness and pleasure of the cared-for will be enhanced—may not provide a sure external sign of caring. We are sometimes thrown into conflict over what the cared-for wants and what we think would be best for him. As caring parents, for example, we cannot always act in ways which bring immediate reactions of pleasure from our children, and to do so may bespeak a desire, again, to be credited with caring.

The one-caring desires the well-being of the cared-for and acts (or abstains from acting—makes an internal act of commitment) to promote that well-being. She is inclined to the other. An observer, however, cannot see the crucial motive and may misread the attitudinal signs. The observer, then, must judge caring, in part, by the following: First, the action (if there has been one) either brings about a favorable outcome for the cared-for or seems reasonably likely to do so; second, the one-caring displays a characteristic variability in her actions—she acts in a nonrulebound fashion in behalf of the cared-for.

We shall have to spend some time and effort on the discussion of non-rule-bound, caring behavior. Clearly, I do not intend to advocate arbitrary and capricious behavior, but something more like the inconsistency advocated long ago by Ralph Waldo Emerson, the sort of behavior that is conditioned not by a host of narrow and rigidly defined principles but by a broad and loosely defined ethic that molds itself in situations and has a proper regard for human affections, weaknesses, and anxieties. From such an ethic we do not receive prescriptions as to how we must behave under given conditions, but we are somewhat enlightened as to the kinds of questions we should raise (to ourselves and others) in various kinds of situations and the places we might look for appropriate answers. Such an ethic does not attempt to reduce the need for human judgment with a series of "Thou shalts" and "Thou shalt nots." Rather, it recognizes and calls forth human judgment across a wide range of fact and feeling, and it allows for situations and conditions in which judgment (in the impersonal, logical sense) may properly be put aside in favor of faith and commitment.

We establish funds, or institutions, or agencies in order to provide the caretaking we judge to be necessary. The original impulse is often the one associated with caring. It arises in individuals. But as groups of individuals discuss the perceived needs of another individual or group, the imperative changes from "I must do something" to "Something must be done." This change is accompanied by a shift from the nonrational and subjective to the rational and objective. What should be done? Who should do it? Why should the persons named do it? This sort of thinking is not in itself a mistake; it is needed. But it has buried within it the seed of major error. The danger is that caring, which is essentially nonrational in that it requires a constitutive engrossment and displacement of motivation, may gradually or abruptly be transformed into abstract problem solving. There is, then, a shift of focus from the cared-for to the "problem." Opportunities arise for self-interest, and persons entrusted with caring may lack the necessary engrossment in those to be cared-for. Rules are formulated and the characteristic variation in response to the needs of the cared-for may fade away. Those entrusted with caring may focus on satisfying the formulated requirements for caretaking and fail to be present in their interactions with the cared-for. Thus caring disappears and only its illusion remains.

It is clear, of course, that there is also danger in failing to think objectively and well in caring situations. We quite properly enter a rational-objective mode as we try to decide exactly what we will do in behalf of the cared-for. If I am ill informed, or if I make a mistake, or if I act impetuously, I may hurt rather than help the cared-for. But one may argue, here, that the failure is still at the level of engrossment and motivational displacement. Would I behave so carelessly in my own behalf?

It would seem, then, that one of the greatest dangers to caring may be premature switching to a rational-objective mode. It is not that objective thinking is of no use in problems where caring is required, but it is of limited and particular use, and we shall have to inquire deeply into what we shall call "turning points." If rational-objective thinking is to be put in the service of caring, we must at the right moments turn it away from the abstract toward which it tends and back to the concrete. At times we must suspend it in favor of subjective thinking and reflection, allowing time and space for *seeing* and *feeling*. The rational-objective mode must continually be re-established and redirected from a fresh base of commitment. Otherwise, we find ourselves deeply, perhaps inextricably, enmeshed in procedures that somehow serve only themselves; our thoughts are separated, completely detached, from the original objects of caring.

Now, before turning to a closer look at the one-caring, perhaps we should consider where we are headed through our analysis of caring.

Ethics and Caring

It is generally agreed that ethics is the philosophical study of morality, but we also speak of "professional ethics" and "a personal ethic." When we speak in the second way, we refer to something explicable—a set of rules, an ideal, a constellation of expressions—that guides and justifies our conduct. One can, obviously, behave ethically without engaging in ethics as a philosophical enterprise, and one can even put together an ethic of sorts—that is, a description of what it means to be moral—without seriously questioning what it means to be moral. Such an ethic, it seems to me, may or may not be a guide to moral behavior. It depends, in a fundamental way, on an assessment of the answer to the question: What does it mean to be moral? This question will be central to our investigation. I shall use "ethical" rather than "moral" in most of our discussions but, in doing so, I am assuming that to behave ethically is to behave under the guidance of an acceptable and justifiable account of what it means to be moral. To behave ethically is not to behave in conformity with just any description of morality, and I shall claim that ethical systems are not equivalent simply because they include rules concerning the same matters or categories.

In an argument for the possibility of an objective morality (against relativism), anthropologist Ralph Linton makes two major points that may serve to illuminate the path I am taking. In one argument, he seems to say that ethical relativism is false because it can be shown that all societies lay down rules of some sort for behavior in certain universal categories. All societies, for example, have rules governing sexual behavior. But Linton does not seem to recognize that the content of the rules, and not just their mere existence, is crucial to the discussion of ethicality. He says, for example: " . . . practically all societies recognize adultery as unethical and punish the offenders. The same man who will lend his wife to a friend or brother will be roused to fury if she goes to another man without his permission." But, surely, we would like to know what conception of morality makes adultery "wrong" and the lending of one's wife "right." Just as surely, an ethical system that renders such decisions cannot be equivalent to one that finds adultery acceptable and wife lending unacceptable.

In his second claim, Linton is joined by a substantial number of anthropologists. Stated simply, the claim is that morality is based on common human characteristics and needs and that, hence, an objective morality is possible. That morality is rooted somehow in common human needs, feelings, and cognitions is agreed. But it is not clear to me that we can move easily or swiftly from that agreement to a claim that objective morality is possible. We may be able to describe the moral impulse as it arises in response to particular needs and feelings, and we may be able to describe the relation of thinking and acting in relation to that impulse; but as we tackle these tasks, we may move farther away from a notion of objective morality and closer to the conviction that an irremovable subjective core, a longing for goodness, provides what universality and stability there is in what it means to be moral.

I want to build an ethic on caring, and I shall claim that there is a form of caring natural and accessible to all human beings. Certain feelings, attitudes, and memories will be claimed as universal. But the ethic itself will not embody a set of universalizable moral judgments. Indeed, moral judgment will not be its central concern. It is very common among philosophers to move from the question: What is morality? to the seemingly more manageable question: What is a moral judgment? Fred Feldman, for example, makes this move early on. He suggests:

> Perhaps we can shed some light on the meaning of the noun "morality" by considering the adjective "moral." Proceeding in this way will enable us to deal with a less abstract concept, and we may thereby be more successful. So instead of asking "What is morality?" let us pick one of the most interesting of these uses of the adjective "moral" and ask instead, "What is a moral judgment?"

Now, I am not arguing that this move is completely mistaken or that nothing can be gained through a consideration of moral judgments, but such a move is not the only possibility. We might choose another interesting use of the adjective and ask, instead, about the moral impulse or moral attitude. The choice is important. The long-standing emphasis on the study of moral judgments has led to a serious imbalance in moral discussion. In particular, it is well known that many women—perhaps most women—do not approach moral problems as problems of principle, reasoning, and judgment. I shall discuss this problem at length in chapter four. If a substantial segment of humankind approaches moral problems through a consideration of the concrete elements of situations and a regard for themselves as caring, then perhaps an attempt should be made to enlighten the study of morality in this alternative mode. Further, such a study has significant implications, beyond ethics, for education. If moral education, in a double sense, is guided only by the study of moral principles and judgments, not only are women made to feel inferior to men in the moral realm but also education itself may suffer from impoverished and one-sided moral guidance.

So building an ethic on caring seems both reasonable and important. One may well ask, at this point, whether an ethic so constructed will be a form of "situation ethics." It is not, certainly, that form of act-utilitarianism commonly labeled "situation ethics." Its emphasis is not on the consequences of our acts, although these are not, of course, irrelevant. But an ethic of caring locates morality primarily in the pre-act consciousness of the one-caring. Yet it is not a form of agapism. There is no command to love nor, indeed, any God to make the commandment. Further, I shall reject the notion of universal love, finding it unattainable in any but the most abstract sense and thus a source of distraction. While much of what will be developed in the ethic of caring may be found, also, in Christian ethics, there will be major and irreconcilable differences. Human love, human caring, will be quite enough on which to found an ethic.

We must look even more closely at that love and caring.